DIVINE COMMITMENT AND HUMAN OBLIGATION

Divine Commitment and Human Obligation

Selected Writings of David Noel Freedman

VOLUME TWO: POETRY AND ORTHOGRAPHY

Edited by

John R. Huddlestun

WILLIAM B. EERDMANS PUBLISHING COMPANY
GRAND RAPIDS, MICHIGAN / CAMBRIDGE, U.K.

255 Jefferson Ave. S.E., Grand Rapids, Michigan 49503 /
P.O. Box 163, Cambridge CB3 9PU U.K.

Printed in the United States of America

02 01 00 99 98 97 7 6 5 4 3 2 1

Library of Congress Cataloging-in-Publication Data

Freedman, David Noel, 1922-
Divine commitment and human obligation: selected writings of
David Noel Freedman / edited by John R. Huddleston.
xx, 269 p. 25 cm.
Includes bibliographical references.
Contents: v. 1. History and religion — v. 2. Poetry and orthography.
ISBN 0-8028-3816-2 (cloth: alk. paper)
1. Bible. O.T. — Criticism, interpretation, etc.
I. Huddleston, John R. II. Title.
BS1171.2.F67 1997
221.6 — dc20 96-6418
CIP

Contents

Editor's Introduction

To survey the writings of David Noel Freedman is tantamount to reviewing the history and development of nearly every facet of American biblical scholarship following the Second World War. From the confidence of the Biblical Theology Movement in the 1950s and 1960s, to the critical response to and subsequent rethinking of many of the assumptions associated with the Albrightian school's approach to ancient Israelite history in the 1970s and beyond, the emergence and rapid rise to popularity of literary approaches beginning especially in the 1970s, the proliferation of newer approaches to the re- (or de-)construction of ancient Israelite history in the late 1980s and 1990s with threatening cracks in — if not crumbling at some points of — the once seemingly invincible towering edifice known as the documentary hypothesis, and in general the uncontrollable bursting forth of countless alternative "criticisms" applied to the interpretation of the biblical text — through it all, as both author and editor, Noel has remained a vibrant and towering presence in the field. The creativity and originality of his many contributions are exceeded only by their prodigious number.

Given the rapidity with which the field has changed in just a few decades, one in Noel's position might be forgiven for being less than enthusiastic about every new development, but nothing could be further from the truth. In fact, through his legendary indefatigable labors as editor and unrelenting author, he has not simply kept up, as it were, but has often taken the lead, paving the way with creative new approaches and interpretations, and in turn challenging others to respond and follow. One thinks, for example, of his collaborative efforts with J. Arthur Baird, Dean Forbes, and Francis Andersen in establishing and promoting the use of computers and statistics in the study of the Bible.[1] While not computer friendly

1. Beginning with the *Computer-Generated Bible* (Lewiston, NY: Edwin Mellen, 1971-), now extending to more than thirty-seven volumes. See also F. I. Andersen and A. Dean Forbes, *Spelling in the Hebrew Bible.* Biblica et Orientalia 41 (Rome: Biblical Institute Press, 1986), and,

himself, Noel's uncanny facility for analyzing nearly anything numerical — from syllable counts to genealogical lists — allows him not only to ask the right questions, but to draw meaningful and relevant conclusions from the raw data.[2]

Noel's contributions to the field of biblical studies are immense, and one could not hope adequately to summarize them in a few short paragraphs. One thinks here particularly of his indelible mark as author and co-author in numerous studies relating to Hebrew poetry ("archaic" and otherwise), including especially verse structure and orthography, biblical history and chronology, the formation and canon of the Dead Sea Scrolls — all of which are represented in the writings collected in these two volumes. The importance of his pioneering work in early Hebrew poetry and orthography has been ably summarized elsewhere by Frank Cross in his preface to an earlier collection of Noel's writings, *Pottery, Poetry, and Prophecy.* Indeed, their earliest collaborative ventures — two joint doctoral dissertations written under William F. Albright (*Evolution of Early Hebrew Orthography,* submitted by Noel in 1948; *Studies in Ancient Yahwistic Poetry,* submitted by Cross in 1950) — remain to this day indispensable reading for any serious student of Hebrew poetry or language.[3] While their conclusions regarding the "archaic" character of particular poems may not command the consensus they once did,[4] none would dispute the seminal nature of these studies as a whole. It is fitting then that the present collection should acknowledge the contributions of this unique and legendary team with the inclusion of one of their early published articles (vol. 2, ch. 1),[5] and a later response (1972) to criticism of their work (vol. 2, ch. 8).

---

most recently, the essays of Noel and others in *Studies in Hebrew and Aramaic Orthography,* ed. D. N. Freedman, A. Dean Forbes, and Francis T. Andersen. Biblical and Judaic Studies from the University of California, San Diego, 2 (Winona Lake: Eisenbrauns, 1992).

2. Note, for example, his comments about the potential of computer-based study in 1980: "Perhaps the most important of these [techniques] will prove to be computer-based research of a mechanical and statistical nature, whereby more ancient and more recent theories can be tested, and material information supplied in unlimited quantity on short notice. Far from displacing original scholarship, computer technology will provide powerful weapons in the scientific assault on the biblical bastion with its unresolved questions and inaccessible secrets, but only for creative and courageous thinkers" (from the Preface to his *Pottery, Poetry, and Prophecy: Studies in Early Hebrew Poetry* [Winona Lake: Eisenbrauns, 1980], ix-x).

3. The latter volume, *Studies in Ancient Yahwistic Poetry,* was published in 1975 (SBL Dissertation Series 21 [Missoula: Scholars Press]) with a "Postscriptum" by the authors and has now been reprinted with new Prefaces by each author (Grand Rapids: Wm. B. Eerdmans, 1996). With respect to the earlier volume, *Early Hebrew Orthography,* see Noel's most recent synthesis, "The Evolution of Hebrew Orthography," in *Studies in Hebrew and Aramaic Orthography,* 3-15.

4. Contrast, for example, the following two studies: David A. Robertson, *Linguistic Evidence in Dating Early Hebrew Poetry.* SBL Dissertation Series 3 (Missoula: Scholars Press, 1972) and Martin L. Brenner, *The Song of the Sea: Ex 15:1-21.* BZAW 195 (Berlin: Walter de Gruyter, 1991).

5. Their first jointly authored article appeared in 1947 ("A Note on Deuteronomy 33:26," *BASOR* 108:6-7).

For Noel, the notion of the canon should be understood in its broadest possible sense to encompass the "process of composition, compilation, edition, and publication" of the writings that comprise the Hebrew Bible. His own work has focused particularly on Genesis through 2 Kings, the "Primary History," nomenclature that, as far as I am aware, was first proposed by him in his entry on the Pentateuch for *The Interpreter's Dictionary of the Bible* (Nashville: Abingdon, 1962; see below, vol. 1, ch. 12). His general thesis concerning the period of composition/compilation and general themes of the Primary History (or "First Bible") was further developed in various articles after 1962 (esp. vol. 1, chs. 14, 32, and 39) and thereafter supplemented and extended to account for the various additions to this initial collection (the "Second Bible"), and eventually the formation of the canon as we know it today (the "Third Bible"; see vol. 1, chs. 40, 42). His views on the development and structure of the canon receive their fullest exposition in his 1991 volume, *The Unity of the Hebrew Bible,*[6] which should be read in conjunction with his slightly later (1992) overview of the process (see vol. 1, ch. 42). Noel's use of symmetry as a defining element in the overall structure and organization of the books of the Hebrew Bible may in part stem naturally from his concern with such symmetry on a much smaller scale in Hebrew poetry, but his uncanny ability to view and play with the text as a whole, to isolate larger correlations between the structure, theme, and purpose — a kind of macro midrash, as it were — is unmatched among modern scholars and in certain respects finds its closest parallel in classic Rabbinic exegesis.[7] While some will inevitably disagree with Noel's analysis at various points, nevertheless, the attempt itself will no doubt generate further discussion and research, which is precisely what he himself would want.

It is perhaps first and foremost as editor of the various Anchor Bible projects that Noel is most widely recognized, and deservedly so given the seemingly inhuman pace at which he is able to edit and return a manuscript (provided he has a generous supply of chewing gum, a suitable classical music radio station, and an electric typewriter capable of withstanding his furious tempo). In the process, the unsuspecting author usually gets more than he or she bargained for in the form of a weighty parcel containing Noel's comments, single-spaced and straining the margins — comments that can sometimes equal (or in some cases even exceed) the length of the originally submitted manuscript. Bur oral tradition tells the story better than I. One need only ask the numerous authors, a veritable Who's Who in the field, who have benefited from his editorial expertise and wise counsel; or, better yet, glance at the acknowledgments to virtually any Anchor Bible volume published under his editorship. Given his enormous input and influence in the writing and development of many of the commentaries, were it

6. Published by the University of Michigan Press (Ann Arbor) as part of the University's Distinguished Senior Faculty Lecture Series.

7. See, for example, my comments on a Rabbinic parallel in *The Unity of the Hebrew Bible*.

not for his position as editor, Noel could easily qualify as co-author. But I suspect he is much more comfortable working behind the scenes where his creative and at times provocative comments and ideas may be offered uncensored, no doubt stimulating their recipients to rethink, reformulate, or even reject cherished positions or interpretations. As the foremost editor in biblical studies of this or probably any century — with the possible exception of Ezra himself — Noel has also done a great deal to promote and nurture the work of colleagues and students, providing encouragement and publishing opportunities for younger or emerging scholars, whether on their own or initially in collaboration with him (see, for example, vol. 2, chs. 5, 9, 12).

One area infrequently discussed (in print at least) in connection with Noel's contributions, but very much a motivating factor in his life and work from the beginning, is his magnanimous, almost obsessive at times, ecumenical spirit. His deep convictions in this area, even to the extent that he may remain silent on certain issues for fear of compromising his carefully guarded neutrality as editor, stem in large measure from his own history. Raised in a secular Jewish environment, it is somewhat ironic that interest in his own Jewish heritage was awakened through the study of Biblical Hebrew and the Hebrew Bible at Princeton Theological Seminary in the early 1940s. (For the record, his first Hebrew teacher was C. T. Fritsch.) At that point, as he himself once put it in conversation, he was hooked and knew where his future lay. A number of pieces illustrative of Noel's early ecumenical leanings, along with his mature forays into the subject, have been included in this collection in order better to give the reader a sense of this aspect of his career (vol. 1, chs. 5, 13, 16, 20, 21, 24). The continued existence and expansion of the Anchor Bible series, showcasing as it does the work of many of the world's foremost Jewish, Catholic, and Protestant scholars, is eloquent testimony to Noel's unparalleled talents in the ecumenical arena. The "credo" for the series, which appeared in 1963 under the joint authorship of Noel and William Albright, surveyed the then current state of biblical studies and the need for an up-to-date commentary series with world-class scholars as contributors. Particular stress was given to the ecumenical nature of the project and the diverse religious and geographical backgrounds of its authors. Although Albright was listed as co-author, Noel once confessed that he himself in fact was the sole author of the statement. Following Albright's death in 1971, Noel sought to solidify the ecumenical stance of the project through the creation of an editorial committee of three, consisting of Frank Cross, (the late) Jonas Greenfield, and Marvin Pope, a kind of "ecumenical triumvirate," as it were.[8] But, as one of the illustrious members of the short-lived committee has noted, "the contribution of the three of us [was]

8. I cannot take credit for the phrase (see the remarks of Frank Cross in "Reminiscences of David Noel Freedman . . . Presented to David Noel Freedman in Celebration of the 25th Anniversary of the Anchor Bible, November 1989," privately circulated pamphlet, Doubleday).

wholly symbolic at best, and Noel soon dropped us from the front matter in dispassionate recognition of our value to the series."

Having studied under Noel at the University of Michigan (his last doctoral student from that institution), I feel compelled to offer a few remarks on the experience of sitting at the feet of one of the great scholars of this century. Despite his massive erudition, Noel graciously — and with amazing patience — allowed and encouraged students to formulate and express freely their own interpretations of the Hebrew text, never insisting that his own views must take precedence over others published or offered in class. He was quick to praise a worthwhile seminar paper when he saw one and would not hesitate to offer assistance in getting it published. His seminars invariably focused on his greatest love, the Hebrew text. The unsuspecting student could dutifully prepare him- or herself by reading all the commentaries and other secondary literature, but once in class he/she soon realized that this was simply not enough — some original thought would be required. His incredibly creative mind never failed to come up with novel ways of looking at a verse or passage long dead, or at least dormant, from over-interpretation. Noel's proposals were frequently deceptively simple, effectively solving a textual dilemma in short order. The overwhelmed student soon realized that here was a scholar who puts the text first and that he would do well to imitate the master. I recall being relieved to discover that I was not the only one who thought Noel had the Hebrew text and its contents committed to memory.[9] In this day and age when it is too easy to become entangled or mired in the secondary literature — sometimes never to emerge — Noel always reminds one of the primacy of the Hebrew text: master the text, then worry about everything else.

Lastly, one cannot help but be struck by Noel's unbounded enthusiasm and love for the field and his great enjoyment of good scholarly debate, welcoming any opportunity to discuss and debate in any forum views contrary to his own. As Editor-in-Chief of the *Anchor Bible Dictionary* project, he on more than one occasion expressed to those on his editorial staff the desire to have ideally not one, but two or even three entries on each topic so as to present fully and fairly all sides of an issue for the benefit of the reader. One thinks, mutatis mutandis, of the words of another scholar of an earlier generation:

> Reasonable men may be allowed to differ, where no one can reasonably be positive. Opposite sentiments, even without any decision, afford an agreeable

9. In his most autobiographical writing to date, Noel explains his unparalleled knowledge of the text as due in part to the fact that in his early days of teaching he began the practice of never going anywhere without the Hebrew text, this being in imitation of his then colleague and teaching mentor, William F. Orr, who did the same with the New Testament. See "He Never Let Me Fall: A Reminiscence," in *He Came Here and Loved Us: A Festschrift in Honor of William F. Orr,* ed. R. C. Curry, T. J. Kelso, and C. S. Maue (Watsontown, PA: The William F. Orr Festschrift Foundation, 1990), 7-13, esp. 8-9.

> amusement. And if the subject be curious and interesting, the book carries us, in a manner, into company, and unites the two greatest and purest pleasures of human life, study and society.[10]

It is this love of learning and scholarly debate, this willingness to reexamine the text with a student's curiosity as though reading it for the first time — Noel has always described himself as a student at heart — that endears him to so many colleagues and students alike. But alas, such legendary figures, such *gedolim,* are increasingly rare among us these days.

The genesis of these volumes dates to the summer of 1991, when Astrid Beck, Program Associate of the Program on Studies in Religion at the University of Michigan, approached me about the possibility of putting together a volume containing some of Noel's most influential articles. Noel himself had already drawn up a rather modest and provisional list of pieces. It soon became apparent, however, that one volume would not suffice. Indeed, given the size of his published output, excluding edited works, one could easily expand such a collection to four or more volumes. In the end, I more than doubled Noel's original list to include not only the most obvious choices, but also others illustrative of the early development of his career. The creation of two separate volumes, one on Israelite history and religion and the other dealing with poetry and orthography, provides a useful means of organization, but the division should not be pressed too far given that some articles could easily fit into either category. In addition, the present collection avoids duplication of earlier pieces reprinted in the author's *Pottery, Poetry, and Prophecy* (1980), as well as those contained in the more recent volume *Hebrew and Aramaic Orthography* (1992) from the University of California at San Diego.

An undertaking of this magnitude of necessity depends and draws upon the goodwill, support, and assistance of others. I am first and foremost indebted to David Noel Freedman, mentor, colleague, and friend, who honored me with the invitation to be a part of this publication. Any attempt to summarize a career as distinguished as his is a most humbling experience.

Throughout the long, and often interrupted, process of preparing the manuscripts, obtaining publisher permissions, and finding a suitable publisher, Astrid Beck provided all the assistance — logistical, financial, and otherwise — that any editor could possibly desire. It was only through her continuing support, advice, and encouragement that these volumes saw the light of day.

The reader will observe that some articles reprinted herein were written in collaboration with others (namely, Frank M. Cross, Chris Franke, and Austin Ritterspach). I sincerely thank the above named scholars for graciously allowing these

10. The quotation comes from the philosopher David Hume, in the prefatory remarks to his *Dialogues Concerning Natural Religion* (1779).

to be included in this collection. In addition, I thank those publishers — here in the United States, in Europe, and in Israel — who granted permission to reprint writings initially published by them.

Lastly, I am most grateful to Eerdmans Publishing Company, especially Senior Editor Allen Myers, for their willingness to take on the project, and the limitless patience they displayed with me in the face of repeated delays and deadline revisions. The tedious and painstaking process of editing, resetting, and proofreading previously published works of this nature is no easy task, and they have done a superb job. For the sake of consistency, minor editorial changes have been made in the text, for example in the use of abbreviations and the transliteration scheme. No attempt has been made by the author to revise the writings reprinted here; however, editorial additions and notes have been inserted at points in order to update the reader on works cited as forthcoming or ones that appeared elsewhere than indicated in the text. Additionally, I have on occasion also updated or supplemented bibliographic citations, but these generally have been kept to a minimum.

JOHN R. HUDDLESTUN
Charleston, S.C., October, 1996

Preface

In the pages of this and the companion volume *(Divine Commitment and Human Obligation: History and Religion)* are representative articles produced during a lifetime career devoted to the study of the Hebrew Bible. I began graduate studies at the Johns Hopkins University in the fall of 1945 under the tutelage of the famous Orientalist, W. F. Albright. Now, fifty years later, I am grateful to those who have assembled this collection of my minor works and have invited me to reflect briefly on my efforts and intentions during those years.

What have fifty years of activity in this field taught me about the Bible, or what have I learned from the energy and effort expended on the investigation of the text of the premier literary work of Western civilization? Chiefly, I have learned to be skeptical about claims (not least, but especially my own), large and small, which purport to resolve this problem or settle that question. In fact, the larger the claim the less likely it is to meet the requirements of evidence and argument. Even small claims rarely pass the tests of coherence and consistency, not to speak of plausibility. This initial reluctance to accept new hypotheses and ideas applies across the board, and not less to my own brilliant notions. So with built-in skepticism there also comes a generous dollop of humility. Progress in understanding the Bible is slow, even in grasping the dimensions of the problems and the depth of our ignorance, much less in being able to make advances or to assess their value when we make them.

These fifty years have seen a great deal of movement and activity, motion and commotion, but to paraphrase an apt political campaign question, How much better off are we now than then? Do we know more and understand better than our academic forefathers, and do we see further than they, even if we are standing upon their shoulders? Perhaps we would be better off if we applied to the Bible not only the standards and methods of scientific research, requiring objective data and logical demonstration — in short, rigorous historical criteria to times and places, persons and occurrences, which often remain elusively beyond our reach — but also the criteria and methods of the Arts. In that way, we might value more a variety of approaches and insights or interpretations and reconstructions, none of which might agree or be compatible with the others, but each or some of which could illuminate texts and contexts, circumstances and settings, in different ways, leading to multiple analyses and syntheses of the various assemblages of data.

Owing chiefly to my heavy and continuing duties as an editor of journals and books, I have pursued a highly eclectic course in my own scholarship, often reacting and responding to the authors of the manuscripts, mainly commentaries on biblical books, which I edited. In cases in which I remained unconvinced by the evidence and arguments offered and in regard to which I had a different opinion — and if persuasion failed as it most often did — I found an opportunity to develop alternate views, and published many of them. Under the circumstances, they deal with details of the text. It is said that the devil is in the details; so also with solutions. One detail can lead to another until a mosaic is formed, one or more patterns discerned, and a larger structure created or developed.

In fact, my first venture in scholarly print was a very brief Note that appeared in the *Bulletin of the American Schools of Oriental Research (BASOR)* in the fall of 1947, while Frank M. Cross, Jr., and I were graduate students at Johns Hopkins. In that issue of the *Bulletin,* which Albright had given us the responsibility of assembling and seeing through the press, we proposed a conjectural emendation of a passage in the Blessing of Moses, specifically Deut. 33:26. This poem was the major topic of the ongoing Seminar that Albright conducted for all graduate students, and the proposal was made jointly by us as our presentation during the term. Albright, who was always on the lookout for any spark of originality and creativity on the part of students, was quite taken with the proposal and gave it his highest accolade, namely, by affirming that it was publishable, and since he was the longtime editor of the *BASOR,* the words were meant literally. As he was about to leave on a trip, he urged us to prepare the Note and put it into the next number of the *Bulletin.* So, in a single transaction, I became both co-author and editor, roles that have persisted in my life and career ever since. Cross was already a published author (in the *Biblical Archaeologist* in the fall of 1947), and he would go on to a prolific career in both categories, but for me this was the true beginning of a life in the writing, editing, and publishing of biblical scholarship.

The experience was intoxicating, and the euphoria was augmented when the late great Semitics scholar H. L. Ginsberg put his approbation in a subsequent issue of the *Bulletin,* while using it as a springboard for a group of additional ingenious emendations to the text of Deut. 33:26-29. It was the end result, typical of Ginsberg's brilliant, slashing style, that also gave both of us our first qualms about this kind of progressive emendation, in which one small change leads to another, and ultimately there are so many of them that the link between the last stage and the first has almost vanished. Inevitably, we both were encouraged to carry on our endeavors to improve and emend difficult texts in subsequent years. Over the years and now certainly, I am less intoxicated than I was then both with the approach and with the application, although I would still contend that the proposed reading is possible and even plausible.

Fifty years later, I am still trying to read and make sense of biblical verses. The primary task of the student-scholar is to read the text closely and carefully and to grapple with problems in and of the text. The Bible: its text remains a great treasury of data, containing vital information about its structure as well as its story. Careful reading and close study are the watchwords, because out of them will come rich rewards, mostly unexpected and unpredictable.

DAVID NOEL FREEDMAN
14 February 1996

Acknowledgments

1. (with Frank Moore Cross) "The Pronominal Suffixes of the Third Person Singular in Phoenician." *JNES* 10 (1951): 228-230.

2. "Archaic Forms in Early Hebrew Poetry." *ZAW* 72 (1960): 101-7.

3. "The Massoretic Text and the Qumran Scrolls: A Study in Orthography." *Textus* 2 (1962): 87-102.

4. "A Second Mesha Inscription." *BASOR* 175 (1964): 50-51.

5. (with Austin Ritterspach) "The Use of Aleph as a Vowel Letter in the Genesis Apocryphon." *RevQ* 6 (1967): 293-300.

6. "The Orthography of the Arad Ostraca." *IEJ* 19 (1969): 52-56.

7. "Orthographic Peculiarities in the Book of Job." *ErIsr* 9 (1969): 35-44.

8. (with Frank M. Cross) "Some Observations on Early Hebrew." *Bibl* 53 (1972): 413-420.

9. (with C. Franke Hyland) "Psalm 29: A Structural Analysis." *HTR* 66 (1973): 237-256.

10. "The Poetic Structure of the Framework of Deuteronomy 33." *The Bible World: Essays in Honor of Cyrus H. Gordon,* ed. Gary Rendsburg, et al. (New York: Ktav, 1980), 25-46.

11. "The Spelling of the Name 'David' in the Hebrew Bible." *Biblical and Other Studies in Honor of Robert Gordis,* ed. R. Aharoni. Hebrew Annual Review 11 (Columbus: Ohio State University Press, 1983), 89-104.

12. (with K. A. Matthews) "Orthography." *The Paleo-Hebrew Leviticus Scroll (11QpaleoLev)* (Winona Lake: Eisenbrauns, 1985), 51-95.

13. "Prose Practices in the Poetry of the Primary History." *Biblical and Related Studies Presented to Samuel Iwry,* ed. A. Kort and S. Morschauser (Winona Lake: Eisenbrauns, 1985), 49-62.

14. "Acrostic Poems in the Hebrew Bible: Alphabetic and Otherwise." *CBQ* 48 (1986): 408-431.

15. "Deliberate Deviation from an Established Pattern of Repetition in He-

brew Poetry as a Rhetorical Device." *Ninth Congress of Jewish Studies* (Jerusalem: Hebrew University Press, 1986), 45-52.

16. "Another Look at Biblical Hebrew Poetry." *Directions in Biblical Hebrew Poetry,* ed. E. R. Follis (Sheffield: Sheffield Academic Press, 1987), 11-28.

17. "On the Death of Abiner." *Love and Death in the Ancient Near East: Essays in Honor of Marvin H. Pope,* ed. J. H. Marks and R. M. Good (Guilford, Conn.: Four Quarters, 1987), 125-27.

18. "The Structure of Isaiah 40:1-11." *Perspectives on Language and Text: Essays in Honor of Francis I. Andersen on His Sixtieth Birthday,* ed. E. W. Conrad and E. G. Newing (Winona Lake: Eisenbrauns, 1987), 167-193.

19. "Patterns in Psalms 25 and 34." *Priests, Prophets and Scribes: A Festschrift in Honour of Joseph Blenkinsopp,* ed. E. Ulrich, et al. (Sheffield: Sheffield Academic Press, 1992), 125-138.

Abbreviations

AB	Anchor Bible
AJSL	*American Journal of Semitic Languages*
ANET	*Ancient Near Eastern Texts,* ed. J. B. Pritchard
AOS	American Oriental Series
ASOR	American Schools of Oriental Research
ATD	Das Alte Testament Deutsch
BA	*Biblical Archaeologist*
BASOR	*Bulletin of the American Schools of Oriental Research*
BDB	F. Brown, S. R. Driver, and C. A. Briggs, *A Hebrew and English Lexicon of the Old Testament*
BH	Biblia Hebraica
BHS	Biblia Hebraica Stuttgartensia
Bibl	*Biblica*
CIS	*Corpus inscriptionum semiticarum*
CBQ	*Catholic Biblical Quarterly*
CMHE	F. M. Cross, *Canaanite Myth and Hebrew Ethic*
DJD	Discoveries in the Judaean Desert
ErIsr	*Eretz-Israel*
HSM	Harvard Semitic Monographs
HTR	*Harvard Theological Review*
HUCA	*Hebrew Union College Annual*
IB	*Interpreter's Bible*
IDB	*Interpreter's Dictionary of the Bible*
IEJ	*Israel Exploration Journal*
JAOS	*Journal of the American Oriental Society*
JBL	*Journal of Biblical Literature*
JNES	*Journal of Near Eastern Studies*
JPOS	*Journal of the Palestine Oriental Society*

JQR	*Jewish Quarterly Review*
LXX	Septuagint
MT	Massoretic Text
OTL	Old Testament Library
PEQ	*Palestine Exploration Quarterly*
PPP	D. N. Freedman, *Pottery, Poetry, and Prophecy*
RevQ	*Revue de Qumran*
RSV	Revised Standard Version
SBL	Society of Biblical Literature
SP	Samaritan Pentateuch
UT	Cyrus H. Gordon, *Ugaritic Textbook*
VT	*Vetus Testamentum*
VTS	*Supplements to Vetus Testamentum*
ZAW	*Zeitschrift für die Alttestamentliche Wissenschaft*

1

The Pronominal Suffixes of the Third Person Singular in Phoenician

The purpose of this paper is to clarify some of the problems connected with the development of the third person singular pronominal suffixes in Phoenician. It has usually been assumed that, with the exception of the Byblian inscriptions, the third person singular suffixes, masculine and feminine, attached to nouns and verbs, always were indicated by *yodh.*[1] In the light of new inscriptional data, it appears that the problem is somewhat more complex than generally thought. Yet these complexities fit into patterns familiar in both Hebrew and Phoenician.

Two readings in the Kilamuwa inscription[2] indicate that in addition to the normal form of the 3rd masc. sg. suffix represented by *yodh,* there was in Phoenician a form of the 3rd masc. sg. suffix not indicated in the orthography (i.e., a pure vowel, probably *-ô* as in Hebrew). These are יד (l. 6), **yadô,* in the expression יד וכל שלח, "And each stretched forth *his* hand," and ראש (ll. 15, 16), **rôšô,* in the expression מי ישחת הספרז ישחת ראש בעל, "Whoever shall smash this inscrip-

1. For standard views see Z. S. Harris, *A Grammar of the Phoenician Language.* AOS 8 (New Haven: American Oriental Society, 1936), 48f.; and *Development of the Canaanite Dialects.* AOS 16 (New Haven: American Oriental Society, 1939), 54f. An exception to this is to be found in the newly published Kilamuwa Sheath Inscription, in which the 3rd masc. sg. suffix is indicated by *he* (as in the Byblian Inscriptions); cf. K. Galling, "The Scepter of Wisdom," *BASOR* 119 (1950): 16f. On the analysis of the forms in the Byblian Inscriptions, see W. F. Albright, "The Phoenician Inscriptions of the Tenth Century B.C. from Byblus," *JAOS* 67 (1947): 159f.

2. There is a considerable literature on the Kilamuwa Inscription. The original publication is F. von Luschan, *Ausgrabungen in Sendschirli* IV (Berlin: W. Spemann, 1911), 374-77. One may find old bibliographical data in M. Lidzbarski, *Ephemeris für semitische Epigraphik III (1909-15)* (Giessen: J. Ricker, 1915), 218-238. Among the more recent treatments are the following: W. F. Albright, "Notes on Early Hebrew and Aramaic Epigraphy," *JPOS* 6 (1926): 75-102; J. A. Montgomery, "Two Notes on the Kalamu Inscription," *JBL* 47 (1928): 196f.; A. Poebel, *Das appositionell bestimmte Pronomen der 1. Pers. sing. in den westsemitischen Inschriften und im Alten Testament* (Chicago: University of Chicago Press, 1932), 33-43.

tion, may Baʿal[-Ṣemed] smash *his* head." The presence of the suffix in both cases certainly is implied by the context, but it must be conceded that a reading without them is possible, though difficult. Regardless of these examples, however, the case for the existence in Phoenician of an alternative form of the 3rd masc. sg. suffix (zero in the orthography) is decisive. In later Phoenician we find the following compelling evidence for this form of the 3rd masc. sg. suffix. Alongside of the frequently repeated phrase כשמע קל יברך appears the expression קלם יברכם . . . כשמע, showing that the former phrase must be read "for he heard *his* voice; may he bless *him*." Moreover, when final vowels begin to be indicated in Punic, this formula appears as כשמע קלא יברכא or ישמע קלא וברכא (the *aleph* being the sign of the 3rd masc. sg. suffix!). The occurrence of two forms of the 3rd masc. sg. suffix in Punic and Neo-Punic, א (= *ō* or *ū*) and יא (= *yū* or *yō;* this form after words ending in long vowels), may now, with confidence, be traced back to Phoenician.

The writers suggest the following picture for the development of the 3rd masc. sg. suffix in Phoenician: one form, derived from **-ahū,* became with syncope of intervocalic *he, *-aw* > **-ô* (as in Hebrew, indicated by *aleph* in Punic); the other form, derived from **-ihū,* became, with the palatalization of *he* after the *i*-vowel, **-iyū* (indicated by *yodh aleph* in Punic). One may compare Phoenician אבי and אחי with Punic אביא, and אחיא (to be read **'abīyū* and **'aḥīyū*), the suffix appearing in the spelling after nouns with long vowels. The development in Hebrew with respect to these words was parallel, except that there was syncope and not palatalization of the *he:* thus *'ābīw* < *'abīhū, 'āḥīw* < *'āḥīhū,* etc. On the basis of this analysis, such prepositional forms as בן (Eshmunʿazar, l. 5), "in it," may readily be explained as **binnū* < **binhū.* Cf. Azitawadd B:III:8, etc., בן, "in it (fem.)," probably to be vocalized **binnā* < **binhā.*

When it comes to analyzing the syntax of these two forms in Phoenician, and in determining the situation in which one or the other is to be used, the criterion applied to Punic will not work.[3] There are many cases in Phoenician in which the suffix in *yodh* is attached to verbal and nominal forms which clearly do not end in a long vowel, e.g., לאלי, "for his god"; לאמי, "for his mother"; לתתי, "for him to give," etc. A more precise distinction in the occurrence and usage of the two forms of the 3rd masc. sg. suffix in Phoenician would seem to be necessary.

The new inscriptions from Karatepe,[4] if the writers' interpretation is correct, supply the necessary evidence to resolve the question. On the basis of the occur-

3. See Harris, *Grammar,* 51.

4. For bibliography, see the most recent treatments: A. M. Honeyman, "Epigraphic Discoveries at Karatepe," *PEQ* 81 (1949): 21-39; C. H. Gordon, "Azitawadd's Phoenician Inscription," *JNES* 8 (1949): 108-115; R. Marcus and I. J. Gelb, "The Phoenician Stele Inscription from Cilicia," *JNES* 8 (1949): 116-120; J. Obermann, *New Discoveries at Karatepe.* Transactions of the Connecticut Academy of Arts and Sciences 38 (New Haven, 1949); R. T. O'Callaghan, "The Phoenician Inscription on the King's Statue at Karatepe," *CBQ* 11 (1949): 233-248.

rence of the 3rd masc. sg. suffix in these inscriptions, it seems clear that the suffix appears as *yodh* in the orthography with nouns or verbs ending in long vowels, and with singular nouns in the *genitive case;* with nouns in the *accusative case,* the suffix appears as zero in the orthography, and its presence must be determined from the context. Throughout the whole mass of Phoenician inscriptions, this distinction is observed carefully, and it is only in later Punic inscriptions that there is a tendency to mix the suffixes.

The cases of the 3rd masc. sg. suffix in *yodh* in the Karatepe inscriptions require no comment; the clearest example of the suffix attached to a noun in the accusative case (not indicated in the orthography) is in B:III:16, ושת שם עלי, "and he sets *his own* name upon it." The same phrase occurs in B:III:14, ושת שם, "and he sets up *his* name." The readings are quite clear; the 3rd masc. sg. suffix is required by the context. In the parallel passages in the A text (IV:16, 18), the phrases under consideration are clearly a continuation of the quotation and should be rendered in the first person ("and I will set *my* name . . .").[5] To decide between the forms שמי (18) and [] שם (16, apparently without the *yodh*) is difficult. In the oblique cases, we would expect the *yodh* for the first person suffix to appear, on the analogy of Ugaritic and Kilamuwa usage.[6]

The 3rd fem. sg. suffix seems to have had a development similar to that of the 3rd masc. sg. suffix: i.e., **-ahā > -ā;* and **-ihā > -iyā.* Cf. Azitawadd B:II:10, 18, where שת אנך שם אזתודי is to be translated, "I made *its* name Azitawaddiy(a)."

The 3rd masc. sg. suffix in the Byblian inscriptions[7] poses a special problem. The *he* in the orthography may reflect a vocalization *-ihū* and/or *-ahū;* the form זרעו in *Yeḥawmilk* (l. 5), "his seed," is to be read **zarʿīw* for older **zarʿihū;* cf. Siloam (l. 2, etc.) רעו, **rēʿēw < rēʿēhū.*[8]

5. This translation also is given by J. Friedrich, "Eine altphönizische Inschrift aus Kilikien," *Forschungen und Fortschritte* 24 (1948): 78.

6. Cf. Harris, *Grammar,* 48; and C. H. Gordon, *Ugaritic Handbook.* Analecta Orientalia 25 (Rome: Pontificium Institutum Biblicum, 1947), I, §6.16. Cf. W. F. Albright, "A Hebrew Letter from the Twelfth Century B.C.," *BASOR* 73 (1939): 12, n. 18. Note, however, in the *Yeḥawmilk* Inscription, l. 8, שמע קל ("she heard my voice").

7. For general bibliography, see Harris, *Grammar;* M. Dunand, *Byblia Grammata* (Beirut: Direction des antiquites, 1945); and Albright, *JAOS* 67 (1947): 153-160. One article has appeared since these publications: C. Brockelmann, "Kanaanäische Miscellen," in *Festschrift Otto Eissfeldt* (Halle: M. Niemeyer, 1947), 61-67.

8. Our treatment of this subject was prepared independently of that of Obermann, *New Discoveries at Karatepe.* He deals with the evidence of the Kilamuwa and Karatepe Inscriptions, and comes to the conclusion that the suffix of the third person (as also the first) may be written with or without the *yodh* depending upon whether the noun ends in a long vowel or stands in the genitive (pp. 25f.). His further observations on the "zero" form of the suffix and the effect of "popular speech" on the orthography of the Karatepe Inscriptions are unwarranted. Thus *šm* in B:III:14 ("his name") is not parallel to *šmy* in A:IV:18 (which must be read "my name"); and the form *bny,* "in it," B:III:8, does not occur, the *yodh* belonging with the following word; cf. p. 27.

2

Archaic Forms in Early Hebrew Poetry

Archaic forms and particles have been identified in increasing number in Hebrew poetry, especially in the earliest Israelite songs.[1] Since none of these features was in regular usage in the language after the 13th century B.C., and since they do not noticeably affect meaning, it would appear that their chief function was aesthetic. Examination of a number of examples indicates that their use was structural rather than ornamental, deliberate rather than haphazard. It seems to the present writer that a specific metrical purpose is deducible in several cases, whereby one colon or half-line is lengthened in this manner in order to balance the parallel colon or half-line. In short, these features were artistically employed to achieve a symmetrical pattern. Such balance or symmetry is a principal characteristic of early Hebrew poetic structure, deriving apparently from its musical framework (i.e., rhythmic dancing and singing, along with simple or complex choral antiphony). In analyzing the metrical evidence, scholars may reduce it to some kind of arithmetic pattern, but this does not mean that the poet consciously used a numerical process. It is not likely that the Israelites counted syllables carefully, or even accents for that matter, when composing their poetry. but it is convenient for us to do so in tabulating the evidence.

It may be desirable to point out that only a small fraction of the original

1. See, e.g., W. F. Albright, "The Oracles of Balaam," *JBL* 63 (1944): 207-233; "The Psalm of Habakkuk," *Studies in Old Testament Prophecy,* ed. by H. H. Rowley (Edinburgh: T. & T. Clark, 1950), 1-18; "A Catalogue of Early Hebrew Lyric Poems (Psalm LXVIII)," *HUCA* 23 (1950-51): 1-39; "The Old Testament and the Canaanite Language and Literature," *CBQ* 7 (1945): 5-31; and most recently, "Some Remarks on the Song of Moses in Deuteronomy xxxii," *VT* 9 (1959): 339-346. F. M. Cross, Jr., and D. N. Freedman, "The Blessing of Moses," *JBL* 67 (1948): 191-210; "A Royal Song of Thanksgiving: II Samuel 22 = Psalm 18," *JBL* 72 (1953): 15-34; "The Song of Miriam," *JNES* 14 (1955): 237-250. B. Vawter, "The Canaanite Background of Genesis 49," *CBQ* 17 (1955): 1-18. H. D. Hummel, "Enclitic *Mem* in Early Northwest Semitic, Especially Hebrew," *JBL* 76 (1957): 85-107.

number of archaic forms in Hebrew poetry are now preserved in the Massoretic Text. In the course of transmission most of them were edited out of the text. The process of grammatical, orthographic, and general linguistic revision is well known in all literatures; that archaisms survive at all in MT is partly the result of accidental circumstances, but also a tribute to the conservatism of the scribal tradition in Israel. Let us look at some examples from early Hebrew poems:

1. The Song of Deborah (Judg. 5:26). It is generally agreed that the Song of Deborah is one of the oldest surviving examples of Israelite poetry, having been composed as early as the 11th century, and written down probably in the 10th. Judg. 5:26 refers to Jael's preparations for killing Sisera. It reads as follows:

Accents		*Syllables*
3	*yādāh layyātēd tišlaḥnâ*	8
3	*wîmînāh lᵉhalmût ʿᵃmēlîm*	9

Two points may be made about the preserved text: a) the conjunction at the beginning of the second colon is probably secondary, perhaps introduced into the text when the material was written down in consecutive fashion (i.e., in prose form, not by line or poetic unit);[2] b) the word *tišlaḥnâ* appears to be a 3rd fem. pl. impf. form, which is anomalous since the subject is "she" (i.e., Jael), 3rd fem. sing. Years ago, C. F. Burney correctly identified the form as the 3rd fem. sing. impf., with energic *nun* (like Arabic *-an, -anna*).[3] This form is quite common in Ugaritic, and has been identified in a number of places in the Hebrew Bible (i.e., the energic form of the verb without suffix).[4] In an attempt to reconstruct an earlier form of the text, we may vocalize as follows:

Accents		*Syllables*
3	*yadah layatid tišlaḥanna*	9
3	*yamīnah lahalmūt ʿamilīm*	9
	Her hand to the tent-peg she stretches,	
	Her right hand to the workmen's mallet.	

The accentual pattern is clearly 3:3; a syllable count gives us 9:9. It will be noted that syllabic equality has been attained only by the addition of the energic ending to the verb *(-anna)*. Without it the first colon would be two syllables short. The implication of this evidence is that the poet deliberately used the energic form of the verb for metrical reasons: to lengthen the first colon so that it balanced the second. It will be seen that a purely accentual system for measuring meter would

2. Cross-Freedman, *JBL* 72 (1953): 17-19, nn. o-v.
3. C. F. Burney, *The Book of Judges* (London: Rivingtons, 1918), 152f.
4. Albright, *JBL* 63 (1944): 212, n. 23; Cross-Freedman, *JBL* 67 (1948): 203, n. 25.

be inadequate to reflect this difference in length, and would offer no basis for the use of this special form of the verb.

2. 2 Sam. 22:16 = Ps. 18:16.[5] In dealing with the passage, we will disregard the initial conjunctions.[6] The verse reads as follows:

Accents			*Syllables*
3	*yērā'ū 'apīqê*	{ *yām* (2 Sam.) / *mayim* (Ps.) }	7
3	*yiggālū môsedōt tēbēl*		8

There is only one significant difference between the two versions: 2 Sam. reads *yām,* Ps. has *mayim* (originally monosyllabic *maym*). The metrical tabulation is the same: accentual 3:3; syllabic 7:8. This is quite regular, and the difference of a single syllable (7:8) hardly disturbs the symmetry. Nevertheless a better reading is possible. It is quite certain that the initial *mem* of *mayim* (Ps.) is the now-familiar enclitic *m(i)* and should be attached to the preceding word. The resultant text is: *'apīqê-mi yām.* This adds a syllable to the first colon, matching the second exactly, 8:8. At the same time, the two texts are harmonized in accordance with what is the more original and superior reading: *yam* for *maym.* We may render thus:

> The channels of the Sea appear,
> The foundations of the world are exposed.

It is to be noted that the passage in 2 Sam. preserves the correct reading, but in a revised form; the enclitic *mem* has been edited out of the text, with the resulting disturbance of the meter. This was undoubtedly the common practice, and may well account for a good deal of apparent metrical irregularity. Where no parallel text or more original variant exists, the damage would be irremediable. Compare, for example, the following case.

3. Deut. 33:11b. MT reads:

Accents		*Syllables*
3	*meḥaṣ motnayim qāmâw*	7
3	*ūmešan'âw min-yeqūmūn*	8

As pointed out by W. F. Albright, the anomalous *motnayim qāmâw* is to be read *motnê-mi qāmâw,* with enclitic *mem* between the members of the construct chain.[7]

5. Cross-Freedman, *JBL* 72 (1953): 26, nn. 40, 41.

6. *Ibid.,* 17-19, nn. o-v.

7. Albright, *CBQ* 7 (1945): 22f.; cf. *JBL* 63 (1944): 219, n. 83. Cross-Freedman, *JBL* 67 (1948): 204, n. 33.

It is to be noted that the Samaritan text has the correct reading: *motnê qāmâw;* but the original enclitic *mem* has been edited out of the text. Moving to the second colon, we may safely omit the initial conjunction, and for the strange *min,* read *man,* "whoever."[8] We vocalize and scan as follows:

Accents		*Syllables*
3	*maḥas motnê-mi qāmâw*	7
3	*masan'âw man yaqūman*	7
	Smite the thighs of his foes,	
	Of those who hate him, whoever arises.	

4. Num. 23:10b (Oracles of Balaam).[9] MT reads:

Accents		*Syllables*
2:2	*tāmōt napšī / mōt y^{e}šārīm*	4:4
3	*ūt^{e}hī 'aḥ^{a}rītī kāmōhū*	10

The plural form *y^{e}šārīm* is difficult to justify, especially in the light of *kāmōhū,* which requires a singular antecedent. As suggested by Albright, we should read here *yāšār* (sg.) with enclitic *mem.*[10] The effect of the use of enclitic *mem* with nouns was to preserve the case ending (here genitive), which was otherwise lost in the evolution of the language: thus, *yašari-mi.* The vowel of the enclitic itself *(mi)* was apparently preserved when the enclitic occurred "medially" (i.e., in a construct chain, or between a noun or verb and its suffix), but was lost when the *mem* was final. When it was dropped, the resulting form would be indistinguishable from the normal masculine plural, as in the present case *(yašarīm > y^{e}šārīm).* Omitting the conjunction at the beginning of the second colon, the resulting text is:

Accents		*Syllables*
2:2	*tamōt napšī / mōt yašari-m*	4:4
3	*tihī 'aḥarītī kamōhū*	9

The metrical pattern 2:2:3 is common in Hebrew poetry.[11] The syllable count in the first line remains unchanged; however, the anomalous plural form has been

8. The last word can be read *y^{e}qīmennū* "(whoever) attacks him," and this may be preferable; cf. Gen. 49:9 = Num. 24:9. Cross-Freedman, *JBL* 67 (1948): 194, and 204, n. 35. Albright, *CBQ* 7 (1945): 23f.; *JBL* 63 (1944): 225.

9. Albright, *CBQ* 7 (1945): 213.

10. *Ibid.,* n. 28a.

11. Albright, *HUCA* 23 (1950-51): 5ff., passim; Cross, "Notes on a Canaanite Psalm in the Old Testament," *BASOR* 117 (1950): 20.

eliminated, while the symmetry has been maintained through the use of enclitic *mem.*

Let me die the death of the upright,
Let my end be like his.

5. Ps. 29:1-2a provides a parallel case.[12] MT reads:

Accents		*Syllables*
2:2	*hābū la YHWH / bᵉnê 'ēlīm*	5:4
2:2	*hābū la YHWH / kābōd wā'ōz*	5:4
2:2	*hābū la YHWH / kᵉbōd šᵉmô*	5:4

The pattern is quite clear and regular though the syllable count is not exactly even (5:4; one may speculate that the monosyllabic Ba'l originally stood in place of bisyllabic YHWH). However, *'ēlīm* in the first line is to be read as El with the enclitic *mem: 'ēli-m,* i.e., the sons of El, the gods. In this case the enclitic preserves the case ending and provides the needed fourth syllable to balance the metrical structure of the tri-colon.

Ascribe to Yahweh O gods (sons of El),
Ascribe to Yahweh majesty and might,
Ascribe to Yahweh the majesty due his name.

6. Exod. 15 (Song of Miriam).[13] There are a number of archaic forms in the poem which have direct bearing on the problem of meter. MT in v. 6 reads:

Accents		*Syllables*
2:2	*yᵉmīnkā YHWH / ne'dārī bakkōᵃḥ*	5:5
2:2	*yᵉmīnkā YHWH / tir'aṣ 'ôyēb*	5:4

The peculiar form *ne'dārī* has been correctly explained by Albright as an archaic infinitive absolute, found also among the Canaanite forms in the Amarna letters.[14] Its metrical function seems clear. At the same time, it may be an improvement to read the plural *'ōyᵉbīm* with the LXX, especially in view of the plural suffixes and nouns in vv. 5 and 7.

Thy right arm, Yahweh is awesome in strength,
Thy right arm, Yahweh destroys the enemy.

12. Cf. my remarks in Hummel, 101f., nn. 101, 102.
13. Cross-Freedman, *JNES* 14 (1955): 237-250.
14. *Ibid.,* no. 14, pp. 245f.

In v. 9, MT preserves two cases of enclitic *mem: timlā'-ēm* for *timlā'ēmô,* and *tôrīš-ēm* for *tôrīšēmô.*[15] We may vocalize and scan the verse as follows:

Accents		Syllables
2:2	*'amar 'ōyīb / 'erdōp 'aśśīg*	4:4
2:2	*'aḥalliq šalal / timla'-im napšī*	5:5
2:2	*'arīq ḥarbī / tôrīš-im yadī*	4:5
	The enemy said, I'll pursue, I'll overtake,	
	I'll apportion the spoil, My desire will be sated,	
	I'll bare my sword, My hand will conquer.	

Metrically we may tabulate as follows: accentual count, 2:2, 2:2, 2:2; syllabic count, 4:4, 5:5, 4:5, in a regualr pattern of four and five syllables. Even greater regularity might be secured by restoring old case and verb endings.

In v. 16, MT has the curious form *'êmātâ,* which is to be understood as the fem. sg. accusative form of original *'ēmatu* (in contrast with the later, normal form *'êmâ*). The longer form has apparently been preserved for metrical reasons. We read as follows:[16]

Accents		Syllables
2:2	*tappīl 'alêhim / 'êmata wapaḥd*	5:5
	Thou dost bring down upon them terror and dread.	

7. Num. 21:17-18 (Song of the Well). This short poem has a strongly marked rhythm and a strikingly regular meter; MT reads:

Accents		Syllables
2:2	*'alī b^e'ēr / '^{e}nū lāh*	4:3
3	*b^e'ēr ḥ^{a}pārūhā śārīm*	8
3	*kārūhā n^{e}dībê hā'ām*	8

The noun *b^e'ēr* was originally monosyllabic, *bi'r(u) > bē'r.* The article before *'am* is to be omitted, on the general rule that the article was not used in early poetry, and specifically because the parallel expression, *śārīm,* does not have it. Other characteristic features of early Hebrew poetic style include the following: omission of conjunctions at the beginning of cola, and of the relative pronoun where it is normally required in Hebrew prose. The last line of the poem poses certain difficulties. It reads:

15. *Ibid.,* nos. 25f., pp. 246f.

16. *Ibid.,* nos. 50f., p. 249. With the noun in the accusative, we should then read the verb as hiphil, *tappīl,* rather than qal.

Accents		*Syllables*
2:2	*bimḥōqēq / b^{e}miš῾^{a}nōtām*	3:5

The rather rigid parallelism of the rest of the poem is somewhat disturbed by the plural form of the second word in this line, and the use of the pronominal suffix. The use of the suffix with only one of a pair of words in parallel construction is a common device in Biblical Hebrew, but we would expect the suffix here to be used with the first member *(m^{e}ḥōqeq)* rather than the second. It seems best, therefore, to regard the final *mem* as enclitic, and to read *bimaš῾anti-m* (or the like), "with staff." We vocalize and scan the poem as follows:

Accents		*Syllables*
2:2	*῾aliyi bi'r / ῾aniyū lah*	4:4
3	*bi'r ḥaparūha šārīm*	7
3	*karūha nadībê ῾am*	7
2:2	*bimahōqiq / bimaš῾anti-m*	4:4

Spring up, O well! Sing to it!
Well which the princes dug,
Which the leaders of the people hewed out,
With scepter — with staff.

The accentual count is 2:2, 3:3, 2:2; the syllabic count is 4:4, 7:7, 4:4.

8. Num. 21:27b (Song of Sihon). This is the only clear example of an unchanged Amorite, i.e., Canaanite, poem in the Bible, dating presumably from the 13th century B.C. We are concerned here only with the opening line, which reads:

Accents		*Syllables*
3	*bō'ū ḥešbôn tibbānēh*	7
3	*w^{e}tikkônēn ῾īr sīḥôn*	7

While the meter is quite satisfactory as the text stands, some changes are in order. The conjunction at the beginning of the second colon ought to be dropped. The form of *tikkônēn,* the so-called hithpo῾l with assimilation of the prefixed *-ṯ,* while apparently attested elsewhere in MT, is questionable. It is more likely that we have here the simple niphal form *tikkōn,* plus the energic ending *-anna,* without suffix. For MT *w^{e}tikkônēn,* we propose *tikkōn-anna.* The occurrence of parallel verb forms, one with energic *nun,* the other without, is attested in Ugaritic poetry.[17] Metrically the situation is unchanged.

{ Come to Heshbon. Let it be built! }
{ *Come! Let Heshbon be built!* }
Let the city of Sihon be established!

17. C. H. Gordon, *Ugaritic Handbook.* Analecta Orientalia 25 (Rome: Pontificium Institutum Biblicum, 1947), I, 62 and nn. 3-4.

The evidence presented is naturally insufficient to draw any far-reaching conclusions about the nature of Hebrew meter. Other explanations of the survival of archaic features are possible; their identification is not always certain, and in other passages their metrical significance is not easily discernible.[18] Furthermore, we have been able to demonstrate metrical regularity only within limited poetic units. It may be suggested, however, that the early Israelites had a strong sense of meter, i.e., a conscious poetic measurement, more precise than the commonly accepted and accentual system, though falling far short of the quantitative metrical systems of Greek or Latin verse. While syllable-counting is both imprecise and pedestrian, it affords a clue to the rhythmic structure of Hebrew poetry, and an occasional glimpse at the Israelite poet composing his verse.

18. E.g., Ps. 29:6, where the enclitic *mem (yarqīd-ēm)* does not seem to improve the metrical pattern. H. L. Ginsberg identified the form (*Kitvê Ugarit [The Ugarit Texts]* [Jerusalem: Bialik Foundation, 1936], 129-131); cf. also "The Ugaritic Texts and Textual Criticism," *JBL* 62 (1943): 115.

3

The Massoretic Text and the Qumran Scrolls: A Study in Orthography

I

Some years ago, Frank M. Cross and I made a systematic study of the orthography of representative inscriptions in the different Northwest Semitic dialects. These could be dated by epigraphic and other means to the period between the 10th and 6th centuries B.C.E., and thus provided a pattern for comparison with Hebrew inscriptions of the same period. The object of the investigation was to determine the basic principles governing orthographic practice and to trace the course of development and refinement in alphabetic spelling of these dialects and of Hebrew in particular. One result of the study[1] was the establishment of a relative chronology, and with the help of related disciplines, especially that of palaeography, an absolute chronology could also be fixed within limits. Thus it was possible not only to determine the general pattern of orthographic development, and to distinguish its principal phases, but also to date these approximately. Our conclusions may be summarized as follows:

1. The Phoenician phase of consonantal orthography, down to the end of the 10th century B.C.E. This was a purely consonantal spelling, without indication of vowel sounds at all, and is the oldest form of alphabetic writing. It is characteristic of the Proto-Canaanite inscriptions found at Sinai and in Palestine. Ugaritic spelling, with different *aleph* signs to indicate various vowels accompanying the *aleph,* is a special phenomenon arising from the peculiar linguistic situation at Ugarit, and has no echoes in later alphabetic spelling. Phoenician inscriptions, from the earliest

1. F. M. Cross, Jr., and D. N. Freedman, *Early Hebrew Orthography.* AOS 36 (New Haven: American Oriental Society, 1952, repr. 1981).

to the latest times, are written in typically consonantal orthography: in fact, they define the nature and details of the system. The earliest Hebrew inscriptions (e.g., the Gezer calendar) exhibit the same characteristics, and clearly belong to this pattern of spelling.

2. The Aramaic phase, from the 9th century, involving the use of *matres lectionis* to represent certain vowel sounds. Two further subdivisions can be distinguished:

a) The introduction of the vowel letters *he, waw,* and *yodh,* to represent long vowels in the final position: i.e., *he* for *ā, ē, ō, waw* for *ū,* and *yodh* for *ī.* We find this pattern in Aramaic inscriptions from the 9th century on, in the Meshaʿ inscription (also 9th century), and in Hebrew inscriptional material from this period (chiefly 8th century on). In short there was a clear shift in Hebrew spelling practice, which may be dated to the 9th century.

b) The gradual introduction of vowel letters, *waw* and *yodh,* in the medial position, to represent *ū* and *ī.* The first examples are found in Aramaic inscriptions from the late 8th century (e.g., *Aššur* spelled with *waw* for *ū*), and now also in Hebrew from approximately the same period, the end of the 8th century (in the so-called Shebna inscription, with the word *'ārūr,* using *waw* for the *ū* vowel). Such usage, however, remains rare and sporadic in Hebrew until the end of the preexilic period. Thus there are only a few examples in the whole of the Lachish correspondence.

II

While some questions could not be decided because of lack of evidence, and others remain obscure, the general pattern, established by inductive analysis from hundreds of examples, has not been seriously undermined by critics, but has been confirmed by subsequent discoveries. On the assumption that some parts at least of the Old Testament were originally written down in the preexilic period, an effort was made to test the usefulness of our studies in early Hebrew orthography for the investigation of the biblical text. For this purpose a series of studies was made of some of the poems, which on other grounds might be regarded as among the oldest compositions in the Old Testament. Professor W. F. Albright pioneered with his important paper on the Oracles of Balaam,[2] followed by studies on Hab. 3,[3] Ps. 68,[4] and, most recently, Deut. 32.[5] Cross and I,

2. "The Oracles of Balaam," *JBL* 63 (1944): 207-233.

3. "The Psalm of Habakkuk," *Studies in Old Testament Prophecy,* ed. H. H. Rowley (Edinburgh: T. & T. Clark, 1950), 1-18.

4. "A Catalogue of Early Hebrew Lyric Poems (Psalm LXVIII)," *HUCA* 23 (1950-51): 1-39.

5. "Some Remarks on the Song of Moses in Deuteronomy xxxii," *VT* 9 (1959): 339-346.

continuing a long Johns Hopkins concern with this early poetry, as attested by the articles of Albright and before him of Paul Haupt, have published papers on Deut. 32;[6] Ps. 18 = 2 Sam. 22,[7] and Exod. 15,[8] and have others as yet unpublished. It is our considered judgment that these papers have generally vindicated the application of orthographic analysis to selected biblical passages. That they have proved useful in text criticism and in the clarification of difficult passages can hardly be denied. Used circumspectly they may be helpful in fixing an original date of written composition. Thus, if any of these poems were written down in the age of David and Solomon, we would expect them to have been written in the prevailing orthographic style, i.e., Phoenician consonantal orthography. While the present Hebrew text of the Old Testament naturally reflects much later spelling techniques, the presence of examples of archaic spelling ("mistakes" from the point of view of later practice, but quite correct according to earlier usage) would be evidence in support of such an hypothesis. We would not wish to press the case beyond this point, since the evidence is limited, and the conclusions depend to some degree on the presuppositions adopted and the method employed in interpreting the data.

The orthographic approach has proved useful not only in identifying the features of the earliest Hebrew spelling, but also in distinguishing orthographically the dialects of northern and southern Palestine (i.e., Israelite and Judahite). A basic difference lies in the pronunciation and spelling of the proto-Semitic diphthongs *aw* and *ay*, which were contracted in the North to *ô* and *ê* respectively while they were preserved uncontracted in the South. Israelite followed Phoenician and Ugaritic in this respect, while Judahite agrees with Aramaic and Arabic. The difference in pronunciation is reflected in the spelling: thus in the North the words for "house" and "death" would be written *bt* and *mt* (pronounced *bêt* and *môt*), while in the South they would be written *byt* and *mwt* (pronounced *bayt* and *mawt*). Comparison of Ps. 18 and 2 Sam. 22 indicated the existence of two recensions of this poem, one written in the standard Judahite spelling characteristic of MT in general, the other in northern orthography.[9] While there has been considerable contamination of the text in the course of transmission, sufficient evidence for the "contracted" orthography survives in the 2 Sam. recension to support substantially the "northern" hypothesis. A further possibility in this direction may be mentioned. The date and provenience of the book of Job have occasioned much debate among scholars, and it cannot be said that any hypothesis has won general approval as yet. Recently the proposal has been advanced that the book is a product of the northern diaspora, i.e., that it comes from the community of Israelites exiled from

6. "The Blessing of Moses," *JBL* 67 (1948): 191-210.
7. "A Royal Song of Thanksgiving: 2 Samuel 22 = Psalm 18," *JBL* 72 (1953): 15-34.
8. "The Song of Miriam," *JNES* 14 (1955): 237-250.
9. *JBL* 72 (1953): 15-17.

Palestine after the fall of Samaria in 722 B.C.E.[10] A number of arguments have been adduced in support of this view, but quite apart from these, a provisional examination of the orthography of the book of Job shows a surprisingly high incidence of peculiar and even unique spellings which are characteristically northern in character. That is, they reflect contraction of the diphthongs *aw* and *ay* in spelling (and presumably therefore in pronunciation), e.g., the particle *ʿôdh* is repeatedly spelled *ʿd* instead of normal Judahite and biblical *ʿwd.*[11] The survival in the book of numerous spellings of this sort can hardly be accidental, and may point to a "northern" recension of the book of Job. [See further Chapter 7 in this volume]

III

In an important sense, however, these studies have been preliminary. The main problem from the beginning has been to determine the place of the MT as a whole (and not simply isolated passages and archaic survivals) in the history of Hebrew orthography, i.e., in what phase of the evolution of Hebrew spelling does the distinctive and characteristic orthography of the MT belong? While the MT is by no means homogeneous, and there is considerable variation not only between the main divisions (e.g., the orthography of the Torah is more conservative than that of the Kethubim, particularly Chronicles) and from book to book, but also on the same page or even in the same verse, there is nevertheless a discernible pattern in the use of *matres lectionis,* though this has not been clearly analyzed or described scientifically. One reason for this is the superimposition of Massoretic vocalization on Massoretic spelling in the ordinary printed text of the Old Testament. For the purpose of clarity in the discussion which follows, let us make the following distinction between spelling and vocalization: by "spelling" we mean the Hebrew letters used to indicate the consonants and certain vowels, i.e., the unpointed text. This is sometimes called the consonantal text, but the term is misleading, since some of the letters represent vowels and not consonants. By "Massoretic vocalization" we mean the full system of vowel indication introduced in the latter half of the 1st millennium C.E., which, while combining with the system of vowel letters, nevertheless superseded and distorted the earlier pattern. There is ample evidence to show that the two systems diverge at many points and reflect different periods in the evolution of Hebrew phonology. Thus the vocalization, while preserving older traditions, is nevertheless considerably later than the pronunciation implied in the spelling of the MT.

10. The suggestion is Albright's. On the North-Israelite diaspora, see his "An Ostracon from Calah and the North-Israelite Diaspora," *BASOR* 149 (1958): 33-36.

11. Job 1:18; 2:3, 9; 8:12, 21.

A cursory examination of MT shows that its spelling does not fit into any phase of preexilic spelling, which even in the latest materials shows only sporadic use of internal *matres lectionis.* On the contrary, MT exhibits consistent use of internal *matres lectionis* for *ū* and *ī* and the contracted diphthongs *aw* and *ay* (*ô* and *ê* respectively). The representation of *ō* varies considerably (i.e., sometimes the *waw* is used, sometimes not), while *ā* and *ē* are not represented by vowel letters. There is no indication of short vowels.

If Massoretic spelling was clearly postexilic — and since the written composition or compilation of any complete book or part of the Old Testament could hardly be attributed to an earlier date, this was only to be expected — it was not at all clear where in the postexilic period the orthography of the Massoretic Text properly fits. The *terminus ad quem* was fixed by the adoption of the Massoretic Text with its particular orthography as the official Bible of the Jewish community toward the end of the 1st century C.E. This view has been fully confirmed by the manuscript discoveries in the Murabbaʿat caves: the biblical manuscripts, which date from the Second Revolt, i.e., before 135 C.E., are Massoretic both in text and spelling. The origins of Massoretic spelling and its emergence as a definable system must be placed much earlier, of course. The discoveries at Qumran in addition to the previously known Nash Papyrus (and to a lesser extent the evidence of Jewish coins of the 2nd and 1st centuries B.C.E.) have enabled us to trace a specifically Massoretic type of spelling back to the latter part of the 2nd century B.C.E., or roughly 100 B.C.E.

For the *terminus a quo* there was in the first place the exile. In view of critical theories concerning the compilation of the principal parts of the Old Testament, and in particular of the Torah and Former Prophets, it seemed reasonable to date the emergence of a canonical text to the century after the exile. When we take into consideration the considerable divergences between the latest preexilic orthography and Massoretic spelling, the 5th century would appear to be the earliest possible occasion for the appearance of Massoretic spelling, while the 4th would be a more reasonable supposition. On general considerations, therefore, the emergence of Massoretic spelling could be narrowed to the period between the 5th-4th and the 2nd centuries B.C.E., since by the latter date distinctively Massoretic spelling appears in biblical manuscripts alongside other more elaborate spelling systems. Greater precision in narrowing the limits could hardly be undertaken because of the deplorable lack of Hebrew inscriptional evidence for the period in question. We are dependent chiefly on seals and stamps, with personal and place names,[12] and these add little to our knowledge of the orthographic practice of the period.

12. Of these, the well-known *yahûd* stamps and the five-letter Jerusalem insignia *(yršlm)* may be mentioned. The *yahûd* stamps are sometimes spelled with the *waw* for *ū*, sometimes without: the former reflects current practice in the 4th (or possibly late 5th) century, while the latter spelling attests the survival of an even older practice. The Jerusalem insignia likewise reflects the persistence of a traditional design and custom of spelling.

IV

While the Qumran scrolls have provided more than ample materials — in fact, an overwhelming and embarrassing quantity — for the orthographic practice, or rather confusion, of the period from the 2nd century B.C.E. through the 1st century C.E., they could hardly have been expected to supply data for the crucial earlier period in which the origins of Massoretic spelling lie. The Qumran community itself does not antedate the latter half of the 2nd century B.C.E., and the bulk of the manuscript materials necessarily belongs to the period following the settlement there. That some of the manuscripts, especially of biblical books, might be of an earlier date was a possibility to be considered: thus the great Isaiah scroll could be dated by experts to the latter part of the 2nd century B.C.E., and a fragment of Ecclesiastes to about the middle of the same century. With the refinement of palaeographical analysis in the last few years, and the examination of hundreds and hundreds of documents from this period, a sequence dating of Qumran manuscripts has proved feasible. Substantial agreement in procedures and results has been achieved by the principal workers in this field, chief of whom is Professor Cross. His provisional study in *JBL*[13] fixed the order and dates of a wide selection of Qumran manuscripts within relatively narrow limits. It has now been superseded by his definitive analysis of all presently available Qumran material (in "The Development of the Jewish Scripts," *The Bible and the Ancient Near East,* ed. G. E. Wright [1961], 133-202).

With the vast amount of material now available, and with absolute control provided by dated documents interspersed through the latter part of the period, the dating of the Qumran manuscripts is virtually certain throughout: we may allow a maximum variation of fifty years in the dating of particular manuscripts. As was to be expected, the large majority of documents from Qumran date from the period of Essene occupation (i.e., from the late 2nd century B.C.E. to the late 1st century C.E.). Nevertheless, Cross has identified several manuscripts of an earlier date, some from the early and middle 2nd century B.C.E., and a few fragments even older than these. They may have been brought to Qumran by the first settlers, or procured from other sources. In any case, there are now three biblical manuscripts which belong, according to Cross's analysis, to the period from *ca.* 275-175 B.C.E., and may reasonably be regarded as the oldest surviving fragments of the Bible. These manuscripts, only one of which has been published in part (4QSam^{b}),[14] now offer us data concerning Hebrew orthographic practice in the 3rd and early 2nd centuries B.C.E., thus enabling us to close partially the gap in the history of postexilic spelling; the situation in the 5th-4th centuries remains obscure. In view of the fact that complete publication of these manuscripts is some years off, and because of their

13. "The Oldest Manuscripts from Qumran," *JBL* 74 (1955): 147-172.
14. *Ibid.,* 165-172.

critical importance for the study of Hebrew orthography in the postexilic period, and particularly for the origins of Massoretic spelling, Cross has made the necessary transcriptions available to me for a provisional orthographic analysis.[15]

Cross classifies the documents as follows:

1. The oldest manuscript is apparently 4QExod[f], containing Exod. 40:8-27 and dating from *ca.* 275-225 B.C.E. or roughly 250.
2. 4QSam[b] contains 1 Sam. 16:1-11; 19:10-17; 20:26–21:6; 23:9-17, and is to be dated *ca.* 250-200 B.C.E., or about 225.
3. The last is 4QJer[a], containing Jer. 12:17–13:6 and 17:10-25, and is to be dated between 225 and 175 B.C.E., or about 200.

There is no need to press for a precise dating of the manuscripts in question at this time, and since the science of Hebrew palaeography has not yet achieved the exactitude or the prestige of Greek epigraphy, we can allow considerable leeway without debate. We intend therefore to treat the documents as roughly contemporaneous and as coming from the latter half of the 3rd century or, at the latest, the early part of the 2nd. The fragments comprise a random selection of sufficient length to secure representative orthographic data, though some characteristic forms are lacking for the reconstruction of a complete picture of the manuscripts' orthography. Our concern is especially with the use of vowel letters in the orthography of the documents, and more particularly with the representation of the medial vowels, since the indication of final vowels had long since been regularized, and the pattern of use remained relatively unchanged from the 9th or 8th century on. There is a significant exception to the general rule: in preexilic inscriptions the 3rd masc. sg. suffix attached to nouns in the singular is regularly represented by the letter *he,* whereas in these documents, as in MT commonly, *waw* is used. The vowel in question was presumably *ô,* though this is not certain for pre-Massoretic vocalization (i.e., we are dependent upon Massoretic vocalization for this pronunciation: it may have been *uh* in preexilic times and possibly *aw* later, contracted to *ô* in postexilic times). Thus the significance of the shift from *he* to *waw* is not altogether clear, though the use of *waw* in this situation is sufficient to demonstrate that our documents belong to a definitely postexilic stratum of Hebrew orthography. A second modification of preexilic spelling relates to the 3rd masc. sg. suffix with plural nouns (Massoretic *-āw*), which is represented in preexilic inscriptions simply by the letter *waw,* while in the present documents, as in MT generally, by *-yw.* There is some difficulty in explaining the appearance of the preexilic form in the southern dialect, though it seems to derive ultimately from *-ayhu.* The postexilic

15. I have consulted with Cross at various stages in the study, and wish to express my appreciation for many helpful suggestions. I must bear responsibility for the conclusions, such as they are.

form *-yw* is incompatible with Massoretic vocalization *-aw,* and reflects rather the vocalization *-ayw* from *ayhū* with syncope of the *he* as very often in spoken Hebrew (so Siloam *rēʿēw* for MT *rēʿēhū,* cf. Jer. 6:21 רֵעוֹ, which is wrongly vocalized.[16] Once again we have a characteristically postexilic form both in our 3rd century documents and MT.

To sum up: the use of vowel letters in the final position in the documents under consideration is identical with prevailing practice in MT. Thus *he* is used to represent final *ā, ē,* and *ô,* e.g., כה *(kô)* in 4QJer[a]. *Waw* is used for final *ū* and *ô* (derived from *aw* — the question of the contraction of the diphthong must be considered further), and *yodh* for final *ī* and *ê* (derived from *ay*). So far as the final vowel letters are concerned, it is clear that the general system, which goes back to the 9th century B.C.E., underwent specific changes in the postexilic period, and that by the 3rd century at the latest they were firmly incorporated into standard orthographic practice. The unanimity of our 3rd century sources, and their identity with Massoretic practice, suggest that the pattern must actually have originated earlier, perhaps in the 4th or even 5th century.

V

It is in connection with the use of medial vowel letters that more fruitful results can be obtained, however. The general pattern is the same in all three documents, and corresponds closely to that of MT, though with certain significant exceptions. We may summarize the evidence as follows:

1. There is no use of vowel letters to represent short vowels, as in MT.
2. The same is true with regard to medial *ā* and *ē.* This is also the common practice of MT.
3. *Waw* is used for *ū* and for *ô,* which results from the contraction of *aw. Yodh* is used for *ī* and for *ê,* which results from the contraction of *ay.* The question as to when these diphthongs contracted is not easily settled. In preexilic orthography the chief evidence for the contraction of the diphthongs is the loss of the original *waw* or *yodh,* while the presence of the *waw* or *yodh* is evidence of its retention. The situation in postexilic orthography is complicated by various factors, including the persistence of historical spelling, i.e., the preservation of *waw* or *yodh* after contraction, so that the letter becomes in effect a vowel indicator, and by the evidence of Massoretic vocalization, which indicates that the diphthong was contracted in certain instances, e.g., the construct state of nouns like *bêt* and *môt,* and preserved in others, e.g.,

16. *Early Hebrew Orthography,* 50, no. 26, and no. 28.

in the artificial forms like *bayit* and *māwet.* If contraction had taken place we would then expect examples of two concomitant phenomena: (1) the occasional loss of originally diphthongal *waw* and *yodh,* since the sounds would fall together with vocalic *ō* and *ē,* which are not always or even regularly represented by the corresponding vowel letters. (2) Extension of the use of *waw* and *yodh* to cases of *ō* and *ē* which did not originate from the corresponding diphthongs *aw* and *ay.* In other words, we would expect similarity in orthographic treatment of sounds which fell together, or at least some overlapping. It is too much to expect that the Hebrew scribes could have maintained a formal, i.e., orthographic distinction for any length of time or with consistency when the phonemic support for the distinction had been lost. Even in modern times with our massive scientific knowledge of linguistics, of etymologies, and the principles governing historical spelling, we continually make mistakes in attempting to preserve and reconstruct older forms, and the mistakes fall into the pattern of contamination described above. It can be safely asserted that once different sounds have fallen together, orthographic distinction between them on the basis of historical practice or etymology cannot be long maintained consistently. In MT, the system of vocalization reflects extensive contraction of the diphthongs *aw* and *ay,* and the resulting vowels *ô* and *ê* are assigned the same value as the *ō* and *ē,* which derive from the original vowels *ā* (or *u*), and *i* (i.e., *ḥōlem* and *ṣēre:* there are undoubtedly distinctions in quantity, and we should reckon with instances of short *ḥōlem* and *ṣēre,* but the system used does not indicate these, while it does indicate an identity in vowel quality). Massoretic spelling, as distinct from vocalization, is less clear on this point. On the one hand, it carefully preserves the distinction between *ê* derived from *ay,* which is consistently represented by *yodh,* and *ē* derived from *i,* which is rarely if ever so indicated. This regularity can hardly be explained as a survival of historical spelling, but is rather rooted in a difference in pronunciation. It may be explained in either of two ways, or a combination of them: either the diphthong had actually been preserved and not contracted, or the *ṣēre* is a short vowel as distinct from the contracted diphthong, which is long, and is therefore not represented in the orthography. Whether the second explanation can be used to cover all cases of the shift *i* > *ē* is debatable, however. On the other hand, the Massoretic treatment of the *ō* vowel *(ḥōlem)* involves extensive representation of vocalic *ō,* derived from *ā* (rather than *u,* which is not indicated by a vowel letter, thus implying that the vowel is short) as well as diphthongal *ô,* derived from *aw.* This can be taken to mean that the *ō* sounds have fallen together, and thus that contraction of the diphthong has taken place. On the whole it would appear that Massoretic spelling and vocalization point in the direction of diphthongal contraction: that the contracted diphthongs *ô* and *ê* are represented by *waw* and *yodh,* that the vowel *ō* derived from $\bar{a}$ is similarly represented by *waw,* although not consistently, while *e* derived from *i* and *o* derived from *u* are not represented in the orthography because they remained short vowels.

VI

When we turn to the new documents from the 3rd century, we find that two of them, Exod[f] and Jer[a], conform closely to the orthographic pattern of MT, while Sam[b] diverges. The latter makes no use of *waw* to represent the vowel $\bar{o}$ *(ḥōlem),* but distinguishes carefully between the diphthong, which is always represented by *waw,* and the vowel, which is not. This implies strongly that the $\bar{o}$ vowel was not represented orthographically, and that the contraction of the diphthong had not yet taken place. Since all three manuscripts come from approximately the same period, it would appear that this was a time of transition, with Sam[b] preserving an older orthographic tradition and the other manuscripts belonging to the newer pattern. We also seem to have reached the point of origin of Massoretic spelling as such.

The only significant distinctions in spelling practice among the manuscripts, and between them and MT, concern the use of *waw* as a medial vowel letter for $\bar{o}$ (derived from $\bar{a}$). There are other differences, but these are minor and may be mentioned in passing. Thus there are a few instances in which Massoretic vocalization indicates an $\bar{\imath}$ vowel, where the manuscripts do not have *yodh* to represent the vowel. Sam(b) spells the name "David" *dwd* regularly, as often in MT, even though the second vowel is apparently long, as the spelling (with *yodh*) elsewhere in MT, and in many places in the Qumran scrolls, shows. In Sam[b] (as MT here), we undoubtedly have a case of historical spelling, the survival of the older, preexilic spelling (which we would expect in the case of names particularly) alongside the development of the more "correct" fuller spelling. In Exod[f] at 40:18, we have **ברחיו** for MT **בריחיו**, which is more regular. This may also be the survival of an older spelling (cf. Jon. 2:7 **ברחיה**) or more likely a scribal slip reflecting the current slurring of the vowel (which is unaccented) in ordinary pronunciation. There are two similar cases in Jer[a]: **הושעני** for MT **הושיעני** (17:14) and **תבאהו** (MT same, 13:1), where the expected *yodh* is omitted, probably as a reflection of current pronunciation of the unaccented pretonic syllable (i.e., the vowel was not heard distinctly or regarded as long). Other explanations are possible; in any case such exceptions do not undermine the general pattern, but only prove that scribes are human.

We may now turn to the evidence for the spelling of $\bar{o}$ in our documents:

1. For Sam[b] we have the following — $\bar{o}$ is never indicated in the orthography, with the possible exception of four words:

a. למועד, *l*^{e}*môʿēd* (1 Sam. 20:35, as in MT). Here the *waw* is etymologic, i.e., derived from the diphthong *aw: *mawʿid > môʿēd.*

b. יונתן, *yônātān* (MT יהונתן, but elsewhere יונתן). Here again the *waw* is etymologic, deriving from an original diphthong. MT spelling is archaizing or hypercorrect, since intervocalic *he* was lost early in ordinary pronunciation (MT vocalization is an artificial backformation from *yônātān*). Thus: **yahunatan > *yawnatan > yônātān.*

c. היום, *hayyôm* (20:27, 34, as MT). Again the *waw* is to be considered etymologic: i.e., **yawm > yôm.* A second root, *ym,* is reflected in the plural *yāmīm,* as also in the curious (but repeated) form *ym* for "day" in preexilic Judahite materials. We must reckon with a more complex dialectic situation in Judah in which biforms of the type *yawm/yam, qawl/qal,* etc., existed side by side.

d. מקום, *māqōm* (20:27, 37; 21:3 as MT). This is the most difficult form, since it is usually derived from **maqām* (root *qm*). If this derivation is correct, then it would be the only case of the use of *waw* for vocalic *ō* (from *ā*) in Sam^{b}. The consistency of usage with this word (all three cases), and the complete absence of any other examples of such use of *waw* (though there are numerous instances of *ō* from *ā* in the materials and an impressive number in which MT has *waw* but where Sam^{b} omits), indicates that another explanation is implied if not required. On the analogy of Arabic and Syriac formations from the same root,[17] we suggest that *māqôm* derives from **maqawm* rather than **maqōm,* and that the *waw* is etymologic here also. The biform *maqām > māqôm* may also have existed, since MT preserves a number of cases in which the *waw* is omitted (though only in combining forms with preposition or suffix, where a possible change in pronunciation may be involved). The plural form *(m*^{e}*qōmōt)* may likewise be derived from the simple form **maqāmāt* rather than one with the diphthong, thus conforming to the pattern suggested in c. above.

As another illustration of metaplastic formations we may suggest the different spellings of the word *Jerusalem.* MT spelling of the last syllable is simply *-lm,* implying a pronunciation *-lēm,* while the vocalization (a permanent Qerē) *-ayim* points to an original diphthong *-aym.* We know now that this vocalization is not artificial but derives from a tradition going back at least to the 2nd century B.C.E., as shown by numerous examples in the Qumran scrolls, in which the *yodh* appears in the last syllable *(-lym).* This can only signify the diphthongal form *-aym,* as *yodh* is not used to represent either *seghōl* or *ṣēre.*

The principal difference between Sam^{b} and MT is in the representation of the *ō* vowel (derived from *ā),* as the following table indicates:

17. Cf. Syriac *qawmā, qawmĕthā* and Arabic *qawm, qawmah,* and *qamah.*

	4QSam^{b}	Verse	MT
1.	בבאם	16:6	בְּבוֹאָם
2.	קמתו	16:7	קוֹמָתוֹ
3.	החלן	19:12	הַחַלּוֹן
4.	טהר	20:26	טָהוֹר
5.	אפד	21:10	הָאֵפוֹד

No. 2, the word *qōmātô* is apparently derived from **qāmat* rather than **qawmat,* although we have argued that *māqōm* derives from **maqawm* rather than **maqām.* Our point is that both basic forms existed in the language, that any given substantive may be derived from either root, and that we may expect considerable mixture in the use of forms.

From the evidence presented it is clear that Sam^{b} not only uses *waw* as a *mater lectionis* less frequently than MT, but follows a consistent pattern which is no longer the case with MT: it distinguishes between diphthongal *ô* and vocalic *ō,* thus implying that there was a difference in the pronunciation of these sounds, i.e., the diphthong had not yet been contracted. We must in view of these data assign orthographic priority to Sam^{b}. It reflects a phase of Hebrew spelling earlier than that of MT. Cross drew this conclusion on general grounds along with the important observation that Sam also preserves a text of Samuel which is demonstrably older than that of MT, and apparently even of the *Vorlage* of the LXX.[18] We are dealing therefore with an archaic manuscript which preserves a tradition, both textually and orthographically, considerably older than the date of the manuscript itself. As a conservative estimate we suggest the 4th century or even late 5th for the pattern, both textual and orthographic, preserved in Sam^{b}.

VII

The evidence for the use of *waw* for *ō* in Ex^{f}, which must now be regarded as the oldest known manuscript of the Bible, is as follows: the usage is not consistent, though a general pattern emerges — there is extensive use of *waw,* contrary to the practice of Sam^{b} and closer to what we find in MT. It is to be noted, however, that the orthography of the manuscript as a whole is somewhat irregular, unlike Sam^{b}, which is a model of consistency, and it must therefore be used with caution. The following cases are clear examples of the use of *waw* for *ō* (from *ā*):

18. *JBL* 74 (1955): 165-172.

	4QEx^f	Verse	MT
1.	אותו	40:9, 13	אֹתוֹ
	אותם	12, 14, 15, 16	אֹתָם
	but אתו	11	אֹתוֹ
2.	עולם	15	עוֹלָם
3.	לדורותם	15	לְדֹרֹתָם
4.	הארון	20 (3 times), 21	הָאָרֹן
5.	צפון	22	צָפֹנָה

These are apparently all cases of *ō* derived from *ā; waw* commonly appears when the *ō* occurs under the accent but not always, cf. לדורותם. There are notable differences in detail between Ex^f and MT, though elsewhere MT spells these words as does Ex^f. However, the spelling of the *nota accusativi* before suffixes with *waw* is very rare in MT, though common in Ex^f and in many later Qumran texts. It is clear that by the 3rd century, and possibly earlier, *waw* was already being used to represent medial *ō*. If we are right in supposing that this usage developed as an extension of the use of *waw* for the contracted diphthong *aw* > *ô,* then it would mean that the diphthong *aw* had contracted by the 3rd century at the latest. Since the evidence of Sam^b points in the other direciton, viz., that contraction had not yet taken place, and the manuscripts are roughly contemporary (in fact, in Cross's opinion Ex^f is somewhat older than Sam^b), we must look for some other explanation of the use of *waw* for *ō* (i.e., it may be independent of the use in connection with the diphthong) or suppose that the two manuscripts reflect a linguistic transition, in which the archaic Sam^b preserves an older pattern of pronunciation and orthography, while Ex^f reflects a later, contemporary usage. The orthographic pattern represented by Ex^f cannot be later than the early 3rd century, and may be as old as the 4th. That of Sam^b must be correspondingly older, though in view of the date of the manuscript itself it can hardly ascend beyond the early 4th century, or possibly the late 5th.

There are additional cases in Ex^f where *waw* is not used although the corresponding word in MT is vocalized with *ḥōlem* (and in one case spelled with *waw* in MT):

	4QEx^f	Verse	MT
1.	אהרן	40:12, 13	אַהֲרֹן
2.	הכתנת	14	כֻּתֳּנֹת
3.	משה	16, 19, 21, 23	מֹשֶׁה
4.	הראשן	17	הָרִאשׁוֹן
5.	הכפרת	20	הַכַּפֹּרֶת
6.	פרכת	21, 22	פָּרֹכֶת

In some cases the omission of the *waw* may be due to carelessness, in others to the survival of historical spelling, and in still others to a difference in pronunciation or interpretation of the word in question. Thus nos. 1 and 3 are proper names where we would expect historical spelling, as in MT. No. 2 may have been understood as a singular form, especially as MT also omits the expected *waw* marking the plural. Nos. 5 and 6 may involve a difference in pronunciation, especially as MT regularly spells without *waw* (the original vowel behind the *ḥōlem* may have been *u* rather than *ā,* and in these manuscripts as in MT *ō* from *u* is not represented in the orthography). No. 4 is the only clear case of omission, and this is doubtless a survival of older spelling practice in Ex[f] (the spelling without *waw* occurs elsewhere in MT).

MT and Ex[f] are closer to each other in the matter of the use of *waw* for *ō* than either is to Sam[b]. At the same time there are important differences between them; particularly as regards the spelling of *'ōt-,* Ex[f] goes beyond MT generally in the direction of the fuller spelling of the later Qumran manuscripts.

VIII

The evidence for the use of *waw* for *ō* for the third manuscript, Jer[a], is as follows: the pattern is very similar to that of Ex[f], and also to that of MT. The following cases illustrate this point:

	4QJer[a]	Verse	MT
1.	נתוש	12:17	נָתוֹשׁ
2.	אזור	13:1, 2, 4	אֵזוֹר
3.	יומהו	17:11	K ימו / Q יָמָיו
4.	הושעני	14	הוֹשִׁיעֵנִי
5.	אצותי	16	אַצְתִּי
6.	מוצא	16	מוֹצָא
7.	(ב)יום	17, 18, etc.	(בְּ)יוֹם
8.	אבושה	18	אֵבֹשָׁה
9.	הלוך	19	הָלֹךְ
10.	יבוא	19	יָבֹאוּ
11.	אבותיכם	22	אֲבוֹתֵיכֶם
12.	שמוע	24	שָׁמֹעַ
13.	עשות	24	עֲשׂוֹת

It is clear that there is widespread use of *waw* for *ō,* comparable to what we find in MT, though more extensive in Jer[a] than MT for this passage. *Waw* is used for the contracted diphthong: nos. 4, 6, 7 and possibly 3 (which is peculiar); *waw* for *ō* from *ā* in the tone position is common: nos. 1, 2, 9, 12, 13. Nos. 5 and 8 involve difficulties in interpretation of the form, though MT usually omits the *waw.* No.

10 is a case of metathesis in Jer^{a} where MT יבאו is the correct reading. No. 11 shows the *waw* used in an unaccented position, though the form may involve a secondary accent: *ʼᵃbōtêkem*. There are in addition a number of cases in which *waw* is omitted although MT vocalizes with *ḥōlem*.

	4QJer^{a}	Verse	MT
1.	קרא	17:11	קֹרֵא
2.	עזביך	13	עֹזְבֶיךָ
3.	יבשו	13	יֵבֹשׁוּ
4.	אמרים	15	אֹמְרִים
5.	מרעה	16	מֵרֹעֶה
6.	רדפי	18	רֹדְפַי
7.	ישבי	20	יֹשְׁבֵי
8.	רכבים	25	רֹכְבִים

The principal examples involve the qal active participle, both singular and plural, where in agreement with regular MT practice *waw* is not used. The careful orthographic distinction in a manuscript not otherwise noted in this fashion suggests that the pronunciation differed, perhaps due to the position of the accent. The $\bar{o}$ of Massoretic vocalization is confirmed, however, by later Qumran scrolls (as well as linguistic analysis). The only other instance of omission in Jer^{a} is no. 3, where MT also omits the *waw*.

IX

The orthography of these three early scrolls from Cave IV of Qumran is the same in all essentials except for the use of *waw* to represent $\bar{o} < \bar{a}$; $\hat{o} < aw$ is regularly represented by *waw*, while $\bar{o} < u$ is never so represented. Sam^{b} apparently does not represent $\bar{o}$ (from $\bar{a}$) at all, while Ex^{f} and Jer^{a} generally do, though with exceptions (discussed above), which arise either as a result of historical spelling or differences in contemporary pronunciation (as distinguished from Massoretic vocalization); these in turn depend upon the position of the accent and the length of the vowel in question. There is also the possibility of scribal error. None of the manuscripts is identical with MT in spelling practice in the passages under consideration, and there are general as well as detailed differences. Nevertheless all three exhibit features which can be matched in MT taken as a whole, and MT could be reconstructed from the evidence of the three manuscripts under consideration.

The earliest or most conservative spelling is that of Sam^{b}, which probably reflects normative Israelite spelling of the 4th century B.C.E. There are numerous significant differences from 6th century practice to suggest an upper limit for

Sam[b]'s orthography in the 5th century. The other two manuscripts exhibit freer use of *waw* as a *mater lectionis,* but may also be based upon usage going back to the 4th century — not earlier in our judgment since it would then be difficult to explain the survival of the older tradition in a 3rd century manuscript like Sam[b]. In addition, the irregularity in the practice of these manuscripts suggests that the extended use of *waw* was of recent origin, and that these manuscripts reflect a period of transition both in spelling and pronunciation.

It may be premature to draw general conclusions about MT on the basis of the material now available, but certain points may be made now. MT shares with all three early manuscripts the same orthographic practice with regard to final and medial vowel letters, with the single exception of the use of *waw* for $\bar{o}$ ($< \bar{a}$), which varies between Sam[b] and the other documents. This alone argues for a long, stable orthographic tradition stemming from scribal schools of the early postexilic period. Massoretic practice with regard to the use of *waw* for $\bar{o}$ might well be described as a compromise between the defective spelling of Sam[b] and the extended orthography of Ex[f], and is in fact very close to that of Jer[a]. It may be further argued that Massoretic spelling was deliberately designed to combine the best features of the different orthographies current in the 4th-3rd centuries, preserving continuity with the older conservative tradition of Sam[b], and at the same time incorporating the helpful features of the newer spelling exhibited in Ex[f] and Jer[a]. We may place the origins of Massoretic spelling as a definite orthographic system in the late 3rd or early 2nd century, and describe it as a learned recension based upon the best practice of the preceding period. Apparently with official support, it gained primacy during the next two centuries, and was ultimately successful as the official biblical spelling, sweeping the field of all rivals.

4

A Second Mesha Inscription

The new Moabite inscription from Kerak is a welcome addition to the scanty epigraphic library of early 1st millennium Palestine, and Messrs. Reed and Winnett are to be commended for prompt and accurate publication of the fragment.[1]

At the same time, a few suggestions about the nature and interpretation of the text may be in order. It will be noted that, so far as it has been preserved, line 1 of the new inscription corresponds exactly with the first line of the Mesha stele.[2] The authors are doubtless correct in identifying the name *[K]mšyt* as that of the father of Mesha, and for that reason the letters *yt* should be restored in line 1 of the Mesha stone. It seems equally clear, however, that the Kerak inscription should be attributed to Mesha, rather than to his father as suggested by Reed and Winnett.[3] We should restore the missing words exactly as in the Mesha stone:

1. *['nk . Mšʿ . bn . K]mšyt . mlk. M'b . h[d]*
2. *[ybny .]*[4]

The paleography of the Kerak inscription conforms closely to that of the Mesha stone, so a common date (within a single reign) is entirely in order. The slight

1. W. L. Reed and F. V. Winnett, "A Fragment of an Early Moabite Inscription from Kerak," *BASOR* 172 (1963): 1-9.

2. *Ibid.,* 7 and figs. 1 and 2. The correspondence, which can hardly be accidental, apparently extends to the break, at the end of the line, in the middle of the word *h[d]-[ybny]* (exactly as in the Mesha stone, ll. 1-2).

3. *Ibid.,* 7.

4. The view that this is an inscription of *Kmšyt* is forced, and the suggestion that the name of his father has been omitted because he was the founder of a new dynasty is not convincing. Even if the latter were true, that would not be sufficient reason for the omission of the patronymic. In the Old Testament, at least, patronymics are regularly given with the names of the founders of new dynasties: e.g., Saul ben Kish; David ben Jesse; Jeroboam ben Nebat; Baasha ben Ahijah; Jehu ben Jehoshaphat ben Nimshi; Shallum ben Jabesh; Menahem ben Gadi; Pekah ben Remaliah; Hoshea ben Elah. Zimri, for obvious reasons, and Omri seem to be exceptional cases.

divergences between the scripts are to be accounted for by the presumption that different stone-cutters were employed at different locations.

If the proposed restoration of the first line is accepted, then it may be possible to reconstruct the full dimensions of the original inscription. Following the pattern of the Mesha stone, the first line will have begun some three words to the right of the present break, but will have ended with the final letters *h[d]*, as does the Mesha stone. The second and third lines will have been correspondingly longer at both ends, but moderately so, allowing room for several words at the beginning of the two lines, but only one or two at the end.

With regard to the name *[K]mšyt*, the authors' suggestion *Kmš-šyt* is not convincing, on grammatical and orthographic grounds.[5] The same comment may be made about H. L. Ginsberg's proposed *K^e^mōš-yatti*, though it cannot be ruled out entirely.[6] Without attempting to interpret the name, and with considerable diffidence, we suggest a connection with the name of the Edomite chieftain *Ytt*, which is apparently a hypocoristicon (Gen. 36:40 = 1 Chr. 1:51).

5. Reed-Winnett, 7-8.
6. *Ibid.*, 8, n. 20a.

5

The Use of *Aleph* as a Vowel Letter in the Genesis Apocryphon

The purpose of this chapter is to examine the use of *aleph* as a vowel letter in the *Genesis Apocryphon.*[1] The analysis is limited to columns xx-xxii, where the forms are generally legible and the context clear. The classification lists column and line, e.g., xx 1 means column xx, line 1 of the edition by Nahman Avigad and Yigael Yadin, *A Genesis Apocryphon* (Jerusalem: Magnes, 1956).

The use of *aleph* falls into two categories: 1) Quiescence of an original consonant which is then retained or restored as a vowel. This phenomenon is to be observed both in final position (I. 1°) and in medial position (I. 2°). So-called *lamedh-aleph* roots form a special group in this category (I. 3°). 2) *Aleph* as a pure vowel letter. Following utilization of consonantal *aleph* as a vowel letter, *aleph* is gradually introduced into the orthography as a pure vowel letter. This occurs at first in final position and is frequent in the *Genesis Apocryphon* (II. 1°). In addition, there are a number of instances where *aleph* occurs as a pure vowel letter in medial position; with only one exception, this occurs after consonantal *waw* or *yodh* (II. 2°).

In order to demonstrate these patterns in the use of *aleph,* all occurrences of *aleph* in medial or final position have been grouped according to the appropriate category:

1. Cases in which *aleph* is clearly consonantal do not figure in this discussion. We would like to acknowledge the helpful counsel of Jonas Greenfield, University of California, Berkeley, California, on a number of issues pertaining to this paper. All responsibility for the material herein presented is, of course, our own.

I. Quiescence of Consonantal *aleph*

1° *In final position.* These cases consist of nouns (substantive and adjectival) in the emphatic state:

'ḥy' (xxi 21)
(wl) 'ymy' (xxi 29)
'lh' (xxi 2, 3, 8; xxii 27, 32)
'mwr'' (xxi 21)[2]
'rḥ' (xxi 28; xxii 4)
'r‘' (xx 13; xxi 4, 10 (twice), 12, 13, 15, 16; xxii 16, 21, 25)
'špy' (xx 19, 20)[3]
bzt' (xxii 13)
gbry' (xxii 23)
(wl)drwm' (xxi 9, 18)
(wl)zwmzmy' (xxi 29)
(l)ḥwry' (xxi 29)
(b)ḥzw'[4] (xxi 8; xxii 27)
ḥkymy' (xx 20)
ḥlt' (xxii 4)
(w)ṭbt' (xxi 3)
(b)ṭwr' (xxi 7)
y'' (xx 4, 8)[5]
ywm' (xxi 5, 23 *[ywmy']*; xxii 21)
ym' (xxi 11, 15, 16, 17 *[lym'],* 18 [twice])
yrdn' (xxi 5)
kwl' (xx 13)
krm' (xxii 14)
(b)lyly' (xx 11, 12, 15, 16; xxi 8; xxii 8, 9)
mdbḥ' (xxi 1)
mdbr' (xxi 11, 28)
(l)mdnḥ' (xxi 9, 16, 17)
mktšy' (xx 18, 24, 29 *[mktš']*)

2. Probable vocalization: *ᵉmōra'ā,* "Amorite." This is a secondary form of the plural; final *aleph* is the emphatic ending. The medial *aleph* is a consonant replacing *yodh;* cf. Biblical Qere/Kethib of *tlyty',* Dan. 2:39, or of *kśdy',* Dan. 5:30.

3. Conjectured reading; but ending is clear, *-yā.*

4. Corrected reading; cf. E. Y. Kutscher, *The Language of the Genesis Apocryphon* (Jerusalem, 1957), 7, 33. [Offprint of *Aspects of the Dead Sea Scrolls. Scripta Hierosolymitana* 4 (1958): 1-35]

5. *yā'ā* < *yā'a',* "beautiful"; masc. sg. with emphatic ending.

mlḥ' (xxi 16)
mlk' (xx 8, 25; *lmlk':* xx 10, 23, 24)
(wl)m'rb' (xxi 9)
(w)ngdy' (xx 18, 24)
nhr' (xxi 15, 17, 19, 28)
nksy' (xxi 3, 33; xxii 17, 19, 24)
npš' (xxii 19)
sdy' (xxi 25)
(w)'ly' (xx 7)[6]
'lmy' (xxi 2, 14)
(l)'mq' (xxi 25)
'rq' (xxii 21)
(l)'tr' (xxi 1)
ptgmy' (xxii 27)
(wl)ṣpwn' (xxi 9)
rbt' (xx 14; xxii 4; *rb':* xxi 11, 12, 16)
rwḥ' (xx 20, 28)
rmt' (xxi 11)
(l)rp'y' (xxi 28)
šby' (xxii 2, 12 [*šbyt'*, twice], 19, 25 [twice])
šḥlny' (xx 26)[7]
śmwq' (xxi 17, 18 [twice])
šmy' (xxii 16, 21)
špr' (xx 7)
twr' (xxi 16 [twice])

2° *In medial position.* In these instances, medial *aleph* is clearly consonantal; whether or not it has quiesced in each case is not certain.

b'dyn (xx 21; xxii 2, 18)
(w)b'š (xxi 7)[8]
b'yš' (xx 17)[9]
dms'n (xxii 21)

6. Translation is difficult but possibly "higher" or "highest." Emphatic form of root *'ly*, "highest" (Biblical Aramaic): *w^e'illāyyā?*

7. Corrected reading; probable vocalization: *šaḥlānāyā*, "purulence." Cf. Joseph Fitzmyer, "Some Observations on the *Genesis Apocryphon*," *CBQ* 22 (1960): 289.

8. Suggested vocalization: *ūb^e'ēš* > *ūbēš*, "it grieved." It is impossible to tell from the orthography whether the *aleph* has quiesced or not (cf. Dan. 6:15, *b^e'eš*).

9. Probable vocalization: *bîšā*, "evil." The medial *aleph* has probably quiesced as in Biblical Aramaic (Ezra 4:12). See also under II.1°c.

y'yn (xx 3, 5)[10]
r'yšh (xx 3)[11]
(l)rpr'y' (xxi 28)[12]
śm'l (xxi 8; xxii 10)
šmy'bd (xxi 25)[13]
(w)t'mr (xx 26)

3° In *lamedh-aleph* forms. In most of these forms, *aleph* has been substituted for original *yodh;* thus, the *aleph* is essentially a pure vowel letter. As a class, however, *lamedh-aleph* verbs represent a secondary formation in Aramaic, and the *aleph* is treated mostly as a quiesced consonant. This is illustrated by the form *hww'* (xxii 9), "they were," 3 masc. pl. *h*^{a}*wō* < *h*^{a}*wō'*.

a) Verbal forms:
(w)bk' (xxii 5)
(w)b‘' (xx 9, 21)
hw' (xx 3, 17, 20; xxi 24; xxii 1, 2, 15)[14]
hww' (xxii 8, 9)[15]
(w)ym' (xx 30)
pṣ' (xxii 11)
qr' (xx 19)[16]
šbw' (xxii 10)[17]
šr' (xxii 13)

b) Miscellaneous:
hw' (xx 10; xxi 6; xxii 7, 9, 14, 15)[18]
hy' (xx 27 [twice]; xxii 13)

10. *yāyān* < *ya'yān,* "perfect"; fem. pl. In this instance, the *ā* of the feminine ending is not represented; we would expect *y'y'n.* See below under II.2° and n. 41.

11. *rē(')šah* < *rēšah* < *ri'šah,* "her head." Although quiesced, the *aleph* reappears as a back formation.

12. Suggested vocalization: *lir*^{e}*pāyyā* < *lir*^{e}*pa'ayyā,* "the Rephaim." It is impossible to tell from the orthography whether the medial *aleph* has quiesced or not; cf. Gen. 15:20, *r*^{e}*pā'īm.*

13. Vocalization is unclear; although *aleph* may have quiesced, it is probably vocalized as a consonant: *š*^{e}*mī'ebed?* Cf. Gen. 14:2: *šem'ēber.*

14. *h*^{a}*wā,* "it is"; 3rd masc. sg. The *aleph,* functioning as a consonant, has quiesced and marks the vowel.

15. As written, this form is the 3rd masc. pl. of *hwy;* hence, *h*^{a}*wō.* The context, however, requires a singular verb; the form is probably a scribal error for *hw'.*

16. In this *lamedh-aleph* verb, the *aleph* is etymologic (cf. Heb. *qr'*); it is the third stem radical. Such forms may have suggested the consonantal function of *aleph* in the other *lamedh-aleph* verbs.

17. *š*^{e}*bō,* "they captured"; 3rd masc. pl. This form of the *lamedh-aleph* verb is parallel to *hww',* in which *aleph* has quiesced but is retained in the orthography. The same verb occurs in xxii 12, written, however, as *šb'w.* The latter is probably a scribal error.

18. 3rd person pronoun, masc.: *hû.* This is a secondary formation analogous to the so-called

II. Use of *aleph* as a Pure Vowel Letter

1° The use of *aleph* as a pure vowel letter occurs at first in final position.

a) In the third femine singular suffix:
ʾnphʾ (xx 3, 4)[19]
ʾrkhʾ (xxi 14)
bhʾ (xx 17)
(l)bʿlhʾ (xx 23)[20]
dbrhʾ (xx 9)
dylhʾ (xx 10 [twice])
drʿyhʾ (xx 4)
(w)ḥzhʾ (xx 9)
(w)ydyhʾ (xx 4, 5, 7)
ydʿhʾ (xx 17)[21]
kpyhʾ (xx 5)[22]
lbnhʾ (xx 4)
mnhʾ (xx 6)
(w)nsbhʾ (xx 9, 27 *[nsbthʾ]*)
ʿynyhʾ (xx 3)
ʿmhʾ (xx 7)
ptyhʾ (xxi 14)
rglyhʾ (xx 5)
šqyhʾ (xx 6)
šprhʾ (xx 7, 9)

b) In verbal forms. Most of these cases involve the infinitive and participle, where *aleph* replaces the common *hē* ending:
(b)ʾtʿṣbʾ (xx 12)
(l)ṭmyʾ (xx 15)[23]
ktšʾ (xx 17)
(l)ṣlyʾ (xx 22)

---

lamedh-aleph verbs. The *aleph* is treated as though it were a consonant and has quiesced. The same is true for the next form, *hyʾ, hî,* "that is."

19. The form in xx 4 is spelled *ʾnpyhʾ* (= *ʾanpayhā*). This spelling preserves the diphthong, as is the common practice in the scroll. The form *ʾnphʾ (ʾanpēhā)* may indicate, however, some fluidity of pronunciation, i.e., a transition in the rendering of the diphthong.

20. Cf. *bʿlh*, xx 25, where the *aleph* of the suffix is omitted.

21. Conjectured reading but suffix is clear, *-hā*.

22. Corrected reading.

23. *lᵉṭammayā,* "to defile"; paʿel infinitive. In this form of the *lamedh-aleph* verb, the *aleph* is a pure vowel letter.

śym' (xxii 10)
šlm' (xxii 28)[24]

c) Miscellaneous forms:
'dm' (xxi 24, 31)[25]
(l)'nt' (xx 9)[26]
b'yš' (xx 17)
br' (xxii 23 [twice], 31)[27]
d' (xx 28; xxi 10, 11, 12; xxii 25)[28]
h' (xx 27; xxii 27)[29]
ḥd' (xx 33; xxi 21, 25; xxii 32)[30]
ḥkm' (xx 7)
km' (xx 3, 4 [3 times], 5, 6)
l' (xx 6, 10, 17, 22; xxi 13 [twice]; xxii 3, 22, 33, 34)[31]
(w)m' (xx 3, 5; xxii 32)[32]
m'' (xxii 6)
md' (xxi 26)[33]
(w)mnḥ' (xxi 20)[34]
(l)'l' (xx 7)[35]
'l' (xxi 20)[36]
(b)'štr' (xxi 28)[37]
r'wtn' (xxi 5)[38]

24. *šᵉlamā,* "they have passed"; 3rd fem. pl. *Aleph* replaces the more common *hē;* cf. *'ṣlth* (xxii 19), *npqth* (xxii 28).

25. *'admā,* "Admah." Cf. *'dmh* in Biblical Hebrew.

26. *lᵉ'intā,* "for a wife"; abs. st. of the noun. Cf. xx 27, *l'nth.*

27. *bārā,* "except for." Occurs in later Aramaic as *br.*

28. *dā,* "this." *Aleph* may originally have been consonantal. Equally ambiguous is the status of *aleph* in *l', h',* and *m'.*

29. Cf. n. 28.

30. This occurs with *lamedh* prefix in xx 33 and xxii 32, meaning "very much." In xxi 21, 25, the form is *kḥd',* meaning "together" or "as one." The root is *ḥd;* cf. Biblical Aramaic *ḥdh, kḥdh.*

31. Cf. n. 28.

32. In xxii 32, the form is *wlm'.* Cf. n. 28.

33. Corrected reading for *mr';* cf. Kutscher, n. 4, p. 32. *middā,* "tribute"; fem. sg. This occurs in later Aramaic as *mdh.*

34. *ūminḥā,* "cereal offering." Cf. *mnḥh,* xxi 2.

35. *lᵉ'ellā,* "above." Cf. Biblical Aramaic. From the noun *'yl ('ēl),* "height"? *Aleph* may, however, be consonantal.

36. *'alā,* "burnt offering." This occurs as *'lwh* in Elephantine papyri; cf. Kutscher, n. 4, p. 32. Note the fem. pl., *'lw'n,* in xxi 2.

37. *bᵉ'aštārā,* "in Ashtaroth." Cf. *b'štrh,* Josh. 21:27.

38. *ra'ᵃwāṯanā,* "our shepherds." Final *aleph* is a pure vowel letter. In this case, medial *ā* following *waw* is not represented; we would expect *r'w'tn'.* See below, II.2°, n. 41.

śgy' (xx 7)[39]
šw' (xxii 14)[40]

2° The next development is the introduction of *aleph* as a pure vowel letter in medial position. It marks the vowel *ā* following consonantal *waw* or *yodh.*[41] Possibly this practice was undertaken to avoid confusion over the consonantal status of *waw* or *yodh.*

a) After consonantal *waw* or *yodh:*[42]
(w)'rgw'n (xx 31), "purple": *wa'arg^e wān.* The reading is partially obscure but legible. The second *aleph* is a pure vowel letter; cf. *'rgwn',* Dan. 5:7, 16, 29.
(w)hw't (xx 17, 27 [partially obscure but legible]; xxii 25), "it was," 3rd fem. sg. *wah^a wāṯ.* Aleph is a pure vowel letter here; cf. *hwt,* Dan. 7:19. It is also possible that the *aleph* was secondarily restored under the influence of other forms of *lamedh aleph* verbs. We may see in this situation the origin of the use of *aleph* as a pure vowel letter following *yodh* or *waw.*
mn lw'ty (xxi 5, 7), "from me": *min l^e wāṯī.* Aleph is a pure vowel letter, following *waw;* cf. Ez. 4:12: *mn lwty.*
mšry'ty (xxi 1), "my camps": *mašr^e yātī.* Aleph is a pure vowel letter after *yodh;* cf. n. 42.
'lw'n (xxi 2), "sacrifices." *'^a lāwān.* Aleph is a pure vowel letter after *waw;* cf. Ez. 6:9: *'lwn.*
(w)tmny't (xxii 6), "eight": *w^e t^e mān^e yāṯ*; fem. pl. *Aleph* is a pure vowel letter after *yodh.*
tny'ny (xxi 1), "a second time": *tinyānī. Aleph* is a pure vowel letter after *yodh;* cf. Dan. 7:5: *tnynh* and Dan. 2:7: *tnynwt.*

b) Use of *aleph* after other consonants:
(w)kl'n (xx 6), "brides": *w^e kallān*; fem pl. of *klt. Aleph* is probably a pure vowel letter, but it may have been misunderstood as a consonant on the analogy of *lamedh aleph* verbs (see above, I. 3°).

39. *śaggīyā,* "great"; fem. sg. *Aleph* is part of the root. We might expect *śaggī'āh* as in later Aramaic. The *aleph,* however, has quiesced in the masculine forms (cf. Biblical Aramaic); hence, it is presumably re-introduced here as the feminine ending.

40. *šāwē,* "Shaveh." Cf. Biblical Hebrew *šwh. Aleph* marks vowel *ē* in this instance.

41. As the analysis has brought out, there are two exceptions to this rule, *y'yn* (see under I.2°) and *r'wtn'* (see under II.1°c).

42. Mention should be made of two instances in column xix noted by Kutscher in his brief reference to the use of medial *aleph* (n. 4, p. 4). The citation for *mšry'ty* is apparently a misprint for xxi 1 (see below). The second form accords with our hypothesis: *w'kly't* (xix 16), "it called": *w^e 'akliyyāṯ.*

Summary

In conclusion, it may be observed that a definite orthographic pattern exists, in which *aleph* is used as a pure vowel letter in medial position after *waw* or *yodh.* Of the three exceptions to this rule, two reflect traditional spelling (cf. n. 41), as would be expected with the introduction of a new orthographic practice.[43] Only once does *aleph* appear in medial position as a pure vowel letter not following *waw* or *yodh* (see above under II. 2° b). In later times this usage became more widespread.[44]

43. Contrary to Kutscher (n. 4, p. 26), the evidence is not clear for an earlier use of medial *aleph,* namely in the Elephantine papyri. The variant spellings of the proper name *ḥsy’rs (ḥsyrs)* may be significant but hardly indicative of a widespread practice. The meaning of *ḥmr’n* is debatable; as Ginsberg has noted, it may be a "synonymous formation" of the masc. pl. *ḥmryn,* meaning "beads." Ginsberg notes further that *aleph* "is not otherwise employed as a *mater lectionis* in the middle of a word in the papyri" (H. L. Ginsberg, "Aramaic Dialect Problems. II," *AJSL* 52 [1935-36]: 100, n. 26) — a claim substantiated by the extensive study on the orthography of the Elephantine papyri by a colleague, Dale Patrick, Graduate Theological Union, Berkeley, California.

44. Cf. Max L. Margolis, *A Manual of the Aramaic Language of the Babylonian Talmud* (Munich: C. H. Beck, 1910), 4; Sabatino Moscati, et al., *An Introduction to the Comparative Grammar of the Semitic Languages* (Wiesbaden: Harrassowitz, 1964), 52; F. G. Uhlemann, *Syriac Grammar,* trans. Enoch Hutchinson, 2nd ed. (New York: D. Appleton, 1875), 30; W. Wright, *A Grammar of the Arabic Language,* 3rd ed. (Cambridge: Cambridge University Press, 1896), 7.

6

The Orthography of the Arad Ostraca*

Dr. Aharoni is to be commended for the prompt and accurate publication of several very interesting ostraca from Tel Arad.[1] Among a variety of features deserving comment, the orthography of these documents can be treated briefly in the following notes.[2]

Ostracon I[3]

Line 1: אלישב, "Eliashib." The word may be vocalized *'elyāšīb.* The *yodh* is consonantal, as the vocalization of the name in MT (1 Chr. 3:24; 24:12, etc.) makes clear. There is no compelling evidence for medial vowel letters in any of the ostraca.

Line 2: עת, "now." Read *'at* or *'ēt.* We have here an alternate form of the common expression *'attā ('th)* of Biblical Hebrew. Since final vowels are represented regularly in Hebrew inscriptions of this period, including these ostraca, there is no reason to suppose a vocalization *'attā* for this word.[4]

* I wish to express my appreciation to Prof. Frank M. Cross, Jr., for reading and correcting this manuscript.

1. Y. Aharoni, "Hebrew Ostraca from Tel Arad," *IEJ* 16 (1966): 1-7 and pl. 7; "The Use of Hieratic Numerals in Hebrew Ostraca and the Shekel Weights," *BASOR* 184 (1966): 13-19. [See Y. Aharoni, *Arad Inscriptions,* ed. and rev. A. F. Rainey (Jerusalem: Israel Exploration Society, 1981), Ed.]

2. On the prevailing pattern of Judahite spelling in the 7th-6th centuries B.C., see F. M. Cross, Jr., and D. N. Freedman: *Early Hebrew Orthography.* AOS 36 (New Haven: American Oriental Society, 1952, repr. 1981), 45-47.

3. Aharoni: *IEJ* 16 (1966): 2-4.

4. See the discussion in Cross-Freedman, 52f. The word *'t* also occurs in Ostracon II, line 3, and Ostracon III, line 1.

לכתים, "to the Kittites." Read *lakkittiyyīm.* Since there are sporadic occurrences of medial vowel letters in preexilic Hebrew inscriptions, it would be possible to interpret the *yodh* as a vowel letter representing *ī.* It is much more probable, however, that the *yodh* is a true consonant, and that the name should be transcribed as shown above, consistent with the spelling of the same word in Isa. 23:12; Jer. 2:10; and Ezek. 27:6. These passages are all roughly contemporary with the ostracon.

Line 3: יין, "wine." Read **yayn* (MT: *yayin*). According to the analysis of Cross and Freedman,[5] the spelling of this word with the second *yodh* would be characteristic of the Judahite or southern dialect, in which diphthongs remained uncontracted. On the other hand, the same word in the Israelite or northern dialect would have been pronounced *yēn* < *yayn,* and spelled *yn,* showing that the diphthong had been contracted. Cf. l. 9, below.[6]

Line 4: הים, "the day." Read **hayyām* (instead of MT: *hayyōm*). The word for "day" in Judahite was apparently **yām* (cf. pl. *yāmīm*), spelled without medial *waw,* unlike MT *ywm* (*yom* < **yawm*). The same form appears in the Siloam inscription and elsewhere.[7]

Line 5: ומעוד, "and from what still (remains)." Read **wamēʿawd* (MT: *ūmēʿōd*). The preservation of the medial *waw* between *ʿayin* and *dalet* indicates that the diphthong was still pronounced. In Israelite, the word would have been written *ʿd* for *ʿōd* > *ʿawd,* as sporadically in MT.[8]

Line 6: הראשן, "the first." Read *hārīʾšōn* (MT). The spelling of this word illustrates the fact that medial vowels were virtually never used in these inscriptions. Following general later practice, we might have expected a *waw* to represent the *ō* of the final syllable. We might also have expected it to be used in *lʿśt* (l. 9; MT: *laʿaśōt*) and *hʾgnt* (l. 10: *hāʾaggānōt;* cf. Isa. 22:24).

Line 9: מיין, "from the wine." Read **miyyayn* (cf. MT *yēn*). It is to be noted that there is no difference in the spelling of the construct form of this noun, as compared with the absolute form (l. 3) discussed above. The Massoretic distinction between the absolute *yayin* and the construct *yēn* is thus not reflected in the inscriptions (which, however, are consistent with the unvocalized biblical text: *yyn*).

5. *Ibid.,* 48f., 57.

6. *Ibid.,* 49 (no. 13), and 57.

7. *Ibid.,* 50 (no. 31), 53 (no. 53); Aharoni: *IEJ* 16 (1966): 3, n. 4.

8. Aharoni, *IEJ* 16 (1966): 3; Cross-Freedman, 50 (no. 24).

Ostracon II[9]

Line 2: יהוה, "Yahweh." Read **yahwē.* The final *he* is used as a vowel letter for *ē.* The same word occurs in l. 9.

Line 3: לשלמך "for your welfare." Read **lišlōmāk.* Normal vocalization of the suffix in MT would be *-kā.* The chief consideration against this vocalization in the ostracon is the generally consistent pattern of representing all final vowels in the orthography. The short form, without final *ā,* is attested in Biblical Hebrew (often in the pausal position), and can be defended as the proper vocalization in the inscriptions. If the suffix were supposed to be pronounced *kā,* we would expect it to be written *kh,* as often in the Dead Sea scrolls, and occasionally in MT. In MT as a whole, the text preserves the short form, which is attested in the ostraca. The vocalization, on the other hand, is based upon the long form *(-kh),* and has been levelled through the Bible.[10]

Line 4: לשמריהו, "for Shemaryahu." Read **lišmaryāhū.* The final *waw* is used as a vowel letter for *ū.*

Line 5: ולקרסי, "and to the Kerosite." Read **wᵉlaqqērōsī.* The final *yodh* is used as a vowel letter for *ī.*

Lines 7-8: צותני, "you charged me." Read *ṣiwwātānī.* The final *yodh* is used as a vowel letter for *ī.* Note that the medial *waw* represents a consonant, a doubled one at that.

Line 9: בית, "house." Read **bayt* (MT: *bēt*). Even in the construct state, the word is spelled with medial *yodh,* showing that the diphthong was preserved in Judahite. In Israelite, however, the word would have been spelled *bt* (as in Ugaritic and Phoenician), and pronounced *bēt.*[11]

Line 10: הא, "he." Read *hū'.* The pronoun is spelled without the medial vowel letter *waw;* cf. MT: *hw'.*

Ostracon III[12]

Line 2: ביתה, "to the house." Read **baytā(h).* See the discussion of *byt* (II, l. 9) above concerning the preservation of the diphthong *ay* in Judahite (represented in the orthography by *yodh*). The *he* directive was originally consonantal, but presumably quiesced in the course of time, serving here as a vowel letter for *ā.*[13]

9. Aharoni, *IEJ* 16 (1966): 5-7.
10. See the extended discussion of this point in Cross-Freedman, 65-67.
11. See the discussion in *ibid.,* 48 (no. 6), 51 (no. 41), 55 (no. 72), etc.
12. Aharoni, *BASOR* 184 (1966): 14-16.
13. Cf. Cross-Freedman, 4, n. 12.

Line 3: אשיהו, "Eshyahu." The final *waw* is used as a vowel letter for *ū.* Cf. above, II, l. 4.

Lines 3-4: ולקחת, "and you shall take." Read **wᵉlāqaḥt.* On the basis of the orthography we posit a short form without final *ā,* which is regularly indicated in Massoretic vocalization. However, the Massoretic form (וְלָקַחְתָּ) is anomalous.[14]

Line 5: מהרה, "quickly." Read *mᵉhērā* (MT). The final *he* is used as a vowel letter for *ā.*

Line 6: אתה, "it." Read *'ōtō* (MT). On the assumption that the antecedent is *šmn* (l. 4), we read the 3rd masc. sg. pronominal suffix, which was represented by *he* in preexilic inscriptions. The spelling would be the same for the 3rd fem. sg. suffix (MT: *'ōtāh*).

Lines 6-7: בחתמך, "with your seal." Read **bᵉḥōtāmāk.* See the discussion of *lšlmk* (II, l. 3) above for the vocalization of the 2nd masc. sg. pronominal suffix.

Line 9: הכתי, "the Kittite." Read **hakkittī.* The final *yodh* is used as a vowel letter for *ī.* Cf. *lktym,* I, l. 2, above.

We may summarize the findings as follows: The orthography of the ostraca conforms throughout with the pattern established for the 7th-6th centuries B.C.E. in Judahite (i.e., southern) inscriptions.[15] More specifically:

a) All final vowels are indicated in the orthography by the appropriate vowel letter: *waw* for *ū, yodh* for *ī,* and *he* for *ā, ē,* and *ō.* Apparent exceptions are susceptible of other plausible explanations.

b) Medial vowels are not represented in the orthography. There is no significant evidence to the contrary, even though there are sporadic occurrences of such medial vowel letters in other preexilic inscriptions.

c) The diphthongs *aw* and *ay* are represented in the orthography of the ostraca by the letters *waw* and *yodh* respectively, indicating that the diphthongs were preserved in the pronunciation of the southern dialect. Both spelling and pronunciation were different in the northern dialect, in which the diphthongs were regularly contracted.

These ostraca both illustrate and confirm the prevailing pattern of orthography in the kingdom of Judah around the year 600 B.C.E.: They are consistent throughout, and also conform to the practice of the Lachish letters and other contemporary documents.

The following notes deal with difficulties in the interpretation of the ostraca:

1. *Ostracon I, lines 6-7: trkb.* While error is always a possibility, and the suggested emendation appears plausible, a defense of the present text can be made. Consideration ought to be given to the noun *rekeb,* "millstone," and to the possible analysis of the verb form as a denominative meaning "to grind (as with a millstone)." The verb could then be parsed as a piel or hiphil imperfect 2nd masc. sg.,

14. Cf. *ibid.,* 65-67.

15. *Ibid.,* 56f.

and be translated, "You shall grind one ephah (?) of meal to make bread for them." The rendering depends for its viability on the view that the coarse flour (i.e., *qémaḥ*) would be re-ground into fine flour *(sólet),* which would then be baked into bread. In any case the verb should be parsed as a 2nd masc. sg. form since such imperfects balance imperatives elsewhere in these ostraca: cf. *ktb* (l. 4, imperative) // *ttn* (l. 10, imperfect); Ostracon II, *tn* (l. 4, imperative // *ttn* (l. 6, imperfect); Ostracon III, *b'* (ll. 1-2, imperative) // *wlqḥt* (ll. 3-4, perfect following *waw* consecutive).

2. *Ostracon II, lines 6-10:* These lines pose serious problems in interpretation as well as offering a tantalizing hint about the "house of Yahweh." Aharoni's approach seems to be essentially correct, but the analysis of the text is dubious at points.[16] The presumed Hebrew is awkward, and the resulting translation is obscure. For *šlm* in l. 8, we suggest the reading *šullam,* the pual perfect 3rd masc. sg., rather than *šālōm,* which is rather abrupt and hardly grammatical. Aharoni's intepretation, "The thing has been done, etc." is correct, but that meaning is best rendered by a verb form of the root *šlm.*[17] The implied subject is *dbr* of ll. 6-7, i.e., the "matter" concerning which the writer received instructions; whatever it may have been, it has been done. With regard to ll. 9-10, I would agree with Aharoni's rendering of *byt yhwh* as "in the house of Yahweh."[18] The phrase in l. 10, *h' yšb* should be analyzed as a 3rd masc. sg. pronoun followed by a participle. While *yšb* could also be analyzed as a perfect form of the verb, or an imperfect, and be derived from one of several roots, the simplest way to explain the presence of the independent pronoun is on the assumption that we have a participial form. In that case the form would be *yōšēb* from the root *yšb,* and the meaning would be "he sits, he dwells, he remains," etc. The whole sentence (ll. 6-10) could then be translated: "As for the matter, concerning which you charged me, it has been settled. In the house of Yahweh he remains." The reference would be to the Temple in Jerusalem, where presumably the writer of the letter was stationed.[19]

16. Aharoni, *IEJ* 16 (1966): 6.

17. *Ibid.,* 6, n. 14.

18. *Ibid.*

19. It may be of interest to note the verbal similarity of the text to 1 Kgs. 9:25, which reads in part: *wšlm 't-hbyt,* "and he completed the Temple." Our text could plausibly be read, "The house of Yahweh has been completed." But it is difficult to imagine circumstances in which such a statement could be made in a letter of the 6th century B.C.E..

7

Orthographic Peculiarities in the Book of Job

The book of Job is a compendium of unsolved problems ranging from the determination of the text of particular verses to broad inquiries into the thought-world of the composer poet. Critical questions concerning the date of composition, authorship, and provenance remain the subject of extensive scholarly debate, and we seem as far as ever from any consensus, much less a final solution. The unusual character of the vocabulary, grammar, and syntax has often been noted; and in recent years much progress in analysis and interpretation has been made through the application of the results of intensive study of the Ugaritic poetic materials.[1] It is not our intention in the present paper to engage directly in a discussion of the matters just mentioned, but rather to point to certain orthographic features of the book of Job, which may indirectly support one or another of the scholarly positions adopted with respect to the provenance and date of composition of the book.

The present text of Job in the Hebrew Bible is the product of a long process of revision and edition, during which its orthography was brought into conformity with generally accepted standards. For the most part, therefore, the spelling of words in Job is typically Massoretic. We mean by this designation the spelling of the official Rabbinic text of the late first and early second centuries A.D. We refer to the Kethib, i.e., the consonants and vowel letters, not to the vocalization which was introduced at a later date. While biblical orthography is not entirely uniform, the range of variation is limited, and exceptions can generally be explained on the basis of scribal option, misinterpretation, or error. In some instances, especially in early poems, we seem to have clear evidence of the survival of archaic spelling patterns, but in no case so far studied do these extend over a whole book or major literary unit. A possible exception would be the early manuscript of Samuel

1. Cf. M. H. Pope, *Job*. AB 15 (Garden City: Doubleday, 1965, ³1973).

(4QSam^b), which consistently preserves a pre-Massoretic orthography, probably that of the 4th century B.C.E., though possibly even earlier.[2]

In view of these general circumstances, the survival of a considerable number of non-Massoretic spellings in Job comes as a surprise. More impressive is the fact that most of these fall together into a consistent pattern which may be described as (North) Israelite or Phoenicianizing.[3] The most important feature of these Canaanite dialects, which distinguished them from Jerusalem (and Biblical) Hebrew, was that the diphthongs *aw* (represented in the orthography by *waw*) and *ay* (represented by *yodh*) were regularly contracted to the vowel sounds $\bar{o}$ and $\bar{e}$, and as such were not indicated in the orthography, except in the final position. It was only in late postexilic times that such vowels, the result of diphthongal contraction, were represented by the corresponding vowel letter; by that time most long vowels were so represented in the medial as well as final position, no distinction being recognized as to their original character.

The number and distribution of these "northern" spellings in the book of Job, and their consistent correlation with an orthographic pattern empirically and independently established from the extant nonbiblical inscriptions, tend to rule out the possibility of accidental collocation, or of a series of scribal whims or mistakes, which coincidentally form a historically validated pattern of spelling practice. Whatever may be said of an occasional doubtful case (see the discussion below), the group as a whole can only be regarded as survivors of an earlier stage of the written transmission of the text either preserved in the course of copying, or restored to the official text on the basis of some old manuscript, newly discovered at a later date. It is legitimate to ask why these examples of dialectic or archaic spelling in particular survived, while the others were routinely modernized. The answer will lie in a study of the procedures involved in manuscript transmission and the operative principles of editors and scribes, a subject not entirely under the control of scholars as yet. We prefer to leave that to another occasion and focus attention rather on the accessible evidence. After it has been presented and discussed we may consider briefly the implications for the dating and provenance of Job.

For the text of Job we have used Kittel's *Biblia Hebraica,* 3rd ed. (henceforth BH^3), and for the occurrences of comparable forms in MT we have relied on Mandelkern. There are some slight variations in spelling in these authorities, as noted.

2. D. N. Freedman, "The Massoretic Text and the Qumran Scrolls: A Study in Orthography," *Textus* 2 (1962): 96-98, 102. [See above, Chapter 3]

3. The essential difference is that in Phoenician orthography final vowel sounds were not indicated, whereas in Israelite (the dialect of the northern kingdom) they were indicated by an appropriate vowel letter. There are few if any clear examples of such defective spelling in Job.

I. Contraction of the Diphthongs *aw* and *ay*

A. Contraction of aw *(originally represented by* waw*) to* ō *(not indicated in the orthography).*

Normally in the Massoretic Text the resultant vowels are represented in the orthography by the same letters, *waw* or *yodh,* which marked the original diphthongs. The reason for this procedure is that Massoretic spelling is based upon the usage of the southern dialect of Judah in which diphthongs were not contracted at all in preexilic times, and then on a partial basis at a much later date. By that time the use of internal vowel letters to indicate long vowels was widespread, so it was natural to retain the *waw* or *yodh* of the original diphthong to represent the resultant long vowel. The examples to be noted exhibit a spelling pattern in which the contracted diphthong is not represented at all, thus reflecting the orthographic practice of countries in which the contraction of diphthongs had taken place at a much earlier stage of the language, as, e.g., in Israel and Phoenicia.[4]

1. Forms derived from *pē waw* roots.

(a) יאל. There are two examples of hiphil forms in Job:

6:9 וְיֹאֵל for normal וְיוֹאֵל < **wayaw'il*
6:28 הוֹאִילוּ, which is normal Massoretic spelling.

Elsewhere in MT there are 17 occurrences of the hiphil of יאל. All of these have the full spelling with *waw,* with the single exception of 1 Sam. 17:39, וַיֹּאֶל. (In the books of Samuel there are two other examples of יאל, both with the full spelling.) It is to be noted that one of the two cases in the Hebrew Bible of defective orthography of this root occurs in Job.

(b) יאשׁ. There is a single example in Job:

6:26 נֹאָשׁ (niphal ptcp. masc. sg.) for normal נוֹאָשׁ.

Note that other printed editions of the text have נואשׁ here, as does Mandelkern. There are four other examples of the niphal in MT, all with the full spelling. The only case in the Bible of defective spelling occurs in Job.

(c) ידע. There are eight examples of hiphil forms in Job, of which two are defectively written:

4. F. M. Cross, Jr., and D. N. Freedman, *Early Hebrew Orthography,* AOS 36 (New Haven: American Oriental Society, 1952, repr. 1981), 19, 57.

10:2; 38:3; 40:7; 42:4 (וְ)הוֹדִיעֵנִי
13:23 הֹדִיעֵנִי for normal הוֹדִיעֵנִי
26:3 הוֹדַעְתָּ
32:7 יֹדִיעוּ for normal יוֹדִיעוּ.

Elsewhere in MT there are 63 occurrences of the hiphil of ידע, of which three (1 Chr. 17:19; Num. 16:5; Judg. 8:16) have defective spelling. It is to be noted that two of the five cases of defective spelling occur in Job.

(d) יחל. There are two examples of the hiphil form in Job:

32:11 הוֹחַלְתִּי
32:16 וְהוֹחַלְתִּי.

There are twelve other occurrences of the hiphil of יחל in MT, all spelled in full with the single exception of 2 Sam. 18:14 אֹחִילָה. There is one example of the derived noun תּוֹחֶלֶת in Job 41:1, תֹּחַלְתּוֹ for normal תּוֹחַלְתּוֹ (Mandelkern reads the full spelling at Job 41:1). There are five other occurrences of the noun in MT, all with the full spelling. It is to be noted that one of the two cases of defective orthography in the Hebrew Bible occurs in Job.

(e) יכח. There are 15 examples of the hiphil of יכח in Job, plus one case of the niphal.

These all have the full spelling with the exception of יֹכִיחֶךָ at Job 22:4:

5:17 יוֹכִחֶנּוּ
6:25 (2) יוֹכִיחַ הוֹכֵחַ
6:26 הַלְהוֹכַח
9:33; 32:12; 40:2 מוֹכִיחַ
13:3 וְהוֹכֵחַ
13:10 (2) הוֹכֵחַ יוֹכִיחַ
13:15 אוֹכִיחַ
15:3 הוֹכֵחַ
16:21 וְיוֹכַח
19:5 וְתוֹכִיחוּ
22:4 יֹכִיחֶךָ for normal יוֹכִיחֶךָ (Mandelkern: יכחך)
23:7 נוֹכָח.

Elsewhere in MT, there are two examples of the niphal form of יכח, of which one is defectively written:

Gen. 20:16 וְנֹכָחַת for normal וְנוֹכָחַת.

There are 39 examples of the hiphil, of which two are defectively written:

Gen. 24:44 הֹכִיחַ
Gen. 24:14 הֹכַחְתָּ.

Note that in both cases the construction and meaning are uncertain.

In addition, there are two occurrences of the derived noun in Job:

13:6 תּוֹכַחְתִּי
23:4 תּוֹכָחוֹת.

Elsewhere in MT, there are 22 occurrences of the derived noun תּוֹכַחַת. There is a single instance of defective spelling at Ezek. 5:15 וּבְתֹכָחוֹת for normal וּבְתוֹכָחוֹת (Ezek. 25:17).

(f) יסף. There are 11 examples of the hiphil form of יסף of which eight are defectively written:

17:9; 34:37 יֹסִיף for normal יוֹסִיף
20:9 תוֹסִיף
27:1; 29:1; 36:1; 42:10 וַיֹּסֶף for normal וַיּוֹסֶף
34:32 אֹסִיף for normal אוֹסִיף
38:11 תֹסִיף for normal תוֹסִיף
40:5 אוֹסִיף
40:32 תּוֹסַף.

Elsewhere in MT, there are approximately 161 examples of the hiphil of יסף, of which 74 (or nearly half) are written defectively. Further analysis produces the following relevant data. The great bulk of the examples are imperfect forms, including all of the cases in Job (150 plus 11 in Job, making a total of 161); of these 150, 71 are defectively written. Limiting ourselves to imperfect hiphil forms the distribution in the major sections of MT is as follows:

	Total	Normal Spelling	Defective
Torah (Pent.)	38	6	32
Former Prophets	48	23	25
Latter Prophets	27	24	3
Writings (excl. Job)	37	26	11
Total	150	79	71
Job	11	3	8

It will be seen that the ratio of full and defective spellings varies considerably as we move from one major section of the Bible to another. Thus, in the Former Prophets the numbers are approximately even (as in the general average), while for the Latter Prophets and Writings the proportion of full spellings is much higher. On the other hand, in the Pentateuch there is a decisive preponderance of defective spellings. The spelling in Job does not conform to that of the Writings but rather to that of the Pentateuch (cf. Gen. 2:10; Exod. 6:7; Num. 1:4; and Deut. 2:9). The spelling of the Pentateuch is generally more defective than other parts of the Bible, and on the whole reflects earlier orthographic practices. The data concerning the hiphil imperfect of יסף suggest that Job's orthography is to be classified with the Pentateuch rather than the later sections of the Bible.

(g) יעל. There are four examples of the hiphil of יעל in Job, of which two are defectively written:

15:3 יוֹעִיל
21:15 נוֹעִיל
30:13 יֹעִילוּ for normal יוֹעִילוּ
35:3 אֹעִיל for normal אוֹעִיל.

Elsewhere there are in MT 19 examples of the hiphil of יעל, all of which have the full spelling. The only two cases of contracted spelling in the Bible occur in Job.

(h) יפע. There are four examples of the hiphil of יפע in Job, of which one is defectively written:

3:4 תּוֹפַע
10:3 הוֹפָעְתָּ
10:22 וַתֹּפַע for normal וַתּוֹפַע
37:15 וְהוֹפִיעַ.

Elsewhere in MT there are four occurrences of the hiphil, all of which have the full spelling. The only instance of contracted spelling of this verb in the Bible occurs in Job.

(i) יצא. There are six examples of the hiphil of יצא in Job, five of which are defectively written:

8:10 יוֹצִאוּ
10:18 הֹצֵאתָנִי for normal הוֹצֵאתָנִי
12:22 וַיֹּצֵא for normal וַיּוֹצֵא
15:13 וְהֹצֵאתָ for normal וְהוֹצֵאתָ
28:11 יֹצִא for normal יוֹצִיא
38:32 הֲתֹצִיא for normal הֲתוֹצִיא.

Elsewhere in MT, the hiphil of יצא occurs 272 times, of which 25 are defectively written. A breakdown of the significant figures shows the contrast between the spelling in Job and the other books of the Bible.

	Job			Others		
	Total	*Full*	*Defect.*	*Total*	*Full*	*Defect.*
Hiphil Perfect	2	0	2	91	89	2
Hiphil Impf.	4	1	3	99	76	23
Total	6	1	5	190	165	25

The additional instances in the other books include the participle, infinitive, and imperative, none of which occurs in Job. The ratio of 5:1 in favor of defective spellings in Job stands in sharp contrast to the almost 7:1 ratio in favor of full spellings for the rest of the Bible.

There are two examples in Job of the derived noun מוֹצָא, one of which is spelled defectively:

28:1 מוֹצָא
38:27 מֹצָא for normal מוֹצָא.

Elsewhere in MT there are 26 examples of the derived noun, four of which are spelled defectively. It will be noted once again that there is a heavy preponderance of full spellings in MT in contrast with Job, though there are not enough examples in Job to make a decisive case.

Taking the overall figures for the root יצא, one finds eight examples in Job, of which six or 75% are defectively written. In the rest of the Hebrew Bible we have 298 cases, of which 29, or about 10%, are defectively written.

(j) יקשׁ. There are two occurrences of the derived noun מוֹקֵשׁ in Job, one of which is defectively written:

34:30 מִמֹּקְשֵׁי for normal מִמּוֹקְשֵׁי
40:24 בְּמוֹקְשִׁים.

Elsewhere in MT the noun occurs 25 times (plus מֹקְשׁוֹת in Ps. 141:9), of which five are defectively written. An interesting example of the two different spelling techniques is to be seen in 2 Sam. 22:6 = Ps. 18:6, where Samuel has the northern contracted spelling מֹקְשֵׁי, while Psalms has the normal spelling מוֹקְשֵׁי.[5]

(k) ירה. There are eight examples of the hiphil form of ירה in Job, of which four are defectively written (for statistical purposes we have lumped together ירה I and II).

5. F. M. Cross, Jr., and D. N. Freedman, "A Royal Song of Thanksgiving: II Samuel 22 = Psalm 18," *JBL* 72 (1953): 23 and n. 8.

6:24 הוֹרוּנִי
8:10 יוֹרוּךָ
12:7, 8 וְתֹרֶךָּ for normal וְתוֹרֶךָּ
27:11 אוֹרֶה
30:19 הֹרָנִי for normal הוֹרָנִי
34:32 הֹרֵנִי for normal הוֹרֵנִי
36:22 מוֹרֶה.

Elsewhere in MT there are 60 examples, of which nine are defectively written.

(l) ישׁב. There is a single example of hiphil of ישׁב in Job; and it is written defectively:

36:7 וַיֹּשִׁיבֵם for normal וַיּוֹשִׁיבֵם.

Elsewhere in MT there are 37 instances of the hiphil, of which 14 are written defectively. These figures may be misleading, however, since seven of these cases of defective spelling occur in Ezra-Nehemiah. In each of these the verb occurs in the same context and has the meaning: "to marry a (foreign) wife"; cf. Ezra 10:2, 10, 14, 17, 18; Neh. 13:23, 27. It seems probable that a different root is involved. If we eliminate these instances, the total would be 30, with seven cases of defective spelling.

(m) ישׁע. There are four examples of the hiphil of ישׁע in Job, one of which is written defectively:

5:15 וַיֹּשַׁע for normal וַיּוֹשַׁע
22:29 יוֹשִׁעַ
26:2 הוֹשַׁעְתָּ
40:14 תּוֹשִׁעַ.

Elsewhere in MT there are 178 cases of the hiphil of the root ישׁע, of which nine are written defectively. A tabular breakdown follows:

	Job			**Others**		
	Total	***Full***	***Defect.***	***Total***	***Full***	***Defect.***
Hiphil Perfect	1	1	0	22	22	0
Ptcp.	0	0	0	33	32	1
Inf. Abs.	0	0	0	2	2	0
Inf. Const.	0	0	0	22	22	0
Imperative	0	0	0	31	31	0
Imperfect	3	2	1	68	60	8
Total	4	3	1	178	169	9

For our purposes the relevant data are to be found in the line for the imperfect forms. In Job there are three examples, of which one is written defectively. For the rest of MT there are 68, of which eight are so written. It is to be noted that six of the eight cases occur in the books of Samuel (and one each in Isaiah and Proverbs), thus pointing to a special orthographic feature of that work:[6]

Hiphil Impf.	*Total*	*Full*	*Defect.*
Job	3	2	1
Samuel	10	4	6
Other books	58	56	2
Total	71	62	9

2. Other cases of contraction: *aw* < *ō*.

(a) עֹד for עוֹד. There are 18 examples of *ʿōd* in Job, of which three are spelled defectively. In addition, there are three instances of עַד, which in all probability should be repointed as עֹד. Thus there would be a total of 21 occurrences of *ʿōd,* of which six have defective spelling. Examples of the full spelling עוֹד occur at 1:16; 1:17; 6:10; 6:29; 7:10 *(bis);* 14:7 (וְעוֹד); 20:9; 24:20; 27:3; 29:5 (בְּעוֹד); 32:15; 32:16; 34:23; 36:2. Examples of the contracted spelling עֹד occur at:

1:18 עַד for עֹד from עוֹד
2:3 וְעֹדֶנּוּ for וְעוֹדֶנּוּ
2:9 עֹדְךָ for עוֹדְךָ
8:12 עֹדֶנּוּ for עוֹדֶנּוּ
8:21 עַד for עֹד from עוֹד.
25:5 עַד for עֹד(?) from עוֹד.

Elsewhere in MT there are 472 occurrences of *ʿōd,* of which 14 are spelled defectively, for a ratio of about 3%, which is significantly less than the frequency of defective spelling in Job, three cases out of 18, or 17%. If we add the three additional cases of mispointed עַד, the ratio rises to 29%. We have made no effort to count the possible cases of עַד for original *ʿōd* elsewhere in MT, though for the books where there is a relatively high proportion of defective spellings of *ʿōd,* we have spot-checked the occurrences of *ʿad* without discovering any probable cases of mispointing, e.g., Jeremiah: four cases of defective spelling out of 54 (7 1/2%); Hosea: two cases out of ten (20%); Micah: one out of four (25% — but the example

6. Cf. Freedman, *Textus* 2 (1962): 98. [See above, Chapter 3] The implications of the data need to be studied further, though the "northern" spelling of 2 Sam. 22, in which two of the examples occur, has already been noted; cf. Cross-Freedman, *JBL* 72 (1953): 15-17, 20; also 22, n. 2 on 2 Sam. 22:3 (משעי and תשעני).

in 1:15 is very questionable); Zechariah: two out of 15 (13⅓%). On the basis of our adjusted findings, Job has the largest number of contracted spellings, and a higher percentage than any other book of the Bible.

(b) וְעֹלָתָה. There is a striking example of contracted spelling in Job 5:16, where we have וְעֹלָתָה for וְעַוְלָתָה, the normal form in MT, which preserves the diphthong *aw* both in the spelling and vocalization. The uncontracted form occurs at Ezek. 28:15; Hos. 10:13; Ps. 125:3. In Ps. 92:16 the Kethib is written defectively as in Job 5:16 עֹלָתָה, while the Qere restores the diphthong, thus confirming our analysis of the reading in Job.

The related noun עַוְלָה occurs nine times in Job, always with the full spelling; cf. 6:29; 6:30; 11:14; 13:7; 15:16; 22:23; 24:20; 27:4; 36:23.

(c) תך. There are six examples of the word *tōk* < **tawk* in Job, one of which is spelled defectively:

1:6; 15:19 בְּתוֹכָם
2:1 בְּתֹכָם for normal בְּתוֹכָם
2:8; 20:13; 42:15 בְּתוֹךְ.

Elsewhere in MT there are 412 cases of *tāwek // tōk* with two instances of defective spelling: בְּתֹכְכֶם in Gen. 35:2 and Num. 32:30 (but note that BH[3] reads בְּתוֹכְכֶם for the latter).

B. Contraction of ay *(originally represented by* yodh*) to* ē *(not represented in the orthography).*

1. Contraction of dual and plural endings.

(a) שורתם. At Job 24:11, for MT שׁוּרֹתָם read the contracted dual *šūrōtēm* < **šūrōtaym,* "between the two rows."[7]

(b) רֵעֵהוּ. At Job 42:10 the word *rēʿēhū* is to be interpreted as a plural noun with 3rd masc. sg. suffix = "his friends," as the context requires. The spelling correctly reflects the "northern" contraction of the diphthong before the suffix: **riʿayhū* < *reʿēhū.* We would expect the normal spelling in MT to be רֵעֵיהוּ, but this form does not actually occur, being displaced by רֵעָיו, which is derived from the same original form **riʿayhū* by a different route involving syncope of intervocalic *he.* The spelling of the contracted form of the plural before suffixes is the same as the singular, with the result that it is not always easy to distinguish between them. Thus we have the singular לְרֵעֵהוּ at 16:21, but the same form at 12:4 should probably be interpreted as plural, "a laughing-stock to his friends." Another

7. Cf. Pope, 161, on Job 24:11a. Consider also *hmrwtm,* "two miry deeps," and *tlym,* "two mounds." I owe these suggestions to M. Dahood, S.J.

possible instance of contracted spelling concealing the plural form of the noun is to be found at 1 Sam. 30:26.

2. Other forms with contracted spelling:

(a) **אימה**. There are five examples of this word in Job, of which three are spelled defectively:

9:34 וְאֵמָתוֹ for normal וְאֵימָתוֹ
13:21 וְאֵמָתְךָ for normal וְאֵימָתְךָ
33:7 אֵמָתִי for normal אֵימָתִי
39:20; 41:6 אֵימָה.

Elsewhere in MT, there are ten occurrences of the word (including the plural וְאֵימוֹת, Ps. 55:5), all with the full spelling.

The related plural form *'ēmīm* occurs once in Job, spelled defectively: 20:25 אֵמִים for אֵימִים. Elsewhere in MT there are two examples of this word, of which one has the contracted spelling (Ps. 88:16, where, however, the text is obscure). There are three occurences of the proper name Emim, two of which have defective spelling (Deut. 2:10, 11). Whether the same root and therefore the contraction of the diphthong is involved may be questioned, but the full spelling in Gen. 14:5, אֵימִים, tends to support the usual etymology.

(b) **איתן**. There are two examples of this word in Job, both of which are spelled defectively:

12:19 וְאֵתָנִים for וְאֵיתָנִים[8]
33:19 אֵתָן for אֵיתָן.

Elsewhere in MT there are nine occurrences of the noun in the singular (not counting eight examples of the proper name Eytan, doubtless derived from the same root), all having the full spelling. The plural form occurs in Mic. 6:2, defectively written (but the text is obscure; see commentaries); and in 1 Kgs. 8:2 we have the old Israelite and Phoenician month name הָאֵתָנִים, also defectively written.[9]

(c) **תימא**. There is a single occurrence of the noun in Job:

6:19 תֵּמָא for normal תֵּימָא.

8. S. Mandelkern, *Veteris Testamenti Concordantiae Hebraicae atque Chaldaicae,* 6th ed. by F. Margolin and M. Goshen-Gottstein (Tel Aviv: Schocken, 1964), lists this form.

9. The contracted form is to be expected since the name is originally Canaanite/Phoenician: ירח אתנם, *CIS* I.1.86a, etc.

The root seems to be ימא; the original spelling representing the uncontracted diphthong is confirmed by Old Aramaic תימא. Elsewhere in MT there are four occurrences of the name, all with full spelling.

(d) תימן. There are two examples of the noun in Job, one of which is written defectively:

9:9 תֵּמָן for תֵּימָן
39:26 לְתֵימָן.

Elsewhere in MT there are 22 occurrences of the noun, all having the full spelling.

(e) תֵּימָנִי. There are six examples of the gentilic form הַתֵּימָנִי, derived from the proper noun תֵּימָן, in Job, of which one is written defectively:

2:11; 4:1; 15:1; 42:7; 42:9 התימני
22:1 הַתֵּמָנִי for הַתֵּימָנִי.

Elsewhere in the MT there are two occurrences of the gentilic התימני and 11 examples of the place name, all written in full. Job has the only examples of contracted spelling in the Bible.

A summary of the information concerning the contraction of diphthongs in the orthography of Job as compared with the rest of the MT is to be found in the table on page 56.[10]

For the words studied, the statistics suggest that less than 10% of the forms are defectively written in the Bible as a whole. If two or three special cases are excluded, the percentage would be considerably lower. For the same words in the book of Job the proportion of defectively written words is much higher, approximately 40%. In my opinion, it would be very difficult to explain this disparity in terms of accidental or coincidental scribal propensities. It looks as though a divergent orthographic tradition underlies the phenomenon.

10. The table confirms the impression that in Job there is much more extensive orthographic evidence for the contraction of diphthongs than in the rest of the Bible. In the case of several words, Job preserves the only extant examples of contracted spelling (marked with an asterisk), another indication of the tendency to standardize orthography in the received text.

Evidence for the Contraction of *aw* > *ō* and *ay* < *e*

Root or Word	Occurrences in Job: Full (With ו)	Occurrences in Job: Contracted (Without ו)	Occurrences in Job: Total	Elsewhere in MT: Full (With ו)	Elsewhere in MT: Contracted (Without ו)	Elsewhere in MT: Total
יאל	1	1	2	16	1	17
יאשׁ	0	1*	1	4	0	4
ידע	6	2	8	60	3	63
יחל	2	1	3	16	1	17
יכח	17	1	18	58	4	62
יסף	3	8	11	87	74	161
יעל	2	2*	4	19	0	19
יפע	3	1*	4	4	0	4
יצא	2	6	8	269	29	298
יקשׁ	1	1	2	20	5	25
ירה	4	4	8	51	9	60
ישׁב	0	1	1	23	7	30
ישׁע	3	1	4	169	9	178
עד / עוד	15	6	21	458	14	472
עולתה, עלוה / עלתה	0	1	1	3	1	4
תך / תוך	5	1	6	410	2	412
Subtotal	64	38	102	1,667	159	1,826
	(With י)	(Without י)		(With י)	(Without י)	
אימה	2	3*	5	10	0	10
אימם	0	1	1	2	3	5
איתן	0	2	2	9	2	11
תימא	0	1*	1	4	0	4
תימן	1	1*	2	22	0	22
תימני	5	1*	6	2	0	2
Subtotal	8	9	17	49	5	54
Grand Total	72	47	119	1,716	164	1,880

II. Other Orthographic Features in Job

A. Omission of vowel letters where MT normally preserves them

1. Omission of י in masc. pl. nouns before 3rd masc. sg. suffix.

(a)	K ואפרחו	39:30 for Q	וְאֶפְרֹחָיו
(b)	K חלצו	31:20 for Q	חֲלָצָיו
(c)	K וידו	5:18 for Q	וְיָדָיו
(d)	K כנפו	39:26 for Q	כְּנָפָיו
(e)	K עינו	21:20 for Q	עֵינָיו
(f)	K שרידו	27:15 for Q	שְׂרִידָיו.

The text (Kethib) in each case is to be interpreted as representing the same plural form of the noun as the Qere, not the singular, though with different spelling. The form without *yodh* appears regularly in Palestinian inscriptions prior to the exile, while the fuller form with *yodh* first appears in 3rd century B.C.E. biblical manuscripts.[11] It is difficult to pinpoint the transition more precisely since Hebrew inscriptional material is almost entirely lacking for the intervening centuries.

The "preexilic" form may be explained as follows: *-ayhū* > *ēhū* > *ēw* (cf. the discussion of רֵעֵהוּ above, involving contraction of the diphthong *ay* > *ē* characteristic of Phoenician and Israelite).

In a similar way the later "biblical" form can be explained in the following manner: *ayhū* > *ayw,* with preservation of the diphthong characteristic of southern or Judahite spelling. The Massoretic pointing ָיו = *āw* apparently reflects a late simplified vocalization of this difficult form.[12]

Since the form without *yodh* occurs regularly in preexilic Judahite inscriptions, in which there are no clear cases of contraction of diphthongs, it is clear that we cannot adduce this form as decisive evidence for contraction or "northern" spelling in Job. Nevertheless, it can be said that these examples fit well into the pattern of "northern" spelling already indicated for Job on the basis of other data, and may be regarded as supporting evidence. In any case, the occurrences of the form without *yodh* point to an earlier stage in the Hebrew orthographic tradition with a *terminus ad quem* somewhere between the 6th and 3rd century B.C.E.

2. Another indication of relatively early spelling is to be found in a group of examples in which the *waw* representing *ō,* normally present in MT, is omitted:

(a)[13] יֹנַקְתּוֹ (8:16) for יוֹנַקְתּוֹ

11. Cross-Freedman, *Early Hebrew Orthography,* 54-55, no. 68 and n. 42. Cf. Freedman, *Textus* 2 (1962): 93-94. [See above, Chapter 3]

12. Cross-Freedman, *Early Hebrew Orthography,* 68-69.

13. Mandelkern has the fuller spelling here; cf. Job 14:7; 15:30.

(b)[14] מֹסְרוֹת (39:5) for מוֹסְרוֹת
(c) נֹצָה (39:13) for נוֹצָה
(d) צֹפַר (11:1) for צוֹפַר (2:11; 20:1)
(e) קֹלוֹ (37:2) for קוֹלוֹ (37:4, 5)
(f) שֹׁפָר (39:25) for שׁוֹפָר (39:24)

B. Defective Spellings

1. There are a few examples in Job involving the omission of final vowel letters. This feature was characteristic of Canaanite/Phoenician spelling, and of early Hebrew orthography through the 10th century B.C.E.[15] Since Hebrew, whether the northern or southern dialect, after the 10th century B.C.E. was written in a standard orthography in which final vowels were regularly indicated and since the orthography of the Hebrew Bible was regularly revised in accordance with dominant practice, few if any examples of authentic archaic spelling have survived. Such cases as do exist are often concealed in the text, in which the letters have been rearranged and the original reading revised, and require extraordinary care in analysis to identify. And there is always the possibility of alternative explanations and interpretations of the materials.

As regards Job we can safely rule out the survival of 10th century spellings. It is possible, however, that Phoenician spelling was used in the autograph or an early copy of Job, especially in view of the literary and stylistic affinities of the book with Canaanite/Phoenician traditions.

Much more evidence would be required to make the case, but these examples may stimulate further research into the problem:

(a) אראה (9:11) for אֶרְאֵהוּ.

Assuming that the proposed reading is correct, the omission of the final *waw* may simply be a case of haplography. Note that the next word begins with ו.

(b) כמים (27:20) for כְּמוֹ יָם.

2. There is an isolated instance of the syncope of intervocalic *he* which deserves notice:

2:6 הִנּוֹ for הִנֵּהוּ.

The resultant form in MT should be vocalized *hinnēw* < *hinnēhū* (cf. Jer. 18:3). The form with the 3rd masc. suffix is rare, the shorter spelling occurring three times in all, and the longer spelling once. The syncope of intervocalic *he* in forms of this kind is a feature of preexilic spelling.[16]

14. This is the only instance in the Bible in which this word is spelled without the first *waw*.
15. Cross-Freedman, *Early Hebrew Orthography,* 19, 56.
16. *Ibid.,* 50, no. 26.

Summary

In view of the factors involved in the transmission of the text of the Hebrew Bible, and especially the following: the pronounced tendency toward uniformity in spelling and the rather late date of surviving manuscripts (particularly Job, for which only small fragments exist before the late medieval texts), the evidence for the persistence of a non-Massoretic orthographic pattern in the book of Job is impressive. The chief feature of this spelling is the contraction of the diphthongs *aw* > *ō* and *ay* > *ē* and the corresponding omission of the letters *waw* and *yodh,* which originally represented the diphthongs. There are approximately fifty examples of such contraction distributed among a variety of verbal, nominal, and adverbial forms, so as to preclude the possibility of arbitrary or accidental spelling variations.

The chief implication of the orthographic data with respect to the composition of Job is that the provenance of the book is northern and its date early. Since the Canaanite/Phoenician affinities in poetic style, mythological allusions, vocabulary, and syntax have been increasingly recognized by scholars, we may regard the evidence of the orthography as substantiating or corroborating these views. All the evidence fits well with the proposal that Job was a product of the (North) Israelite diaspora some time in the 7th or early 6th century B.C.E.

It is altogether fitting to conclude the article with a statement on the date, authorship, and provenance of the book of Job by Professor W. F. Albright, to whom this volume is dedicated [the quoted material is from a personal letter dated 7 February 1965]:

Following are some of my arguments for a Phoenician-influenced origin in Galilee or the Syrian diaspora (or, of course, the Coastal Plain of Palestine or Phoenicia) during the 7th or — possibly — the early 6th century B.C.E.

1. The total absence of quotations from Scripture, the closest being a few word sequences and common themes. This would be virtually inconceivable in the work of a man of Judah at this time.

2. The profound influence of Phoenician cosmology and cosmogony, Phoenician speech, trade, etc. Note especially the culture heroes Taḥut (originally Thoth), whom Sanchuniathon called the wisest man that ever lived under the sun, and Shekwi (so — the name is now attested from a Phoenician seal).

3. The religious ideas, which share the incipient skepticism of the age in Phoenicia and Ionia, but at the same time provide us with remarkable precursors of later Pharisaic concepts, though couched in unmistakably Canaanite language.

4. The textual evidence which you cite. In my opinion the new Qumran Job offers an earlier ending than MT, G (and the otherwise unknown Aramaic Targum which it mentions), or the Targum to which some of the rabbis objected. I also believe that the Elihu insert was made by the original author in response to orthodox criticism of his original text; it shares the characteristics of the rest of

the book without equalling the latter in literary skill (cf. the two Fausts of Goethe!).

5. Job's knowledge of Arabia came chiefly from Phoenician sources: e.g., Bûz is the Phoenician pronunciation of Bâz (Akkadian Bāzu).

8

Some Observations on Early Hebrew

The present study is a review article of a monograph by D. W. Goodwin based upon his doctoral dissertation accepted at Brown University in 1965.* In spite of the somewhat grandiose title, the work consists mainly of a critical evaluation of six articles on poems in the Hebrew Bible, three by W. F. Albright, and the rest written jointly by his pupils, F. M. Cross, Jr., and D. N. Freedman; the latter incorporated many of Albright's suggestions and were originally written under his supervision. All were drafted in the decade of the 40s, although some did not appear in print until somewhat later (the earliest was published in 1944, the latest in 1955). In addition to the main section, entitled "Archaic Forms" (ch. 4, pp. 45-136), there are separate studies devoted to related subjects: "Dialects of the Second Millennium" (ch. 2); "Orthographic Theory" (ch. 3); and "Metrical Theory and Hebrew Poetic Style" (ch. 5).

The initial question is whether such a narrowly limited selection of material warrants the sort of full-dress treatment offered here and also whether the results justify the effort and energy expended by the doctoral candidate and his advisors. In view of the extraordinary impact which Albright's contributions have had on biblical and Near Eastern studies, perhaps any investigation, especially of methods, however restricted, should be welcomed. Nevertheless, it would have enhanced the worth of the present undertaking if Goodwin had extended the scope of his inquiry to bring it more fully up to date and include more recent contributions to the subject by the principals under consideration, and the work of others who belong to the same Baltimore group. As it is, the monograph is itself archaic and obsolescent, although published as recently as 1969.

The author expresses his purpose as follows: ". . . to examine the ways in which he [William Foxwell Albright] and those pupils, namely Frank Moore Cross,

*Donald Watson Goodwin, *Text-Restoration Methods in Contemporary U.S.A. Biblical Scholarship.* Pubblicazioni del Seminario di Semitistica, Ricerche, 5 (Naples: Istituto Orientale di Napoli, 1969), x-178pp. 24.5 x 17.

Jr. and David Noel Freedman, have restored the texts of certain poetic passages of the Old Testament, Exod. 15, Dt. 33, 2 Sam. 22 and Ps. 18 (parallel texts), the poetic portions of Num. 23-24, Hab. 3, and Ps. 68" (Goodwin, 1). Goodwin goes on to identify the criteria which were used in making decisions about the text, and to classify them under eight headings:

1. Scribal errors;
2. Versions;
3. Parallel texts;
4. History;
5. Motifs;
6. Poetry;
7. Orthography;
8. Archaic forms.

The first three belong to the general and traditional equipment of the text-restorer, and in Goodwin's opinion do not require special notice; they are subsumed in his critique of our methods under the other headings. He analyzes nos. 4 and 5 as part of the general attempt to date the poems under consideration in the 2nd millennium B.C.E. and to interpret them in their historical setting. The last three items require individual attention, and a separate chapter of the work is devoted to each of these.

Chapter 3 is entitled "Orthographic Theory." After summarizing briefly the views expounded by Cross and Freedman in their monograph *Early Hebrew Orthography* (New Haven: American Oriental Society, 1952), Goodwin adds his own critique. He objects strenuously to our use of the expression "principle of consonantism" in referring to the orthography of the Phoenician inscriptions, remarking that this so-called principle is "a modern simplification" (29). He prefers to speak of an "acrophonic principle" (30) from which consonantal spelling is derived as a "direct and mechanical corollary" (29: the quotation is taken from Z. Harris, *A Grammar of the Phoenician Language* [New Haven: American Oriental Society, 1936], 15). He is disturbed that the word "principle" has been transferred and, what is worse, "consonantism" has been separated from "acrophony." He concedes that the "acrophonic principle" served as a "sort of 'principle of orthography' " in the Phoenician language; but "acrophony" had to be kept in mind (31), or else presumably the orthography would not have functioned effectively. Harris is probably right in supposing that an acrophonically-derived alphabet is the source of consonantal spelling,[1] but whether this hypothesis is valid or not, our concern in

1. As a matter of fact we, too, have championed this view, as Goodwin should have known; see, e.g., F. M. Cross and T. O. Lambdin, "A Ugaritic Abecedary and the Origins of the Proto-Canaanite Alphabet," *BASOR* 160 (1960): 21-26.

Early Hebrew Orthography was not with theoretical and speculative factors, but with developing a typological description of the orthographic practice of the inscriptions.

He goes on to say that the "orthographic timetable which Cross and Freedman have developed rests on the assumption that the scribes of the Old Aramaic dialects adopted 'consonantal spelling' along with the Phoenician alphabet" (32). He gives no reference for this statement, because we did not make it. It is an inference from our description of the process by which a spelling system with a complete set of final vowel letters was developed in Old Aramaic. We suggested that the time lapse was very brief, and twice used the expression "almost immediately" (*Early Hebrew Orthography,* 10 and 31). Admittedly we cannot prove this because, as both we and Goodwin observe, the earliest Old Aramaic inscriptions already exhibit *matres lectionis* (from the 10th and 9th centuries; cf. *Early Hebrew Orthography,* 23-24). At the same time, his assumption that vowel letters were employed "from the very beginning" (33) is equally unproved. His notion (34) that such an orthography developed from reading "foreign inscriptions in their own dialect, reading the new vowels in place of the consonants which the original writers had intended," is sheer speculation and has no visible connection with the actual practice of these scribes.

Goodwin's conclusion is that "there never was such a principle of orthography as 'consonantism' . . . . The term becomes meaningless when an effort is made to apply it as a criterion in the analysis of orthographic practice. As a 'rigid rule' it never existed. If there is no 'principle of consonantism', then it is hardly profitable to talk about a counter-principle of *matres lectionis.* All we can do is explore the ways in which symbols which had originally represented only consonants came to be employed as symbols for vowels" (33). He continues that his primary concern is not with "principles of orthography . . but the practice of orthography as it was handed down within one dialect and adapted from one dialect by another" (33). Finally he says, "Nevertheless, it would be possible to discover a time-table for the development of vowel-letters if we could note a progression within a dialect from 'acrophonic' to 'vocalic' spelling, as Harris has pointed out for us in the case of Phoenician" (33-34).

So this is what the vehement protest was all about. Substitute the words "acrophonic" and "vocalic" for "consonantism" and "vowel letters" and the crisis subsides.

Goodwin then deals with our treatment of the orthography of the Gezer calendar. Following Baumgartner and Moscati, he echoes the claim that the Gezer calendar is the "pivot of their orthographic theory." If the analysis of the Gezer calendar which we presented can be successfully challenged, the orthographic theory collapses with it. This is misleading, since our views of the development of orthography in the territory of Israel do not depend upon a specific determination of the date, dialect, or spelling of the calendar. Although we see no reason to alter our views of the latter in the slightest, in spite of continuing efforts of scholars to re-analyze and reinterpret the material, we could ignore the calendar entirely in making our basic case. All alphabetic inscriptions from the territory under consideration in the proto-Canaanite period (from the end of the 13th to the end of the 11th century B.C.E.) exhibit the same orthographic phenomena which we have associated with Phoenician inscriptions, namely consonantal spelling. To the list of these given in *Early Hebrew Orthography,* pp. 8ff. (which Goodwin never mentions in his monograph), a number of other items are now to be added (for a general survey, see F. M. Cross, "The Origin and Early Evolution of the Alphabet," *Eretz Israel* 8. *E. L. Sukenik Memorial Volume* [1967]: 8*-24*). On the other hand, all inscriptions dating from the 9th century on show consistent use of vowel letters in the final position. A significant change took place in this area between the end of the 11th century and the middle of the 9th century, regardless of what we think of the Gezer calendar.

With regard to the latter, Goodwin offers nothing new, but simply rehashes arguments already dealt with in *Early Hebrew Orthography.* Concerning the word *pšt* in the inscription, he says, "The reading **pištā* . . . is probably no more, nor no less, probable than *pēšet*" (35). It is not quite clear to us what "probably . . . probable" is supposed to signify, or the remarkable collocation of negatives in "no more, nor no less," but presumably he means that the two readings have equal standing. This, however, is hardly the case. The word *pištā* is the common word in Biblical Hebrew, a thoroughly attested dialect for this time and area, whereas **pēšet* does not occur in the Bible at all, but is a hypothetical construct from the attested form *pištī,* which occurs twice in the book of Hosea (2:7, 11), and is evidently the result of mispointing by the Massoretes (cf. the note by Freedman in "פשתי in Hosea 2_7," *JBL* 74 [1955]: 275).

Goodwin's conclusion about our orthographic study is inevitably negative. He repeats his charge for the fourth time in the chapter that "consonantal spelling" is a glib modern simplification (39), and urges that "orthography in Northwest Semitic dialects was determined by scribal practice rather than abstract principles" (39). He has added "glib" to "simplification" and "abstract" to "principles," apparently feeling that the second terms alone are insufficient to end the discussion.

Had Goodwin read more carefully he would have discerned that our concern was to draw up a typology of orthographic practice and to describe in general terms the patterns (or principles) immanent in this typological sequence. Our conclusions give, we believe, the most "parsimonious" explanation of the data comprehended. Goodwin's assertions to be valid either must demonstrate that our description fails to comprehend the full data or must present a simpler or more parsimonious explanation of the full data. He makes no serious attempt to do either.

Goodwin summarizes our conclusions on pp. 39-40, and then offers his evaluation on p. 42. He rejects the first point, that vowel letters were not used before the 9th century, on the basis of his analysis of the Gezer calendar; but, as already indicated, he has ignored the cumulative evidence of the alphabetic inscriptions from the 13th through the 11th centuries, in none of which do vowel letters occur. He appears to accept the second point, that after the middle of the 9th century all final vowels were indicated in the orthography. With respect to the third point concerning the late sporadic appearance of medial vowel letters, he agrees in part, but insists that the use of *waw* for *ō* is attested in the Siloam inscription and in the Lachish letters. He does not provide evidence or argument for this position, however. Presumably he has in mind forms like *b‘wd* and *hmwṣ’;* but there is only the evidence of Massoretic vocalization to indicate that the diphthong *-aw* was contracted to *-ō*. How does Goodwin know that contraction had already taken place by the 8th century B.C.E. in Judahite Hebrew? How does he explain in this case how the scribes *always* distinguish between *-ô* < *-aw* and *-ô* < *-ā,* without error, always marking *ô* < *-aw* with *waw,* never marking *-ô* < *-ā?* Does he believe that the ancient scribe resorted to historical linguistics, reconstructing etymologies? In this case we must suppose also that while the Judaeans were historical linguists, the Phoenicians and North Israelites were less sophisticated since the latter two *never* distinguished *-ô* < *aw* and *-ô* < *ā* in their orthography. On the contrary, we must insist that the simplest explanation of the data is rather that in the South, as in Aramaic, the diphthong *-aw* had not contracted in preexilic times.

On the fourth point, namely that *waw* does not signify *-ô* until postexilic times, Goodwin claims that the evidence contradicts our position. He states that there are instances in the Samaria ostraca, the Siloam inscription, and the Lachish ostraca, without, however, specifying the instances, citing any new evidence or offering any argument to refute our analysis and explanation of forms in which *waw* appears in the final or medial position. Since he has stated elsewhere that our criteria are derived from "abstract principles," any conclusions we might reach would be dismissible, whereas he needs only to assure us that his methods and conclusions are scientific and inductive to guarantee their validity. How can such a cavalier approach to contestable points advance our understanding of the problems?

At no point does Goodwin offer evidence for his conclusions, which echo the views of an older scholarship (see our discussion of the history of such scholarship, *Early Hebrew Orthography,* 1-7). Nor, in spite of his devotion to scientific method, does he mention a single one of the dozens of inscriptions which have been found and published since our monograph appeared. Such new data provide the nearest equivalent to experimental verification in the exact sciences, and can be used to test previously propounded hypotheses. There is ample orthographic information in these inscriptions; tested against these materials, our proposed scheme for the evolution of Hebrew orthography passes on all major points and most minor ones. The only significant modification is in the third point. Although Goodwin takes no notice of the evidence, there is now at least one clear example of the use of *waw* as an internal vowel letter in the 8th century (let it be noted that it represents the vowel *-ū,* not *ō*); the word is *’rwr* = *’ārūr,* "cursed" (cf. N. Avigad, "The Epitaph of a Royal Steward from Siloam Village," *IEJ* 3 [1953]: 137-153).

Goodwin's own theory about spelling practices is offered on p. 40. He suggests that "the speakers of a dialect in which sound changes had occurred would read consonantal signs of older and of foreign inscriptions as representing the vowels which they pronounced in their dialect." It is difficult to judge the validity of such a hypothesis, especially since Goodwin does not trouble to offer any examples or other supporting data. But he does point out that the conflicting tendency toward defective spellings and the persistent tradition of consonantal spelling would have sufficed to create the impression that such signs need not always be written. This statement seems to be Goodwin's version of our remarks concerning the relation of consonantal spelling to orthography in which vowel letters are used, a statement which he castigated vigorously a few pages earlier (33).

In any case, he concludes: "The result would be precisely the kind of spelling which we find in the non-Phoenician dialects and languages . . . in which certain symbols represent vowels as well as consonants, but are used in this fashion somewhat sporadically, especially in the medial position" (40). What is concealed in the statement is that final vowel letters are used consistently and systematically in these inscriptions, a fact which is somewhat inconvenient for a theorizer who holds that vowel letters developed from the misreading of consonants, and might or might not be used, at the discretion if not whim of the scribe.[2]

Chapter 4 on "Archaic Forms" constitutes the main part of the book (45-136). In it Goodwin deals with the bulk of the textual restorations made in the six studies under consideration. Throughout, Goodwin raises the question whether the presence of archaisms demonstrates or even implies an early date for the composition. The question is entirely legitimate. One must define the archaic and distinguish it from the archaistic (i.e., imitation of archaic) or merely dialectic. Precisely this question is raised methodologically and carried through in a painstaking linguistic analysis in the Yale dissertation of David A. Robertson, *Linguistic Evidence in Dating Early Hebrew Poetry* (1966). [Published as *Linguistic Evidence in Dating Early Hebrew Poetry.* SBL Dissertation Series, no. 3 (Missoula, MT: SBL, 1972). Ed.] His methods are much more stringent than those of Goodwin, and his conclusions independent of, if often in agreement with, those of the reviewers.

Goodwin raises questions about a number of specific proposals and offers his own alternatives in some cases. Certainly we would regard the published studies as work in progress, subject to criticism and correction. In a number of instances, we have already revised our views and some of these have found their way into print. We will comment briefly on some of the points he makes.

1. Dt 33:2. He queries our reading *'ittō-m,* "with him" (preposition + pronominal suffix + enclitic *mem*) and asks more than once where there is evidence

2. On the postexilic development of Hebrew orthography, see now M. E. Sherman, "Systems of Hebrew and Aramaic Orthography: An Epigraphic History of the Use of *Matres Lectionis* in Non-Biblical Texts to ca. A. D. 135" (diss., Harvard, 1966).

of comparable constructions in related languages, or elsewhere in Hebrew. At the time, it was rather a daring suggestion but, in view of more recent developments, it now seems rather staid. We can now refer Goodwin to the studies of this phenomenon by H. D. Hummel, "Enclitic *Mem* in Early Northwest Semitic, Especially Hebrew," *JBL* 76 (1957): 91 and n. 42, and 99; and M. Dahood, *Psalms III.* AB 17a (Garden City: Doubleday, 1970), the section entitled "Grammar of the Psalter," 408, for a list of examples; see discussion of these examples in the Comments on the individual Psalms. Such data do not demonstrate the correctness of our reconstruction, but they establish the reading as a legitimate possibility.

2. Ps. 68:34-45a (pp. 71-72). For additional evidence and discussion of the vocative *lamed* in Biblical Hebrew, see Dahood, *Psalms III,* 407, and the Indices of *Psalms I, II,* and *III.* [Published respectively in 1966, 1968, and 1970 by Doubleday. Ed.]

3. Goodwin's discussion of the Hebrew article is unsatisfactory on several grounds. He appears to be unaware of the evidence that the article originated only after the loss of case endings in Canaanite and hence is a phenomenon of the 1st millennium. The most satisfactory discussion of the linguistic data may be found in the paper of T. O. Lambdin, "The Junctural Origin of the West Semitic Definite Article," *Near Eastern Studies in Honor of William Foxwell Albright,* ed. H. Goedicke (Baltimore: Johns Hopkins, 1971), 315-333. The first appearance of the article in Canaanite, is 10th century in date, and this cannot be long after its origin. In no case can we suppose that the definite article as such is older than the general loss of case endings in Canaanite which began no earlier than the 13th century B.C.E. Moreover, there is no demonstrative adjective or pronoun to which it can be traced back (Lambdin). One would expect the definite article to penetrate very slowly into poetic language, especially into the stereotyped metrical formulae of oral poetry; this expectation is confirmed by its extreme rarity in the bestpreserved archaic Hebrew poetry. Goodwin admits its rarity in early Hebrew poetry but insists that the definite article be retained "where it conforms to known usage in Old Phoenician more or less closely. . . ." This is a remarkable proposal. He is suggesting that the use in Phoenician *prose* be extended to early Hebrew *poetry.* In view of the fact that Hebrew poetry in the early period does owe much to Canaanite language, it may be of interest to compare Hebrew and Phoenician *poetry.* Unfortunately, we possess only the Phoenician incantations from Arslan Tash[3] (7th century B.C.E.), which contain fully formal Phoenician poetry. To these may be added the Gezer calendar, which is metrically patterned, and the couplets from the caves of Khirbet Beit Lei (6th century B.C.E.).[4]

3. See F. M. Cross and R. J. Saley, "Phoenician Incantations on a Plaque of the Seventh Century B.C. from Arslan Tash in Upper Syria," *BASOR* 197 (1970): 42-49, esp. 48.

4. See F. M. Cross, "The Cave Inscriptions from Khirbet Beit Lei," *Near Eastern Archaeology in the Twentieth Century. Festschrift N. Glueck,* ed. J. A. Sanders (Garden City: Doubleday, 1970), 299-306.

In none of these, Phoenician or Hebrew, is there a single instance of the use of the definite article. In short, all data presently known point to the absence of the article in early Hebrew poetic language.

4. Ps. 68:9, the use of *zh* in the expression *zeh sīnay* (pp. 88-89). After reviewing the evidence (but unaccountably not referring to the article by Cross, "Yahweh and the God of the Patriarchs," *HTR* 55 [1962]: 225-259), Goodwin concludes that the expression "*'elōhīm zeh sīnay* could mean, 'God, this one, the one of Sinai' and be judged as Hebrew which is syntactically correct . . ." (89). But who would compose such a monstrosity in any language? And Goodwin has to create a new meaning for *sīnay,* "the one of Sinai," in the process, not otherwise attested (88-89). With T. Meek's final capitulation on the structure and sense of the expression "the one of Sinai" (cf. "Translating the Hebrew Bible," *JBL* 79 [1960]: 331-32), one might have hoped that the matter would be settled, but clearly that is not the case. For further discussion, see Dahood, *Psalms II,* 139, on Ps. 68:9.

5. On pp. 107-8, Goodwin discusses the noun *bāmāh,* which occurs in Hab. 3:19bc and Ps. 18:34 (= 2 Sam. 22:34). Albright has supplied the word *ym,* "Sea," in Hab. 3, and we have supplied the word *mt,* "Death," in Ps. 18. Goodwin queries the interpretation of *bāmōtē* as "back" and the emendation in both places. We believe that his doubts about the restorations may be justified and that the texts should be reconsidered.

In ch. 5, Goodwin deals with "Metrical Theory and Hebrew Poetical Style." On the whole his comments are cautious and sound. Thus far at least, no theory of meter and strophic structure in Hebrew poetry is sufficiently stabilized and precise to provide a firm basis for textual emendation. It may be hoped that with the accumulation of statistical data and a more extensive study of distributional patterns, we may be able to proceed in that direction and ultimately be able to decide when something has fallen out and when something has been added. Recent studies by Cross ("The Song of the Sea and Canaanite Myth," *Journal for Theology and the Church* 5 [1968]: 1-25; note especially the samples of Ugaritic meter, 3-7), Dahood *(Psalms I, II, III, passim),* and Freedman ("The Structure of Job 3," *Bibl* 49 [1968]: 503-8; soon to appear are studies of Ps. 137; Exod. 15; and Ps. 29) indicate that syllable-counting may prove to be the most effective way of analyzing poetic structure in Hebrew as well as Canaanite. [See F. M. Cross, *CMHE* (1973). For Psalm 137, see *PPP,* 303-322, and for Exodus 15, 179-227 in the same volume. For Psalm 29, see Chapter 9 in this volume. Ed.]

In the conclusion of his work, Goodwin suggests rather strongly that a hidden theological or historical motivation (i.e., a "cause," 159) guided the methodology and seriously affected the results of our work. He notes a common desire, even passion, for dating the poems early in Israel's history (the 2nd millennium is the watchword), and thus to use them to reconstruct that history. To the extent that we shared Albright's opposition to prevailing critical theories about Israel's history in the 1940s, and in particular scholarly views about the setting, date, and character of the poems, there may be an element of truth in the suggestion. The studies were composed in the heat of the battle, and reflect the effort to challenge the confident assumptions and assured results of two generations of scholarship. This challenge to the establishment developed out of the great renewal of archaeological activity after the First World War, a movement in which Albright played the leading part. In Albright's opinion, archaeology provided a solid base and viable framework on which biblical history could be recovered and reconstituted. By using the firm historical pegs thus provided, it would be possible to analyze, organize, and interpret the biblical materials in a new and much more effective way. The poetry studies were one of the products of this approach. To suggest or imply that other considerations influenced the conclusions is not worthy of the scholarly profession and does not belong in this book.

In conclusion, we wish to express our appreciation to Dr. Goodwin for spending so much time and effort on these studies and related exercises. We regret that he did not find them more rewarding, and we regret even more that his own work was not more productive. Instead of advancing beyond our perimeters and staking out new territories, he has been content to rework plowed fields, and not to advantage. His work has been regressive, in the sense that he has largely revived old views, restated old positions, not on the basis of new evidence, but by ignoring it.

The book is marred by an inordinate number of typographical errors, a list of which has been sent to the author in the event that there is a second printing or edition of the work. In addition, the author has adopted a specialized transcription of Biblical Hebrew which is not adequately explained in the Acknowledgments (p. v): e.g., the letter *he* with *mappiq* is transcribed "hh" as though the latter were a *dagesh forte.* It is often difficult to distinguish between eccentricities and errors.

9

Psalm 29: A Structural Analysis

In 1935, H. L. Ginsberg published an article demonstrating the existence of Canaanite elements in Psalm 29.[1] Among these were: 1) the mention of the *b^enē 'ēlīm* related to the assembly of the *banu ili* in the Ugaritic texts; 2) the glorification of the voice of Yahweh, an adaptation of the praises of Baal, the Canaanite storm god; 3) topographical references to Lebanon, Sirion, and Kadesh, all located in Syria; 4) the first discovery in the Bible of an enclitic *mem* (v. 6); 5) the kingship of Yahweh, similar to the formula of Baal's triumph over his foes. Since then, others have developed and supplemented this original investigation, especially with the aid of recent work in Ugaritic.[2] Linguistic and textual problems remain, however.[3] The present paper suggests that a structural analysis of the psalm not only supports the integrity of the present text but also points to some complex and sophisticated techniques of Hebrew poetry.

1. "A Phoenician Hymn in the Psalter," *Atti del XIX Congresso Internazionale degli Orientalisti* (Rome, 1935), 472-76; *Kitvê Ugarit [The Ugarit Texts]* (Jerusalem: Bialik Foundation, 1936), 129ff. [Hebrew]; an expanded version is to be found in "The Rebellion and Death of Baʿlu," *Orientalia,* N.S. 5 (1936): 180ff.

2. T. H. Gaster, "Psalm 29," *JQR* 37 (1946-47): 55-65; F. M. Cross, Jr., "Notes on a Canaanite Psalm in the Old Testament," *BASOR* 117 (1950): 19-21; H. J. Kraus, *Die Psalmen,* I/2 (Neukirchen: Neukirchener Verlag, 1961), Eng. trans.: *Psalms 1–59* (Minneapolis: Augsburg, 1989), ad loc.; A. Weiser, *The Psalms.* OTL (Philadelphia: Westminster, 1962); M. Dahood, *Psalms I.* AB (Garden City: Doubleday, 1965); H. L. Ginsberg, "A Strand in the Cord of Hebraic Hymnody," *ErIsr* 9. Albright Volume (1969): 45-46.

3. Both Ginsberg and Cross regard v. 7 as incomplete. Cross speaks of haplography (*BASOR* 117 [1950]: 20), while Ginsberg offers the following restoration: "The voice of Yahweh kindles flames / [Yea, Yahweh kindles flames] of fire" ("A Phoenician Hymn," 474). Dahood, on the other hand, reverses the order of vv. 6 and 7 (*Psalms I,* 174).

Transliteration and Translation

habū layahweh binē ʾēlīm	(1) Give praise to Yahweh, O sons of El
habū layahweh kabōd waʿōz	Give praise to Yahweh, the Glorious and Victorious
habū layahweh kabōd šimō	Give praise to Yahweh, whose name is Glorious
hištaḥwū layahweh bihadrat qōdš	(2) Prostrate yourselves before Yahweh, when he appears in the sanctuary —
qōl yahweh ʿal hamaym	(3) Yahweh's voice is upon the waters
ʾēl hakabōd hirʿīm	El the Glorious thunders
yahweh ʿal maym rabbīm	Yahweh upon the mighty waters
qōl yahweh bikōḥ	(4) Yahweh's voice in power
qōl yahweh bihadār	Yahweh's voice in majesty
qōl yahweh šōbēr ʾarazīm	(5) Yahweh's voice breaks the cedars
wayašabbēr yahweh ʾet-ʾarzē halibanōn	Yahweh shatters the cedars of Lebanon
wayarqīdēm kimō ʿēgl libanōn	(6) It makes Lebanon skip like a calf
waśiryōn kimō ben-rēʾmīm	and Sirion like a young wild bull.
qōl yahweh ḥōṣēb (bi)lahbōt ʾēš	(7) Yahweh's voice hews (with) flames of fire
qōl yahweh yaḥīl midbār	(8) Yahweh's voice shakes the plain
yaḥīl yahweh midbar qadēš	Yahweh shakes the plain of Kadesh
qōl yahweh yaḥōlēl ʾayyalōt	(9) Yahweh's voice makes the hinds writhe
wayaḥśōp yaʿarōt	and strips the forests —
wabihēkalō kullō ʾōmēr	and in his temple everyone will say:
kabōd yahweh lamabbūl yašab	(10) "Glorious is Yahweh, enthroned since the Flood
wayēšeb yahweh malk laʿōlām	Yahweh the king has been enthroned for ages
yahweh ʿōz laʿammō yittēn	(11) Let Yahweh give victory to his people
yahweh yabarrēk ʾet-ʿammō bišalōm	Let Yahweh bless his people with peace."

In determining metrical patterns we have adopted a syllable-counting method. In general we follow MT, but modify the vocalization when there is compelling evidence for a more original pronunciation. The following variations from MT may be noted:

1. Segolate formations are treated as monosyllabic: e.g., *ʿēgl* for MT *ʿēgel* (v. 6), and *malk* for MT *melek* (v. 10). The same treatment is accorded resolved diphthongs: e.g., *maym* for MT *mayim* (v. 3).

2. We do not count secondary vowels, introduced into MT mainly in connection with laryngeals: e.g., *hištaḥwū* for MT *hištaḥᵃwū* (v. 2), *kōḥ* for MT *kōaḥ* (v. 4), *rē'mīm* for MT *rᵉ'ēmīm* (v. 6), *lahbōt* for MT *lahᵃabōt* (v. 7), *yaḥśōp* for MT *yeḥᵉśōp*.

3. The definite article is represented as *ha-*, but without doubling the following consonant (e.g., *hakabōd* for MT *hakkābōd,* v. 3). Its presence has been ignored where the sole indication is the Massoretic vocalization (e.g., *bikōḥ* for MT *bakkōaḥ,* v. 4, and *bišalōm* for MT *baššālōm,* v. 11).

4. Without adhering to the intricacies of Massoretic classification of vowels according to quality and quantity, we attempt to distinguish between long and short vowels. However, because of widespread uncertainty concerning the effect of the accent on syllable length, and the historical development of the language, we have avoided assigning relative time values to the vowels. Perhaps naively, we assume that the differences will tend to cancel out; hence all syllables are considered equal for our purposes. We have also been somewhat arbitrary in identifying the vowels which underlie vocal shewa in the text (e.g., *bi* for *bᵉ, la for lᵉ).*

Since formal analysis and interpretation go hand in hand, and one type of evidence cannot easily be separated from the other, it will be necessary to move back and forth from one area to the other in order to integrate the data and the argument. We will begin with a brief account of the strophic structure, and then turn to a more detailed examination of the text. Psalm 29 has an ordered structure, which may be outlined as follows:

		Number of Syllables
Vv. 1-2	Introduction	37
Vv. 3-4	Stophe I	29
Vv. 5-6	Strophe II	38
Vv. 7-9	Strophe III	47
Vv. 10-11	Conclusion	36

We follow the verse divisions of MT with a single exception. In accordance with the proposal of B. Margulis, we mark the end of v. 9 after *'ōmēr,* and read *kābōd* as the first word of v. 10.[4]

The Introduction and Conclusion each consist of four lines, with the following metrical pattern:

4. "A Ugaritic Psalm (RŠ 24.252)," *JBL* 89 (1970): 303.

	Introduction		Conclusion
V. 1	5 + 4 = 9	V. 10	4 + 5 = 9
	5 + 4 = 9		5 + 4 = 9
V. 2	5 + 4 = 9	V. 11	3 + 5 = 8
	6 + 4 = 10		5 + 6 = 11
Total	37		37

If we adopted a more conventional procedure and counted only the stressed syllables, the results would be equivalent:

V. 1	2 + 2 = 4	V. 10	2 + 2 = 4
	2 + 2 = 4		2 + 2 = 4
V. 2	2 + 2 = 4	V. 11	2 + 2 = 4
	2 + 2 = 4		2 + 2 = 4

The Introduction and Conclusion not only correspond in structure, but they also are linked by theme and content. In the Introduction the "sons of El" are summoned to give praise to Yahweh, and in the Conclusion we have their proclamation of Yahweh's eternal sovereignty, and their prayer in behalf of his people. The centrality and ubiquity of Yahweh are emphasized by the repetition of the name of the deity, which occurs in each of the eight lines of the Introduction and Conclusion. In the former Yahweh is the indirect object (always preceded by the preposition *la-*) of the series of imperative verbs, while in the latter he is the subject, the sole and sufficient actor in the drama of rule and redemption. A correlative pattern, also keyed to the name Yahweh, appears in the body of the poem as well.

The link between the Introduction and Conclusion is provided by v. 9c, "and in his palace everyone will say," which complements v. 2b, "Prostrate yourselves before Yahweh in the holy place when he appears." It locates the scene of the divine assembly, and describes its response to the manifestation of the supreme deity, which is indicated in v. 2b, and amplified in the main part of the poem, vv. 3-9. We hold, then, that v. 9c, while belonging to the main section of the poem, nevertheless serves as the transition from the Introduction to the Conclusion, which constitutes the utterance referred to in v. 9c. A defense of this view will be presented in the Notes.

The main part of the poem (vv. 3-9) is dominated by the theme of *qōl yahweh,* the thunderous voice of Yahweh. The expression occurs seven times,[5] while the

5. The number seven figures in other texts dealing with the storm god theme. Ugaritic Text no. 17 lists the gods of Mt. Casius, including El, Dagan (the father of Baal), and seven storm gods *(bʿlm).* The parallel Akkadian text (RS 20.24) has Adad^{ḫursag} Ḫazi, followed by Adad$_1$ through Adad$_6$. Cf. W. F. Albright, *Yahweh and the Gods of Canaan* (Garden City: Doubleday, 1968), 140-43. An Assyrian text from Assur also gives seven Adads. M. Astour suggests that the seven were differentiated "not for theological reasons, but according to the most renowned shrines of the storm god" ("Some New Divine Names from Ugarit," *JAOS* 86 [1966]: 279). In the Hymn

name Yahweh appears by itself an additional three times, making a total of ten for the latter. Since these numbers are used repeatedly in the Bible for organizational and symbolic purposes, we may infer not only that the selection was deliberate but also that the poem is substantially complete in the form in which we have it. This section consists of three strophes, vv. 3-4, 5-6, and 7-9: the lines of division are indicated by shifts in tone and texture, and confirmed by the distribution of the key terms already mentioned. Thus, in the first strophe the storm gathers force over the Mediterranean. In the second, it shatters the mighty cedars of Lebanon, while shaking the highlands of Syria. In the third, it thunders on into the plains, having left a trail of devastation in the forests. Each strophe begins, appropriately, with *qōl yahweh.* The expression occurs three times in the first strophe, and an equal number of times in the third strophe; the remaining occurrence is in the second strophe. The word Yahweh by itself occurs once in each strophe. The distributional pattern is outlined in the following table:

	qwl yhwh		yhwh		
Strophe I (vv. 3-4)	3		1		
Strophe II (vv. 5-6)	1		1		
Strophe III (vv. 7-9)	3		1		
	7	+	3	=	10

It may be added that v. 6 is characterized by an impressive chiasm, which fittingly marks the midpoint of the poem:[6]

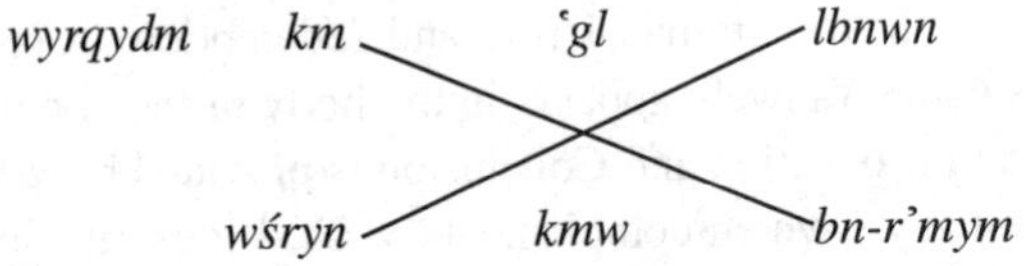

to Iškur, when Enlil gives the storm winds to his son Iškur, he says, "The 'seven' winds I have harnessed for you as a team, the storm winds I have harnessed for you. . . ." Cf. A. Kapelrud, "The Number Seven in Ugaritic Texts," *VT* 18 (1968): 494-99: the number seven is seen to be loaded with strength and danger, a number of completion, a number of denoting intensity and quality.

6. Ps. 137 is approximately the same length as Ps. 29, and has a similar structure. The midpoint of the psalm (vv. 5-6ab) is marked by a double chiasm:

ʾm ʾškḥk yrwšlm tškḥ ymyny
tdbq lšwny lḥky ʾm lʾ ʾzkrky

For further details see D. N. Freedman, "The Structure of Psalm 137," *Near Eastern Studies in Honor of William Foxwell Albright,* ed. Hans Goedicke (Baltimore: Johns Hopkins University Press, 1971), 187-205, esp. 193-98.

Notes

Vv. 1-2. *bny 'lym.* In view of the Canaanite background of this psalm, and the presence in Canaanite myths of the *bn ilm,* "the sons of El," it is more likely that the *mem* is to be interpreted as enclitic than as the plural ending.[7]

kbwd w'z. These are generally regarded as attributes of Yahweh, and so translated: "glory and strength" (RSV) or "glory and praise" (AB). Later on in this psalm, however, *kābōd* is identified as a name of Yahweh (v. 2a; cf. also vv. 3 and 9c); cf. also Ps. 4:3; 62:8; 66:2, where Yahweh is called *kbwdy*). Here it is to be read similarly, in conjunction with *'z* as a double name: "Glorious and Victorious."[8] Other biblical passages which associate divine titles with Yahweh's manifestation in the storm include the Song of Hannah:

> It is Yahweh who crushes his opponents
> it is the Exalted One who thunders in heaven.
> (1 Sam. 2:10)[9]

kbwd šmw. Instead of the construct chain: "the glory of his name," we read a name formula: "Glorious is his name"; cf. *yhwh šmw,* "whose name is Yahweh" (Exod. 15:3).

bhdrt qdš. LXX has "in the court of his sanctuary," apparently reading *ḥṣrt* for the difficult *hdrt;* cf. Ps. 96:8-9, where the expressions *bhdrt qdš* and *lḥṣrwtyw* are in parallel construction. Others connect it with a root meaning "ornament" and translate "in holy array" (RSV). As shown by F. M. Cross, Jr., however, the same term *hdrt* is found in Ugaritic, in the Keret poem, where it is in parallel with the word *hlm,* meaning "dream."[10] In the story Keret falls into a trance, in which he has a vision of El, who descends to speak to him (Col. I, ll. 35-36). After the dream, Keret awakens:

krt . yḥt . wḥlm	Keret awoke and it was a dream
'bd . il. whdrt	the servant of El, and it was a vision
	(Lines 154-55)

7. This is apparently Dahood's view; *Psalms I,* 175-76. For an example of *bn 'lm* in Phoenician, see Dahood, "G. R. Driver and the Enclitic *mem* in Phoenician," *Bibl* 49 (1968): 89f.

8. The following double divine names in Ugaritic may be noted: *Gapnu-wa-Ugāru,* "Vineyard-and-Field" (cf. W. F. Albright, *Archaeology and the Religion of Israel* [Baltimore: Johns Hopkins, 1942], 89) and *Kothar-wa-Khasis,* "the Very Skilful and Intelligent One" (Albright, *Yahweh and the Gods of Canaan,* 136-37). Double and multiple divine epithets abound in the Psalter; cf. Dahood, *Psalms I, II, III,* Indices under "Appellatives" and "Epithets." On *'z,* "victory," see Dahood, *Psalms I,* 180.

9. Albright, *Yahweh and the Gods of Canaan,* 21.

10. Cross, *BASOR,* 117 (1950): 21.

In other words, the dream consisted in a vision of El, along with an audition. In Hebrew, on the other hand, the root *hdr* has connotations of splendor, majesty, glory; cf. Ps. 96:6; Job 40:10; Ps. 111:3, where it is parallel with *hōd;* Ps. 8:6; Isa. 35:12, where it is parallel with *kābōd.* It also appears in v. 4 of this psalm in the description of Yahweh's manifestation in the storm. Interpreting the term in v. 2 in the light of Hebrew and Ugaritic usage, we arrive at the following rendition: "theophanic vision," "divine appearance."[11]

Since the theophanic vision takes place in the heavenly temple where the *bny 'lym* are, it is reasonable to interpret *qdš* as parallel or complementary to *hykl* in v. 9c. The relationship will be seen more clearly if we put the lines in sequence:

hištaḥwū layahweh	(2b) Prostrate yourselves before Yahweh
bihadrat qōdš	in the holy place of his appearing
wabihēkalō kullō 'ōmēr	(9c) and in his temple every one will say:

A careful examination of the passages in which the expression *bhdrt qdš* occurs (Ps. 96:9; 1 Chr. 16:29; 2 Chr. 20:21; cf. Prov. 14:28) indicates that *qōdeš* designates "the holy place," i.e., the heavenly temple of Yahweh, as well as its earthly counterpart in the central sanctuary (Ps. 96:7-9). Support for this analysis is to be found in a closely related passage, Hab. 2:20, in which the terms *hykl* and *qdš* are combined:

wayahweh b^{e}hēkal qodšō	Now Yahweh is in his holy temple
has mippānāw kol-hā'āreṣ	Let all the earth be silent in his presence!

Further comparison with Ps. 96:9 brings out the essential synonymity of the expressions: *hdrt qdš* and *hykl qdšw.*

hištaḥ^{a}wū layahweh	Prostrate yourselves before Yahweh
b^{e}hadrat qōdeš	in the holy place of his appearing
ḥīlū mippānāw kol-hā'āreṣ	Tremble before him, all the earth!

11. Cross, *ibid.;* and C. Gordon, *Ugaritic Handbook.* Analecta Orientalia 25 (Rome: Pontificium Institutum Biblicum, 1947), 225. Ginsberg renders the word "fantasy" (*The Legend of King Keret, BASOR* Sup 2-3 [1949]: 71). J. Aisleitner proposes "eine [hehre] vision" (*Die mythologischen und kultischen Texte aus Ras Shamra* [Berlin: Akadémiai Kladó, 1959], 92). J. Gray favors "vision" (*The KRT Text in the Literature of Ras Shamra,* 2nd ed. [Leiden: Brill, 1964], 55), and offers in support of his view the following translation of ll. 35-36:

wbḥlmh . 'el . yrd	And in his dreaming El comes down
bẓhrth . 'ab . 'adm	Yea, in his vision, the father of men.

The passage in Ps. 96:7-9 is almost identical with the opening lines of Psalm 29, but there are significant minor modifications. The substitution of *mišp^{e}ḥōt ʿammīm* for *b^{e}nē ʾēlīm* reflects the shift from the heavenly to the earthly domain, or from mythological to cultic conceptions. The language used of the temple remains the same, showing that there was no sharp differentiation between the two sanctuaries. The cultic addition in Ps. 98:6,

ś^{e}ʾū minḥāh ūbōʾū l^{e}ḥaṣrōtāw	Bring an offering, and enter into his courts

fixes the setting in the temple area, and lends further support to the identification of the *qōdeš* in v. 9 as the holy place. It is noteworthy that v. 10 continues with the proclamation of Yahweh's kingship, as does Ps. 29:9c-10, though the imagery in the latter is more archaic; cf. *ʾimrū . . . yhwh mālāk* (96:10) with *ʾomer . . . (wayēšeb) yhwh melek* (29:9c-10).[12]

The last instance of the expression *hdrt = qdš* occurs in 2 Chr. 20:21, where we read:

wayyiwwāʿēṣ ʾel-hāʿām	Then he took counsel with the people
wayyaʿ^{a}mēd	and he appointed
m^{e}šōr^{a}rīm layhwh	those who sing to Yahweh
ūm^{e}hal^{e}līm l^{e}hadrat-qōdeš	and those who offer praises to the theophanic holy place
b^{e}ṣēʾt lipnē heḥālūṣ	as they were going before the army
w^{e}ʾōm^{e}rīm hōdū layhwh	and saying, "Give thanks to Yahweh,
kī l^{e}ʿōlām ḥasdō	for his kindness is everlasting."

While the event is located in the plain of Tekoa (2 Chr. 20:20), the setting is typically cultic. The king, Jehoshaphat, is described as assembling the temple singers (lit.: "those who sing praises to Yahweh, to the holy place of the theophany") to pass before the troops, singing the refrain: "Give thanks to Yahweh, for his kindness is everlasting." The key terms are complementary: *mšrrym* and *mhllym* = those who sing praises, i.e., one of the priestly or levitical choirs; *layahweh* and *lhdrt* = *qdš* = to Yahweh in the holy place where he reveals himself. This would normally be interpreted as the heavenly sanctuary, though it is possible that the songs of praise would be directed to the sanctuary in Jerusalem, as suggested in Solomon's prayer (1 Kings 8:22-53; note especially the prayer to be offered by the army when it goes out against the enemy, vv. 44-45). In either case the prayer is heard by Yahweh in his heavenly sanctuary.

12. In view of the imperatives in Ps. 29:1-2, and *ʾimrū* in Ps. 96:10, it would be plausible to read *ʾ^{e}mōr* "(all of you) say." But it is not necessary to change the text, since variation in verb forms is to be expected in Hebrew poetry; cf. Dahood, *Psalms III,* 426, "Participle functioning as imperative."

In sum we propose that vv. 2b and 9c form an envelope around the body of the poem, which describes the awesome physical effects of the manifestation of the great God in his heavenly temple, and in particular of his thundering speech from the throne.[13] The Introduction and Conclusion supply details of the scene in the temple at the appearance of the deity in all his refulgent splendor. The presence of Yahweh in his palace and the impact of his thunder upon the world could hardly be stressed more effectively than by the persistent repetition of the name, and the voice of Yahweh. Thus the whole poem is a celebration of the manifestation of the deity in glory and splendor, power and majesty, symbolized by the seven claps of thunder, each compelling the obeisance of his subjects, and exacting an appropriate acknowledgment from the world at large.

As already indicated, the *bny 'lym* of Psalm 29 are reminiscent of the *bn ilm* of the Ugaritic texts, the retinue of minor deities in the Canaanite pantheon. In the Baal-Anath cycle, the *bn ilm* are assembled for a dinner in the company of El.[14] Similar to this gathering, and pertinent to the opening lines of Psalm 29, is the banquet of the gods at which the construction of Esagila, Marduk's heavenly temple, is celebrated.[15] At the banquet one of the functions of the gods is to praise the chief god Marduk by reciting his fifty names (ll. 121ff.). Another ancient composition dealing with the theme of the storm god is the Hymn to Iškur, the Babylonian counterpart of Hadal-Baal.[16] In this poem the various names of Iškur are listed. In fact, the first half of the hymn is devoted to the "name of Iškur."[17]

> Great Bull, who shines brightly, your name reaches to the end of the heavens
> Father Iškur, great bull, who shines . . .
> Iškur, son of An, great bull . . .
> Lord of Enigi, great bull . . .
> Iškur, lord of plenty, great bull. . . .[18]

13. Cf. 2 Sam. 22:7 = Ps. 18:7; Isa. 6:1; Mic. 1:2; Hab. 2:20; Ps. 11:4. N. Habel points out that the theophany of Baal in the storm emanates from the palace in the heavens (*Yahweh Versus Baal: A Conflict of Religious Cultures* [New York: Bookman, 1964], 76).

14. UT 51:111:14.

15. Enuma Elish, VI, ll. 71ff. See T. Gaster, *Thespis* (New York: Schuman, 1950), 74ff. [rev. ed. 1961 (Doubleday), 443-46] for a comparison between the psalm and the Enuma Elish.

16. A. Falkenstein and W. von Soden, *Sumerische und Akkadische Hymnen und Gebete* (Zurich: Artemis, 1953), 248-250.

17. Other parallels can be drawn between Iškur on the one hand and Hadad-Baal and Yahweh on the other. Just as Baal and Yahweh are "riders of the clouds," so Iškur rides the storm wind. His voice is a roaring wind like the voice of Yahweh in Ps. 29.

18. El also has the title of "Bull" in the Ugaritic texts. See Albright's discussion of El in *Yahweh and the Gods of Canaan,* 119ff.

In Psalm 29, the "sons of El" are commanded to call out the names of Yahweh: *Kabōd, ʿOz,* and in the course of the poem, *ʾEl haKabōd, Kabōd . . . Malk,* and above all *Yahweh,* which occurs not fewer than eighteen times in the eleven verses of the poem.[19]

Strophe I (vv. 3-4)

According to our count, v. 3 consists of 18 syllables, with approximately 8 of them stressed. The proper division into lines and cola poses a problem. There are several possibilities, but none is entirely satisfactory. We may follow the arrangement of BH[3], which has a structure of three lines with 6 syllables each, or a stress count of 2:2 (or 3):3.

qwl yhwh ʿl hmym	Yahweh's voice upon the ocean
ʾl hkbwd hrʿym	El the Glorious thunders
yhwh ʿl mym rbym	Yahweh upon the great ocean

In this pattern, lines one and three, which are linked by the repetition of key words (the pattern would be abcd // bcde), form an envelope around the somewhat isolated middle clause, giving rise to the view that it may be intrusive in this verse.

Another possibility would be to take the verse as a couplet with the division after *hkbwd:*

qwl yhwh ʿl hmym ʾl hkbwd	The voice of Yahweh-El the Glorious is upon the ocean
hrʿym yhwh ʿl mym rbym	Yahweh thunders over the great ocean.

The syllable count is 10:8, while the stress pattern is apparently 2:2/2:2. The two-line scheme with its repetitive style is perhaps more like other couplets in the poem; cf. vv. 5 and 8. In the latter verses, the line with *qwl yhwh* is followed by a line with *yhwh* alone; in these instances the divine name is preceded immediately by a verb: *wyšbr* (v. 5) and *yḥyl* (v. 8). We are inclined therefore to link *hrʿym* with *yhwh* in v. 3. We note in the first line the composite original divine name *yahweh-*

19. There is similar mention of the name of Yahweh in Ps. 66:2; 79:9; 96:10; 1 Chr. 16:29. J. Muilenburg states: ". . . in worship men would pronounce the name. . . . To name the name is the central cultic act" ("The Speech of Theophany," *Harvard Divinity School Bulletin* 28 [1964], 39).

'ēl, here divided for stylistic reasons: to isolate *qwl yhwh* at the beginning of the unit in conformity with the prevailing pattern of the poem.[20]

Whatever the proper division, the sense of the verse can be rendered through a combinatory approach to the component parts: "The voice of Yahweh-El the Glorious thunders over the great ocean." A notable feature of the unit, which among other things serves to fill out the presumed metrical requirements, is the expanded repetition, or ballast variant: *'l hmym // 'l mym rbym.* The device is also found in v. 5, *'rzym // 'rzy hlbnwn,* and in v. 8, *mdbr // mdbr qdš.* A reverse pattern is to be seen in the sequence *qwl yhwh // yhwh,* in which the force of the term *qwl* is carried over to the abbreviated expression *yhwh,* since it is Yahweh's voice which is the active agent throughout; cf. vv. 5 and 8, in which the verbs are repeated in connection with *qwl yhwh* and *yhwh.*

The definite article occurs three times in Psalm 29, twice in v. 3: *hmym* and *hkbwd* in v. 3, and *hlbnwn* in v. 5; we do not count those instances in which its presence is indicated by the Massoretic vocalization, not by the letter *he: bakkōaḥ* and *behādār* (v. 4) and *baššālōm* (v. 11). We need not decide the latter cases, since they do not affect materially either the meaning or the meter. While the use of the definite article in early Hebrew poetry is rare, its occasional occurrence cannot automatically be regarded as secondary. Its use as a relative pronoun is firmly established, and as an attenuated demonstrative entirely in order.[21] Since the usage is sporadic rather than regular, we should regard it, not as a normal grammatical feature, but as an emphatic particle. At the same time we must reckon with the possibility, perhaps inevitability, that in the course of time and transmission the article may appear more often than was intended by the original poet. Distinguishing between those instances which belong to the poem and those which are the result of editorial or scribal activity is not an easy task. Of the three occurrences in Psalm 29, the article with *lbnwn* in v. 5 is the least likely to be original, but even in this instance there can be no certainty.[22] A curious aspect of the use of the article

20. On the divine name *yhwh-'l,* see D. N. Freedman, "The Name of the God of Moses," *JBL* 79 (1960): 156 [See Volume I, Chapter 9]; and F. M. Cross, Jr., "Yahweh and the God of the Patriarchs," *HTR* 55 (1962): 250ff. For a discussion of its use in the Psalter, see Dahood, *Psalms I,* 64, 104-5, 177, 188. The original combination is preserved in Ps. 10:12 and 31:6; the elements are separated in Ps. 18:3 and 29:3. Cf. Dahood, "The Name *yišma'-'ēl* in Genesis 16, 11," *Bibl* 49 (1968): 88, n. 3.

21. E.g., in David's Lament, *hmlbškm,* "the one who clothed you," and *hm'lh,* "the one who put [golden ornaments] upon [your clothes]" (2 Sam. 1:24); also *hn'hbym,* "the beloved ones," and *hn'ymm,* "the lovely ones" (1:23): Cf. *hhr ḥmd* in Ps. 68:17 (Albright, *Yahweh and the Gods of Canaan,* 26-27, and references to earlier work cited there). The phrase *n'm hgbr,* which occurs in the Oracles of Balaam (Num. 24:3, 15) and the Last Words of David (2 Sam. 23:1), is to be rendered: ". . . the utterance of that man whose / whom. . . ."

22. We have the following data for the use of the definite article with *lbnwn* in MT: of the total of 70 occurrences 18 are not useful for our purposes. One is followed by the *he* directive

is that the same word occurs both with and without it, usually in the same or adjoining verses: e.g., *hmym* and *mym* in v. 3; *hlbnwn* in v. 5, and *lbnwn* in v. 6; *hkbwd* in v. 3, and *kbwd* in vv. 1, 2, and 9. In all cases, the word with or without the article is definite, which shows that the use of the article is not purely functional, but stylistic, possibly metrical.

Verse 4 is a bicolon with a syllable count of 5 + 6 = 11 (or a stress count of 2:2). It emphasizes those aspects of *qwl yhwh,* its majesty and power, which are equally applicable to the action described and to those which follow.

(*lbnwnh* in 1 Kgs. 5:28), and is naturally without the article. There are 17 others, all preceded by the inseparable prepositions *b* and *k.* In accordance with standard procedure, the *he,* if any, has been elided; the only indication of its original presence would be the vocalization: *ball-* and *kall-*. In every instance, the vocalization indicates the presence of the article, showing that the Massoretes interpreted the forms in accordance with normal prose usage (i.e., with the article). In view of the other data for the use of the article with *lbnwn,* it is clear that the vocalization presupposing the article has been levelled through artificially, thus erasing possibly helpful information about the distribution. These data may also provide a clue as to what has happened in the course of transmission, though there is a significant difference between normalizing vocalization and standardizing the form of the word. Of the 52 occurrences remaining, there are 30 with the article and 22 without. Dividing the passages between poetry and prose (in accordance with the practice of BH[3] or RSV), we find that there are 28 instances in poetry and 24 in prose. The distribution may be tabulated as follows:

	With the article	Without the article	Totals
Prose	21	3	24
Poetry	9	19	28
	30	22	52

Two of the prose occurrences without the article are in Ezek. 31:15-16. While this passage is commonly treated as prose, it is very much like the surrounding material in Ezekiel, which is commonly treated as poetry: in BH[3], Ezek. 31:2-9 is poetry, 10-12 is prose, 13 is poetry, and 14 is divided between prose and poetry; vv. 15-18 are considered prose, but ch. 32 is divided between prose and poetry. The other three passages in Ezekiel in which *lbnwn* occurs are all taken to be poetry. Regardless of a final decision about these two occurrences, the evidence is overwhelming for the use of the article with *lbnwn* in prose passages (the only other occurrence without the article is in 2 Chr. 2:7). While the corresponding association of *lbnwn* (without the article) with poetic passages is not as strongly supported, nevertheless the preponderance of poetic passages have *lbnwn* without the article. On the basis of the present text, we can affirm the correlation and say that the use of the article with *lbnwn* is characteristic of prose, and the use without the article is typical of poetry. In view of the data it would be reasonable to suppose that several of the cases in poetry where the article does occur are the result of inadvertent or deliberate scribal activity, tending to make the practice uniform (as is true of the vocalization of the inseparable prepositions). With respect to Ps. 29, we can say that *lbnwn* in v. 6 is perfectly proper and what we would expect. On the other hand, *hlbnwn* is suspect, and we would have some basis for regarding the article as secondary. But the evidence is not conclusive.

The syllable count for Strophe I is:

V. 3	10 + 8 = 18
V. 4	5 + 6 = 11
Total	29

Strophe II (vv. 5-6)

Verse 5 refers to the destructive power of the storm as it sweeps in from the sea and breaks over the mountains of Lebanon with their fabled cedars. The syllable count is 8 + 13 = 21 (the stress count would be 3 : 2 . 2 or 3:4). The second line of the couplet seems unduly long; otherwise the maximum length of a single line in the poem is 11 syllables, v. 11b, and even that may be excessive. It may be, therefore, that one or more of the following "prosaic" elements in the line is secondary: *'t,* the sign of the definite direct object, the definite article, or the *waw* consecutive at the beginning of the line. The case for and against the definite article has already been considered. The use of the sign *'t* is less well attested for early poetry than the definite article.[23] There are very few occurrences in the entire corpus, and those which do turn up may well belong to secondary or intrusive elements in the poem. Its presence in v. 5b may therefore be questioned, as also in v. 11b, which, interestingly, are the two longest lines in the poem. It would be reasonable to regard their appearance in Psalm 29 as the result of an inadvertent hypercorrection on the part of a grammatically oriented scribe.

In v. 6, the *mem* of the group *wyrqydm* was identified by Ginsberg as enclitic rather than the 3rd masc. pl. suffix.[24] It was the first such occurrence noted in the Bible; since that time hundreds of other examples have been identified, confirming the fact that classical Hebrew shares this phenomenon with Ugaritic and other Canaanite dialects.[25] While the enclitic *mem* does not affect the meaning at all, and does not seem to have any syntactical function, it does serve to preserve the vowel at the end of the word to which it is attached: e.g., the modal ending of the verb, or the case ending of the noun. Thus its use would affect the syllable count, and it may have had a metrical function.

23. It does not occur at all in such early poems as Exod. 15:1-18; Judg. 5:1-31; 2 Sam. 1:19-27. Gen. 49 provides an interesting study: the particle does not occur in the body of the poem (*'t* in v. 25 is a scribal error for *'l*), but it does occur in v. 1b, which is regarded by most scholars as a late secondary introduction, since the poem has its own introduction, v. 2.

24. Cf. n. 1.

25. H. D. Hummel, "Enclitic *Mem* in Early Northwest Semitic, Especially Hebrew," *JBL* 76 (1957): 85-107. For examples in the Psalter, see Dahood, *Psalms III,* 408-9, and under "Enclitic *mem*" and "*mem encliticum*" in the Indices to Vols. I, II, and III.

The syllable count for Strophe II is:

V. 5	8 + 12 =	20
V. 6	10 + 8 =	18
Total		38

Strophe III (vv. 7-9)

Verse 7 adds the element of fire to the destructive action initiated in v. 5. Bolts of lightning shatter the great trees and ignite a blaze in the fallen and standing timber. This picture of disaster is completed in v. 9b *(wyḥśp yʿrwt),* with the forests left bare and ruined. We suggest that v. 9b forms an *inclusio* or envelope, with v. 7 enclosing the separate unit vv. 8-9a, to be identified by the repetition of the verbal root *ḥw/yl.* In support of this proposal we point to the continuity of theme and action between the two passages (vv. 7 and 9b), the congruity of sense, and the paronomasia involving the words *ḥōṣēb* and *wayaḥśōp;* note the sequence of consonants: the same laryngeal, *ḥ,* followed by a sibilant and a labial. The order of the verbs — participle followed by imperfect with *waw* consecutive — is the same as v. 5 *(šōbēr . . . wayašabbēr)* with which this unit (vv. 7, 9b) is linked by subject matter.

It is possible that we should read the preposition *b*ᵉ before *lhbwt ʾš.* It may have been lost by haplography after the *b* of *ḥōṣēb;* or we may have an example of the single writing of a double consonant, an occasional scribal practice when the last letter of one word was the same as the first letter of the next word.[26] It is just as likely that the reading *lhbwt ʾš* is correct as it stands; in that case, the expression should be interpreted as a dative of means after the verbal form *ḥṣb.*

With v. 9b, the description of *qwl yhwh* is completed. As we have pointed out, v. 9c is a continuation of v. 2b, and serves as the link between the Introduction and the Conclusion.[27]

26. On this phenomenon, see Dahood, *Psalms II,* 81, and literature cited there; also under "Single writing of consonant . . ." in Index. Cf. *Psalms III,* 371-72. There can be no doubt that the practice existed, since it is attested in the Lachish letters: the expression *ḥay yhwh* is written *ḥyhwh,* with one *yodh* instead of two. On the other hand, it was not widely adopted, and was ultimately abandoned, at least in the writing of official texts. Individual cases must be judged on their merits.

27. Although most translations take v. 9c as a continuation of 9ab, there is a sharp break between the units. Gaster acknowledges the fact, and attempts to resolve the difficulty by restoring a lost line: ". . . the missing subject is the divine assembly. We must restore '. . . the assembly of the deities acclaiming him' . . ." *Thespis,* 75f.; cf. *JQR* 37 (1946-47): 62. We render *klw* as "everyone, all of you," taking the suffix as the nominative sg. case ending (*-u* > *-ō*), instead of the 3rd masc. sg. pronoun: "all of it."

Verse 8 has a structure very much like that of vv. 3 and 5, with incremental repetition (abcd // cbde), and chiasm of verb and subject *(. . . yhwh yḥyl / yḥyl yhwh . . .).* Verse 9a deals with a concomitant phenomenon, and is bound to the preceding couplet by a common or homonymous verbal root: *yḥwll // yḥyl.*

The metrical data are arranged so as to bring out the relationships among the several components:

V. 7	8		
V. 8			7 + 8 = 15
V. 9a			9
V. 9b	6		
V. 9c			9
Totals	14	+	24 + 9 = 47

The metrical structure of the main section (vv. 3-9) may be summarized as follows:

Strophe I	29
Strophe II	38
Strophe III	47
Total	114

It will be observed that Strophe II is not only the middle unit, but the median and average of the three. Further, Strophe III is as much longer than Strophe II as Strophe I is shorter, a matter of 9 syllables. In our opinion, this is not an accidental figure, but exactly the length of v. 9c, which, as we have argued, does not belong to the description of *qwl yhwh,* but serves to connect the Introduction and the Conclusion. If we suppose that the poet was working with a stanza length of 38 syllables, and intended to have three such stanzas making a total of 114 syllables, we can understand his procedure in adding a 9-syllable line to the last strophe, while reducing the first by the same amount. In this way, he was able to supply the needed connection to the Conclusion (vv. 10-11), while at the same time suggesting that v. 9c could also be read before the first strophe (vv. 3-4), as a continuation of the Introduction (v. 2b).

Conclusion

For metrical and other reasons we follow Margulis in reading *kbwd* (at the end of v. 9) as the first word in v. 10.[28] Since the two lines of v. 10 are bound closely by the chiastic repetition of *yhwh . . . yšb* and *wyšb yhwh,* we are inclined to interpret the other structurally parallel terms in complementary or combinatory fashion. The related items would then be: *kbwd* (v. 10a) and *mlk* (v. 10b), and *lmbwl* (v. 10a) and *lʿwlm* (v. 10b). In the first pair we find the components of the well-known expression *melek hakkābōd,* "the Glorious King," which occurs repeatedly in Ps. 24:7-10; we interpret accordingly, "Yahweh the Glorious King." With regard to the latter pair, we follow Dahood in analyzing the terms as a reference to the Primeval Flood, with the preposition *le* having the meaning "from, since."[29] Paraphrasing the verse as a whole, we arrive at the following rendering: "Yahweh the Glorious King has been enthroned since the Primeval Flood."

Verse 11 consists of two parallel lines in a partially chiastic arrangement. Aside from the name Yahweh, which stands emphatically at the beginning of each line, the order of the corresponding terms is reversed in v. 11b as compared with v. 11a:

ʿz lʿmw ytn	Victory to his people let him give
ybrk (ʾt) ʿmw bšlwm	Let him bless his people with peace

In v. 11a, the grammatical order is: direct object, indirect object (with preposition), and verb. In v. 11b, the order is: verb, direct object, and indirect object (with preposition). The organization of the couplet is somewhat more subtle, however, since the synonymous or related terms are in different syntactical relationships: *lʿmw,* which is the indirect object, and *ʿmw,* which is the direct object: *ʿz,* which is the direct object, and *bšlwm,* which is the indirect object. It may also be observed that *ʿz* in v. 11 is a complement and echo of *ʿz* in v. 1: Let Yahweh the Victorious now bestow victory upon his people.[30]

28. Cf. n. 4.

29. Dahood, *Psalms I,* 180. In a number of psalms the theme of Yahweh's kingship is associated with his victory over the primeval flood. In Ps. 93 Yahweh's power over the cosmic waters is extolled. Cf. H. G. May, "Some Cosmic Connotations of *Mayim Rabbîm* 'Many Waters,' " *JBL* 74 (1955): 9-21. Ps. 93:3-4 have been described as "the triumph of Yahweh over the oceans of origins." Cf. E. Lipiński, "*Yāhweh mâlāk,*" *Bibl* 44 (1963): 435. Ps. 89, in which the heavens praise Yahweh in the assembly of the holy ones, proclaims Yahweh's successful combat with Rahab, and his victory over the sea. Isa. 51:9 describes the destruction of the chaos monster in the days of old *(dwrwt ʿwlmym).* The link between victory over cosmic foes and enthronement or eternal dominion is also to be seen in the formulas of Baal's triumph. Cf. Ginsberg, "A Phoenician Hymn," 474; Gaster, *Thespis,* 75.

30. Other passages in Hebrew poetry associate the storm theophany with Yahweh's coming

We close with a summary of the metrical data, listing in successive columns the syllable count defended in the paper and the actual count according to Masoretic vocalization:

Psalm 29

Syllable Count:	Proposed	MT
Introduction:		
V. 1	9 + 9 = 18	9 + 9 = 18
V. 2	9 + 10 = 19	9 + 12 = 21
Total	37	39
Strophe I		
V. 3	10 + 8 = 18	11 + 9 = 20
V. 4	5 + 6 = 11	6 + 6 = 12
Total	29	32
Strophe II		
V. 5	8 + 12 = 20	8 + 13 = 21
V. 6	10 + 8 = 18	11 + 9 = 20
Total	38	41
Strophe III		
V. 7	8	9
V. 8	7 + 8 = 15	7 + 8 = 15
V. 9ab	9 + 6 = 15	9 + 7 = 16
V. 9c	9	9
Total	47	49
Conclusion		
V. 10	9 + 9 = 18	9 + 10 = 19
V. 11	8 + 10 = 18	8 + 11 = 19
Total	36	38

There is no significant difference between the proposed figures and those of MT. The ratios remain essentially the same, though the absolute numbers are somewhat higher for MT. As might have been expected, the Introduction and Conclusion are practically equal in length (37 and 36 syllables). The Strophes of the main section are arranged in ascending order: 29, 38, 47. As already pointed out, the second Strophe is both mean and average for the three; put another way, Strophe II with 38 syllables is exactly half of the total of the other two: 29 +

---

to redeem his people: Exod. 15, Judg. 5, Hab. 3, Pss. 68, 89. Cf. N. Habel, *Yahweh Versus Baal,* 80. Gaster compares the closing verse of Ps. 29 with Enuma Elish: in Marduk's appearance after his victory over Tiamat, he is hailed as "the help of his people, salvation of his people," *Thespis,* 76. Ginsberg suggests that the fact that Yahweh is to give ʿz to his people rather than to his anointed one (as in 1 Sam. 2:10) may be an indication of premonarchic composition (*ErIsr* 9 [1969]: 45).

47 = 76. This median figure (38) is roughly the same as that for the Introduction and Conclusion. It would be possible to project an hypothetical norm from these numbers and their relationships: e.g.,

Introduction:	18 + 18 = 36
Strophe I	15 + 12 = 27
Strophe II	18 + 18 = 36
Strophe III	21 + 24 = 45
Conclusion:	18 + 18 = 36

Variations from the norm can be explained in the following ways: changes in the text and vocalization from the time of composition until the final fixing of the text, whether deliberate or accidental, and variations adopted by the poet himself. The surviving structural symmetry shows that none of these factors has seriously affected the text, in spite of the long period of transmission. We may be confident that we have the hymn substantially as it was composed for liturgical use in early Israel.

10

The Poetic Structure of the Framework of Deuteronomy 33*

Much progress has been made in the elucidation of the framework of the Blessing of Moses (Deut. 33:2-29),[1] but obscurities and difficulties persist.[2] In a renewed effort to clear up some of the problems, I have given greater attention than in the past to structural components, metrical and rhythmic factors, and prosodic devices which link the several parts of the framework, the Opening, the Midsection, and

1. Deut. 33:2-29. It seems best to retain the title "Blessing," in preference to "Testament" in the light of Deut. 33:1, which emphasizes the former term: "This is the blessing with which Moses, the man of God, blessed the sons of Israel before his death." Perhaps it would serve to call the poem a Testamentary Blessing, and thus bring out its character as a final pronouncement within the genre of "blessings." The same combination is present in the "Blessing of Jacob" (Gen. 49:1-27; cf. Gen. 48:21).

2. This study should be regarded as a supplement to the detailed article on Deut. 33 published by Frank M. Cross and me years ago: "The Blessing of Moses," *JBL* 67 (1948): 191-210; a slightly different version of this article is found in F. M. Cross and D. N. Freedman, *Studies in Ancient Yahwistic Poetry.* SBL Dissertation 21 (Missoula: Scholars Press, 1975), 95-122. [Repr. Grand Rapids: Wm. B. Eerdmans, 1995] Inevitably, after thirty years, there are changes in perspective and views concerning a number of details. These modifications are presented and defended in the current chapter; for matters not mentioned in this article, the reader is referred to the fuller treatment. Naturally, I bear full responsibility for the assertions made here, and my longtime colleague and friend is not obliged to share that burden along with that of our joint work; he has discussed various features of the text in his *Canaanite Myth and Hebrew Epic* (Cambridge, Mass.: Harvard University Press, 1973), especially 101, 157-59. For a full study of the syntax and structure of the whole Blessing, cf. M. O'Connor, *Hebrew Verse Structure* (Winona Lake: Eisenbrauns, 1980). Concerning the monograph by D. K. Stuart, *Studies in Early Hebrew Meter.* HSM 13 (Missoula: Scholars Press, 1976), see the review by A. M. Cooper, *BASOR* 233 (1979): 75-76.

---

* I wish to express my gratitude and appreciation to M. O'Connor for his help in the preparation of this chapter.

the Closing.[3] Because of space requirements, I will limit the present study to the three units mentioned, although there is no reason to suppose that they were composed or circulated independently of the tribal blessings which constitute the body of the work (Deut. 33:6-20, 22-25).[4]

Given the context in Deuteronomy, and the assumed circumstances, the attribution of the poem to Moses is quite understandable, though doubtless more sentimental than factual. Nevertheless, it can only apply to the "blessings," not to the framework, the contents of which are partly about Moses, not by him. That Moses is the central human figure in this material can only be doubted if the verse (4) in which he is mentioned is excised, a questionable procedure at best. In my opinion, the blessing is part of the epic or heroic cycle of poems celebrating the man and his greatness, his extraordinary achievement in the life of Israel, fragments of which have survived, embedded in the great prose work, in which he is the most prominent person (the Pentateuch, or more correctly the books from Exodus through Deuteronomy). I have examined other passages (especially in Numbers) illustrating this point; if they were put together, they would afford roughly contemporary testimony to the status and reputation of Moses among Israelites of an early generation when his influence and memory were fresh, when the tribal league flourished, and before the rise of the monarchy with its very different set of national heroes.[5] For the present, I will confine my remarks to the passages in Deut. 33.

With respect to the date of composition of the Blessing of Moses, Frank M. Cross and I have maintained for at least thirty years that the poem is a product of the premonarchic era, and should be dated in the 11th century B.C.E.[6] We have seen no compelling evidence or argument to alter that opinion. In a more recent attempt to date a number of the poems in the Pentateuch and Former Prophets, I proposed a sequence dating of these works, both relative and absolute, with similar results for the Blessing of Moses. It belongs to Phase II of the series, which covers the 11th century. The same data and line of reasoning apply to the framework as to the body of the poem. Since these points have been made in some detail elsewhere, there is no need to repeat them here.[7]

3. For discussion and bibliography on recent developments in the study of Hebrew poetry, with special attention to structural patterns and metrics, see in addition the works cited in n. 2 of my "Prolegomenon," in *The Forms of Hebrew Poetry* by G. B. Gray (New York: Ktav, 1972), vii-lvi; the Bibliography is on xlvii-liii. Cf. also articles on Hebrew poetry by N. K. Gottwald in *IDB* 3 (1962): 829-838; and M. Dahood, *IDB* Supplementary Volume (1976), 669-672.

4. I plan to publish soon a detailed study of the tribal blessings including not only the Blessing of Moses, but also the list in Gen. 49, and the materials in Judg. 5, in order to compare the early patterns. [See Volume 1, Chapter 35]

5. D. N. Freedman, "The Aaronic Benediction (Numbers 6:24-26)," in *No Famine in the Land,* ed. J. W. Flanagan and A. W. Robinson (Missoula: Scholars Press, 1975), 35-48.

6. Cross-Freedman, *Studies in Ancient Yahwistic Poetry,* 97-98.

7. "Divine Names and Titles in Early Hebrew Poetry," *Magnalia Dei: The Mighty Acts of*

When it comes to the time and place of the contents of the poem, i.e., what it purports to describe and relate, we must emphasize the association with Moses, and refer the material to the last days of his life and work. The setting is the Moabite plain, in the vicinity of Mt. Nebo (and Mt. Pisgah), where Moses was to die and be buried. I have argued elsewhere that the Exodus from Egypt is to be dated early in the 12th century B.C.E.;[8] hence this penultimate activity in the life of Moses must be put somewhat later, perhaps in the second quarter of that century, and in any case not later than about 1150 B.C.E. In other words, the poem reflects circumstances and events around the middle of the 12th century, but was composed about a century later, roughly in the middle of the 11th century. While the gap is substantial, I assume that traditions persisted, memory was tenacious, and therefore that the poem as a whole faithfully reflects the period of which it speaks, while being, nonetheless, a product of a later age. A certain telescoping effect may be observed, or a blending of data from both periods. For the purposes of this paper it is sufficient to posit the mixture, without attempting to sort out the differences in detail.

Of great importance in understanding the transition from the Wilderness to the Promised Land is the transjordanian settlement. Much of the content of Numbers and the whole of Deuteronomy are located in that region. It was to Transjordan that Israel turned when other alternatives proved impractical (staying at Kadesh), or impossible (invading Canaan from the south). They were able to evade conflict with Edom and Moab, and to establish a foothold in territory north of the Arnon River, and along the east bank of the Jordan, by defeating in succession the two Amorite kings, Sihon and Og. According to the tradition, both the conquest and the assignment of these territories to the two-and-a-half eastern tribes were attributed to Moses. Thus the final convocation of the people of Yahweh in Moses' lifetime was held on the territory belonging to the firstborn son, Reuben, now firmly in the possession of Israel. The purpose of such a conclave would be not only to hear the last words of the old leader, and to affirm allegiance to the divinely chosen successor, but to plan the immediate future, the conquest of the cisjordanian sector, and the allocation of districts to the remaining tribes.

The poem therefore presupposes the existence of the twelve-tribe league at the time of the assembly in Transjordan, as well as Moses' presence and partici-

---

God, ed. F. M. Cross, W. E. Lemke, and P. D. Miller, Jr. (Garden City: Doubleday, 1976), 55-107; the discussion of the data and date of Deut. 33 is to be found on 68-70.

8. The dating is based in part on an analysis of the Song of the Sea, Exod. 15:1-18 and v. 21; cf. D. N. Freedman, "Early Israelite History in the Light of Early Israelite Poetry," in *Unity and Diversity: Essays in the History, Literature, and Religion of the Ancient Near East,* ed. H. Goedicke and J. J. M. Roberts (Baltimore: Johns Hopkins University Press, 1975), 3-35 [reprinted in *PPP,* 131-166]; the discussion of the events described in the Song of the Sea is on 4-12, and nn. 5-47. Cf. also *Magnalia Dei,* 57-60; and "Early Israelite Poetry and Historical Reconstructions," in *Symposia,* ed. F. M. Cross (Cambridge, Mass.: American Schools of Oriental Research, 1979), 85-96 [= *PPP,* 167-178].

pation in its deliberations. In my view it is precisely this convention which reflects and represents the successful linkup of the Mosaic movement out of Egypt with the already existent twelve-tribe Israelite league located in Canaan. Israel was a political-geographic entity with roots in the patriarchal age and traditions. The patriarch Jacob is described as the immediate progenitor of the twelve tribes (= Israel), who are called his sons; and its existence is affirmed for pre-Mosaic times (cf. Gen. 49). This league was unified by faith in a single God (El-Shadday of patriarchal tradition; cf. אל אלהי ישראל, Gen. 33:20), and claimed and occupied territory in Canaan (e.g., Shechem, Gen. 48:22), some time in the Late Bronze Age, perhaps much earlier.[9] According to information provided in the Merneptah stele of about 1225 B.C.E., Israel was overwhelmed and devastated by an Egyptian raiding force at that time.[10] While skepticism has been expressed about this pharaonic claim, there is no reason to doubt either the capacity of the concern of the Egyptians to inflict damage of this sort, especially when rebellion in the provinces was involved. Archaeological evidence from Palestine for this period reflects the destruction of numerous cities, some presumably by the Egyptians (capture of Ashkelon, Gezer, and Yanoam is mentioned in the stele). Simeon and Levi seem to have borne the brunt of the attack (cf. Gen. 49:5-7, although the episode may have occurred much earlier): the latter apparently ceased to function as a secular tribe, while the former was displaced and ultimately absorbed by Judah. We may assume that the league itself was shattered by the experience and continued to exist largely in name and memory, until revived by Moses and Joshua and their successors.

Shortly thereafter we may date the beginnings of the Mosaic movement and the Exodus from Egypt. Persistent tradition associates Moses and his family with the tribe of Levi, while names of members, including Moses himself, have strong Egyptian affinities. It may well be that many associated with Moses and his group derived from or were affiliated with one or another of the twelve tribes, since there was continuing traffic between Canaan and Egypt. For centuries, even millennia, Semites had drifted down to Egypt as visitors, traders, and beggars, or been taken under duress as prisoners of war to be pressed into service as public slaves, or otherwise brought for sale as domestic slaves.

The movement led by Moses was at first not a league of tribes in any formal sense, but a new society based upon a revelation of the God Yahweh granted to Moses in the Sinai wilderness at the sacred mountain of the deity. Ultimately this new community found a permanent home in Canaan as an integral if not the central

9. See L. E. Toombs, "Shechem: Problems of the Early Israelite Era," in *Symposia,* 69-83, on the evidence for the capture and destruction of Shechem in LB II; provisionally I associate the statement in Gen. 48:22 with this destruction. Israelite occupation of this area, including Shechem, in pre-Mosaic times is asserted by a number of scholars.

10. For a convenient rendering of the Merneptah stele, see the translation by J. A. Wilson in *ANET,* 376-78.

component in the twelve-tribe league, Israel. The linkup took place in Transjordan under the leadership of Moses and his henchman, Joshua. Here the two groups joined forces to establish a base of operations in the territory of Reuben (one of the twelve tribes and the first according to seniority). Possession of the region was gained through the defeat of Sihon the Amorite king of Heshbon, who had wrested the land from the Moabites only a short time before (Num. 21:26-30). With the revival of the confederation under the banner of Yahweh, it became feasible to cross the Jordan and reclaim lost territory on that side of the river. Then by battle or treaty or some combination of the two, the Israelites were able to capture essential parts of the land, and reconstitute a Palestinian state. The final amalgamation of Wilderness Wanderers and Israelite Leaguers was achieved formally by Joshua in the course and at the conclusion of his military campaigns.

The territorial acquisitions and assignments were officially ratified and reunification was celebrated at the covenant-renewal convocation described in Josh. 24. Prior to that, however, the groundwork had been laid and the strategy formulated at the transjordanian meeting over which Moses presided, and to which the poem in Deut. 33 bears witness.

The situation reflected by the poem is complex, and no doubt the individual oracles touch on more than one occasion and circumstance in the history of the league and its members. Comparison with the earlier and more original list in Gen. 49 shows that both Simeon and Levi have experienced serious changes in status: Simeon is not mentioned directly in Deut. 33, while Levi is no longer the secular tribe of Gen. 49, but a sacral group with special responsibility for the Thummim and Urim, the Covenant and the Torah (Deut. 33:8-10). In this respect the later list reflects the disastrous consequences of the dire pronouncement in Gen. 49:5-7. To make up the sacred number, twelve, in the present circumstances, Joseph, the largest and most important of the tribes, is divided into two entities (denominated sons): Ephraim on the West Bank of the Jordan, and Manasseh on both sides of the river (subject to further division at a later date). This provisional arrangement did not last, nor did a different one reflected in the Song of Deborah. The official solution was to preserve all the names, and at the same time to respect the realities: the double-tribe status of Joseph was confirmed; Simeon was restored to the list, though actually a part of expanded Judah, and Levi was given special status and token territory among the tribes, so it became a supernumerary in charge of the sanctuary and the ark, a thirteenth tribe in a system designed for twelve.[11]

It is now time to turn to the poem itself and more particularly to the framework, vv. 2-5, 26-29. To begin with, I shall provide a transliteration and translation, and then defend both in the accompanying notes. In order to determine structural features, metrical and rhythmic patterns, I shall follow the received Hebrew text throughout, and adopt the Massoretic vocalization in all but a few cases. Since I

11. See my discussion in *Unity and Diversity,* 12-23.

believe that syllable-counting constitutes the best descriptive method in dealing with quantity and comparison of poetic units, it is important to define these as carefully and precisely as possible.[12] Hence, I eliminate obviously secondary developments reflected in MT: segolate formations are treated as monosyllables (e.g., **malk* for *melek*); compound *shewas* added after laryngeals are not counted (**yaʿleh* for *yaʿaleh*), but otherwise vocal shewa in any position is counted; *pataḥ furtive* is secondary and therefore not counted (**rûḥ* for *rûaḥ*). Since mine is a minimum count by intention, contractions in MT are accepted (e.g., *mîmînô* for **miyyamînô*), but are not generated where MT has the standard or longer form. With respect to the anomalous pointing of 2nd masc. sg. pronominal suffix forms (i.e., those vocalized *-tā* and *-kā,* but without final vowel letters), I have adopted the short form throughout, in accordance with the principle of minimal count, and because the underlying written text presupposes the short form of the suffix. No doubt, both forms were in use simultaneously over long periods of time: the short form was normalized in the text, while the long form was standardized in the vocalization. Choosing between them in given cases is not easy. In a few instances, a different vocalization is proposed, where MT is clearly faulty: e.g., *ʾᵃsēdôt* for אֶשְׁדָּת (v. 2), where the vocalization of MT is based upon a highly improbable interpretation of the text.

In the Notes, however, I will supply substitute readings and renderings, which I think are superior to MT. While these readings have been proposed on the basis of textual (i.e., versional), contextual, linguistic, and other nonmetrical factors, they might affect the structure of the units, if adopted. On the whole, I would rather describe, analyze, interpret, and make claims about the surviving text, rather than create one that fits my notions about meter and stanza construction in Biblical Hebrew poetry. In this poem, the differences are very slight, but emendations *metri causa* have become so suspect, and for cause, that I would rather avoid emendations entirely in the debate about poetic structure.

Elsewhere I have called attention to certain common particles, the presence or absence of which is considered diagnostic for the distinction between prose and poetry in the Bible.[13] Generally speaking, the relative pronoun אשר, the sign of the definite direct object את, and the definite article ה, occur regularly in normal prose usage, whereas their incidence is markedly reduced in poetry; they hardly occur at all in the earliest poems, those contained in the Pentateuch and Former Prophets. In gross figures the particle count in standard prose regularly exceeds

12. On the theory and practice of syllable-counting, cf. *The Forms of Hebrew Poetry,* xxxii-xxxv; also my detailed study of the Song of the Sea in "Strophe and Meter in Exodus 15," *A Light Unto My Path,* ed. H. N. Bream, R. D. Heim, and C. A. Moore (Philadelphia: Temple University Press, 1974), 163-203. [See also Chapter 16 below]

13. Cf. D. N. Freedman, "Pottery, Poetry, and Prophecy," *JBL* 96 (1977): 6-8 [reprinted in *PPP,* 1-22]; for an elaborated statement on the subject, see the forthcoming volume on Hosea in the Anchor Bible, vol. 24; this is a joint effort with F. I. Andersen. [Garden City: Doubleday, 1980]

15% of the total number of words, while in classic poetry (e.g., the Psalter and other poetic books of the OT), the particle count is usually under 5%, often below 3%. In any particular piece of poetry, the lower the count of these particles, the greater the likelihood that the text has not been tampered with in the course of transmission. The normal expectation would be that such particles might be added through the inadvertence of scribes more accustomed to prose conventions.

It is important to note therefore the almost total absence of such prose particles in the framework of the Blessing of Moses. While the sample is small, out of a total of ninety-four words there is only one instance of these particles, a glaring example in v. 29 (**ואשר**). The ratio of particles to total word count, 1.1%, is in the lowest bracket for Hebrew poetry, and consistent with the proposed date of composition. While it cannot be proved, I would argue that the presence of **אשר** in v. 29 is secondary and intrusive. The fact that it occurs before **חרב**, but is omitted before the parallel term **מגן**, is indicative. In ordinary prose one would expect to see it with both words, or at least the first, whereas in poetry, as already indicated, it would not be needed at all. An analogous example is found in the Oracles of Balaam, Num. 24:4 and 16. In Num. 24:4, we have the following bicolon:

אשר מחזה שדי יחזה	**נפל וגלוי עינים**

whereas in v. 16 we have the same bicolon, with the exception that **אשר** has been omitted. Since without **אשר** the two cola match elegantly, and one of the two parallel passages omits the particle, it seems all but conclusive that **אשר** has been added in v. 4, and was not originally part of the poem here any more than in v. 16. In the case of **ואשר** in Deut. 33:29, removal seems to be justified, and I have excised it from the text.[14]

Deut. 33:2-5, 26-29**

6	*yahweh missînay bā'*	(2) Yahweh — from Sinai he came
8	*w*^{e}*zāraḥ miśśēʿîr lāmô*	and shone from Seir for them
6	*hôpîʿ mēhar pā'rān*	he burst forth from Mt. Paran
8	*w*^{e}*'ātâ mērīb*^{e}*bōt qōdš*	and went from the myriads of holiness

14. Dahood recognizes that **אשר** should not be interpreted as the relative pronoun; he analyzes the term as a form of **'iššer,* "to bless," but this can be rated no more than a possibility. He renders as follows:

'šryk yśr'l my kmwk	Happy are you, O Israel! Who is like you,
ʿm nwšʿ byhwh	a people saved by Yahweh?
miggēn ʿzrk	who gave you help
we'iššer ḥrb g'wtk	and blessed your victorious sword.

Cf. Dahood, "Hebrew-Ugaritic Lexicography I," *Bibl* 44 (1963): 298. On **מגן** cf. D. N. Freedman and M. O'Connor in *TWAT,* Bd. IV, 646-659. [*TDOT* 8 (forthcoming)]

8	*mîmînô ʾ^{a}šēdōt lāmô*	from his Southland to the mountain slopes for them.
5	*ʾap ḥōbēb ʿammîm*	(3) Indeed, the protector of peoples
7	*kol-q^{e}dōšâw b^{e}yādek(ā)*	all his holy ones are at your hand
7	*w^{e}hēm tukkû l^{e}raglek(ā)*	and they bow themselves at your feet
7	*yiśśāʾ middabb^{e}rōtêk(ā)*	he carries out your pronouncements.
8	*tôrâ ṣiwwâ-lānû mōšeh*	(4) Instruction Moses charged to us
8	*môrāšâ q^{e}hillat yaʿqōb*	possession for the assembly of Jacob
7	*way^{e}hî bîšūrûn malk*	(5) and he became king in Jeshurun
7	*b^{e}hitʾassēp rāʾšê ʿām*	when the chiefs of the people gathered together
6	*yaḥd šibṭê yiśrāʾēl*	in conclave the tribes of Israel.
6	*ʾên kāʾēl y^{e}šūrûn*	(26) There is none like El, O Jeshurun
7	*rōkēb šāmêm b^{e}ʿezrek(ā)*	who rides the skies for your help
8	*wab^{e}gaʾwātô š^{e}ḥāqîm*	and in his majesty the clouds
7	*m^{e}ʿōnâ ʾ^{e}lōhê qadm*	(27a) a dwelling is the ancient God
8	*wamittaḥt z^{e}rōʿōt ʿôlām*	and an undergirding are the arms of the Eternal.
9	*way^{e}gāreš mippānêk(ā) ʾôyēb*	(27b) And he drove out from your presence the enemy
5	*wayyōʾmer hašmēd*	and he said, "Destroy."
7	*wayyiškōn yiśrāʾēl bitḥ*	(28) So Israel settled securely
5	*bādād ʿān yaʿqōb*	alone dwelt Jacob
7	*ʾel-ʾarṣ dāgān w^{e}tîrôš*	in a land of grain and must
7	*ʾap-šāmâw yaʿr^{e}pû-ṭāl*	indeed, his skies drip dew.
8	*ʾašrêk(ā) yiśrāʾēl mî kāmôk(ā)*	(29a) Happy are you, Israel! Who is like you?
6	*ʿam nôšaʿ bayahweh*	a people delivered by Yahweh
8	*māgēn ʿezrek(ā) ḥarb gaʾwātek(ā)*	shield of your help, sword of your splendor.
9	*w^{e}yikkāḥ^{a}šû ʾōy^{e}bêk(ā) lāk*	(29b) Then your enemies will come cringing to you
10	*w^{e}ʾattâ ʿal-bāmôtêmô tidrōk*	and you, upon their backs you shall trample.

**The Hebrew appears in transliteration here and elsewhere in order to highlight Freedman's syllabification [eds.].

Before proceeding with the analysis of the opening and closing units of the poem, I wish to call attention to v. 21, which is obviously related to the third stanza of the Opening (vv. 4-5). While scholars have noted the close similarity between v. 21b (including the last word of v. 21a, ספון, which is to be joined with the first word of v. 21b, ויתא, to form ויתאספון; this reading is reflected partially in the LXX of that verse, συνηγμένων, and corresponds to בהתאסף in v. 5) and v. 5bA: in addition to the use of the same verbal root אסף in the hithpael (the only occurrence of this form in the Hebrew Bible), the following pair of words are identical: ראשי עם. It is my contention that the remaining cola in the verse (21) belong to the same context as the middle passage just mentioned, and that all five cola refer to the tribal assembly, in which Moses plays the leading role.

5	*wayyar' rē'šît lô*	(21a) And he provided the first share for him
7	*kî-śām ḥelqat meḥōqēq*	Indeed, he assigned the commander's portion (to him)
8	*wayyit'assepûn rā'šê 'ām*	(21b) Then the chiefs of the people gathered together
6	*ṣidqat yahweh 'āśâ*	the righteousness of Yahweh he executed
8	*wamišpāṭâw 'im-yiśrā'ēl*	and his judgments with Israel.

In my view, v. 21 has nothing to do with the Blessing of Gad, which is contained in a tricolon, v. 20. A number of the blessings in both Gen. 49 and Deut. 33 have this form: Zebulun (v. 13) and Benjamin (v. 27) in Gen. 49; and Benjamin (v. 12) and Naphtali (v. 23) in Deut. 33. In addition, the first unit of the Blessing of Judah in Gen. 49:8-12 is a tricolon (v. 8).[15] Against the idea of including v. 21 in the blessing is not only the strong shift in imagery, but the evidence and argument adduced above. Furthermore, in all the tribal blessings, no composite of eight cola is attested. It might be argued that the blessing on Gad continues through the first two cola of v. 21, and that only the last three cola are intrusive at this point. There is a five-colon blessing in this poem (on Asher, vv. 24-25), so that possibility for Gad cannot be ruled out, but the other division, separating v. 20 from v. 21, and assigning the latter to the framework of the poem, is more attractive and more likely. Hence, v. 21 constitutes a five-colon unit comparable in structure with those in the Opening and Closing (vv. 2, 4-5, 26-27a, 27b-29a), serves to break the sequence of blessings in the body of the poem, and links the Opening and Closing.[16]

15. That it is an independent unit is confirmed by the appearance of the name Judah at the beginning of the following blessing (v. 9; the image is quite different). The second of these units also is independent, since the third unit expresses another change in imagery, and the name Judah appears again in the first colon (vv. 10-12). With respect to the blessing on Gad, therefore, a tricolon seems eminently feasible.

16. A very similar pattern in the Opening and Closing of Ps. 137 was identified by me in "The Structure of Psalm 137," *Near Eastern Studies in Honor of William Foxwell Albright,* ed. H. Goedicke (Baltimore: Johns Hopkins University Press, 1971), 187-205, esp. 190-91, 201-2, and 203-5. A different five-colon pattern occurs in Exod. 15; *A Light Unto My Path, passim.*

The anomalous and perhaps liturgical element, v. 18, in the Blessing of Jacob (Gen. 49:1-27) has a similar function. It may be purely coincidental that the break in each poem comes between the blessings on Gad and Dan (although the order is reversed: Gad followed by Dan in Deut. 33, Dan followed by Gad in Gen. 49).

In view of the close association between Deut. 33:21 and vv. 4-5, it becomes clear that Moses is the focus of attention, and that Yahweh is the subject of the verbs in v. 21a. In addition to וירא in the first colon, I read MT שָׁם as *śām,* "he appointed/assigned." MT is conceivable, and perhaps defensible as a reference to the locale of the assembly, in which case וירא would govern both objects ראשית and חלקת מחקק, which are themselves synonymous or rather complementary. The other reading fits the context better. It also makes for an impressive chiasm with the fourth colon of the verse: צדקת יהוה עשה, an example of perfect reciprocity. "He (Yahweh) assigned a commander's share (to him: Moses) . . . the righteousness of Yahweh he (Moses) performed." In the larger structure, the first two cola (21a) balance the last two (21b). The action of Yahweh in appointing Moses as leader, and awarding him the victor's share, is matched by that of Moses in executing the judgments of Yahweh both within and on behalf of his people Israel. The sense attributed to וירא in v. 21 is confirmed by the usage in Gen. 22:8, יראה לו השה אלהים "God himself will provide the sheep" (while the reading שָׁם is reinforced, and strengthens that analysis). Just as חלקת מחקק explicates and complements ראשית, so צדקת יהוה and משפטיו are complementary, and form a combination: "the righteous judgments of Yahweh." Structurally, v. 21 constitutes a unit, corresponding to several in the Opening and Closing; its content confirms and amplifies the statements in the latter part of the Opening (vv. 4-5). And it establishes the centrality of Moses in the tribal configuration. I note the appearance of the key words, Yahweh and Israel, in conformity with the pattern we find in the Opening (Yahweh in v. 2, and Israel in v. 5) and Closing (Yahweh in v. 29, and Israel in vv. 28, 29).[17]

The Opening divides into the following sections: 1) v. 2: 5 cola, 36 syllables; 2) v. 3: 4 cola, 26 syllables; 3) vv. 4-5: 5 cola, 36 syllables.

The Closing divides into the following sections: 1) vv. 26-27a: 5 cola, 36 syllables; 2) v. 28: 4 cola, 26 syllables; 3) v. 27b and v. 29a: 5 cola, 36 syllables; 4) v. 29b: 2 cola, 19 syllables.

In comparing the two large units, note the excellent structural correlation between v. 3 (4 cola, 26 syllables) and v. 28 (4 cola, 26 syllables), and also between vv. 4-5 (5 cola, 36 syllables) and vv. 26-27a (5 cola, 36 syllables). For the remaining matchup, we have v. 2 (5 cola, 36 syllables) and v. 27b (2 cola, 14 syllables) and v. 29a (3 cola, 22 syllables). While the latter pair are not contiguous, they form an envelope around v. 28, an unusual but not unattested arrangement. Apart from

17. For a discussion of the two-part framework of Gen. 49 and the three-part framework of the Blessing of Moses, in the contexts of both poems, cf. O'Connor, ch. 10, *ad loc.*

common subject matter, vv. 27b and 29a are linked by the occurrence of the second person pronominal forms referring to Israel (v. 27b: מפניך; v. 29a: אשריך, כמוך, עזרך, גאותך), whereas in v. 28 the corresponding forms are consistently in the third person. That leaves v. 29b, which forms a conclusion to the entire poem (cf. Judg. 5:31, which serves the same purpose and has a similar tone). The final couplet (v. 29b) is substantially longer than any other bicolon in the framework of the poem, and stands somewhat apart from the rest of the material. The chiastic pattern which dominates the framework, along with the details of the correlations, can be seen in the following schematic table:

	The Opening		The Closing
(2)	2 + 3 + 1 = 6		2 + 2 + 1 + 3 = 8
	3 + 3 + 2 = 8		1 + 2 + 3 = 6
	2 + 2 + 2 = 6	(29a)	2 + 3 + 1 + 2 = 8
	3 + 4 + 1 = 8		3 + 2 = 5
	3 + 3 + 2 = 8	(27b)	4 + 3 + 2 = 9
	36		36
(3)	1 + 2 + 2 = 5		1 + 2 + 3 + 1 = 7
	1 + 3 + 3 = 7		1 + 1 + 2 + 3 = 7
	2 + 2 + 3 = 7		2 + 1 + 2 = 5
	2 + 5 = 7	(28)	3 + 3 + 1 = 7
	26		26
(4)	2 + 2 + 2 + 2 = 8		3 + 3 + 2 = 8
	3 + 3 + 2 = 8	(27a)	3 + 3 + 1 = 7
(5)	3 + 3 + 1 = 7		5 + 3 = 8
	4 + 2 + 1 = 7		2 + 2 + 3 = 7
	1 + 2 + 3 = 6		1 + 2 + 3 = 6
	36		36
		(29b)	5 + 3 + 1 = 9
			3 + 1 + 4 + 2 = 10
			19

With respect to the matching units, i.e., the Opening and the Closing, each consists of 14 cola having 98 syllables, for an average count of 7 syllables per colon. The actual distribution around that figure is symmetrical, as shown in the following table:

Syllables	The Opening	The Closing
5	1	2
6	3	2
7	5	5
8	5	4
9	0	1
	14	14

The prevailing pattern consists of bicola of 14 syllables, either 7 + 7, or 8 + 6, or 6 + 8. There are some tricola and more complex arrangements, but the basic scheme is fixed within a narrow range of variation.

Correlations in detail occur in matching sections. Thus in vv. 3 and 28 there are 4 cola, 3 with 7 syllables, 1 with 5 syllables. In vv. 4-5 and 26-27a, there are 2 cola with 8 syllables, 2 with 7 syllables, and 1 with 6 syllables. In vv. 2 and 27b and 29a, there are 3 matching cola, 2 with 8 syllables, and 1 with 6 syllables: the only variation is a bicolon, 6 + 8 = 14, in v. 2, which is balanced by a bicolon, 9 + 5 = 14, in v. 27b. There can hardly be any doubt that the composition, organization, and arrangement of the two units and their several sections are part of a deliberate pattern.

In support of the case for structural chiasm and symmetry, we note the following phenomena: the key word Yahweh occurs at the beginning (v. 2) and at the end of the poem (v. 29), and nowhere else in the Opening and Closing (but it does occur in the Divider, v. 21). The very unusual term for Israel, Jeshurun, which occurs only two other times in the Hebrew Bible (Deut. 32:15 and Isa. 44:2), occurs twice in this poem: at the end of the Opening (v. 5) and at the beginning of the Closing (v. 26). The combination of the key terms Yahweh and Jeshurun forms a symmetrical and chiastic framework for the poem. A slightly different example is the pair: עם and ישראל. In v. 5 (the Opening) the sequence is עם at the end of the second colon, followed by ישראל at the end of the third colon. In v. 29 (the Closing) the same pair occurs, but in reverse order: ישראל occurs in the first colon, followed by עם in the second. Other relevant data include the name Jacob, which occurs twice in the framework, in vv. 4 and 28; there is an additional occurrence of the name Israel in v. 28 for which there is no counterpart in the Opening, but it turns up in the Divider, v. 21. I turn now to the details of the units.

Part I: Proem, Deut. 33:2-5

A. Prologue, Verses 2-3

1. Verse 2: The correct interpretation of this deceptively difficult verse depends to a great extent on the proper analysis of its structure. The emphatic position of Yahweh at the very beginning of the passage shows not only that he is the dominant figure of this piece, but that each line or colon is directly related to him and his activity. Thus **יהוה** is the subject of all the verbs in the verse: **בא**, **זרח**, **הופיע**, and **אתה**. While LXX and many scholars interpret the last of these terms as the prep. **את** with or without the 3rd masc. sg. suffix, it is best to follow MT and take it as the verb **אתה**. The basic structure of the unit is a sequence of bicola, with a fifth colon constituting an expansion of the second bicolon. The first bicolon is balanced and chiastic: **יהוה מסיני בא // וזרח משעיר למו**; the *waw* at the beginning of the second colon is nonconsecutive since the verbs in the two cola have the same form (perfect) and the same tense (past). In Hebrew poetry, the conjunction tends to appear more frequently at the beginning of the second colon of a bicolon than at the beginning of the first colon; this pattern is exemplified in the two bicola in v. 2. Thus the second bicolon begins with **הופיע** (without *waw*); this verb is balanced by **ואתה** in the same way that **וזרח** matches **בא**. The final (fifth) colon of v. 2 is an expansion or extension of the previous clause, and adds a poetic flourish to the unit, which consists of 5 cola and 36 syllables, a repeated pattern in this poem.[18]

A more intricate internal arrangement may also be discerned. The verbs **בא** and **אתה** are more closely parallel to each other than either is with the other two verbs (**זרח** and **הופיע**), which are themselves synonyms. In Prov. 1:27 there is the sequence: **בבא . . . יאתה . . . בבא** (the arrangement is chiastic, but while the order of the verbs is the same as in Deut. 33:2, at least for the first two occurrences, the chiasm is reversed; **בבא** begins the first colon, and **אתה** opens the fourth colon). The chiasm in Deut. 33:2 has been achieved by shifting **בא** to the end of the colon in order to give special prominence to **יהוה** at the beginning of the Opening. In Job 3:25, **ויאתיני** is balanced by **יבא לי** (an interesting inversion because we would expect **בוא** as the A-word to precede **אתה** as the B-word). The same sequence occurs in Mic. 4:8, where **תאתה** is matched with **ובאה**. The same roots are associated in somewhat different fashion in Isa. 44:7 (**ואתיות ואשר תבאנה**) but the essential synonymy of the terms is confirmed. In Cant. 4:8, we find the pair **אתי תבואי**.

Similarly, **זרח** and **הופיע** have more in common with each other than either has with the other two verbs. Both depict the action of Yahweh in his role as sun-god or light-bearer: rise, come forth (**זרח**), shine forth (**הופיע**). Thus the envelope

18. Cf. n. 16.

construction: ואתה . . . בא is balanced by וזרח . . . הופיע in reverse order. The syllable count is symmetrical in either arrangement: 6 + 8 = 14, and 6 + 8 = 14.

The principal structural element binding the five cola of the section is the fivefold repetition of the prep. מ(ן): מסיני — משעיר — מהר פארן — מרבבת — קדש — מימינו. Together with the four overlapping verbs, they emphasize motion away from, the procession of the deity from his own mountain sanctuary. All the parts should be understood as sharing in this movement away from the southern, Sinai sanctuary to the new location. The place names generally are familiar to us from other references to the abode of Yahweh. Sinai is the most common term, but Seir and Paran also occur with some frequency (e.g., Judg. 5 and Ps. 68).[19] Under the circumstances it is tempting to read *m^eribat qādēš* (cf. Deut. 32:51) for the anomalous and confusing מרבבת קדש, since a fourth place name is desiderated, but in spite of LXX κάδης, the temptation should be resisted. Apart from the problem of the textual changes involved, there is the point that the expression מריבת קדש occurs only in prose accounts, never in poetry. It is preferable to adopt the more difficult reading of MT, and to link the fourth and fifth cola of v. 2 in the process of analysis and interpretation.

The phrase מימינו אשדת should be regarded as parallel with and complementary to מרבבת קדש. With respect to the expression אשדת, MT cannot be followed in its analysis of the term into two words, אש דת, which is a counsel of despair.[20] Rather, the word should be read as *'^ašēdōt,* "mountain-slopes." The term אשדת is singularly appropriate to the region from which Yahweh has departed, and to which he has come. It is used in conjunction with Mt. Pisgah, which is close to the place where the tribal assembly in Deut. 33 takes place (cf. Deut. 34:1 for Pisgah = Nebo; the expression אשדת הפסגה, "the slopes of Pisgah," occurs in Deut. 3:17; 4:49; Josh. 12:3; 13:20). Since nothing thus far has been said of the goal of Yahweh's march, but only of the place or places from which he has departed, it may be that we should see in אשדת the designation of this geographical objective, the locale of the tribal gathering near the slopes of Pisgah. It is possible to interpret the term in this fashion, since direction need not be expressed by the preposition. On the other hand, after the fivefold repetition of the prep. מ(ן) we would expect a more positive differentiation if direction toward somewhere were intended. It is more likely therefore that אשדת is part of the description of the southern scene along with the rest of the terms used in v. 2. Hence מימינו אשדת is to be taken as a unit (in spite of the order of the words) and in balance with מרבבת קדש. If מימינו means "from his right hand," i.e., from his southern region = southland, then this expression is to be combined with קדש, which as it stands describes the original holy homeland of Yahweh (cf. Exod. 3:5 where the expression אדמת קדש occurs,

19. On the Southland, cf. Cross, *Canaanite Myth and Hebrew Epic,* 86, 100-103.

20. M. Dahood, *Psalms II.* AB 17 (Garden City: Doubleday, 1968), 44, proposes *'ōš^edōt,* "those striding," a verbal form derived from *'ešed,* "leg, foundation."

referring not merely to the spot on which Moses was standing, but to the whole area).[21] The combination may be translated "his southland sanctuary." Along the same lines, the words רבבת and אשדת agree in form (and can be interpreted as having the same gender and number). They can then be combined with the following sense: "myriads of mountain slopes," an appropriate description of the mountainous region which was believed to be Yahweh's homeland. We paraphrase cola 4 and 5 of this verse: "He proceeded from the myriad mountain slopes of his southland sanctuary."

It is also possible to analyze רבבת as referring to the heavenly hosts, the agents and messengers of Yahweh who show up en masse in the next verse. But given the context, we would not expect departure from these hosts in the description, but accompaniment by them, as v. 3 states. So it seems better to identify רבבת with the physical features of the sacral region from which Yahweh has departed. In support of this view, note the following pattern: in the first bicolon, the prep. מ(ן) is used with single-word objects: מסיני // משעיר; in the second pair a construct chain of two terms occurs: מהר פארן // מרבבת קדש. The corresponding terms in the final colon would be מימינו אשדת (in reverse order). All of the geographic terms in v. 2, so far as we can tell, refer to the same general area, the region primordially associated with Yahweh: Sinai and Seir, the mountainous region of Paran and Qadeš (itself an expression of the holiness of the area, doubtless the site of an ancient sanctuary); "the mountain-slopes of his southland" is the summation of the preceding descriptions. Yahweh has come from this region for the sake of his servant Moses and his people Israel. The term למו is difficult, but its importance is underscored by its repetition at the beginning and end of the verse. Whether the pronominal suffix is 3rd masc. pl. or sg. cannot be resolved here, but in either case the reference is likely to be to the people, Israel (= עם נושע ביהוה). The force of the prep. ל is not altogether clear, but it seems to be ethical: i.e., "for the sake of him (it, them)."

LXX offers a beguiling alternative to MT and the interpretation proposed here. Not only does it supply κάδης as the fourth geographic term, but also the intelligible ἄγγελοι for the difficult אשדת. The Greek rendering goes well with μυριάσι (= רבבת) of the previous colon, and anticipates and confirms the picture of the deity surrounded by a heavenly retinue as he proceeds from his southland residence. It is difficult, however, to derive ἄγγελοι from the word אשדת, or any similar combination of letters. The reading is too simple and hence suspect. It is certainly better, and in fact obligatory, to struggle with the much more difficult reading of MT.

2. Verse 3: In this verse we have a couplet consisting of balancing bicola. While the cola can be read consecutively, both syntax and grammar point to an

21. I owe this observation to Professor Benjamin Mazar of Hebrew University.

envelope construction in which the outer cola (numbers one and four) are linked, as well as the two interior ones (numbers two and three). Thus v. 3a1 has a 3rd masc. sg. form (the ptcp. חבב) to which the verb ישא in v. 3b2 (3rd masc. sg. impf.) corresponds. Similarly, the masc. pl. noun in v. 3a2, קדשיו, agrees with the plural verb in v. 3b1: תכו. The words בידך and לרגלך in v. 3a2 and v. 3b1 respectively form a closely linked pair (perhaps a kind of merismus, as in English, "hand and foot," meaning "in every way, entirely"), and reinforce the proposed arrangement. The appearance of 2nd masc. sg. pronominal suffixes complicates the syntactical analysis of this material. Three different pronoun groups can be identified in this verse: 3rd masc. sg. (חבב probably, ישא, and the suffix on קדשיו); 3rd masc. pl. (קדשיו, the noun, not the suffix; הם תכו); and 2nd masc. sg. (בידך, לרגלך, מדברתיך). While sporadic shifts between third and second person forms relating to the same subject are observable in the biblical text, it is difficult to equate here the 3rd masc. sg. suffix on קדשיו with the 2nd masc. sg. suffix on בידך // לרגלך. If three different parties are depicted in v. 3, then the problem of identification becomes acute and urgent. Assuming that v. 3 is a continuation of v. 2, we would naturally identify the third person singular subject of ישא (v. 3b2), who is also חבב עמים (v. 3a1), with Yahweh. The 3rd masc. pl. term קדשיו (v. 3a2), along with the pair הם תכו, would in any case be the holy ones who constitute the divine retinue. That leaves the words with the 2nd masc. sg. pronominal suffix (בידך, לרגלך). In the Closing, the 2nd masc. sg. forms are all identified with Israel (cf. v. 29, also v. 27b; on v. 26 see the notes), and that would be a possible choice here: the shift from third to second person postulated between vv. 2 and 3 is matched by the shift from third person forms in v. 28 to second person forms in v. 29. While the picture of divine beings accompanying Israel is quite reasonable, and is thematic in the book of Exodus for the departure from Egypt and the wanderings in the Wilderness, the specific description of these heavenly beings being prostrate and subservient, waiting in attendance ("hand and foot"), rather reflects the imagery of fawning courtiers surrounding a king. Finally, the notion that the deity accepts the demands, or carries out the commands, of any other party is intrinsically improbable (v. 3b2). The setting in v. 3 is the heavenly court, with the chief God surrounded by his entourage of retainers and servants, who wait on him hand and foot, and execute his royal commands. Thus the "holy ones" are the angels or lesser divine beings (3rd masc. pl. forms), and God is represented by the 2nd masc. sg. forms. That leaves the 3rd masc. sg. forms to be examined and explained. That referent seems to be an intermediate figure, like the archangels of a later period of theological speculation, with special characteristics and responsibilities. It is this "protector of peoples" (or we may read with LXX, "of his people") who carries out the commands of the supreme Deity, and who may be the immediate superior of the bodyguard or retinue which surrounds the divine throne. It is possible that behind this rather murky arrangement is an earlier pattern in which Yahweh functioned as this intermediate figure, while the chief god was El (cf. Deut. 32:8-9, which in the *Vorlage* of LXX seems to reflect such a mythological pattern: Elyon being an epithet of El, while Yahweh was depicted as the guardian of Israel).[22]

Regarding the difficulties in the analysis and interpretation of v. 3b, there is little to be added to the earlier discussion. Whether הם תכו is to be read as two words, or combined into a single verb form **himtakkû* or the like, the problem of morphology remains; but the sense is much the same: "submit, prostrate yourself, be subservient," which suits the context admirably.[23] The meaning of the last colon seems to be: "carry out, execute words of command," although the exact combination of verb and noun is not elsewhere attested. The form מדברתיך is unusual and anomalous, but it seems best to derive it from the common root **dbr,* meaning "word."[24] Whether the initial *mem* is to be taken as enclitic with the preceding word (ישא) or as a preformative with דברתיך is not easy to decide. It is also possible to follow MT and read the preposition here, although the sense is not clear (a partitive usage would hardly be appropriate).

B. Introduction, Verses 4-5

This unit is structurally comparable to v. 2 and vv. 26-27a (not to speak of vv. 27b and 29a), and consists of 5 cola, with a total of 36 syllables. In view of the repetition of this pattern in the Opening and Closing, it would be unwise to tamper with the existing text. It is highly unlikely that precise symmetrical patterns would emerge accidentally or incidentally as a result of accretions and alterations made by editors and scribes.

1. Verse 4: The explicit reference to Moses explains the placement of the poem in the book of Deuteronomy, and the particular setting in these chapters at the end of the book. Nevertheless, the passage should not be regarded as secondary or unhistorical, since, as we have shown elsewhere, Moses figures prominently in a poetic tradition parts of which have been preserved in the Pentateuch, and which is older than the oldest prose accounts. Doubtless there is a recollection here of a tribal conclave at which Moses himself presided, and delivered his farewell remarks in the form of Instruction (= Torah). Whether the specific tribal blessings derive from Moses or this particular assembly would be difficult to establish, and is not of concern in this paper. But there is no reason to doubt, once the wilderness wanderers had arrived at and settled upon land belonging to or claimed by one or

22. On the Mari background of *ḥpp* (Akk. *ebēbu*), see G. E. Mendenhall, *The Tenth Generation* (Baltimore: Johns Hopkins University Press, 1973), 105-121, 170; and Cross, *Canaanite Myth and Hebrew Epic,* 107, n. 38. Cf. חפץ in Deut. 33:12.

23. On the proposed verb form, cf. Cross-Freedman, *Studies in Ancient Yahwistic Poetry,* 108-9. Note that the reading המתכו is presented in *BHS.* J. T. Milik preserves MT, reading a form of תכך; "Deux documents inédits du Désert de Juda," *Biblica* 38 (1957), 252-54.

24. For a different interpretation of this difficult text, see Dahood, 233. He translates, "They carry your train," deriving the key word from *dbr,* "to follow."

more of the tribes, that they would have joined forces with the still-existent tribal league. If the independent existence of a tribal league is assumed, then a meeting of representatives of all the surviving tribes with the group coming from Sinai and Kadesh in transjordanian territory (i.e., on the Plains of Moab) would be quite natural. The occurrence of the 1st person pl. pronoun (v. 4, לנו) shows that the poem is a community-sanctioned product, although no doubt the work of one or more individuals, and reflects the self-awareness of the holy congregation. The penetration and success of the new faith in Yahweh are embodied in this poem. Yahweh has accompanied the wilderness group as it enters the territory of the tribal league, and in the process of conquest and consolidation of gains, has been accepted as the dominant deity of Israel (and equated with patriarchal El, the original creator of the covenant community). The reorganization and restructuring of the league is the principal business of the conclave, spurred by the defeat of the two Amorite kings and the capture of claimed territories (previously and continuously occupied by members of the transjordanian tribes). From this land base, the liberation of cisjordanian tribal territories could be projected, and would be carried out in the future by the new leader, Joshua. The climax and culmination of the struggle with the Canaanite kings will come with the battle at the Wadi Kishon in the days of Deborah and Barak, and the end of Canaanite hegemony in the heartland west of the Jordan.

The term מורשה in the second colon is not only parallel to תורה, but is bound to it also by assonance and rhyme. The terms are not synonymous, but complementary. The Instruction of Moses must relate to the possession and inheritance of the land, the primary civil interest and responsibility of the confederation. This is the territory promised to the patriarchs, and occupied by their descendants, united through the overriding imperative of Yahweh's newly asserted claim to the same area. What Moses commanded, therefore, concerned the efforts to gain or regain possession of the land, the principles governing league action, and the final determination of boundary lines, initially for the transjordanian tribes, but ultimately for the entire territory of Israel.

2. Verse 5: The different terms for the assembly of the tribes have interlocking connections, all dependent upon לנו in the first colon. Thus קהלת יעקב in v. 4b is parallel to שבטי ישראל in v. 5b: both are construct chains defining the group as a congregation (קהלת) and tribal league (שבטי), while the pair יעקב // ישראל is a standard expression. In addition, we have the rare term ישרון in association with יעקב, a pairing which is attested in Deut. 32:15 and Isa. 44:2. Furthermore, ראשי עם in v. 5b1 combines with שבטי ישראל in v. 5b2 to provide a detailed description of the members of the ruling council: the chiefs of the tribes of the people of Israel. It has been argued elsewhere that the king (מלך) in this passage (v. 5a) is Yahweh himself (cf. יהוה ימלך, "Yahweh reigns," in Exod. 15:18), and that one of the purposes of the tribal conference was to affirm solemnly that fundamental truth: that Yahweh, and no one else, was king of the worshipping congregation of Jacob // Jeshurun.

Part II: The Closing, Deut. 33:26-29

The case for the structural relationship between this section and the Opening (vv. 2-5) has already been presented. Here the pattern is essentially the same but the order is reversed, so that vv. 26-27a match vv. 4-5, v. 28 is equivalent to v. 3, and vv. 27b, 29a, which form an envelope around v. 28, balance v. 2. Verse 29b is a coda, attached to v. 29a, to bring the whole poem to a fitting close. It has no direct correspondent in the opening unit. Assorted data have been adduced in support of these views, and need not be repeated. We will turn instead to details of the verses under consideration.

A. Verses 26-27a, Apostrophe to אל ישרון*, "the God of Jeshurun" the sky-rider*

In this context, אל seems to be the generic term for deity, and a surrogate for Yahweh. Behind that connection is doubtless one of the high gods of the West Semitic pantheon. The sky-rider par excellence in Near Eastern mythology must be the sun-god (cf. v. 2, where Yahweh is described as beaming forth and rising). In addition, the storm-god Baal-Hadad is described as a sky-rider (strictly speaking, "rider of the clouds"; cf. Ps. 68:5, which connects the description with Yah).

In the transcription and translation of v. 26b, I have followed MT. A substantially better reading is obtained through a very modest group of changes, as noted in the earlier article by F. M. Cross and D. N. Freedman:[25]

7	*rōkēb šāmêm bᵉʿuzzô*	Rider of the skies in his power
8	*rōkēb gaʾwātô šᵉḥāqîm*	Rider in his majesty of the clouds

Oddly enough, the syllable count is unchanged, so the metrical analysis is not affected. The pair of combinations, in chiastic order, may be paraphrased as follows: "on clouds of the skies" and "in his majestic strength."

Verse 27a remains problematic. Following the analysis in "The Blessing of Moses" by Cross and Freedman, we may parse the initial word מענה as the noun מעון, "refuge, habitation," with the 3rd masc. sg. pronominal suffix. Then the difficult expression מתחת can be interpreted as the prepositional phrase "underneath him," with the suffix from מענה serving double-duty. The unit could then be rendered: "His refuge is the Ancient God / and underneath him (i.e., supporting him) are the arms of the Eternal One."[26]

25. *Studies in Ancient Yahwistic Poetry,* 120. There is no need to supply the preposition in the second colon, since the preposition with *ʿzw* also serves *gʾwtw*.

26. O'Connor, *ad loc.,* reads a fem. pass. ptcp. of מתח, "to spread out," otherwise only known in Isa. 40:22 in the Hebrew Bible, but well attested in other Semitic dialects.

B. Verse 28

On the reading *ʿān* for MT עין, see the discussion in "The Blessing of Moses."[27] It is possible that the received Hebrew text reflects a supposed piel form of the same root, with intensive force.

With respect to the sequence אל ארץ, I have accepted the arrangement in MT, although elsewhere I proposed that the prep. אל be detached from the following noun, be read as the divine appellative, and be attached to the preceding noun יעקב, to produce the original full form of the name: Jacob-el.[28] The effect of this rearrangement would be very slight, but it would change the internal counts as follows: from 7:5, 7:7 to 7:6, 6:7. The difference is minute, and perhaps irrelevant, but the fact remains that the pattern for the corresponding unit in the Opening (v. 3) has 4 cola, 3 with 7 syllables, and 1 colon with 5 syllables, or exactly the same as the present arrangement in MT. Under the circumstances, I think it best to stay with MT in v. 28.

C. Verses 27b and 29a

The third unit consists of two parts, vv. 27b and 29a, which form an envelope around v. 28. As already noted, v. 27b is to be dissociated from v. 28 because of the shift from second to third person pronominal forms in the latter; but v. 27b is to be connected with v. 29a by the recurrence of the same second person forms, all of which refer to Israel. The resultant unit exhibits the same pattern repeated elsewhere in the Opening and Closing (and in slightly modified form in the Divider, v. 21). The correspondence is almost exact, not only with regard to total syllable count (5 cola and 36 syllables) but in the correlation of individual lines. It was necessary to revise the text of v. 29a by the removal of the single prose element (ואשר), which we regard as intrusive.

D. Verse 29b, Peroration

While the last unit is linked grammatically with what precedes through the presence of second person pronominal forms, it also serves to close the entire poem on a triumphant note. As noted, the bicolon is heavier in metrical terms than any other in the Opening and Closing, and since there is no correspondent passage in the Opening in an otherwise completely symmetrical structure, it may be regarded as an added ornamentation, a conclusion to the unit and to the poem as a whole.

27. *Studies in Ancient Yahwistic Poetry,* 121, n. 87.

28. "The Original Name of Jacob," *IEJ* 13 (1963): 125-26. Cf. the comments by M. Dahood, *Psalms I.* AB 16 (Garden City: Doubleday, 1966), 242, 273.

11

The Spelling of the Name "David" in the Hebrew Bible*

The name David occurs 1073 times in the Hebrew Bible.[1] Of these, approximately 788 have the standard three-letter orthography *(dwd),* while the remainder (*ca.* 285) are spelled with four letters *(dwyd),* the internal vowel-letter *yodh* being added. While the four-letter spelling is less frequent, it is sufficiently common to warrant

1. The numbers are provided by F. I. Andersen-A. D. Forbes from their computer-based analysis of the Hebrew text. Their counts and calculations are derived from the Kittel BH (3rd ed.), which represents the text of the Leningrad Manuscript also used for the BHS. The distribution of the name and its alternate spellings is as follows:

	dwd		dwyd
Samuel	575		0
Kings	93		3
Isaiah	10		0
Jeremiah	15		0
Ezekiel	3		1
Minor Prophets	1		8
Psalms	87		1
Proverbs	1		0
Ruth	2		0
Song of Songs	0		1
Ecclesiastes	1		0
Chronicles — Ezra-Nehemiah	0		271
Totals	788	+	285 = 1073

These figures should now be adopted as normative in place of those listed in Brown, Driver, and Briggs (1907: 187b), for which only a claim of approximate accuracy was ever made: BDB

* I wish to acknowledge the valuable assistance of my colleague, M. P. O'Connor, who edited the manuscript, incorporating numerous changes in the wording and occasionally in the meaning; he prepared the footnotes and bibliography, which are included substantially as he wrote them.

the designation of alternate official spelling. The phenomenon of two official or correct spellings side by side in the Hebrew Scriptures is sufficiently rare and intriguing to warrant further analysis and discussion.[2]

A similar but essentially different phenomenon is the occurrence of different forms of the same name, in which a phonological distinction is reflected in the spelling, e.g., *yônātān* and *y^e^hônātān* as alternate forms of the name of the son of Saul.[3] In the case of David, however, there is no reason to suppose that the name was pronounced differently depending on the spelling, or that there is any difference at all except in the orthography. Other examples of this phenomenon occur, especially when a medial *yodh* or *waw* is omitted or added in the spelling in contrast with the prevailing pattern, but such deviations in defiance of an established spelling are sporadic (e.g., Assyria is regularly spelled *'šwr,* but there is a single case of defective spelling in 1 Chr. 5:6);[4] in certain cases of relatively rare names, tone variant spellings may occur (e.g., Gehazi occurs 12 times: it is spelled with five letters, *gyḥzy,* eight times, and with four letters, *gḥzy,* the other four times — all of these occurrences are in 2 Kings, chs. 4, 5, and 8).

More often, an alternate, generally fuller, spelling is found in biblical and nonbiblical texts from Qumran, generally those which lie clearly outside of the Massoretic tradition. Thus the name Moses is always spelled with three letters in the Massoretic Text *(mšh),* but frequently with four letters *(mwšh)* in the Qumran scrolls. Similar variation obtains for the name David, which is spelled with four letters in the extensive (but fragmented) text 4QSam[a], whereas in MT it is always spelled with three letters in the books of Samuel.[5] The defective spelling is also

---

gives 1066 as the total with *ca.* 790 for the three-letter spelling, and *ca.* 276 for the four-letter spelling. Needless to say, the general argument in this chapter is not affected by the slight discrepancy between the two sets of figures. There are two exceptions in the readings of the Leningrad MS which will be considered at appropriate places in the paper. No count is foolproof, but *dw(y)d* seems to present special problems. The only previous study of the spelling patterns known to me, that of Hugo Bonk 1891: 127-29, reckons with 889 occurrences, by Bonk's own count. I cannot accept Bonk's conclusion that the use of the *dwd*-spelling in Psalms, Proverbs, Qoheleth, and Ruth represents a post-Chronicler revival of the oldest spelling (p. 129), but it is interesting to note that some contemporaries would. The total of 790 occurrences given in Carlson-Ringgren (1978: 157) seems to be an error based on a misreading of BDB.

2. For references to recent discussions of the name David, see W. Baumgartner, et al. (1967: 207), and Carlson-Ringgren 1978.

3. For discussion, see Freedman-O'Connor 1980.

4. Though others may be suggested, given that *'šr* is such a common combination in the Bible, F. I. Andersen and I have proposed to recognize such an instance of *'šr, "Assur,"* in Hos. 7:12 (Andersen-Freedman 1980: 469-470; cf. 463).

5. The text remains unpublished, though most of the material readings can be found in McCarter's commentary on I Samuel (1980) and the forthcoming companion volume [*II Samuel.* AB 9 (Garden City: Doubleday, 1984)]. 4QSam[c] (Ulrich 1979) probably showed the same pattern,

found in the Qumran text 4QSam*b*, which has the distinction of being among the oldest of all manuscripts preserved there (dating from about 250 B.C.E., and in any case from the 3rd century B.C.E., much earlier than 4QSam*a*).[6]

In the case of the name David, we are dealing with a remarkable set of circumstances and data, which should enable us to pose questions, propose hypotheses, make inferences, and even draw conclusions about a set of issues, all of which are of interest, and some of which may have important bearing on matters of canon, the dating of various compositions, and the evolution of official orthography. In the first place, the name is well known, occurs frequently, and is widely distributed in the biblical text. Secondly, both spellings are well represented and hence can be regarded as correct or acceptable to editors and scribes. It is reasonable to ask how such a development took place, why there are two acceptable spellings, why they occur where they do, and what the relation of one group is to the other. In attempting to provide an answer to these questions, we will also endeavor to sketch a picture of orthographic development in Biblical Hebrew which will account for the divergence or evolution in spelling and correlate that with the compilation of the different biblical books and their incorporation into the Hebrew canon.

Let us consider first the distribution of the name in the Bible. The three-letter spelling (i.e., the so-called defective spelling, which is also the older and original spelling of the name in an alphabetic script using only consonants — *dwd*) is predominant in the narrative of the so-called Deuteronomic History (= Former Prophets): all the hundreds of occurrences in Samuel are defectively written, as are the vast majority of cases in Kings (about 79 in all, of which three are written plene: 1 Kgs. 3:14; 11:4, 36).

The defective spelling also predominates in the Latter Prophets: this is true of all instances of the name in Isaiah (including the occurrence in Isa. 55:3) and Jeremiah, as well as in three of the four examples in Ezekiel (the exception is Ezek. 34:23; the spelling is defective in Ezek. 34:24 and 37:24, 25). The three-letter spelling also occurs, without exception, in Psalms, Proverbs, Ruth, and Ecclesiastes.[7]

---

though no instances of the name are preserved. The full spelling is attested in some 1Q texts: 1Q7:3 (2 Sam. 21), and 1Q7:4 (2 Sam. 23); both are published in Barthélemy 1955: 65.

Among the nonbiblical cases of the plene form, we may cite these cases: (1) 6Q9 (= 6Qap-Sam/Kgs) 22:4 (Baillet 1962: 119); (2) 4Qp161 (= Isa[a]) 7-10.iii 22 (reedited in Horgan 1979: I,18,II,76,85); the passage treats Isa. 11:15 and so does not reflect a MT occurrence of David; (3) 4QPBless 2,4 (discussed in Fitzmyer 1971); (4) 4QFlor 1–2i 11 (discussed in Fitzmyer 1971); (5) 4Q504 (= DebHam[a]) 1-2.iv.6 (Baillet 1982: 143).

6. The treatment in Freedman 1962 has not yet been superseded by the *editio princeps*. [See above, Chapter 3]

7. There is an exception in the spelling of the name in Ps. 122:5 in BH^3 and BHS, where we find *dwyd* instead of the expected *dwd*. Comparison, however, with the spelling in the Aleppo Codex, which must be regarded as the best of all the Medieval MSS, shows the three-letter spelling. It is more likely, in my judgment, that the Aleppo Codex preserves the correct spelling for the

The four-letter spelling is used regularly in the Chronicler's work: 1 and 2 Chronicles, Ezra-Nehemiah.[8] It is stated in BDB that the defective spelling is found at 1 Chr. 13:6, and doubtless such a reading occurs in the printed text used by the editors, and possibly in the manuscripts on which it was based. But it is to be noted that BHS, which is based on the Leningrad MS, gives the full spelling at 1 Chr.13:6, and the same is true of the Aleppo Codex. So we must conclude that the defective spelling in 1 Chronicles claimed in BDB is not derived from the best and oldest manuscripts of the Hebrew Bible, but is based on an aberrant text arising probably from a scribal slip easily induced by the fact that scribes were trained to spell the name both ways and may from time to time have substituted one spelling for the other unintentionally. What is surprising is how consistently the spelling, whether of three or four letters, is maintained throughout single books. With only the two exceptions already noted (in Ezekiel and Kings), the spelling, whether plene or defective, is the same throughout individual books.

In addition to the Chronicler's work, the full spelling is found throughout the Minor Prophets, including instances in Amos (twice) and Hosea (once),[9] as well

---

Psalter, consistent with all other examples in that book, than the Leningrad MS, which is generally not as reliable as the Aleppo, has the original spelling, which was modified inadvertently in the Aleppo Codex. It is possible, of course, that the original edition of the complete Psalter as we have it contained four-letter examples of the name, since publication of the whole Psalter could not have been earlier than the exile, and might well have been later. If the Psalter should be regarded as containing both spellings, it would then be grouped with Kings and Ezekiel in the transition period. But one doubtful exception should be viewed skeptically.

8. BDB (1907: 187b). Furthermore, Mandelkern's *Concordance* (1947) and Baumgartner, et al. (1967: 207), support the full reading of the name in the passage mentioned in the text (1 Chr. 13:6).

9. The Leningrad MS has the three-letter spelling at Hos. 3:5, and that might be taken as a reflection of the original spelling in some preexilic form of the book or partial collection of prophetic works. However, the Aleppo Codex has the four-letter spelling here, so we must treat the Leningrad reading with caution. The latter may reflect an older spelling in the transmission of the book of Hosea, but it seems more likely to have been a deliberate or inadvertent alteration by a medieval scribe. The Hosea passage in question is often treated as a later Judahite insertion in the prophetic text, and the spelling might be adduced to support this view. I shall propose another explanation for the spelling below; I continue to recognize the passage as proper to the text (cf. Andersen-Freedman 1980: 307).

In the case of the Book of the Twelve Prophets and of the Psalter the Aleppo Codex reflects the consistency of spelling within books which we have pointed out as characteristic of the scribal tradition. It is always possible to regard such consistency as artificial and to see in the variations of the Leningrad MS evidence for diverse spellings preserved by very careful and attentive scribes. Perhaps it is best to leave the question open in these cases. The general argument would be modified only to the extent of recognizing that the Book of the Twelve might contain an older spelling in the book of Hosea, which would be quite in keeping with the date of the prophet and an early edition of this book. In the case of the Psalter, the example of four-letter spelling would support the inevitable and necessary conclusion that the Psalter is a product of the transition period (the exile) at the earliest.

as Zechariah (six cases). In addition, the Song of Songs has a single example of the name (it is spelled in full: Cant. 4:4).

Now what is to be made of this bundle of data? The first, most obvious, and yet important point is that there is a correlation between the older spelling and the earlier books of the Bible, and a similar correspondence between the later spelling and the later books of the Bible. Just as we know that the defective three-letter spelling is the original alphabetic spelling of the name David, and that it preceded the four-letter fuller spelling in time, so we also know that the books of Samuel and Kings are older than the Chronicler's work; and in a general way the data correspond to this elementary observation about the spelling of the name David in the books of the Bible. With certain equally obvious exceptions, it is clear that the older books (not just in content but in composition, compilation, and publication) have the earlier spelling and the later books have the more developed spelling.

This commonplace can now be coordinated with a theory of date of composition and implied canonization, as follows: The form of spelling of the name David reflects the period in which the book in question reached substantially present form or was published under the aegis of some significant authority.[10] Thus the occurrence of the three-letter name in a book would point to an earlier date of composition in its present form, while the presence of the four-letter spelling of the name would point to a later date. The value for relative dating or for helping to confirm a dating already arrived at on other grounds can hardly be questioned. Thus Samuel-Kings is the older work and has the defective earlier spelling of the name David, while the Chronicler's work is admittedly later (postexilic), and correspondingly has the fuller spelling of the name David.

We plan to examine the situation in other books of the Bible, but before doing so we must make or concede two points:

1) In other books, with the exception of the Psalter, the name does not occur very often, and we should exercise caution in making inferences or drawing conclusions on the basis of one or two instances, especially when these are restricted largely to titles (as, e.g., in the case of Proverbs or Ecclesiastes, where the name occurs only once, or in the Psalter, where most of the approximately eighty-eight occurrences are in the titles).

2) As already noted, there must have been a tendency to normalize the spelling throughout individual books. The dominant spelling in a book would tend to spread over the book, and possible instances of the other spelling would tend to disappear under the pressure toward conformity. Such a process is typical and to be expected.

10. I have discussed the basic theory often (Freedman 1962 [See above, Chapter 3]; 1963 [See Volume I, Chapter 27]; 1976 [See Volume I, Chapter 27]; 1983 [See Volume I, Chapter 32]; Cross-Freedman 1975).

What is surprising is that this tendency has developed in opposite directions, so that the defective spelling is consistent in some books and the plene spelling predominant in others. In only two books is there any overlap, and it is in them perhaps that we should look for clues to the transition from one official spelling to the other. What is clear thus far is that the early spelling is dominant in the Former Prophets and the later spelling exclusive in the Chronicler's work. A transitional phase (if these mixed spellings are not the result of inadvertence or inattention on the part of scribes) may be observed toward the end of the Primary History (three occurrences of plene spelling in Kings) and in the book of Ezekiel (one instance of plene spelling). Since on other grounds it can be argued that the completion of these major works occurred in the same period or generation, we may be able to pinpoint the transition from one spelling to the other in the period between the initial compilation of Samuel-Kings on the one hand and that of the Chronicler's work on the other.

Speaking in terms of relative dating, we can examine the distribution of the name David in other books of the Bible: among the Latter Prophets, both Isaiah and Jeremiah have the three-letter spelling consistently. That evidence would argue for an early date of compilation. I think this conclusion is entirely satisfactory for Jeremiah, but less so for Isaiah, since the latter part of the book is considerably later than the time of Isaiah, or Jeremiah for that matter. This occurrence of the three-letter form of the name in Isa. 55:3 is a particular problem, but we may appeal to the consistent use of that form in the earlier part of Isaiah to explain its occurrence in the later chapter. An earlier version of Isaiah (including chs. 1–33, 36–39) would have had the older spelling and that spelling would have prevailed even after the consolidated edition (including chs. 34–35, 40–66) was made. We have already discussed the book of Ezekiel and its mixed spelling. The defective spelling ought to have prevailed, and the occurrence of a plene form may be the result of scribal inadvertence.[11] Nevertheless the spelling in Ezekiel may be transitional. When we come to the Book of the Twelve, the situation is reversed. Here the spelling is plene throughout, although presumably the name David was originally spelled with three letters instead of four in early books such as Amos and Hosea. To explain the occurrence of the four-letter spelling throughout the collection of Minor Prophets, we must appeal again to the principle of consistency, only this time the late spelling was dominant and it displaced any examples of early spelling. The source of the late spelling is to be found inside the group, specifically in the book of Zechariah, where the name occurs six times in chs. 12–13. In every case the spelling is full, and doubtless it was this preponderance that determined the spelling in the remaining cases (2 in Amos, 1 in Hosea). It is also inviting to suggest that the full spelling was predominant at the time that Zechariah (II or III) was put together and pub-

11. Or does the pattern recognized by Andersen (1970) obtain here, as O'Connor suggests to me?

lished. The date of this work might provide us with a terminus for the completion of the transition from the three-letter to the four-letter form of the name.

We can now state the case in terms of relative chronology:

1) The early three-letter spelling predominates in the basic narrative that stretches from Genesis to Kings (Primary History) and in the Major Prophets. It is also found in a variety of other books such as Ruth (several examples) and Proverbs and Ecclesiastes (only in the title and hence less persuasive). The old spelling is found throughout the Psalter as well, and while most of the occurrences are in titles and headings, there are a number of cases in the body of the Psalms. While most scholarship supports a late date for the compilation of the Psalter, it is nevertheless true that the Hebrew of the Psalms is good classical Hebrew for the most part, and an early date for earlier editions of the Psalms would be quite plausible. Here again we must appeal to the force of the system in regularizing the spelling, although it is surprising that the older spelling prevailed in this case (as probably also in the case of Ecclesiastes). The prevalence of the old spelling in the book of Ruth is not surprising, however, since it is being recognized increasingly that Ruth belongs to the literary tradition of classical Hebrew and is more likely a product of the First Temple period than the Second.[12]

2) The transitional phase between older and newer spellings is reflected in the book of Ezekiel, where both spellings occur, and in Kings, where a few instances of the longer later spelling are to be found. In both cases the preponderance is in favor of the old spelling, so these books in their original form probably belong to the last period of the old spelling and the early part of the transition (i.e., the early part of the exile).

3) The period of late spelling dominance is reflected especially in the Chronicler's work (1 and 2 Chronicles — Ezra-Nehemiah).[13] Every example has the new spelling: the transition is now complete, and the longer spelling has displaced the older one. The longer spelling is also found in the Song of Songs. While we might have expected the older spelling in view of the association with Solomon, the newer spelling does not surprise us particularly, since it is widely believed that in its present form the book is a late postexilic compilation (perhaps from the Persian period).[14] Had the name occurred in the title or heading we might have expected the older spelling as a conscious archaism, but its presence in the text itself shows that it reflects the same time as the completion of the book.

Now we come to the question of absolute (or relatively absolute) dating. If

12. See, e.g., Campbell 1975: 23-28. Sasson suggests a date in the time of Josiah but ends with a more agnostic view (1975: 249-251). Robert Gordis has well stated the arguments for a later date (1976: 243-46).

13. See Freedman 1961: 436-442.

14. See the cautious formulation of Gordis (1971b: 368-69), as well as the more agnostic report of Pope (1977: 22-33, esp. 27). This is not to deny the antiquity of much of the material — cf. Sekine 1982: 9.

the relative sequence in the chronological order of the books in their canonical form can be established or at least indicated by the orthographic criterion (as illustrated by the name David), is it possible to tie the sequence to objective data from external sources, to dates that can be fixed, at least within certain limits?

We wish to make two preliminary observations, and then proceed to the formulation of a specific theory of dating of the books of the Hebrew Bible:

1) It is to be noted and emphasized that the orthographic shift is developmental or evolutionary, and that the progression is from the shorter defective spelling to the longer fuller spelling. Regardless of other factors (and there are many), in principle the shorter spelling reflects the older tradition, while the longer spelling reflects a development in the system. Broadly speaking, then, the three-letter spelling should point to earlier composition and four-letter spelling should reflect later composition and publication. It is important to point out that at Qumran the later spelling predominates not only in the books of the Bible where the long spelling occurs but in nonbiblical documents, showing that the long spelling was the standard spelling of that period. Furthermore many of the books of the Bible in which the short spelling predominates in MT have the long spelling at Qumran. This is true of the great Isaiah scroll, where in every instance in which MT has *dwd* 1QIsa^{a} has *dwyd.*[15] The shift is especially striking in the case of 4QSam^{a}, in which the long spelling is found, although in MT the short spelling is ubiquitous. It is all the more important to observe that the short spelling prevails in 4QSam^{b}, one of the few Qumran biblical scrolls to preserve the older and original spelling of the name. The general principle established earlier is confirmed by the observation that 4QSam^{b} is one of the oldest manuscripts at Qumrân (around 250 B.C.E.), while 4QSam^{a} is at least a century later.

We can also explain the survival or preservation of the old spelling in such books in MT. Clearly the proto-Massoretes (or scribes or rabbis) made a choice and preferred, where possible, to select older and better manuscripts to establish their text, including orthography. Where the older and shorter spelling could be found, presumably in old manuscripts, it was adopted and the spelling along with the text preserved. The occurrence of the short spelling in various books of the Hebrew Bible can thus be explained and justified. Regarding books of MT in which only the long spelling is found, the conclusion must be that there were no manuscripts of those available or accessible with the shorter spelling. That could result from accident, but it is much more likely that such manuscripts never existed, because when the books were written the longer spelling was official or dominant and had displaced the older, shorter spelling.

2) The development of Hebrew orthography can be traced in the available inscriptional evidence and in the Bible.[16] In general preexilic or First Temple

15. Burrows 1950.

16. The basic pattern was first worked out in Cross-Freedman 1952, which is to be supplemented with the material in Cross-Freedman 1975; Sarfatti (1982: 58-65) has brought the

orthography is characterized by a paucity of medial vowel letters, although their use is attested as early as the 8th century (final vowel letters were introduced in the 9th century and were used regularly from that time on). Typically *waw* was used for medial long *û* (e.g., *'ārûr* spelled *'rwr*), while *yodh* was used for medial long *î* (e.g., *zîp,* spelled *zyp,* or *'îš,* spelled *'yš;* in the Arad ostraca hiphil forms occasionally include *yodh* to indicate the characteristic long *î* of that conjugation, e.g., *hbqyd* for *hibqîd,* an unusual form, but there is no question about the use of *yodh* as a vowel letter for long *î*). The use is sporadic, and becomes more frequent in the later preexilic inscriptions. We can say that medial vowel letters were introduced in Hebrew inscriptions probably in the 8th century, and that their use increased but was still sporadic at the end of the 7th century.

Developments in Hebrew during and after the exile are a little harder to trace, but it is reasonable to argue that the use of internal vowels increased so that by the 3rd century B.C.E. there was consistent and regular use of such *matres lectionis* for all so-called pure long medial vowels. By analysis of the few Hebrew inscriptions we have along with judicious use of the more extensive repertoire of other West Semitic inscriptions, including Aramaic and Ammonite materials for the 6th and 5th centuries, we conclude that the process in Hebrew was probably complete by the beginning of the 5th century (i.e., around 500 B.C.E.), even though decisive evidence (from the earliest Dead Sea Scrolls) is not available in substantial quantity until the 3rd century B.C.E. The conclusion would be that the general and regular use of medial vowel letters was firmly established by the end of the 6th century, i.e., with the advent of the Second Temple period. The transition period during which internal vowel letters were used irregularly but with increasing frequency occupies most of the 6th century, roughly the period of the exile or the period between the destruction of the First Temple and the building or dedication of the Second Temple (587/6-516/5).

Summarizing, we may now describe the development in the spelling of the name David as reflected in the Bible as follows:

1) From earliest times until the end of the 7th century B.C.E. the original three-letter spelling *(dwd)* was used consistently and probably without exception.

2) Occasional use of the four-letter spelling occurs in the transition period (6th century), and this phenomenon is reflected in the mixed spelling of the name in books such as Kings and Ezekiel.

3) Consistent use of the four-letter spelling is characteristic of the Second

---

discussion up to date. The linguistic basis of the development of Hebrew orthography is treated in O'Connor 1983. The major new source of data was the work of the late Yohanan Aharoni at Arad. My preliminary treatment of the first Arad texts published (Freedman 1969 [See above, Chapter 6]) has been overtaken by the full edition (Aharoni 1975; cf. Rainey 1977 and, in English, Aharoni 1981); there are rough surveys of the orthographic patterns in Aharoni 1981: 142; and Parunak 1978; cf. also Sarfatti's essay.

Temple period. Beginning with the book of Zechariah and continuing with the Chronicler's work, the evidence is both uniform and unanimous in support of the longer spelling.

Then, if we may be so bold, we may suggest how the history and distribution of the two spellings of the name David point toward or offer support for a proposal (already presented on other grounds) about the composition, publication, and authorization of various books of the Hebrew Bible.

The viewpoint propounded here is that the books of the Hebrew Bible which contain the name of David reflect, in the predominant spelling of each book, the period during which they were compiled and formally published. Thus the books containing the three-letter spelling would be assigned to the First Temple period, the books with the four-letter spelling to the Second Temple period, and those with mixed spelling to the transitional period between the two others. Inevitably this is a rather crude division made with an imprecise tool, and we must reckon with other factors which could and probably did affect the outcome. But allowing for all possible sources and elements of contamination, there remains a remarkable correlation between the spelling practice involved and the generally accepted dating of the books of the Bible, which provides support both for the methods used and for the principles proposed in this paper.

Thus we would say that the Primary History (Genesis-2 Kings) is predominantly a product of the First Temple period, a contention made first on other grounds and now supported by the overwhelming preponderance of the three-letter spelling of the name David. Since, however, it is certain that the whole work in its present form could not have been produced before the thirty-seventh year of the exile of King Jehoiachin (*ca.* 561/60 B.C.E.), we are not surprised at the occurrence of a few instances of the longer spelling; out of many hundreds of instances of the name, there are three with the longer spelling. In its final and present form the work is a product of the exilic transitional period.

Correspondingly, the Chronicler's work, in which the four-letter spelling is uniform and without exception, must be, as it undoubtedly is, a product of the Second Temple period (earliest possible date toward the end of the 5th century).

Turning to the Latter Prophets, we note that the books of Isaiah and Jeremiah have the older spelling of the name throughout. With respect to Jeremiah we might have expected a few examples of the four-letter spelling, since the book is a product of the 6th century at the earliest and may in some parts be somewhat later (although I fail to find anything in it that brings us past the Neo-Babylonian era). Since we posit that during the latter part of the 7th century and early part of the 6th the older spelling predominated, we conclude that that spelling was preserved throughout the book by design. The same would be true of the book of Isaiah; that the three-letter spelling would be preserved in First Isaiah seems reasonable, since some such book, ending with chs. 36–39 (attached to chs. 1–33), seems to have been compiled about the same time as Jeremiah. The extension of the same spelling to Second Isaiah (55:3), when the normative spelling had already shifted to the four-letter variant, can be explained as a result of the desire for uniformity in single books, and possibly the effect of traditional patterns on writing which was deliberately designed to be part of a canonical anthology.

The book of Ezekiel, as already noted, exhibits the mixed orthography that should be characteristic of the middle exilic period. The proposed date of publication of Ezekiel (*ca.* 570-567 B.C.E., on the basis of the content and dates in the book itself) would fit well with the mixed picture of spelling: even the ratio of three to one in favor of the older spelling would reflect the period before the return from exile and compare well with the roughly contemporary work, the Primary History.

When we come to the Book of the Twelve Minor Prophets, the picture changes dramatically, but understandably. Since the book as a whole could not have been compiled before the latest individual prophetic works were written, it has to be assigned to the Second Temple period (not earlier than 518 B.C.E. and perhaps "as much as half a century later").[17] Such an analysis is supported by the uniform four-letter spelling of the name David throughout the whole work. The bulk of the instances occur in Second (or Third) Zechariah, and the correlation of date and spelling is exact and exactly what we have come to expect. In fact, the data in the book of Zechariah provide us with compelling evidence for the official adoption of the four-letter spelling in authoritative religious works. The examples of the longer spelling in Amos and Hosea, while technically anachronistic (although we have no external evidence for the publication of these prophetic works before the exile), nevertheless reflect the date of publication of the composite work. No doubt the principle of spelling consistency within a given scroll is at work here as well, if we assume that in earlier editions of Hosea and Amos the older spelling of the name David was used.

Turning to other books of the Bible in which the name David occurs (the *Ketubim*), we may comment briefly.

1) *Psalms.* The name occurs frequently, mostly in titles and extended headings, but also in the body of various psalms. The spelling is consistently with three letters. Even if we apply the principle of consistency, it is clear that the prevailing orthography of the name derives from manuscripts in which that spelling was used, and which therefore reflects a preexilic or early exilic setting. By contrast, the Psalms scroll from Cave 11 of Qumran uses the four-letter spelling regularly.[18] We would therefore assign the Psalter, with its conservative spelling in MT, in its essential content and orientation to the First Temple period.

2) *Proverbs.* The name occurs only once, in the heading, with the three-letter spelling. If the latter points in any direction, it suggests that the book of Proverbs was compiled in the First Temple period. Certainly that is not the majority view among

17. The hypothesis of earlier editions of the "Minor Prophets" is discussed in Andersen-Freedman 1980: 40-52, 143-49.

18. Sanders 1965.

scholars, but it is not an impossible notion. The origins of the book are rooted in the royal court (just as the Psalms come from First Temple practice) and much of the contents must go back to the same source. An association with the "men of Hezekiah" is not unlikely, so the spelling may accurately reflect an authentic tradition. Since it is in the heading only, we must exercise some reserve, especially in view of the fact that all the headings with the name of David use the same spelling. Since the books in question are attributed to David or Solomon, we might expect the older traditional spelling to be used, regardless of the actual date of composition. Such an argument, however, should not be pressed unduly because in later periods scribes had no hesitation in using the longer spelling for many prominent biblical names, whether they were copying biblical manuscripts or others.

3) *Ruth.* The name occurs several times toward the end of the book, and in every case the name is spelled with three letters. The spelling supports the view, mentioned earlier, that Ruth is a product of the classical period of Hebrew literature, i.e., the time of the First Temple.

4) *Song of Songs.* There is a single instance of the name David in this book. It is spelled with four letters, which points us to the Second Temple period for compilation and publication. Since the name occurs in the body of the poem (4:4) rather than the heading, we can regard it as a reliable indicator of the date of the book in its present form. It is possible that in a more original form, or in terms of various components, it should be dated to the First Temple period, and that the spelling of the name was revised in the course of transmission. We would argue, however, that if the scribes had known of or could gain access to a manuscript with the older spelling they would have preserved that spelling in their copies. We conclude that no such manuscript existed.

5) *Ecclesiastes.* Here, as in the case of Proverbs, the name David occurs only once, and that is in the heading. As is true of all headings and titles, the spelling here is with three letters. If it points in any direction, it suggests a First Temple date for the book. Here we should probably demur, since most scholars hold firmly to a postexilic date for the work. We can explain the archaizing spelling of the title in terms of the general practice in all the books with such headings, as well as the possible influence of the attribution of the book to Solomon the son of David. It must be admitted, however, that the evidence, a single example in a given book, is hardly sufficient to form a basis for judgment.

The books of the Bible, broadly speaking with respect to their compilation and publication (in the form in which they have been preserved), can be dated according to the spelling of the name David, which is preserved in the Massoretic Text. Again, generally speaking, those with the three-letter spelling belong to the First Temple period (or not later than the first part of the 6th century), while those with the four-letter spelling may be assigned to the Second Temple period. Those which have a mixed spelling may be assigned to the transitional period between the other two, or roughly the middle part of the 6th century.

Bibliography

Aharoni, Y.

1975 *Kĕtūbōt ʿĂrād [Arad Inscriptions].* Jerusalem: Bialik Institute and Israel Exploration Society.

1981 *Arad Inscriptions.* Jerusalem: Israel Exploration Society.

Andersen, F. I.

1970 "Orthography in Repetitive Parallelism." *JBL* 89:343-44.

———, and D. N. Freedman

1980 *Hosea.* AB 24. Garden City: Doubleday.

Baillet, M.

1962 "Textes des grottes 2Q, 3Q, 6Q, 7Q à 10Q." In M. Baillet, et al., *Les 'Petites Grottes' de Qumrân.* DJD 3. Oxford: Clarendon, 45-164.

1982 *Qumrân Grotte 4 III (4Q 482-4Q 520).* DJD 7. Oxford: Clarendon.

Barthélemy, D.

1955 "Textes bibliques." In D. Barthelemy and J. T. Milik, *Qumrân Cave I.* DJD 1. Oxford: Clarendon, 49-76.

Baumgartner, W., et al.

1967 *Hebräisches und aramäisches Lexikon zum Alten Testament,* I. Leiden: Brill.

Bonk, H.

1891. "Über die Verwendbarkeit der doppelfonnigen mit *yohô* und *yô* anlautenden Namen." *ZAW* 11:125-156.

Brown, F., S. R. Driver, and C. A. Briggs

1907 *A Hebrew and English Lexicon of the Old Testament.* Oxford: Clarendon.

Burrows, M., ed.

1950 *The Dead Sea Scrolls of St. Mark's Monastery.* New Haven: ASOR.

Campbell, E. F.

1975 *Ruth.* AB 7. Garden City: Doubleday.

Carlson, A., and H. Ringgren

1978 "דָּוִד *dāvidh.*" *TDOT* 3, ed. G. J. Botterweck and H. Ringgren. Grand Rapids: Wm. B. Eerdmans, 157-169.

Cross, F. M., and D. N. Freedman

1952 *Early Hebrew Orthography.* AOS 36. New Haven: American Oriental Society, repr. 1981.

1975 *Studies in Ancient Yahwistic Poetry.* SBL Dissertation 21. Missoula: Scholars Press. [Repr. Grand Rapids: Wm. B. Eerdmans, 1995]

Fitzmyer, J. A.

1971 "The Son of David Tradition." *Essays on the Semitic Background of the New Testament.* London: G. Chapman, 126.

Freedman, D. N.

1961 "The Chronicler's Purpose." *CBQ* 23:436-442. [See Volume I, Chapter 10]

1962 "The Massoretic Text and the Qumrân Scrolls: A Study in Orthography." *Textus* 2:87-102. [See above, Chapter 3]

1963 "The Law and the Prophets." *VTS* 9:250-265. [See Volume I, Chapter 14]

1969 "The Orthography of the Arad Ostraca." *IEJ* 19:52-56. [See above, Chapter 6]

1976 "Canon of the OT." *IDB,* Supplementary Volume. Nashville: Abingdon, 130-36. [See Volume I, Chapter 27]

1983 "The Earliest Bible." *The Bible and Its Traditions.* Michigan Quarterly Review 22/3:167-175. [See Volume I, Chapter 32]

———, and M. O'Connor

1986 "יהוה *YHWH.*" *TDOT,* 5. Grand Rapids: Wm. B. Eerdmans, 500-521.

Gordis, R.

1971a *The Biblical Text in the Making: A Study of the Kethibh-Qere.* 2nd ed. New York: Ktav, repr. 1981. (Originally published in 1937)

1971b *Poets, Prophets and Sages: Essays in Biblical Interpretation.* Bloomington, Ind.: Indiana University Press.

1976 *The Word and the Book: Studies in Biblical Language and Literature.* New York: Ktav.

Horgan, M. P.

1979 *Pesharim: Qumrân Interpretations of Biblical Books.* CBQ Monograph 8. Washington: Catholic Biblical Association.

McCarter, P. K.

1980 *I Samuel.* AB 8. Garden City: Doubleday.

Mandelkern, S.

1947 *Veteris Testamenti Concordantiae Hebraicae atque Chaldaicae,* 7th ed. F. Margolin and M. Goshen-Gottstein. Tel Aviv: Schocken.

O'Connor, M. P.

1983 "Writing Systems, Native Speaker Analyses, and the Earliest Stages of Northwest Semitic Orthography." *The Word of the Lord Shall Go Forth,* ed. C. L. Meyers and M. P. O'Connor. Winona Lake: Eisenbrauns, 439-465.

Parunak, H. V. D.
1978 "The Orthography of the Arad Ostraca." *BASOR* 230:25-31.

Pope, M. H.
1979 *Song of Songs.* AB 7C. Garden City: Doubleday.

Rainey, A. F.
1981 "Three Additional Hebrew Ostraca from Tel Arad." *Tel Aviv* 4 (1977): 97-104. Repr. in Aharoni 1981, 122-25.

Sanders, J. A.
1965 *The Psalms Scroll of Qumrân Cave 11 (11QPs*[a]*).* DJD 4. Oxford: Clarendon.

Sarfatti, G. B.
1982 "Hebrew Inscriptions of the First Temple Period — A Survey and Some Linguistic Comments." *Maarav* 3:55-83.

Sasson, J. M.
1979 *Ruth: A New Translation with a Philological Commentary and a Formalist-Folklorist Interpretation.* Baltimore: Johns Hopkins University Press.

Sekine, M.
1982 "Lyric Literature in the Davidic-Solomonic Period in the Light of the History of Israelite Literature." *Studies in the Period of David and Solomon,* ed. T. Ishida. Winona Lake: Eisenbrauns, 1-11.

Ulrich. E. C.
1979 "4QSam[c]: A Fragmentary Manuscript of 2 Samuel 14–15 from the Scribe of the *Serek Hayyaḥad* (1QS)." *BASOR* 325:1-25.

12

Orthography (of the Paleo-Hebrew Leviticus Scroll)

Orthography: Preexilic

Over twenty-five years ago, F. M. Cross and D. N. Freedman published their study of the origin and development of Northwest Semitic orthographic practices in the Iron Age. Their monograph *Early Hebrew Orthography,* published in 1952 as one of two joint dissertations, was born out of the observations of W. F. Albright, who had recognized the need for orthographic controls for assessing and dating the earliest strata of Hebrew poetry preserved in the Pentateuch.[1] By a systematic analysis of representative Northwest Semitic epigraphic materials, Cross and Freedman were able to isolate and describe the orthographic systems employed by different Northwest Semitic dialects from the twelfth to sixth centuries B.C.E. as well as trace these spelling principles as they evolved in the various dialects.

The orthographic rules derived from Cross and Freedman's investigation have been tested by the hoard of new epigraphic finds recovered in the past quarter-century from the Near East. No forthcoming evidence has seriously undermined the fundamental principles proposed in their initial studies, and only some modification has been necessary (Cross-Freedman 1975: 182-83; Freedman 1969 [See above, Chapter 6]; Jackson 1983).[2]

1. See Albright 1944, where he restores the biblical text of the Balaam oracles and determines the antiquity of their composition by applying principles of historical orthography; also, see his treatment of the Psalm of Habakkuk (1950). Cross and Freedman followed their orthographic study with an analysis of ancient biblical poetry in a second dissertation submitted in 1950 (recently republished in 1975) where they employed their newly derived principles; also see their published papers conveniently cited under "Recent Bibliography" (1975: 189-191).

2. Those who offer serious objections are most recently Zevit 1980; Bange 1971; and Tsevat 1960. Even Zevit remarks at one point: "Epigraphic material discovered since the publi-

For our purposes, we will focus only on the state of Judahite orthography at the time of the exile (outlined in section *A* below); a survey of developments in the Judahite language from the time of the exile (section *B*) will follow. Against this background, the postexilic spellings which emerged in Judahite from the fifth to first centuries B.C.E. will be surveyed. The phonological-morphological changes in Judahite language and the spellings reflecting them, distinguished by certain traits, will be grouped according to type. From this endeavor we will be able to examine the spellings occurring in 11QpaleoLev and their place in the development of orthographic practices in the last half of the first millennium B.C.E.

Judahite Orthography at the Time of the Exile

Resources

The preexilic sources for Judahite orthography consist of the epigraphic materials, ranging in date from the eighth to sixth centuries B.C.E. and coming from many sites throughout Judah (e.g., Jerusalem, Arad, Yavneh-Yam, Wadi Murabbaʿat, and Kuntillet ʿAjrud). The inscriptional materials yield reliable orthographic information for characterizing the developmental pattern of preexilic orthography.

Development

The development of preexilic Hebrew spellings follows a chronologically unilinear pattern with the exception of the dialectical divergence of Judahite and Israelite regarding the status of diphthongs *aw* and *ay.* In Israelite the vowels *ô* and *ê,* derived from diphthongal contractions, were not represented in the orthography and therefore the northern orthography did not preserve historical spellings (e.g., *qēṣ* < *qayṣ; yēn* < *yayn*). Judahite, on the other hand, did not experience diphthongal contraction before the 5th century B.C.E., and the dialectal differences in pronunciation between north and south were reflected in their divergent spellings: e.g., ייו *(yayn)* in the south against יו *(yēn),* and מות *(mawt)* against מת *(mōt)* in Israelite.

The state of Judahite orthography at the time of the exile (A) is summarized below; outline numbers (e.g., *A1b*) are listed for each feature and the outline number will be referred to later in the chapter for cross-reference purposes.

---

cation of *EHO* [*Early Hebrew Orthography*] has tended to conform to the general pattern of development described by the authors, but not to their timetable" (1980: 2).

Fitzmyer (1979: 64-66) finds that Aramaic texts recovered subsequently to the dissertation of Cross and Freedman have supported their proposal for the origin and development of the use of vowel letters. He notes that modification is necessary, but "the evidence, such as it is, merely confirms the basic thrust of their original contention" (1979: 65).

A1. Major phonological-positional phenomena

A1a. Long vowels in final position always written (no later than 800 B.C.E.).[3]

sound	*graph*
î (high front vowel)	י
û (high back vowel)	ו
ê, â, ô (non-high vowels)	ה

A1b. Long, high vowels in medial position erratically written (*ca.* 700 B.C.E.)[4]

sound	*graph*
î	י
û	ו

A1c. Long mid and low vowels in medial position not written

A1d. Short vowels in any position not written

A2. Minor morphological phenomena

3rd masc. possessive suffix for sg. nouns

sound[5]	*graph*
uncertain	ה

3. For a recent discussion of the vowel system of the Northwest Semitic dialects with respect to the vowel triangle (analyzed into high and non-high groups, with the latter further analyzed into high and back groups) and also a phonological explanation for the first developmental stage (i.e., representing final, long vowels) away from a purely consonantal system, see O'Connor 1983: 448-49. The vowel triangle below reflects the vowel system of the Northwest Semitic languages.

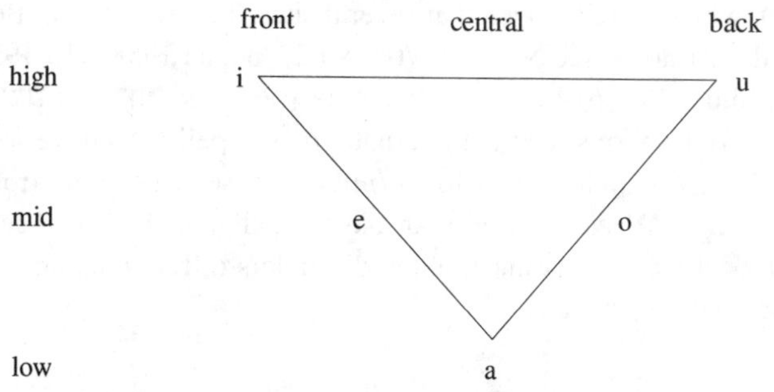

4. Recent epigraphic studies at Arad have shown that the high front vowel *(î)* is erratically written in the hiphil stem and for radical *î* (Aharoni 1970: 20-21; 1975; Parunak 1978: 30). The high back vowel *(ū)* is also sporadically written: written in the qal passive stem in the Royal Steward Inscription *('arûr)* and absent in personal and geographical names at Arad (cf. זכר for biblical *zakkūr;* Aharoni 1975 and Parunak 1978: 30).

5. Reconstructions by Cross and Freedman (1952: 54-55) and Harris (1939: 26, 55) indicate that *he* was pronounced *ô* < *aw* < *ahū* and *waw* pronounced *aw* < *ayū* < *ayhū* (Cross-Freedman 1952: 54, 68) or *aw* < *ahū* (Harris 1939: 25).

3rd masc. possessive suffix for pl. nouns

sound[5]	*graph*
uncertain	ו

A3. Dynamics of preexilic system

1. vowel length
2. vowel height
3. parsimony

Preexilic spellings are based on the priority of vowel length (only long vowels marked) over height with parsimony in the use of *matres lectionis.*[6]

Hebrew Orthography: Postexilic

Developments in the Judahite Language

Resources

The sources which provide information about the orthographic practices of the postexilic period include both inscriptional and manuscript materials. The inscriptional data (seals, stamps, coins, and ossuaries) coming from the 5th to 1st centuries B.C.E. are numerous but of limited usefulness for orthographic history, since seals and stamps with personal and place names often preserve historical spellings. Those of particular interest are the stamps ירשלם, יהוד/יהד, and מוצה/מצה, which were recovered at several sites, Tell-en-Naṣbeh, Bethany, Ramat Raḥel, and Jerusalem (see Naveh 1970: 58-62; Avigad 1958: 113-19; 1974: 52-58; 1976; Garbini 1962: 61-68). The defective spellings, יהד and מצה, are archaic survivals of older forms, and the alternate, *plene* spellings utilize *waw* as a *mater lectionis:* ו for *û (yahûd)* and ו for *ô (môṣâ);* these seals come from the Persian period. The ירשלם seals preserve an old, preexilic spelling of "Jerusalem," but the dating of these seals is uncertain and scholars differ, assigning dates from the 4th to 2nd centuries B.C.E.[7]

5. See note 5 on p. 125.

6. O'Connor (1983: 449) shows that parsimony explains why among the extrabuccal glides (', *h*), the *h* was preferred for the non-high vowels.

7. For a discussion of the seals, see Avigad 1974: 55. The spelling ירשלם, pronounced *y^{e}rūšālēm,* is attested in the 6th century B.C.E., inscriptions of Khirbet Beit Lei (Naveh 1963; Cross 1970); the full spelling ירושלים occurs in manuscripts at Qumran. The two spellings probably have independent and parallel histories; the MT reflects both traditions: the customary spelling in the Kethib is ירושלם and the vocalization in the Qere has *y^{e}rûšālayim.*

In general we may expect manuscripts and inscriptions to differ in orthography since each group had its traditional pattern and development. Such a division is not uncommon in cultures in which there is a strong inscriptional tradition, such as in Latin epigraphic materials in which the orthography is quite different from what is found in literary Latin (Sandys 1919: 189-195; Rushforth 1930: ix-x). In any case, the epigraphic evidence is of little help, so we will concentrate on the manuscripts.

The massive corpus of manuscript materials from Qumran dates to the lower end of our spectrum (2nd century B.C.E.-1st century C.E. for the most part) and is contemporary with the Essene settlement at Qumran. Among the manuscripts of Cave 4 three have been identified as antedating the settlement, probably brought there by the initial settlers of this desert community. The texts (4QEx^{f}, 4QSam^{b}, 4QJer^{a}) date from the mid to late 3rd century and thereby supplement our evidence for postexilic spelling practices from the end of the Persian period to the first Christian century. From such a corpus we are able to discern the development characteristic of postexilic spellings as well as to identify four orthographic types.

Development

Unlike the preexilic system, the development of postexilic spelling has no simple chronological basis; various types of orthography coexist side by side between 300 B.C.E. and 100 C.E. Therefore, we will examine the *typological* range of orthographies; the chronological orientation of the types will be indicated, but until the full range of the Qumran biblical material is available no absolute correlation is possible.

Before isolating and identifying the postexilic spelling patterns and testing them against selected exemplars, we will state below the major phonological and morphological changes in Judahite which occurred from the time of the exilic period.

B1. Major phonological and morphological developments

- *B1a.* Diphthongs *ay* and *aw* reduce to *ê* and *ô* (*ca.* 4th century B.C.E.).[8]
- *B1b.* Collapse of sounds *ō* < *aw* and *ō* < *ā́*
- *B1c.* Lengthening and lowering of *u* to *ō* (*ca.* 2nd century B.C.E.)
- *B1d.* Collapse of *ô* < *aw*, *ō* < *ā́*, and *ō* < *u*

8. The date for this change is according to the reconstruction of the comparative linguistic forms of our earliest Qumran manuscripts (Freedman 1962); see our discussion below under "Conservative Spelling."

B2. Minor morphological developments

B2a. (1) 3rd masc. sg. possessive suffix with sg. nouns[9]

sound	*graph*
ô	ו

(2) 3rd masc. sg. possessive suffix with pl. nouns[10]

sound	*graph*
āw	יו

B2b. Long forms of suffixes develop[11]

(1) 2nd masc sg. possessive כה-

(2) 2nd masc. sg. perfect קטלתה

(3) 2nd masc. pl. possessive כמה-

(4) 2nd masc. pl. perfect קטלתמה

(5) 3rd masc. pl. possessive ־המה/מה-

(6) 3rd fem. pl. possessive ־הנה

B2c. Long forms of 3rd masc./fem. sg. pronouns

(1) 3rd masc. הואה *hû'ā(h)*

(2) 3rd fem. היאה *hî'ā(h)*

B3. Collapse of the pharyngeal-laryngeal system

B3a. Laryngeal collapse *(aleph/he)*

(1) *aleph* used in vowel notation in medial position

(2) *aleph/he* interchange

B3b. Pharyngeal collapse *(ayin/ḥeth)*

(1) proto-*ayin*/proto-*aleph* collapse (e.g., אל/על)

(2) *ḥeth/he* interchange

(3) *ḥeth/ayin* interchange

9. *Contra* preexilic practice (see above, *A2*). MT vocalizes as *ô.* Two explanations for this development are possible, with the quiescence of final *he:* (1) *ahu > au > aw > ô;* (2) *uhu > uh > u > ō.*

10. *Contra* preexilic practice (see above, *A2*). MT vocalizes *āw.* The orthography conforms to the pronunciation found in the northern dialect *(êw),* but the vocalization derives from Judahite pronunciation. Two traditions then overlap in the MT: the spelling is Israelite *(ayhū > êhū > êw);* the pronunciation is Judahite *(ayhū > ayū > āw).* See Cross-Freedman 1952: 68-69.

11. The longer forms developed slowly and became paradigmatic in the Hasmonean spellings. Nos. 1 and 2 are taken to be older since they are preserved in the MT; the other forms eventually faded out of use. Cross and Freedman (1952: 65-68) posit that both the short and long forms coexisted in preexilic times; the longer form was common in literary works and the shorter in common, informal material. The longer spelling *kâ* is attested in a poetic inscription (אלהיכה) of the 6th century B.C.E. at Khirbet Beit Lei (Cross 1970: 301, 305 n.11), and the shorter form is well attested in Judahite (Parunak 1978: 27). Apparently the shorter spellings predominated in those texts chosen for the Rabbinic Bible and the longer forms were lost except where frozen in the MT. We might compare the longer form *tiqṭōlnâ* of the 2nd and 3rd fem. pl. which persevered in the orthography of the MT, though there are several places in the Hebrew Bible where the shorter tradition is evidenced (Cross-Freedman 1952: 67).

Survey of Qumran Manuscripts

Most of the major manuscripts from Qumran have been published, but only a small portion of the 4Q biblical material is available (for instance, we have no complete publication of any paleo-Hebrew text, only a small fragment of 4QpaleoEx*m*; see Skehan 1955); we will examine eight representative texts ranging in date from about 300 B.C.E. to 50 C.E., which were recovered from the caves of major manuscript discoveries (1Q, 4Q, and 11Q). In some cases our survey is restricted by the fragmentary nature of the material or the absence of a full publication; for those reasons, we cannot offer an exhaustive or definitive statement but only a provisional one which will enable us to evaluate the significance of the spelling pattern found in 11QpaleoLev.

Some of the available data of these eight manuscripts will be surveyed with regard to types, distinguished by comparison to the state of Judahite orthography at the time of the exile (see above, *A1, A2, A3*) and the developments in Judahite from the time of the exile (see above, *B1, B2, B3*). We will not consider personal or geographical names in our survey since they preserve historical or otherwise fixed spellings.

We do not expect to find complete regularity for spellings in these materials for several reasons: (1) the scribal observance or neglect of the general practice of avoiding double *plene* spellings in words; (2) differences in pronunciation reflected in various spellings [e.g., a defective spelling due to the unaccented long medial vowel, ברחיו/(בריחיו) and הושעני/(הושיעני) (see Freedman 1962: 96)]; and (3) the scribal tendency to harmonize different spelling traditions, and to substitute contemporary for older or archaic orthography.

Manuscript	Information Available	Date	Source of Date
4QSam*b*	description	275-250	E. Ulrich/F. M. Cross (personal communication) Cross 1975; 1963: 120-21.
4QJer*a*	description	225-175	Ulrich/Cross (above)
4QEx*f*	description	275-250	Ulrich/Cross (above) also Cross 1961: 166
4QpaleoEx*m*	partial publication	200-175	Skehan 1979: 809
4QSam*a*	description	100-50	Ulrich 1978: 10
4QSam*c*	full publication	100-75	Ulrich 1979: 3
11QPs*a*	full publication	50 C.E.	Sanders 1965
1QIsa*a*	full publication	125-100	Cross 1961: 138

Types of Orthography

Conservative orthography

The archaic spelling pattern found among the Qumran texts (represented by 4QSam*b*) more closely parallels the state of Judahite orthography at the time of the exile than the other postexilic systems and is antecedent to the later developmental changes in Judahite phonology and morphology (cf. *B*, except *B2a*).

Proto-Rabbinic orthography[12]

The orthographic system which is the parent of the Rabbinic spelling pattern adopted for the authoritative texts of the 1st century C.E. occurs at Qumran and reflects the extension of *A1* and the changes *B1ab, B2a.* As we shall learn below, the spellings of 11QpaleoLev closely reflect this type of postexilic orthography; a redundant exemplar of this kind is 4QJer*a*. This type does not follow precisely what we find in the MT, however, because the proto-Rabbinic texts underwent systematic spelling revisions in the 1st century C.E. and the leveling of standard forms throughout the biblical text.

Proto-Samaritan orthography

The parent of the SP spelling system, with its extensive use of internal *matres lectionis,* dominates the spelling patterns of the Cave 4 manuscripts and is found among most paleo-Hebrew texts and many texts in square characters. We will examine three exemplars: 4QEx*f*, 4QpaleoEx*m*, and 4QSam*a*. Like the MT, the Samaritan biblical manuscripts underwent spelling revision (e.g., the reduction of *matres lectionis;* the adoption of the shorter spellings היא/הוא) and were modified toward a more conservative pattern (but still more fully written than the MT).

12. Cross (1979: 39) calls for the adoption of the term "proto-Rabbinic" to displace the designation "proto-Massoretic," previously used by him and by most scholars today, to identify the pre-Christian textual family adopted by the rabbis. Cross is speaking of text-type here and not orthography, but the term is appropriate for orthography too, particularly since we are discussing spellings, i.e., the consonantal text, standardized in the Rabbinic period and not the pointing appended later by the Massoretic schools of the late-1st millennium C.E.

Hasmonean orthography[13]

The exemplars of this system reflect the linguistic tradition of Judahite during the 2nd-1st centuries B.C.E. This type has all the morphological changes of *B1, B2, B3* and presents a new system by the reevaluation of *A3:* vowel height is given priority over vowel length as indicated by its lavish use of *matres lectionis* for long vowels in any position and short vowels sporadically. For those spellings in which short vowels are said to be written, we are working roughly within the boundaries of the phonological tradition of the MT. It is possible that in the later stages of the Hasmonean system phonological phenomena existed, about which we know little, that are linguistically unrelated to the MT and, correspondingly, words took on different shapes. Such an interpretation may seem intuitively correct, but it underestimates the new priority given to vowel height which is aptly demonstrated in the spellings of the Hasmonean type.

Our exemplars are three biblical texts which span the most prolific period of scribal activity at Qumran: 4QSam[c], 11QPs[a], and 1QIsa[a]. As Purvis (1968: 67-69) has shown, the SP has common linguistic features with the Hasmonean tradition; its spelling has been influenced by this type too, primarily in the proliferation of internal *matres lectionis* and also the behavior of the pharyngeal-laryngeal system *(B3).*

Conservative Spelling

Exemplar: 4QSam[b]

A1, A2, A3 apply, but with these exceptions; (1) *A1b:* high, long vowels always written; (2) *A2:* ו and יו attested (see *B2a* below).

B1 has not occurred (all spellings henceforth in parenthesis are of the MT). Evidence:

diphthong *aw*

למועד	20:35	*lamaw'id*
היום	20:27, 34	*yawm*
מקום	20:27, 37; 21:3	*maqawm*

13. While none of our designations for these postexilic spelling systems is adequate, the Hasmonean title is least satisfying since it has chronological implications and we want to focus solely upon typological ones at this juncture; typologically, we are describing a system which presents a reevaluation of the dynamics of the preexilic system and by doing so distinguishes it from all other systems.

vocalic *ō* < *ā́*

בבאם	16:6	*(b^{e}bô'ām)*
קמתו	16:7	*(qômātô)*
החלן	19:12	*(haḥallôn)*
טהר	20:26	*(ṭāhôr)*

B2a applies. Evidence:

מראשתיו	19:6	*(m^{e}ra'^{a}šōtayw)*
עמו	20:35	*(ʿimmô)*

B2bc, B3 do not apply.

By reconstructing the comparative linguistic forms of the earliest Qumran texts (4QEx^{f}, 4QSam^{b}, and 4QJer^{a}), Freedman (1962: 98) discovered that the spellings of 4QSam^{b} indicate that the reduction of *aw* > *ô* had not occurred. 4QSam^{b} spellings consistently differentiate diphthongal *aw* > *ô* by the writing of etymologic *waw* from vocalic *ō* < *ā́* where the *waw* is absent, implying thereby a difference in pronunciation. If contraction had occurred, we would expect two concurrent phenomena: (1) occasional loss of original diphthongal *waw* and *yodh,* since the pronunciation would be indistinguishable from vocalic *ō* and *ē,* which are not written in the orthography; (2) the extension of *waw* and *yodh* to vowels *ō* and *ē,* which are not derived from *aw* and *ay,* since the sounds would have fallen together. In 4QEx^{f} and 4QJer^{a} (see below), the distinction becomes blurred and *waw* is increasingly used as a vowel letter for vocalic *ō* < *ā́,* suggesting that contraction of *aw* > *ô* has taken place.

For the remaining exemplars surveyed below, *A1a* applies and change *B2a* has occurred; these features are characteristic of all forms of postexilic spellings and will not be discussed again. For the most part, *A1b* does not apply since the writing of *î/û* became more consistent in postexilic spellings; of course, there are occasional exceptions where defective spellings occur. All spellings in our lists which appear in parentheses are those of the MT.

Proto-Rabbinic Spelling

Exemplar: 4QJer^{a}

A1, A3 apply. *A1b* occurs by the erratic use of medial י for the high front vowel *(ī):*

הושעני	17:14	*(hôšîʿēnî)*
תבאהו	13:1	*(t^{e}bīʾēhû)*
שנית	13:3	*(šēnît)*
אמרים	17:15	*(ʾōm^{e}rîm)*

A1c does not apply (see *B1b* below).
B1a has occurred:

הושעני	17:14	*(hôšîʾēnî)*
מוצא	17:16	*(môṣāʾ)*
יום	17:17, 18	*(yôm)*

B1b in process; evidence: *waw* extended to ō < ắ

qal inf. abs.:

(1) נתוש	12:17	*(nātôš)*
(2) הלוך	17:19	*(hālōk)*
(3) שמוע	17:24	*(šāmōaʿ)*

qal inf. constr.:

(4) עשות	17:24	*(ʿ^{a}śôt)*

II-*waw* verb:

(5) יבשו	17:13	*(yēbōšû)*
(6) אבושה	17:18	*(ʾēbōšâ)*

qal. act. ptcp.:

(7) קרא	17:11	*(qōrēʾ)*
(8) עזביך	17:13	*(ʿōz^{e}be[y]kā)*
(9) אמרים	17:15	*(ʾōm^{e}rîm)*
(10) רדפי	17:18	*(rōd^{e}pay)*
(11) ישבי	17:20	*(yōš^{e}bê)*
(12) רכבים	17:25	*(rōk^{e}bîm)*

I *waw* noun:

(13) מוצא	17:16	*(môṣāʾ)*

II *waw* noun:

(14) קול	9:9	*(qôl)*
(15) מעוף	9:9	*(mēʿôp)*
(16) מעון	9:10	*(m^{e}ʿôn)*

qaṭāl noun:

(17) [ה]אזור	13:1 + 3 times	*(hāʾēzôr)*

qāṭal noun:

(18) עולם	10:10	*(ʿôlām)*
(19) נכח	17:16	*(nōkaḥ)*

$\bar{a}$n suffix:

(20) [מרא]שן	17:12	*(mērî'šôn)*
(21) שברון	17:18	*(šibbārôn)*
(22) בלשון	18:18	*(ballāšôn)*
(23) אביון	22:16	*('ebyôn)*

$\bar{a}$t suffix:

(24) נאות	9:9	*(n^{e}'ôt)*
(25) נתיבות	18:15	*(nĕtîbôt)*
(26) מדות	22:14	*(middôt)*

particle:

(27) לוא	12:4	*(lō')*
(28) לו	17:16, 23; 18:15	*(lō')*
(29) הלוא	22:15	*(h^{a}lô')*

B1cd do not apply.

B2cd, B3 do not apply with the exception of *B3a:* וארפה/ *(w^{e}'ērāpē')* 17:14, in which ה appears as a *mater lectionis* for *ē*. This phenomenon occurs often in Hasmonean spellings (see discussion below); its appearance here is probably a scribal slip and reflects the scribe's linguistic tradition.

The linguistic change in *B1ab* has taken place and *waw* is written for *ō* < *ā́* in a wide range of categories; the pattern of spellings closely follows the MT, particularly in the defective spellings of the qal act. ptcp. The fuller writing of the qal inf. abs. (nos. 1-3) may be a device to distinguish it from the more common participial forms since it is rarer.

The spelling of לוא/לא (nos. 28-30) becomes important for comparative purposes; no. 30 agrees with the MT, whose spelling of this word generally is defective. 4QJer^{a} has the full spelling on one occasion (no. 28), a spelling which is common in the proto-Samaritan and Hasmonean types; the shorter writing is attested twice (no. 29). The full spelling again indicates the scribe's linguistic tradition. Also, the spelling מבחור / *(mibḥar)* at 22:7 is a morphological exception and indicates a reshaping of the form.

Proto-Samaritan Spelling

Exemplar 4QEx^{f}

A1, A3 apply with exceptions; *A1b:* long, high vowels generally written [but בריחיו/ *(b^{e}rîḥāyw)* 40:18]. *A1c* does not apply (see below).

A2 does not apply.

B1ab have occurred; evidence: *waw* extended to new categories for vocalic *ō* < *ắ*. I *waw* noun:

(1) עולם	40:15	*(ʿôlām)*

II *waw* nouns:

(2) לדורותם	40:15	*(l^{e}dōrōtām)*
(3) הארון	40:20, 21	*(hāʾārōn)*

qaṭāl noun:

(4) צפון	40:22	*(ṣāpōnâ)*

*ā*t* suffixes:

(5) כהנות (pl.)	40:15	*(likhunnat)* (sg.)
(6) לדורותם	40:15	*(l^{e}dōrōtām)*

**ān* suffix:

(7) הדאשן	40:17	*(hārīʾšôn)*

nota accusativi:

(8) אותו	40:9, 13	*(ʾōtô)*
(9) אותם	40:14-16	*(ʾōtām)*
(10) אתו	40:11	*(ʾōtô)*

B1cd, 2bc do not apply.

B3b may find supporting evidence in 4QEx^{f} through the על/אל interchange:

אל הארון	40:20	*(ʿal hāʾārōn)*
אל הארון	40:21	*(ʿal ʾ^{a}rôn)*
אל ירך	40:24	*(ʿal yerek)*

The changes in *B1ab* are in process; diphthongal *ô* < *aw* and *ô* < *ắ* have collapsed and as a result the morphological developments resulting in *ō* are growing obscure. Unfortunately, there are no examples of participles, infinitives, or I-*waw*/II-*waw* finite verbs for comparative purposes. The writing of *ô* for the *nota accusativi* in nos. 8, 9 (but not always; cf. no. 10) indicates that the use of the *waw* for the vocalic *ō* < *ắ* is being extended. The spellings of 4QEx^{f} are fuller than 4QJer^{a} and present a *transitional* style of orthography which moves in the direction of the *plene* spellings to be examined in the following examples.

Those forms in 4QEx^{f} without *waw* are probably survivals of historical spellings: e.g., אהרן (40:12, 13); משה (40:16, 19, 21, 23) and no. 7 above. The spellings הכפרת/ *(hakkappōret)* 40:20 and פרכת/ *(pārōket)* 40:21, 22, without *waw,* probably are normal since the ō is derived from *u.* The writing with *waw* of ō < *u* has not occurred *(B1c).*

Exemplar: 4QpaleoEx*m*

A1, A3 apply; exception *A1c* (see below).

B1ab apply. Evidence:

I-*aleph* verb:

(1) ויאומר	32:26	*(wayyō'mer)*

qal inf.:

(2) ענות	32:18	*(ʿanôt* or *ʿannôt)*

nouns:

(3) גדול	32:10	*(gādôl)*
(4) בזרוע	32:12	absent
(5) לעולם	32:13	*(leʿōlām)*
(6) קול	32:17, 18	*(qôl)*

pronoun:

(7) זאות	(cf. Skehan 1955: 183)	*(zō't)*

nota accusativi:

(8) אותך	32:10	*('ôtekā)*
(9) אותם	32:12	*('ōtām)*

B1cd, B2bc, B3 do not apply.

Nos. 1 and 7 suggest that *aleph* has quiesced and the retention of *aleph* is a historical spelling.

The fragment available from 4QpaleoEx*m* (Skehan 1955) is a small sample, but its spellings show the sporadic introduction of *waw* for vocalic ō < *á* in additional categories. This type of orthography is a moderate form of the usage for *waw* which appears in spellings of the Hasmonean type (Cross 1966: 90).

Spellings ממוחרת/ *(mimāḥarat)* 32:30 and והרוגו/ *(wehirgû)* 32:17 are morphologically reanalyzed forms and therefore exceptional (cf. דרושו of 1QIsa*a* at 1:17).

Exemplar: 4QSam*a*

A1, A3 apply with exceptions; *A1a: aleph* occurs as an *avia lectionis* ("grandmother of reading") after a long vowel already marked by a *mater:* כיא/ *(kî)* 1 Sam. 2:21, 25.[14]

14. For a discussion of the *avia lectionis* and its purpose, see O'Connor (1983: 450).

A1c does not apply (see below).
B1ab apply: Evidence that *waw* is extended to participial forms and pronouns.
qal act. ptcp.:

(1) **היוצא**	1 Sam. 1:23	absent
(2) **שומע**	1 Sam. 2:23, 24	*(šōmēaʿ)*
(3) **הולך**	2 Sam. 3:1	*(hōlēk)*

inf. constr.:

(4) **להפתותך**	2 Sam. 3:25	*(l^{e}pattōt^{e}kā)*
(5) **ולעשות**	2 Sam. 7:23	*(w^{e}laʿ^{a}śôt)*

inf. abs.:

(6) **חטוא**	1 Sam. 2:25	absent

II *waw* nouns:

(7) **טובות**	1 Sam. 2:24	*(ṭôbâ)*
(8) **קול**	1 Sam. 2:25	*(l^{e}qôl)*

qaṭāl nouns:

(9) **קדוש**	1 Sam. 2:2	*(qādôš)*
(10) **אפוד**	1 Sam. 2:28	*(’ēpôd)*
(11) **אלוהי**	1 Sam. 6:3	*(’elōhê)*

pronoun:

(12) **אנוכי**	2 Sam. 11:5	*(’ānōkî)*

nota accusativi:

(13) **אותו**	1 Sam. 1:24	*(’ōtô)*
(14) **אותם**	2 Sam. 12:17	*(’ōtām)*

B1cd beginning; evidence for *ō* < *u* marked by *waw:*
yiqṭōl forms:

(15) **יעבור**	1 Sam. 1:11	absent
(16) **יפולו**	1 Sam. 2:33	absent

inf. constr.:

(17) **לאמור**	1 Sam. 6:2	*(lē’mōr)*

nouns:

(18) **בכול**	1 Sam. 2:32	*(b^{e}kōl)*
(19) **נחושת**	2 Sam. 8:8	*(n^{e}ḥōšet)*

B2bc do not apply.

B3 does not apply with exceptions; *B3a: aleph/he* interchange in עזא/ (*ʿuzzâ*) for "Uzzah" (2 Sam. 6:6), *aleph* marking the final *ā* vowel.

Changes described in *B1cd* appear to be in process; in this regard 4QSam^a has a spelling system that is *transitional,* possessing features which become common in the exemplars of the following type of orthographic system.

The spelling of אנוכי (no. 12) shows an interest in vowel height, a growing priority in the Hasmonean style of spellings. The spelling חודשים/ (*ḥ^{a}dāšîm*) at 1 Sam. 6:1 in 4QSam^a exemplifies another case of an analogical reanalysis.[15]

For summary purposes, the appended chart includes those categories where *ō* < *ā́* (written or not) appears in the above texts; "Y" indicates where the examples occurred and "X" where *no* examples appeared and therefore limited our comparative purposes.

	4QEx^f	4QpaleoEx^m	4QSam^a
I-*aleph* verb	X	Y	X
qal act. ptcp.	X	X	Y
qal inf. abs.	X	X	Y
qal inf. constr.	X	Y	Y
nouns	Y	Y	Y
pronouns	Y	Y	Y
*āt suffixes	Y	X	X
*ān suffixes	Y	X	X
nota accusativi	Y	Y	Y

Hasmonean spelling

Exemplar: 4QSam^c

A1a applies with the exception of *aleph* occurring as an *avia lectionis* after final long vowels:

כיא	2 Sam. 14:22	(*kî*)
ישמניא	2 Sam. 15:4	(*y^{e}śīmēnî*)

A1b applies.

A1c does not apply (see *B1abcd* below).

A1d does not apply; two examples have *waw* marking the short mid-vowel *o:*

קודקדו	2 Sam. 14:25	(*qodq^{o}dô*)

15. Examples from 4QSam^a are gleaned from Ulrich's work (1978), which focuses upon textual studies and is without a treatment of the orthographic system. A systemic study must await the publication of the critical edition.

(scribal error for קודקדו, with first *daleth* omitted)

כול   2 Sam. 15:2   *(kol)*

B1ab apply. *Waw* marking *ô* < *ā́* is extensively used and appears for the negative particle לא.

I *aleph* verb:

(*plene* 9 times)

(1) ויאומר   2 Sam. 14:11   *(wayyō'mer)*

but ויאמר   2 Sam. 14:10   *(wayyō'mer)*

2 Sam. 15:4

II *waw* verb:

(2) ויבוא   2 Sam. 15:13   *(wayyābō')*

qal inf. constr.:

(3) לנגוע   2 Sam. 14:10   *(lāgaʿat)*

nouns:

(4) נכוחים   2 Sam. 15:3   *(n^ekōḥîm)*

(5) ל[אדוני   1 Sam. 25:30, etc.   *(la'dōnî)*

nota accusativi:

(6) אותך   2 Sam. 14:18   *('ōtāk)*

pronoun:

(7) זאות   1 Sam. 25:31   *(zō't)*

כזו[את   2 Sam. 14:13   *(kāzō't)*

particle:

(8) לוא   1 Sam. 25:31   *(lō')*

B1cd in process. Evidence of *waw* for *ô* < *u: yiqṭōl* form:

(1) יסוב   2 Sam. 14:24   *(yissōb)*

qal inf. constr.:

(2) לאמור   2 Sam. 14:32   *(lē'mōr)*

B2b applies. Long suffix form כה attested ten times (Ulrich 1979: 3): e.g., בכה, 2 Sam. 14:10; עבדכה, 2 Sam. 14:20.

B2c applies. Evidence of long forms: הואה, 2 Sam. 14:19; היאה, 2 Sam. 14:27.

B3b is in process; אל/על (2 Sam. 14:30) confusion is attested: אליו, 2 Sam.

15:3 (עליו). The alternate spellings of nos. 1 and 7 indicate the quiescence of *aleph.* Also, the omission of *aleph* in ברם (2 Sam. 15:8), which is corrected in the text, supports that interpretation.

4QSam^{c} has an inconsistent orthography, sometimes defective but usually full. The scribe of 4QSam^{c} shows a tendency to write full spellings; we can see how he attempts to standardize the *plene* forms of אמר (Ulrich 1979: 3). However, three examples of defective spellings occur: שם (2 Sam. 14:7), אלו (2 Sam. 14:30), and עבדכה (2 Sam. 14:31). Also, we note that the long form of the suffix כה predominates. The processes in *B1cd, B2,* and *B3* are underway and the orthographic pattern — which is more fully developed in the next two exemplars — of this type "may be seen blossoming in 4QSam^{c} before our very eyes" (Ulrich 1979: 20).

Exemplar: 11QPs^{a}

A1ab apply: high long vowels generally are written, but there are some exceptions in the hiphil stem: e.g.,

והעבר	136:14	*(w^{e}heʿ^{e}bîr)*
יחשך	139:12	*(yaḥšîk)*
הוצא	142:8	*(hôṣîʾâ)*
יכתרו	142:8	*(yaktīrû)*

A1c does not apply; the long mid-vowel *ē* is written by י: e.g.,

זידים	119:35	*(zēdîm)*
כמיתי	143:3	*(k^{e}mētê)*

For the long mid-vowel *ō,* see below at *B1abcd.*

A1d does not apply; the mid-short vowels *o* and *e* are occasionally written: e.g.,

עוזרנו	124:8	*(ʿezrēnû)*
אוזנכה	130:2	*(ʾozne[y]kā)*
קודשכה	138:2	*(qodš^{e}kā)*
אוכלמה	145:15	*(ʾoklām)*

A3 no longer applies; the dynamics of the old system are obscured by the changes which have occurred in *B1, B2, B3.*

B1abcd apply. Evidence for *ō* < *ā́:* e.g.,

I *aleph* verb:

יואמר	129:1	*(yōʾmer)*

II *waw* verb:

אבוש	119:46	*(ʾēbôš)*
יבוא	121:1	*(yābōʾ)*

qal inf. abs.:		
הלוך	126:6	*(hālôk)*
qal act. ptcp.:		
רודפי	119:157	*(rōd^{e}pay)*
עושה	121:1; 148:8	*(ʿōśeh)*
שומריכה	121:3	*(šōm^{e}rekā)* (sg.)
הבוטחים	125:1	*(habbōṭ^{e}ḥîm)*
nouns:		
אדוני	128:5	*(ʾ^{a}dōnay)*
הרואש	133:2; 141:5	*(hārōʾš)*
והצואן	151:3	
pronoun:		
אנוכי	119:141; 141:10	*(ʾānōkî)*
זואת	145:21	*(zōʾt)*
particle:		
לוא	102:18	*(lōʾ)*
Evidence for *ō* < *u:* e.g.,		
yiqṭōl forms:		
יעמוד	130:3	*(yaʿ^{a}mōd)*
יגמור	138:8	*(yigmōr)*
ימלוך	146:10	*(yimlōk)*
qal imper.:		
זכורה	119:49	*(z^{e}kōr)*
qal inf. constr.:		
לשמור	119:60	*(lišmōr)*
quṭl noun forms:		
חושך	105:28	*(ḥōšek)*
לבוקר	130:6	*(labbōqer)*
קודש	134:2	*(qōdeš)*
B2b applies; e.g.,		
שמכה	109:21	*(š^{e}mekā)*
גערתה	119:21	*(gāʿartā)*
במה	119:93	*(bām)*
יברכה	128:5	*(y^{e}bārekā)*
אוכלמה	145:15	*(ʾoklām)*

B2c applies; הואה occurs once (154:9).

B3a applies; evidence for laryngeal collapse in process: e.g., omission of aleph:

תובד	Sir. 51:10	*tw'bd*
בתרה	Sir. 51:2	*btw'rh*

11QPs[a] has extended the use of *waw* for marking *ô < u;* the *ō* sounds have fallen together. The longer suffixes are in full use now *(B2a).* The laryngeal system is generally stable but evidence points to the beginnings of laryngeal collapse *(B3a),* which will become fully evident in 1QIsa[a].

Exemplar: 1QIsa[a]

A1a applies with the exception of *aleph* occurring for final long vowels *ā* and *ē* due to the processes of *B3* (see examples below).

A1c does not apply; long mid-vowels are written with the addition of the erratic spelling of the mid/low vowels *ē* and *ā.*

sound/graph

ē/y	מית	38:1	*(mēt)*
	ליץ	29:20	*(lēṣ)*
ē/'	נאלכה	2:3	*(nēl^ekā)*
	עואר	43:8	*(ʿiwwēr)*
ē < i/y	היטיב	1:17	*(hêṭêb)*
ā/'	יאתים	1:17, 23	*(yātôm)*

Evidence for the spelling of *ō* is below at *B1abcd.*

A1d does not apply; short vowels are erratically marked.

sound/graph

high	*u/w*	שולחן	65:11	*(šulḥān)*
	i/w	משוסה	42:22	*(m^ešissâ)*
	i/y	רינה	14:7	*(rinnâ)*
mid	*o/w*	בוצרה	34:6; 63:1	*(boṣrâ)*
	e/w	רוגע	54:7, 8	*(regaʿ)*
	e/y	שריצר	37:38	*(śar'eṣer)*

A3 does not apply; the dynamics of the old system are replaced by the new priority of height over length and the proliferation of *matres lectionis.*

B1abcd have occurred. Examples of marking *ō < ā́* and *ô < u* illustrate that the distinction in the sounds has been lost:

I *aleph* verb:

יואמר	1:11, 18	*(yō'mer)*
יאומר	8:1, 3	*(y'ōmer)*

qal inf. abs.:		
אכול	22:13	*(ʾākōl)*
qal act. ptcp.:		
שומע	1:15	*(šōmēaʿ)*
שופטיך	1:26	*(šōpeṭayik)*
suffix **ān:*		
שלמונים	1:23	*(šalmōnîm)*
suffix **āt:*		
תורות	24:5	*(tôrōt)*
nouns:		
צאון/צואן	13:14; 53:6	*(ṣōʾn)*
זרועו	40:10, 11	*(zerōʿô)*
pronoun:		
זאות/זואת	3:6; 19:20	*(zōʾt)*
nota accusativi:		
אותה	1:7 *passim*	*(ʾôtāh)*
particle:		
לוא	*passim*	*(lōʾ)*
ô < u, e.g.,		
yiqṭōl forms:		
ידרוש	8:19	*(yidrōš)*
יעמוד	36:2	*(yaʿamōd)*
qal imper.:		
כתוב	8:1	*(ketōb)*
qal inf. constr.:		
לפקוד	26:21	*(lipqōd)*
quṭl noun forms:		
חודש	1:13	*(ḥōdeš)*
אוהל	38:12	*(ʾōhel)*
בושת	54:4	*(bōšet)*

B2b applies. Evidence:

2 masc. sg. possessive	כה	אפכה	12:1
perfect	תה	אמרתה	6:9
2 masc. pl. possessive	כמה	בושתכמה	41:7
perfect	תמה	שאבתמה	12:3
3 masc. pl. possessive	המה/מה	ארצמה	34:7
3 fem. pl. possessive	הנה	יושביהנה	37:27

B2c applies. Evidence: e.g.,

המה	1:2	*(hēm)*
אתמה	3:14	*('attem)*
הואה	34:17	*(hû')*
היאה	47:10	*(hî')*

B3ab apply. Evidence for pharyngeal-laryngeal collapse (for examples of *aleph* used for medial vowel notation, see above at *A1c*): e.g.,

B3a

ā / א for ה	(1) וגבורא	36:5	*(ûgᵉbûrâ)*
	(2) והיא	8:14	*(wᵉhayâ)*
ā / א after ה	(3) עליהא	34:11	*('ālêhā)*
	(4) ומאציליהא	41:9	*(ûmē'ᵃṣîle[y]hā)*
ē/i for ה	(5) שדא	66:3	*(śᵃde[h])*
א after *î*	(6) פיא	40:5	*(pî)*
	(7) אניא	66:9	*('ānî)*
א after *ô*	(8) בוא	37:7, 10	*(bô)*
	(9) עמוא	63:11	*('ammô)*
aleph omitted	(10) משריך	3:12	*(mᵉ'aššere[y]kā)*
	(11) זות	14:26	*(zō't)*

B3b (for exhaustive listing, see Kutscher, 305-7)

א/ע	(12) עלוהי	2:2	*('ēlāyw)*
	(13) על	6:9 *passim*	*('el)*
ayin omitted	(14) יבור	28:15	*(Kethib: 'br)* (y absent) *(Qere: ya'ᵃbor)*
ה/ח	(15) אשיתחו	5:6	*('ᵃšîtēhû)*
	(16) הגורח	3:24	*(ḥᵃgôrâ)*
ח/ע	(17) שעיס	37:30	*(šāḥîs)*
ה/א	(18) אסר	5:5	*(hāsēr)*

The quiescence of *aleph* made it available for vowel notation; *aleph* is used in 1QIsa[a] for marking final *ā/ē* replacing the *he* (nos. 1, 2, 5) and after *he (â)* especially for the 3rd fem. sg. suffix (nos. 3, 4). The use of *aleph (avia lectionis)* after final long vowels *(î/ô)* which are themselves already marked (nos. 6, 7, 8, 9) is a feature distinguishing this type from preexilic spellings or other postexilic systems (see examples above). *Aleph* also occurs for medial vowel notation (יאתום).[16]

The collapse of the pharyngeal-laryngeal system produced the omission, addition, and interchange of the pharyngeals-laryngeals as illustrated in nos. 10-19. Earlier, we saw the beginnings of this phenomenon in 4QSam^c and 11QPs^a, but in 1QIsa^a the spellings show that the collapse has occurred.

Historical Summary

We have reviewed four postexilic spelling systems and surveyed exemplars of each type with regard to *typological* development only; now we want to add a historical framework for the origins of these systems. No unilinear development occurred, as in the preexilic system, and therefore it is not surprising to see later exemplars reflecting older orthographic systems.

Conservative spelling

The practice preserved in 4QSam^b illustrates the earliest orthographic pattern of the postexilic period; its tradition is closest to preexilic systems and antedates the Qumran texts exhibiting the contraction of diphthongs *ay* and *aw* and the collapse of the $\bar{o}$ sounds *(B1abcd).* It probably preserves 5th to 4th century B.C.E. practice, as Freedman has shown (1962: 102); it cannot be earlier since, though close, it is different from 6th century B.C.E. practice *(A2).* The absence of more exemplars of this type at Qumran is probably due to the age of these manuscripts. These older texts were probably master scrolls which were copied by scribes who, in the process, updated the orthography and afterward disposed of the aging manuscripts. In 4QSam^c we have evidence of this activity; we can see how the scribe changes (in his copy) the orthography of his *Vorlage* (Ulrich 1979: 20).

Proto-Rabbinic spelling

The origins of this system are probably in the 3rd century B.C.E.; the exemplar 4QJer^a has an erratic, more conservative usage of the new spelling feature (*waw* for $\hat{o} < \acute{\bar{a}}$) which fully develops in later systems. The spellings of 4QJer^a are close, though not exact in every detail, to the spelling tendencies of the MT and illustrate the beginnings of this system during this period. The identification of 4QJer^a as a congener of the proto-Rabbinic system is not determined solely by comparing its spellings with those of the MT. By this procedure we would find that the spellings of 4QJer^a (or any text of this type) is not glaringly different from what we have in

16. The use of *aleph* as a pure vowel letter in medial position *($\bar{a}$),* following consonantal *waw* or *yodh,* occurs in 1QapGen (Freedman-Ritterspach 1967).

the extant SP since the latter underwent systematic revisions toward the proto-Rabbinic texts. Rather, the comparison must begin with the spelling systems evidenced within the Qumran texts themselves prior to the revisional activities of the 1st-2nd centuries C.E. Among the texts, then, different spelling patterns are clearly discerned, although some texts seem to be transitional, and the roots of what became the MT and SP systems are identified. The spelling traditions of the MT and SP, in spite of having been modified, still bear the earmarks of their origins as we have found them attested in the Qumran exemplars.

The rabbis adopted a system somewhere between the conservative, archaic type of 4QSam*b* and those which have a proliferation of vowel letters. The spelling pattern was chosen and revised for the official biblical texts no later than the late 1st century C.E., as shown, for example, by the Murabbaʿat manuscripts (from the period between the First and Second Jewish Revolts); these pentateuchal texts are the same in spelling and text-type as the Massoretic tradition (Cross 1964: 287-88).

Proto-Samaritan spelling

The orthographic pattern illustrated in our three exemplars (4QEx*f*, 4QpaleoEx*m*, 4QSam*a*) emerged in the 3rd century B.C.E.; it is distinguished primarily by its preference for the fuller use of internal *matres lectionis (yodh/waw)* for long vowels and the occasionally erratic behavior of the pharyngeal-laryngeal system.

Cross indicates that many manuscripts from Cave 4 appear in this orthography (1966: 89-90); in particular, many pentateuchal texts have this moderately full orthography which is reflected in the SP (1972: 309-10). The spelling system was adopted and modified for the writing of the SP by the sectarian community; the SP spellings were revised in the 1st century C.E. toward the more conservative Rabbinic texts, but still retained their essentially fuller tendencies. The spellings of the SP tend to be more consistent than those in the MT.

Hasmonean spelling

This final spelling type reflects the linguistic tradition of the 2nd to 1st century B.C.E. and is a new system which has reevaluated the preexilic pattern, giving priority of vowel height over vowel length for its basis. Long vowels are noted in any position and short vowels are sporadically written by the graphs ו/י/א. The collapse of the pharyngeal-laryngeal system made *aleph* available for vowel writing and it appears erratically for final and medial *ā/ē* vowels. The Hasmonean spellings are marked by laryngeal interchange, omission, and addition. The pronunciation of a final long vowel for possessive suffixes and verbal afformatives became paradigmatic and we have this in the spellings of the long forms of the second and third person (masc. and fem.) suffixes. There are no long forms for the first person since they already end in a long vowel *(î/nû)*.

As Purvis has shown (1968: 66, 68), the SP spellings have been influenced by the linguistic tradition of the Hasmonean period and its spellings; this linkage is evidenced primarily by the fuller use of internal ו/י for vowel notation and the behavior of laryngeals.[17] Also, like Hasmonean exemplars, the *aleph* is occasionally used as a medial *mater* for *ā* (e.g., קאמה/*qāmâ,* Gen 37:7) in the SP (more so than in the MT).

Mansoor (1958: 46-49) notes several common linguistic features between the SP and the Hasmonean texts: (1) elision of quiescent *aleph;* (2) elision of consonantal laryngeals; (3) omission of *he* in the infinitive construct with *lamedh;* and (4) the commutation among laryngeals. There are, however, significant spelling differences, e.g., the absence of the long suffixes and pronoun forms in the SP orthographic tradition.

Both the conservative spelling system (illustrated by 4QSam^b) and the Hasmonean type fell out of use, though some features of the latter are preserved in the SP; the spellings of the proto-Rabbinic and proto-Samaritan types were adopted and perpetuated by the Jewish and Samaritan socio-religious communities of the 1st century C.E. for the writing of their scriptures.

11QpaleoLev Orthography

The Leviticus readings of orthographic interest are listed and categorized below. Where the MT spelling differs in any way, it appears in parentheses beside the scroll's spelling; this does not include textual variants in the MT. The location of the spelling in the scroll is noted by fragment or column and line number. Where a spelling occurs more than twice, the first occasion is listed and followed by the siglum "+". Letters within brackets [ ] are supplied for lacunae, but the spellings

17. Talmon (1952: 147, n.1) and Purvis (1968: 52-59) demonstrate the unreliability of von Gall's edition for evaluating spellings of the SP; von Gall has spelling reconstructions on the basis of what he expects them to be and not what they are in the manuscripts he consulted. He does not always include in his apparatus spelling variants which are fuller. Working from Ṣadaqa's edition (1964) of a single manuscript, Purvis found in general that the Samaritan manuscripts "show preference" for the fuller orthography (1968: 54). His computation of *waw* as a *mater* in the oldest portion of the *'Abiša'* scroll gave these results for Deuteronomy: in about 270 cases the *mater* appears in the scroll where it is absent in the MT and in only 72 cases does the fuller spelling occur in the MT where the SP is defective; of these latter instances, in 21 occurrences another significant SP manuscript has the fuller spelling. Likewise, Gesenius found for Genesis that there are about 200 or more occurrences of *waw* as a *mater* than in MT (cf. Gerleman 1948: 13). My own counting of the Leviticus text, based on the edition of Ṣadaqa, yielded similar results: there are 200 more instances of *waw* as a *mater* in SP than in MT, and about 75 more occurrences of *yodh.* MT has the longer spelling with *waw* on roughly 35 occasions and *yodh* about 15 times when the SP does not.

listed below are based on sure readings (at least for the point in question) and not supplied ones. Elements affixed to a word which are in parentheses indicate that the element does not always appear with the word whose spelling is under consideration: e.g., (ה)זה; זה occurs with and without the definite article. Following the spelling in the scroll is the biblical reference.

Spellings

I. Final Vowels Consistently Marked
  A. *Waw*
    1. *Waw* marks *û*
      a. Verbal suffixes
        (1) nominative (3rd masc. pl.)
          B:2 וי]קרבו (10:5)
          H:7 יביאו (17:5)
          H:8 יזבחו (17:5)
          I:1 תירשו (20:24)
          I:5 נעשו (18:30)
          I:8 תהיו (19:2)
          I:9 תיראו (19:3)
          I:9 תפנו (19:4)
          J:5 יעלמו (20:4)
          K:3 יקחו (21:7)
          1:3 תקרבו (22:22) *(taqrîbû)*
          1:6, 2:5 תעשו (22:23; 23:25)
          1:7 ירצו (22:25)
          3:5 וינצו (24:10)
          3:6 ויביאו (24:11)
          4:5 יחשבו (25:31)
          5:4 תלכו (26:21)
          5:4 תבו (26:21) *(tōʾbû)*
          5:6 ונשמו (26:22)
          5:6-7 תוסרו (26:23)
          6:2 יגאלנו (27:13)
        (2) accusative (3rd masc. sg.)
          D:1 וראהו (13:3)
          J:3 יר]גמהו (20:2)
          3:1-2 ו]א[כלהו (24:9)
          3:7 ויניחו (22:12)
      b. Possessive suffix (3rd masc. sg.)
        6:7-8 שדהו (27:17)
    2. *Waw* marks *ô*

a. Possessive suffix (3rd masc. sg.)
E:3 בקרחתו (13:42)
G:6 טמאתו (15:3)
G:7; 4:9 בו (15:3; 25:35)
G:9 במשכבו (15:5)
H:7 עמו (17:4)
I:8; 3:7 אמו (19:3; 24:11)
J:4 מזרעו (20:3)
J:7 ב]משפחו (20:5) *(ûbᵉmišpaḥtô)*
K:8; 4:8 י]דו (21:10; 25:35)
3:2 + לו (24:9)
3:6 + אתו (24:11)
4:2, 3 גאלתו (25:29)
4:2 ממכרו (25:29)
4:7 אחזתו (25:33)
6:2 חמישיתו (27:13) *(ḥāmîšītô)*
6:3 ביתו (27:14)
6:5 אחזתו (27:16)
6:6 זרעו (27:16)
b. Objective suffix (3rd masc. sg.)
K:4 וק]דשתו (21:8)
6:3 והעריכו (27:14)
c. Conjunction
C:7 + או (11:32)

B. *Yodh*
1. *Yodh* marks *î*
a. 1st singular pronoun
(1) independent
I:6 + אני (18:30)
(2) verbal nominative suffix
J:3, 5 והכרתי (20:3, 4)
5:2 ושברתי (26:19)
5:2 ונתתי (26:19)
5:4 ויספתי (26:21)
5:5 + ושלחתי (26:22)
5:7 והכיתי (26:24)
5:8 והביאתי (26:25) *(wᵉhēbē'tî)*
(3) nominal possessive suffix
I:5 משמרתי (18:30)
J:4 מקדשי (20:3)
5:4, 7 עמי (26:21, 23)
5:4, 7 לי (26:21, 23)

5:9 בשברי (26:26)

b. Nominal endings

(1) gentilics

3:4 מצרי (24:10)

3:5 הישראלי (24:10)

(2) ordinal number

2:3-4 השבעי (23:23, 27) *(hašš^{e}bîʿî)*

c. Other nouns

3:7 דברי (24:11)

5:4, 7 קרי (26:21, 24)

d. Particle

I:5 לבלתי (18:30)

2. *Yodh* marks *ê* < *ay*

H:1 + בני (16:34)

H:5 + לפני (17:4)

I:2 אנשי (18:27)

3:2 מאשי (24:9)

4:4 + (ו)בתי (25:31)

4:5 + (ו)ערי (25:32)

C. *He*

1. *He* marks *ē* > *(ē)*

a. Verb and participle (III-*he* type)

I:4 יעשה (18:29)

K:4 + יהיה (21:8)

1:5 ירצה (22:23)

4:3, 5, 6 תהיה (25:21, 31, 32)

4:4 לקנה (25:30)

b. Noun

H:4-5 לן[מ]חנה (17:3)

H:8 ה]שדה (17:5)

2:5, 8 אשה (23:25, 27)

3:5 במחנה (24:10)

3:7; 5:9 (ל)מטה (24:11; 26:26)

c. Pronoun

F:2 + (וה)זה (14:16)

I:1; 5:1 (ה)אלה (18:27; 27:18)

d. Personal names

A:2 + יהוה

I:7 + משה (19:1)

e. Particle

E:4 והנה (13:43)

2. *He* marks *â*

a. Verb
H:1 צוה (6:34)
1:8 והיה (22:27)
b. Feminine marker
(1) verb
4:2 והיתה (25:29)
4:8 ומטה (25:35)
5:5 ושכלה (26:22)
5:5-6 והכריתה (26:22)
5:6 והמעיטה (26:22)
(2) participle
K:3 גרושה (21:7)
(3) nouns
A:3 העלה (4:25)
B:4 העדה (10:6)
F:8 לת]נופה (14:21)
K:3; 3:4 (ו)אשה (21:7; 24:10)
2:4 תרועה (23:25)
2:5 עבדה (23:25)
2:8 מלאכה (23:28)
4:2 חומה (25:29)
(4) adjective
4:3 תמימה (25:30)
4:5 גאלה (25:31)
5:3 כנחה (26:19) *(kanne̱ḥušâ)*
5:4-5 מכה (26:21)
c. Piel inf.
5:1 לי]סרה (26:18)

II. Internal Long Vowels Marked
A. *Waw*
1. *Waw* marks *û*
a. Verb (II *waw* type)
4:8 ימוכ (25:35)
6:4, 7 יקום (27:14, 17)
b. Nominative verbal suffix
H:8 והביאום (17:5) *(wehebîʾūm)*
c. Passive stem
J:2 יומת (20:2)
K:3 גרושה (21:7)
K:7 יו]צק (21:10)
1:4 שרו]ע (22:23)

1:5 ומעוכ (22:24)
1:5 וכתות (22:24)
d. Noun
F:8 לת]נופה (14:21)
G:2 + מחוצ (14:53)
1:2, 7 מומ (22:21, 25)
2:4 תרועה (23:25)
5:3 יבולה (26:20)
e. Afformative *û*
4:4 לצמיתות (25:30) (*laṣṣ^{e}mîtût)*
f. Pronoun
D:1+ הוא (13:3)

2. *Waw* marks *ô* < *aw*
a. Nouns from II *yodh/waw* verbs
B:5 + מועד (10:7)
4:2 מושב (25:29)
4:9 ותושב (25:35)
b. Others
D:2 העור (13:4)
D:3 + ביומ (13:5)
H:4; 1:4 ו)שור) (17:3; 22:23)
3:2 במקומ (?) (24:9) [**māqawm* > *māqôm;* cf. also below at 3b(1)]
3:4; 4:7 בתוכ (24:10; 25:33)

3. *Waw* marks *ô* < *ā́*
a. Verbal stem
K:9 יבוא (21:11) *(yābō')*
b. Noun stems
(1) *qaṭāl*
E:2 ט]הור (13:40)
K:3; 3:2 קדוש (21:7; 24:9) *(qādōš)*
K:7 הגדול (21:10)
2:6 בעשור (23:27)
3:2 במקומ (?) (24:9) (**māqā́m* > *māqôm;* cf. above also at 2b)
(2) *qāṭal*
3:3 + עול (24:9)
4:2 + חומה (25:29) *(ḥōmâ)*
(3) *qiṭāl*
4:3 מלאות (25:30) *(m^{e}lō't)*
(4) *qāṭil*
4:1 + בי]ובל (25:28) *(bayyōbēl),* always *plene*
c. From **ān*
1:2 ל]רצונ (22:21)

2:4 שבתונ (23:24)
2:4 זכרונ (23:24)
5:2 גאונ (26:19)

d. From **āt*
I:4 התעבות (18:29) *(hattôʿēbôt)*
5 הת]עבות (18:30) *(hattôʿēbôt)*
I:4 העשות (18:30) *(hāʿōśōt)*
I:9 שבתותי (19:3) *(šabbetōtay)*
K:9 נפשות (21:11) *(napšōt)*
6:8 הנתרות (27:17) *(hannōtārōt)*

e. Qal act. ptcp.
C:1 הולכ (11:27)

f. Qal inf. abs. (II *waw* type)
J:2 מות (20:2)

g. Qal inf. constr. (II *waw*/III *yodh* types)
C:6 במותמ (11:31) *(bemōtām)*
I:5 עשות (18:30)
J:7; K:5 לזנות (20:4; 21:9)

h. Other
6:1, 3 טוב (27:12, 14)

B. *Yodh*

1. *Yodh* marks *ê < i*
5:7 והכיתי (26:24)
5:8 והביאתי (26:25) *(wehēbēʾtî)*

2. *Yodh* marks *î*

a. In the hiphil stem
H:5 לה]קריב (17:4)
H:7 יביאו (17:5)
I:2 תקיא (18:28)
J:6 המית (20:4)
K:2 + מקריב(ימ) (21:6)
3:7 ויניחו (24:12)
5:5 והכריתה (26:22)
5:6 והמעיטה (26:22)
6:3 + יקדיש (27:14) *(yaqdīš)* but *(yaqdîš)* 27:16, 17
6:3 והעריהו (27:14)
6:4 יעריכ (27:14)
6:4, 9 (ה)מקדיש (27:15, 19)

b. Radical *î*
G:2 + (ל)עיר (14:53)
H:3 + איש (17:3)
5:3 לריק (26:20)

c. Noun stems
(1) *qaṭīl*
5:8 ברית (26:25)
(2) *qaṭīlīt*
6:2 חמישיתו (27:13) *(ḥamîšītô)*
6:5 חמשית (27:15) *(ḥamîšît)*
6:9 חמשית (27:19) *(ḥamīšît)*
(3) *qaṭīlut*
4:4 לצמיתות (25:30)
(4) *taqṭīl*
4:9 ותרבית (25:36)
d. Pronoun
4:7, 8 היא (25:23, 24) (היא *ktb;* 25:33)
e. Adjective
4:3 תמימה (25:30)
f. Particle
4:5 סביב (25:31)
g. Masculine plural suffix
D:4; 4:2 ימים (13:5; 25:29)
H:7 זבחים (17:5)
I:8; 3:2 קדשים (19:2; 24:9)
J:8 הידענים (20:6)
K:2 מקריבים (21:6)
K:8 הבגדים (21:10)
1:7 משה]תים (22:25)
2:7 הכפרים (23:27)
4:4 החצרים (25:31)
6:6 בחמשים (27:16)
6:8 השנים (27:18)
h. With possessive suffix
4:8, 9 אחיכ (25:35, 36)
i. Personal names
B:3 ולאית]מר (10:6)
3:7 שלמית (24:11)
3. *Yodh* marks *ê* < *ay*
a. Possessive suffix *(yw)*
G:8 עליו (15:4)
J:7 אחריו (20:5)
4:4 לדרתיו (25:30)
b. Prepositions with suffixes
I:3 לפניכם (18:28)
2:9; 5:4 עליכם (23:28; 26:21)

c. Plural nouns with suffixes
H:7 זב]היהמ (17:5) *(zibḥêhem)*
I:8 + אלהיכמ (19:2)
K:1 אל]היהמ (21:6)
K:4; 4:9 אלהיכ(מ) (21:8; 25:36)
2:7 נפשתיכמ (23:27)
4:7-8 עריהמ (25:34)
5:2 חטתיכמ (26:18) *(ḥaṭṭōʾtêkem)*
5:2 שמיכמ (26:19)
5:6 דרכיכמ (26:22)
d. Nouns in construct
D:2 מראיה (13:4) *(marʾehā)*
H:3 + בית(מ) (17:3)
6:3, 4 ביתו (27:14, 15)
e. Particles
4:4; 5:1 אינ (25:31; 26:17)
6:1, 3 בינ (27:12, 14)

III. Unmarked Internal Long Vowels
A. *ā* (consistently unmarked)
C:2, etc. בנבלתמ (11:27)
B. *ē*
1. *ē* < *ay*
G:4; H:3 אלהמ (15:2; 17:2) *(ʾalêhem)*
K:7 מאחו (21:10) *(mēʾeḥāyw)*
2. *ē* < *i*
B:4, etc. העדה (10:6)
C. *ī*
1. In the hiphil stem
J:5 יעלמו (20:4) *(yaʿlîmû)*
K:5 מקדשמ (21:9)
1:3 תקרבו (22:22) *(taqrîbû)*
2. Ordinal number
2:3-4, 6 השבעי (23:24, 27) *(haššᵉbîʿî)*
D. *ō*
1. *ō* < *u*
a. Qal prefixing conj.
3:5 ויקב (24:11)
4:2 ימכר (25:29)
b. Qal inf. constr.
K:8 ללבש (21:10)
2:3 לאמר (23:23)

3:8 לפרש (24:12)
c. *quṭl* segolates
B:5; H:5 אהל (10:7; 17:4)
C:4 החלד (11:29)
C:5 והחמט (11:30)
F:3 אזנ (14:17)
2:4, 5 (ל)חדש (23:24, 25)
2:4 + קדש (23:24)
6:6 חמר (27:16)
2. *ō* < *ā́*
a. Qal prefixing conj.
5:4 תבו (26:21) *(tō'bû)*
b. Qal inf. abs.
6:2 גאל (27:13)
c. Qal act. ptcp.
D:7 + כהנ (13:8)
H:7 זבחימ (17:5)
4:4 לקנה (25:30)
5:1 רדפ (26:17)
5:8 נקמת (26:25)
5:9 איב (26:25) *('ôyēb)*
d. Noun stems
(1) *qaṭāl*
I:8; K:4 קדש(ימ) (19:2; 21:8) *(qādôš,* 21:8)
I:8 + אלהיכמ/אלהיהמ/אלהיכ (19:3)
(2) *qiṭāl*
2:5 עבדה (23:25)
6:6 שערימ (27:16)
(3) *qaṭṭāl*
5:2 + חט(א)תיכמ (26:18)
e. Suffixes with *ā*
(1) **ān*
J:8 הידענימ (20:6)
(2) **āt*
2:7 נפשתיכמ (23:27)
4:4 לדרתיו (25:30)
f. Accusative marker
I:3; 6:1 אתה (18:28; 27:12)
J:3 + את[ו] (20:3)
g. Personal names
H:2 אהרנ (17:2)
I:7 משה (19:1)

J:2, 4 למלכ (20:2, 3)
h. Particle
I:2 + (ו)לא (28:18)
3. *ô* < *aw*
G:6 בזב[ו] (15:3)
I:4 + התעבות (18:28) *(hattô'ēbôt)*
6:8 הנתרות (27:18) *(hannôtārōt)*

IV. Consonantal Remarks
A. Elision of *aleph*
4:9 וירת (25:36) *(w^e^yārē'tā)*
5:2, 5 חטתיכם (26:18, 21) *(ḥaṭṭo'têkem)*
5:4 תבו (26:21) *(tō'bû)*
B. Elision of *ḥeth* and *resh*
4:6 אזתמ (25:32) *('aḥuzzatām)*
4:7 מגש (25:34) *(migraš)*
C. Confusion of *he* and *ḥeth*
H:7 זב[היהמ (17:5) *(zibḥêhem)*
D. Elision of *šin*
5:3 כנחה *(kanne^ḥušâ)*

11QpaleoLev and the Proto-Rabbinic Orthographic System

A study of the spellings in 11QpaleoLev leads us to conclude that its orthographic system reflects the MT protòtype and is representative of the same orthographic tradition chosen by the rabbis for the official text of the Jewish Pentateuch. The distribution of vowel letters in 11QpaleoLev is similar to that of 4QJer[a], our proto-Rabbinic exemplar, and is unlike the fuller orthographies reflected in the proto-Samaritan and Hasmonean exemplars.

The spellings of 11QpaleoLev are remarkably close to those of the MT, and the few that vary are limited to insignificant details or to the slips of the scribe who from time to time betrays his own linguistic tradition. The problem with defining "MT-type spellings" is the apparent inconsistency of spellings throughout the Hebrew Bible which defies — at least at this point in our knowledge — definitive explanations for its irregular patterns of *plene* and defective spellings.[18] Regardless of the direction in which the use of *matres lectionis* was moving with regard to the fixation of the biblical texts — toward the *plene,* the defective, or the alternation of both — once the text was fixed, the spellings were in a "mixed status quo" never to be leveled through

18. E.g., note this fourfold spelling: *b^e^tūlōt* (Lam. 5:11); *b^e^tûlōt* (Lam. 2:10); *b^e^tūlôt* (Zech. 9:17); and *b^e^tûlôt* (Isa. 23:4) (Weinberg 1975: 462).

again (except through vocalization). The mixture and distribution of *matres lectionis* do not conform to any set of consistent, definite rules and, thereby, cannot be rationalized in any clear-cut fashion (Weinberg 1975: 461).

However, the spellings of the MT do not escape tendencies or preferences and "there is nevertheless a discernible pattern in the use of *matres lectionis,* though this has not been clearly analyzed or described scientifically" (Freedman 1962: 90). These tendencies include: (1) the consistent use of *waw* and *yodh* as internal *matres lectionis* representing long vowels *û* and *î;* (2) contracted diphthongs *ô* < *aw* and *ê* < *ay* generally retain *matres lectionis;* (3) the writing of *ō* < *ā́* is inconsistent (e.g., the tendency toward defective spellings for the qal act. ptcp.); (4) the general absence of medial vowel letters for long vowels *ā* and *ē* < *i;* (5) no representation of short vowels; and (6) the succession of two *matres lectionis* in consecutive syllables is avoided (e.g., *n*^{a}*bîʾ,* but *n*^{e}*bīʾîm)* (Weinberg 1975: 462; Freedman 1962: 90-91).

The spellings of 11QpaleoLev indicate the same tendencies and reflect the orthographic practices prevailing in the MT. They are clearly dissociated from the *plene* tradition known in the Hasmonean period and those texts of the proto-Samaritan type.

The use of final vowel letters follows the same pattern as in the proto-Rabbinic type: *waw* occurs for final *û* and *ô* and *yodh* appears for final *î* and *ê. He* is written to indicate *ā* and *ē,* but there is no occasion where *he* represents *ō,* a preexilic practice which occasionally escaped revision in the MT (Sperber 1966: 265; Bauer-Leander 1922: #29k). The 3rd fem. sg. morpheme *(ā)* is marked by *he* and not *aleph* as found among the *plene* texts of the Hasmonean type.

The writing of medial vowel letters is also consistent with MT practices: *waw* occurs for *ô* < *ā́* and *ô* < *aw; yodh* appears for *î, ê* < *ay,* and *ê* < *i* (two occasions). There are some exceptions; the scroll has spellings in which the *ī* of the hiphil stem (יעלמו, 20:4; תקרבו, 22:22) or of other words (השבעי, 23:24, 27) is not represented, but where the MT has the full orthography. In the first two cases, the scribe may have failed to recognize the stem and understood it as piel rather than hiphil. This is unlikely, though, particularly for יעלמו since עלם is not attested in the piel. These spellings are probably orthographic archaisms or survivals.

The distribution of *waw* for *ō* < *ā́* corresponds to the usage of the MT and is close to 4QJer^{a} in its defective spellings, particularly the qal act. ptcp. and the *nota accusativi.* Like the MT, vocalic *ō* < *u* is not represented in its orthography, as in the *qutl* segolates (e.g., אהל / *(ʾōhel),* 10:7; 17:4; קדש / *(qōdeš),* 23:24, 27; 24:9). The divergent spellings of the *ō* sounds indicate the persistence of phonetic distinctions. In the Hasmonean type, these distinctions are lost since the *ō* sounds collapse, and thus the writing of *ō* < *u* occurs.

Medial *û* in an open or tone-long closed syllable is consistently marked by *waw,* except for the defective spelling of הכפרם / *(hakkippūrīm),* which is probably a frozen form.

Short vowels in closed, unaccented syllables, unlike the spellings of the Hasmonean type, are not indicated in the orthography, e.g., גאלתו / *(ge'ullātô),* 25:29; כל / *(kol),* 10:6 *passim;* and קרבנ / *(qorban),* 17:5.

Again, like the MT, historical spellings persist in the scroll, e.g., משה / *(mōšeh),* אהרנ / *('aharōn),* ראש / *(ro'š),* and צאנ / *(ṣō'n).*[19] The retention of etymological *waw* and *yodh* is common too, e.g., במותם / (but MT has *b^{e}mōtām),* 11:31; מות / *(môt),* 20:2; מרשב / *(môšab),* 25:29; בני / *(b^{e}nê),* 16:34; ביתו / *(bêtô),* 27:14, 15.

The short forms for 2nd masc. sg. suffix *kā* and verbal afformative *tā* are regular in the scroll, which is the Massoretic spelling. The longer orthography (כה and תה), characteristic of the *plene* texts of the Hasmonean type, appears occasionally in the MT, suggesting that a mixed orthographic tradition has been preserved in the Hebrew Bible.[20]

We have already noted the correspondence between the treatment of laryngeals in the SP and the Hasmonean tradition, particularly the elision of quiescent *aleph* and the commutation of certain laryngeals. The behavior of laryngeals in 11QpaleoLev indicates that our scribe's own linguistic tradition was that of Hasmonean times. For the most part, he faithfully carries out the more restrictive orthographic tradition he seeks to preserve (proto-Rabbinic), but his own speech or familiarity with contemporary, alternative spellings influences him. On occasion, for example, he drops the quiescent *aleph* in his spellings. His treatment of חטאתה is most instructive since he alternates spellings of the word within the same paragraph. The elision of *aleph* occurs in Lev 26:18 and 26:21, but the historical spelling occurs immediately afterward in Lev 26:24. Also, in this passage we have the elision of *'alep* in תבו (26:21). It is as though the scribe is subconsciously lapsing into his accustomed orthographic habits. We know that the linguistic collapse of the laryngeal-pharyngeal system resulted in three orthographic traits (Goshen-Gottstein 1960: 106): (1) the foremost practice was omission; (2) the addition of a letter [e.g., יאכה / *(yakkeh),* 1QIsa^a/30:31] and (3) the change in place of the vowel letter *waw* with the historical *aleph* [e.g., יואר / *(y^e'ôr)*]. The spellings of חטתה and תבו in our scroll illustrate the first result, but there are none where a letter is added (2). An excellent example of the third trait is attested in our scroll by the *plene* spelling מלאות (Lev. 25:30) for *m^{e}lō't* (MT). The absence of *ḥeth* in אזתמ (25:32) and perhaps *resh* in מגש (25:34) is not due to scribal haplography but the instability of the laryngeal system.[21]

19. The *aleph* is a historical spelling and was not pronounced after the Amarna age: **ra'š > rāš > rōš* and **ṣa'n > ṣān > ṣōn.* Compare 1QIsa^a spelling: צאונ/צונ and ראוש/רוש (Harris 1939: 42-43; Bauer-Leander 1922: #25b).

20. Compare *bō'^{a}kāh/bō'^{a}kâ; kappekāh/kappekâ; nātattāh* or *nātattâ* and *natattā* (Bauer-Leander 1922: #29c; Gesenius-Kautzsch-Cowley 1910: #44g).

21. *Resh,* when pronounced as a palatal, approximates the sound of a laryngeal and takes on some of its characteristics (Gesenius-Kautzsch-Cowley 1910: #6g, 22gr).

There is a tendency in the MT orthographic system to avoid consecutive *matres lectionis* in successive syllables (or double-*plene* words), though not always or regularly; the scroll on the whole reflects this same concern. A sampling from the text will illustrate this point:

קדשימ	19:2	*(q^{e}dōšîm)*
הידענימ	20:6	*(hayyidd^{e}ʿōnîm)*
לצמיתת	25:30	*(lāṣṣ^{e}mîtūt)*
שערימ	27:16	*(ś^{e}ʿōrîm)*

On other occasions there is a disparity in spellings. The scroll has double *plene* spellings where the MT does not: e.g., מקריבימ / *(maqrîbīm),* 21:6. The three different spellings of חמ(י)ש(י)ת are informative in this regard because *plene* and defective modes are found interchanged both in the scroll and the MT:

27:13	חמישיתו	*(ḥ^{a}mîšītô)*
27:15	חמשית	*(ḥ^{a}mîšît)*
27:19	חמשית	*(ḥ^{a}mīšît)*

The scroll has fuller spellings than the MT, as is true of 4QJer^{a} of the proto-Rabbinic type, but the general pattern of *plene* spellings versus defective ones in the scroll appears to be very close to that of the MT. Below are gathered those spellings in 11QpaleoLev which differ from the MT in the writing of vowel letters.

Defective:

G:4, H:3	אלהמ	15:2; 17:2	*(ʾ^{a}lêhem)*
G:6	בזב[ו	15:3	*(b^{e}zôbô)*
I:4	התעבות	18:29	*(hattôʿēbôt)*
J:5	יעלמו	20:4	*(yaʿlîmû)*
K:7	מאחו	21:10	*(mēʾeḥāyw)*
1:3	תקרבו	22:22	*(taqrîbû)*
2:3-4, 6	השבעי	26:24, 27	*(hašš^{e}bîʿî)*
5:9	איב	26:25	*(ʾôyēb)*

Plene:

C:6	במותמ	11:31	*(b^{e}mōtam)*
D:2	מראיה	13:4	*(marʾehā)*
E:1	לב]נות	13:39	*(l^{e}bānōt)*
H:8	והביאומ	17:5	*(wehebîʾūm)*
I:1, 5	הת(ו)]עבות	18:27, 30	*(hattôʿēbōt)*
I:4	העשות	18:30	*(hāʿōśōt)*

I:9	שבתותי	19:3	*(šabb^{e}tōtay)*
K:2	מקריבימ	21:6	*(marqrîbim)*
K:3; 3:2	קדוש	21:7; 24:9	*(qādōš)*, but *qādôš*, 21:8
K:9	נפשות	21:11	*(napšōt)*
K:9	יבוא	21:11	*(yābōʾ)*
4:1 +	ביובל	25:28	*(bayyōbēl)*
4:3 +	חומה	25:29	*(ḥōmâ)*
4:3	מלאות	25:20	*(m^{e}lōʾt)*
4:4	לצמיתות	25:30	*(laṣṣ^{e}mîtût)*
5:8	והביאתי	26:25	*(w^{e}hēbēʾtî)*
6:2	חמישיתו	27:13	*(ḥ^{a}mîšitô)*
6:3	יקדיש	27:14	*(yaqdīš)*, but *yaqdîš*, 27:16
6:5	חמשית	27:15	*(ḥ^{a}mîšit)*
6:8	[ה]נתרות	27:17	*(hannōtārōt)*

Conclusion

11QpaleoLev reflects the same orthographic tradition chosen by the rabbis for the standardized text of the Pentateuch. We found that *A1ad, A3,* and *B1ab, B2a* apply to the scroll's spellings:

1. Long vowels in final position are always written.
2. High long vowels *(î/û)* are generally written with exceptions for *î* of the hiphil stem and radical *î*.
3. Long mid-vowels are generally written (with exceptions) for diphthongs *(ô < aw; ê < ay)* but *waw* for vocalic *ō < ā́; ō < u* is not written.
4. Short vowels in any position are not written.
5. Possessive suffixes (3rd masc. sg.) ו and יו for singular and plural nouns, respectively, occur.
6. The graphic representation of the pharyngeal-laryngeal system has not collapsed; the occasional exceptions are through scribal slip as a result of the scribe's own linguistic tradition.

The *terminus ad quem* for this system, as we noted earlier, must be at the end of the 1st century C.E. when the text and orthography were stabilized, as shown by the manuscript finds at Wadi Murabbaʿat, Maṣada, and Naḥal Ḥever, which are Rabbinic both in spelling and text-type and come from the time of the Bar Kochba revolt (*ca.* 135 C.E.). The upper limit for the beginnings of the Rabbinic system would be the 5th century B.C.E. since preexilic spellings differ notably from it.

Freedman (1962: 102) has narrowed this gap considerably in his analysis of the earliest Qumran texts and concludes:

> Massoretic practice with regard to the use of *waw* for *ō* might well be described as a compromise between the defective spelling of Sam[b] and the extended orthography of Ex[f], and is in fact very close to that of Jer[a]. It may be further argued that Massoretic spelling was deliberately designed to combine the best features of the different orthographies current in the 4th-3rd centuries, preserving continuity with the older conservative tradition of Sam[b], and at the same time incorporating the helpful features of the newer spelling exhibited in Ex[f] and Jer[a]). We may place the origins of Massoretic spelling as a definite orthographic system in the late 3rd or early 2nd century, and describe it as a learned recension based upon the best practice of the preceding period.

The distribution of *waw* for *ô* < *ā́* in 11QpaleoLev is very close to that of the MT; it demonstrates that this kind of spelling pattern persevered into the 2nd-1st centuries B.C.E. alongside other spellings at Qumran. The system would undergo further refinement and modification by the end of the 1st century C.E. before it became the archetype for the Rabbinic Bible.

Although paleo-Hebrew texts (Cave 4) from Qumran regularly are written in the proto-Samaritan style (Cross 1966: 89), the scribe of 11QpaleoLev preferred the more restricted system, as we know it in the MT. The proto-Rabbinic orthographic system was becoming authoritative for scribes at Qumran.

Perhaps scholars will someday discover why this system continued to undergo refinement until it was stabilized in the Rabbinic texts and why it had gained acceptance over rival orthographic systems by the 1st century C.E. We only know that the Rabbinic decision, affected perhaps by the Samaritan schismatics (whose texts are more *plene*) and by a desire to retain some of the archaic flavor of the more conservative spellings, carried the official and final verdict.

Bibliography

Aharoni, Y.

1970 "Three Hebrew Ostraca from Arad." *BASOR* 197:16-42.

1975 *Kětūbōt ʿĂrād [Arad Inscriptions].* Jerusalem: Bialik Institute.

Albright, W. F.

1926 "Notes on Early Hebrew and Aramaic Epigraphy." *JPOS* 6:75-102.

1944 "The Oracles of Balaam." *JBL* 63:207-233.

1950 "The Psalm of Habakkuk." *Studies in Old Testament Prophecy,* ed. H. H. Rowley. Edinburgh: T. & T. Clark, 1-18.

1955 "New Light on Early Recensions of the Hebrew Bible." *BASOR* 140:27-33.

Allegro, J. M., and A. A. Anderson
1968 *Qumrân Cave 4, I (4Q158–4Q186).* DJD 5. Oxford: Clarendon.

Avigad, N.
1958 "New Light on the MṢH Seal Impressions." *IEJ* 8:113-19.
1960 "*Yehûd* or *Ha'îr*." *BASOR* 158:23-27.
1974 "More Evidence on the Judean Post-Exilic Stamps." *IEJ* 24:52-58.
1976 *Bullae and Seals from a Post-Exilic Judean Archive.* Qedem Monograph 4. Jerusalem: Hebrew University/Institute of Archaeology.

———, and Y. Yadin
1956 *A Genesis Apocryphon: A Scroll from the Wilderness of Judaea.* Jerusalem: Magnes/Hebrew University.

Baillet, M., J. T. Milik, and R. de Vaux
1962 *Les 'Petites Grottes' de Qumran: Planches.* DJD 3. Oxford: Clarendon.

Bange, L. A.
1971 *A Study in the Use of Vowel-Letters in Alphabetic Consonantal Writing.* Munich: UNI-Druck.

Barnes, W. E., et al.
1914 *Pentateuchus Syriace.* London: Societatem Bibliophilorum Britannicam et Externam.

Bauer, H., and P. Leander
1922 *Historische Grammatik der hebräischen Sprache des Alten Testaments.* Halle: M. Niemeyer. Repr. Hildesheim: Georg Olms, 1962.

Ben-Hayim, Z.
1958 "Traditions in the Hebrew Language, With Special Reference to the Dead Sea Scrolls," *Aspects of the Dead Sea Scrolls.* Scripta Hierosolymitana 4:200-213.

Birnbaum, S. A.
1950 "The Leviticus Fragments from the Cave." *BASOR* 118:20-27.
1954-57 *The Hebrew Scripts, Part Two: Plates.* London: Palaeographia.

Brooke, A. E., and N. McLean
1906 *The Old Testament in Greek,* I: *The Octateuch,* pt. 1: *Genesis.* Cambridge: Cambridge University Press.
1909 *The Old Testament in Greek,* I: *The Octateuch,* pt. 2: *Exodus and Leviticus.* London: Cambridge University Press.

Burrows, M.
1949 "Orthography, Morphology, and Syntax of the St. Mark's Isaiah Manuscript." *JBL* 68:195-211.

———, ed.
1950 *The Dead Sea Scrolls of St. Mark's Monastery,* I. New Haven: ASOR.

Cross, F. M.
1955 "The Oldest Manuscripts from Qumran." *JBL* 74:147-172.
1956 "Lachish Letter IV." *BASOR* 144:24-26.
1958 *The Ancient Library of Qumran and Modern Biblical Studies.* Garden City: Doubleday, repr. Sheffield: Sheffield Academic Press, 1994.
1961 "The Development of the Jewish Scripts." *The Bible and the Ancient Near East,* ed. G. E. Wright. Garden City: Doubleday, 133-202.
1962a "Epigraphic Notes on Hebrew Documents of the Eighth-Sixth Centuries B.C.: II. The Murabbaʿat Papyrus and the Letter Found Near Yabneh-Yam." *BASOR* 165:34-46.
1962b "Epigraphical Notes on Hebrew Documents of the Eighth-Sixth Centuries B.C.: III. The Inscribed Jar Handles from Gibeon." *BASOR* 168:18-23.
1963 "The Discovery of the Samaria Papyri." *BA* 26:110-121.
1964 "The History of the Biblical Text in the Light of Discoveries in the Judean Desert." *HTR* 57:281-299.
1966 "The Contribution of the Qumrân Discoveries to the Study of the Biblical Text." *IEJ* 16:81-95.
1970 "The Cave Inscriptions from Khirbet Beit Lei." *Near Eastern Archaeology in the Twentieth Century,* ed. J. A. Sanders. Garden City: Doubleday, 299-306.
1972 "The Evolution of a Theory of Local Texts." *RB* 79: 101-113. Repr. *Qumran and the History of the Biblical Text,* ed. F. M. Cross and S. Talmon. Cambridge, Mass.: Harvard University Press (1975), 306-320.
1979 "Problems of Method in the Textual Criticism of the Hebrew Bible." *The Critical Study of Sacred Texts,* ed. W. Doniger O'Flaherty. Berkeley: Graduate Theological Union, 31-54.

———, and D. N. Freedman
1952 *Early Hebrew Orthography.* AOS 36. New Haven: American Oriental Society, repr. 1981.
1975 *Studies in Ancient Yahwistic Poetry.* SBL Dissertation 21. Missoula: Scholars Press. [Repr. Grand Rapids: Wm. B. Eerdmans, 1995]

Díez-Macho, A.
1968 *Neophyti 1: Targum palestinense, Ms. de la Biblioteca Vaticana,* I: *Génesis.* Textos y estudios 7. Madrid: Consejo superior de investigaciones científicas.
1971 *Neophyti 1: Targum palestinense, Ms. de la Biblioteca Vaticana,* III: *Levítico.* Textos y estudios 9. Madrid: Consejo superior de investigaciones científicas.

Field, F.

1875 *Origenis Hexaplorum,* I: *Genesis-Esther.* Repr. Hildesheim: Georg Olms, 1964.

Fitzmyer, J. A.

1970 Review of A. Díez-Macho, *Neophyti 1. CBQ* 32:107-112.

1975 "Correction" [to Freedman 1974]. *CBQ* 37:238.

1977 *The Dead Sea Scrolls: Major Publications and Tools for Study.* Sources for Biblical Study 8. Missoula: Scholars Press.

1979 *A Wandering Aramean: Collected Aramaic Essays.* SBL Monograph 25. Missoula: Scholars Press.

Freedman, D. N.

1962 "The Massoretic Text and the Qumran Scrolls: A Study in Orthography." *Textus* 2:87-102. [See above, Chapter 3]

1969 "The Orthography of the Arad Ostraca." *IEJ* 19:52-56. [See above, Chapter 6]

1974 "Variant Readings in the Leviticus Scroll from Qumran Cave 11." *CBQ* 36:525-534.

———, and A. Ritterspach

1967 "The Use of Aleph as a Vowel Letter in the Genesis Apocryphon." *RevQ* 6:293-300.

von Gall, A. F.

1914-18 *Der hebräische Pentateuch der Samaritaner.* Repr. Giessen: Alfred Topelmann, 1966.

Garbini, A.

1962 "The Dating of Post-Exilic Stamps." *Excavations at Ramat Raḥal: Season 1959 and 1960,* ed. Y. Aharoni. Rome: Universita degli Studi/Hebrew University, 61-68.

Gasquet, A.

1929 *Biblia Sacra Iuxta Latinam Vulgatam Versionem,* II: *Libros Exodi et Levitici.* Rome: Vatican.

Gerleman, G.

1948 *Synoptic Studies in the Old Testament.* Lunds Universitets Årsskrift, N.S. 44/5. Lund: C. W. K. Gleerup.

Gesenius, G.

1815 *De Pentateuchi Samaritani: origine, indole et auctoritate commentatio philologico-critica.* Halle: Libraria Rengerianae.

———, E. Kautsch, and A. E. Cowley

1910 *Gesenius' Hebrew Grammar,* 2nd ed., ed. A. E. Cowley. Oxford: Clarendon.

Ginsburger, M.
1903 *Targum Pseudo-Jonathan (Thargum Jonathan ben Usiel zum Pentateuch).* Repr. Hildesheim: Georg Olms, 1971.

Goshen-Gottstein, M. H.
1960 "Linguistic Structure and Tradition in the Qumran Documents." *Text and Language in Bible and Qumran.* Jerusalem: Orient, 97-132.

Grossfeld, B.
1971 "Bible, Translations, Ancient Versions, Aramaic: the Targumim." *Encyclopaedia Judaica.* Jerusalem: Keter, 4:841-851.

Hanson, R. S.
1964 "Paleo-Hebrew Scripts in the Hasmonean Age." *BASOR* 175:26-42.
1974 "Toward a Chronology of the Hasmonean Coins." *BASOR* 216:21-23.
1976 "Jewish Paleography and Its Bearing on Text Critical Studies." *Magnalia Dei: The Mighty Acts of God. Essays in Honor of G. E. Wright,* ed. F. M. Cross, W. E. Lemke, and P. D. Miller. Garden City: Doubleday, 561-576.

Harris, Z. S.
1939 *Development of the Canaanite Dialects.* AOS 16. New Haven: American Oriental Society.

Holmes, R. and J. Parsons
1798 *Vetus Testamentum Graecum cum variis lectionisbus,* I. Oxford: Clarendon.

Jackson, K. P.
1983 *The Ammonite Language of the Iron Age.* HSM 27. Chico: Scholars Press.

Jastrow, M.
1903 *A Dictionary of the Targumim, the Talmud Babli and Yerushalmi, and the Midrashic Literature.* 2 vols. Repr. Brooklyn: P. Shalom, 1967.

Kadman, L.
1954 "The Hebrew Coin Script: A Study of the Epigraphy of Ancient Jewish Coins." *IEJ* 4:150-167.

Kennicott, B.
1776 *Vetus Testamentum Hebraicum cum variis lectionibus,* I. Oxford: Clarendon.

Kindler, A.
1974 *Coins of the Land of Israel: Collection of the Bank of Israel.* Trans. R. Grafman. Jerusalem: Keter.

Kutscher, E. Y.
1974 *The Language and Linguistic Background of the Isaiah Scroll (1QIsa[a]).* Studies on the Texts of the Desert of Judah 6. Leiden: E. J. Brill.

Mansoor, M.

1958 "Some Linguistic Aspects of the Qumran Texts." *Journal of Semitic Studies* 3:40-54.

Martin, M.

1958 *The Scribal Character of the Dead Sea Scrolls,* I. Bibliothèque du Muséon 44. Louvain: Publications Universitaires/Institut Orientaliste.

Mathews, K. A.

1980 "The Paleo-Hebrew Leviticus Scroll from Qumran." Diss., University of Michigan. [Rev. ed. with David Noel Freedman, *The Paleo-Hebrew Leviticus Scroll (11QpaleoLev).* Winona Lake: Eisenbrauns, 1985]

Meshorer, Y.

1967 *Jewish Coins of the Second Temple Period.* Trans. I. H. Levine. Tel Aviv: Am Hassefer.

1974 "The Beginning of the Hasmonean Coinage." *IEJ* 24:59-61.

Morag, S.

1974 "On the Historical Validity of the Vocalization of the Hebrew Bible." *JAOS* 94:307-315.

Naveh, J.

1963 "Old Hebrew Inscriptions in a Burial Cave." *IEJ* 13:74-92.

1968 "Dated Coins of Alexander Jannaeus." *IEJ* 18:20-25.

1970 *The Development of the Aramaic Script.* The Israel Academy of Sciences and Humanities Proceedings 5/1. Jerusalem: Israel Academy.

O'Connor, M.

1983 "Writing Systems, Native Speaker Analyses, and the Earliest Stages of Northwest Semitic Orthography." *The Word of the Lord Shall Go Forth,* ed. Carol L. Meyers and M. O'Connor. Winona Lake: Eisenbrauns, 439-465.

Parunak, H. V. D.

1978 "The Orthography of the Arad Ostraca." *BASOR* 230:25-32.

van der Ploeg, J. M. P.

1962 *Le Targum de Job de la grotte 11 de Qumran (11QtgJob), Premiere communication.* Medelingen koninklijke nederlandse Akadamie van Wetenshappen, Afd. Letterkunde 25/9. Amsterdam: N. V. Noord-hollandische Uitgevers Maatschappij.

Pritchard, J. B.

1959 *Hebrew Inscriptions and Stamps from Gibeon.* Philadelphia: University Museum, University of Pennsylvania.

Purvis, J. D.

1968 *The Samaritan Pentateuch and the Origin of the Samaritan Sect.* HSM 2. Cambridge, Mass.: Harvard University Press.

Quell, G.

1973 *Exodus et Leviticus. BHS,* ed. K. Elliger and W. Rudolph. Stuttgart: Deutsche Bibelstiftung.

Reifenberg, A.

1950 *Ancient Hebrew Seals.* London: East and West Library.

de Rossi, G. B.

1784-85 *Variae Lectionis Veteris Testamenti Librorum,* I. Parma: Ex Regio. Repr. Bibliotheca Rossiana 7. Amsterdam: Philo, 1969-71.

Rushforth, G. M.

1930 *Latin Historical Inscriptions.* 2nd ed. London: H. Milford.

Sabatier, P.

1743 *Bibliorum Sacrorum latinae versiones antiquae, seu Vetus Italica,* I. Rheims: Reginald Florentain. [Repr. Turnhout: Herder, 1976]

Ṣadaqa, A., and R. Ṣadaqa

1964 *Samaritan Version of the Pentateuch,* III: *Sēpher Wayyiqrāy.* Tel-Aviv: TaSHYaT.

Sanders, J. A.

1962 "The Scroll of Psalms (11QPss) from Cave 11: A Preliminary Report." *BASOR* 165:11-15.

1965 *The Psalms Scroll of Qumrân Cave 11.* DJD 4. Oxford: Clarendon.

Sandys, J. E.

1919 *Latin Epigraphy: An Introduction to the Study of Latin Inscriptions.* Cambridge: Cambridge University Press.

Sherman, M. E.

1966 "Systems of Hebrew and Aramaic Orthography: An Epigraphic History of the Use of *Matres Lectionis* in Non-Biblical Texts to ca. A.D. 135." Diss., Harvard Divinity School.

Skehan, P. W.

1955 "Exodus in the Samaritan Recension from Qumran." *JBL* 74:182-87.

1957 "The Qumran Manuscripts and Textual Criticism." *VTS* 4:148-160.

1964 "A Psalm Manuscript from Qumran (4QPs^{b})." *CBQ* 36:313-322.

1965 "The Biblical Scrolls from Qumran and the Text of the Old Testament." *BA* 28:87-100.

1978 "IV. Littérature de Qumran. A. Textes bibliques." *Supplément au Dictionnaire de la Bible* 51, ed. H. Cazelles and A. Feuillet. Paris: Letouzey & Ané, 805-822.

Sperber, A.

1959 *The Bible in Aramaic,* I: *The Pentateuch according to Targum Onkelos.* Leiden: E. J. Brill.

1966 *A Historical Grammar of Biblical Hebrew.* Leiden: E. J. Brill.

Sukenik, E. L.

1933 "The 'Jerusalem' and 'The City' Stamps on Jar Handles." *JPOS* 220, pl. 17.

1955 *The Dead Sea Scrolls of the Hebrew University.* Jerusalem: Magnes.

Talmon, S.

1952 "The Samaritan Pentateuch." *Journal of Jewish Studies* 2:144-150.

1964 "Aspects of the Textual Transmission of the Bible in the Light of Qumran Manuscripts." *Textus* 4:95-132.

1970 "The Old Testament Text." *The Cambridge History of the Bible,* I: *From the Beginnings to Jerome,* ed. P. R. Ackroyd and C. F. Evans. Cambridge, Mass.: Harvard University Press, 159-199.

1975 "The Textual Study of the Bible — A New Outlook." *Qumran and the History of the Biblical Text,* ed. F. M. Cross and S. Talmon. Cambridge, Mass.: Harvard University Press, 332-400.

Torczyner, H., et al.

1938 *Lachish I (Tell ed-Duweir),* I: *The Lachish Letters.* London: Oxford University Press.

Tov, E.

1978-79 "The Textual Character of the Leviticus Scroll from Qumran Cave 11." *Shnaton* 3:238-244 (Hebrew).

Trever, J.

1977 *The Dead Sea Scrolls: A Personal Account.* Grand Rapids: Wm. B. Eerdmans. [Rev. ed. of *The Untold Story of Qumran.* Westwood, N.J.: Revell, 1965]

Tsevat, M.

1960 "A Chapter on Old West Semitic Orthography." *The Joshua Bloch Memorial Volume,* ed. A. Berger, et al. New York: New York Public Library, 82-91.

Turner, E. G.

1971 *Greek Manuscripts of the Ancient World.* Oxford: Clarendon.

Ulrich, E. C.

1978 *The Qumran Text of Samuel and Josephus.* HSM 19. Missoula: Scholars Press.

1979 "4QSam^c: A Fragmentary Manuscript of 2 Samuel 14-15 from the Scribe of the *Serek Hayyaḥad* (1QS)." *BASOR* 235:1-26.

de Vaux, R.

1949 "La Grotte des Manuscripts hébreux." *RB* 56:586-609.

1956 "Fouilles de Khirbet Qumrân: Rapport préliminaire sur les 3e, 4e et 5e Campagnes." *RB* 63:533-577.

1973 *Archaeology and the Dead Sea Scrolls.* Schweich Lectures 1959. Rev. ed. London: Oxford University Press and British Academy.

Waltke, B. K.

1965 "Prolegomena to the Samaritan Pentateuch." Diss., Harvard University.

1970 "The Samaritan Pentateuch and the Text of the Old Testament." *New Perspectives on the Old Testament,* ed. J. B. Payne. Waco: Word, 212-239.

Weinberg, W.

1975 "The History of Hebrew *Plene* Spelling: From Antiquity to Haskalah." *HUCA* 46:457-487.

Wevers, J. W.

1974a *Text History of the Greek Genesis.* Abhandlungen der Akademie der Wissenschaften in Göttingen, Philologische-historische Klasse, 3rd ser. 81. Göttingen: Vandenhoeck & Ruprecht.

1974b *Septuaginta: Vetus Testamentum Graecum,* I: *Genesis.* Academiae Scientiarum Gottingensis. Göttingen: Vandenhoeck & Ruprecht.

1978 *Text History of the Greek Deuteronomy.* Abhandlungen der Akademie der Wissenschaften in Göttingen, Philologische-historische Klasse, 3rd ser. 106. Göttingen: Vandenhoeck & Ruprecht.

Yeivin, S.

1950 "The Date and Attribution of the Leviticus Fragments from the Cache in the Judaean Desert." *BASOR* 118:28-30.

York, A. D.

1974 "The Dating of Targumic Literature." *Journal for the Study of Judaism in the Persian, Hellenistic and Roman Period* 5:49-62.

Zevit, Z.

1980 Matres Lectionis *in Ancient Hebrew Epigraphs.* ASOR Monograph Series 2. Cambridge, Mass.: ASOR.

13

Prose Particles in the Poetry of the Primary History*

A long-recognized distinctive feature of biblical poetry is the striking rarity of certain familiar particles found regularly and frequently in biblical prose, specifically, *'ᵃšer* (the relative pronoun), *'ēt* (the sign of the definite direct object), and *h* (the definite article). Although it is generally agreed that prose and poetry differ sharply in their use of these particles, and although their use as a reliable criterion in distinguishing prose from poetry has long been asserted and relied upon, the statistical data for a given set of poems and a comparable prose corpus have never been developed and published; the empirical base for this important and useful distinction has not been established. Similarly, the implications of the particles' occurrence for genre-classification, both within the two categories and between them, and possible patterns of evolution in their use have not been seriously examined. The present study of the three "prose particles" is intended as a model for the analysis of material comprising both prose and poetry. Its findings and inferences are available for application on a broad scale to the rest of the literature of the Hebrew Bible.

Eleven substantial poems of varying length have been incorporated into the Primary History of the Hebrew Bible, i.e., the Torah and the Former Prophets, the prose narrative that runs consecutively from Genesis through Kings. These easily identified poems constitute an interesting group for various kinds of research. Not only do most of them derive from the earliest period of Israel's history, but they share a similar if not common transmissional history as part of the canonical core of the Hebrew Bible, the oldest part to be standardized and fixed textually. Four of them have been transmitted in metrical form as far back as scholars can trace them through

*After this article was submitted for publication, all the data about the prose particles appeared in print in the article by Andersen-Forbes listed in the Bibliography. The present paper, however, was written and submitted in final form before the Andersen-Forbes article appeared.

the manuscript tradition: (1) the Song of the Sea, Exod. 15 (not preserved in the Aleppo Codex, but confirmed by other medieval manuscripts in a stichometric arrangement); (2) the Song of Moses, Deut. 32 (not only in the Aleppo Codex, but also in metrically arranged fragments from the Dead Sea Scrolls, about a thousand years earlier); (3) the Song of Deborah, Judg. 5 (metrically arranged in the Aleppo Codex, although in a pattern different from that in the Pentateuch), and (4) the Psalm of David, 2 Sam. 22 (equivalent to Ps. 18). The seven other poems, while not metrically specified in the manuscripts, have been identified through recent scholarly research; there exists broad agreement as to their existence and boundaries: (1) the Blessing of Jacob, Gen. 49; (2) the Oracles of Balaam, Num. 23–24; (3) the Blessing of Moses, Deut. 33; (4) the Song of Hannah, 1 Sam. 2:1-10; (5) the Lament of David over Saul and Jonathan, 2 Sam. 1:19-27; (6) the Testament of David, 2 Sam. 23:1-7, and (7) the Prayer of Hezekiah, 2 Kgs. 19:21-28 = Isa. 37:22-29.

Recent critical editions of the Hebrew text reflect the scholarly consensus regarding these poems; this paper follows the delimitation and demarcation of the poems in the recent Stuttgart edition of the *Biblia Hebraica.* Ten of the eleven relate and reflect events and circumstances of the early history of Israel, from the 13th to the 10th centuries B.C.E., and are the products of roughly the same period, perhaps the 12th to 9th centuries B.C.E. These ten will be treated together. The eleventh, the Prayer of Hezekiah, clearly belongs to a much later period; it will be dealt with separately, for purposes of control and comparison.

A principal value of these poems, separately and together, is that they originated apart from the prose narrative in which they are embedded. At the same time they share the transmissional history of those books which constitute the Primary History from the time that it was formally promulgated as the canonical core of the Hebrew Bible, probably by the middle of the 6th century B.C.E. Preserved differences in the treatment of poetry and prose in this corpus probably reflect the standard but separate forms of the two literary types at the time of incorporation rather than later developments in the principles or techniques of scribal copying.

As this study aims centrally to confirm the hypothesis that the three particles *ʾašer,* *ʾēt,* and *h* occur significantly more often in prose than in poetry, each poem is examined in company with a corresponding prose passage. Tables below list the occurrence of particles in each poem and in its corresponding prose passage. This approach allows comparison of materials similar in content and textual history so as to emphasize the essential distinction between poetry and prose while eliminating all incidental or accidental factors. As the ordinary use of the particles in prose varies considerably from literary type to literary type, and even from sentence to sentence within a single genre, it is important to examine a large sample, one drawn from radically different segments of the narrative.

The data in this study have been derived from a standard text of the Hebrew Bible, the Stuttgart edition, and the same method of analysis has been followed in all passages, prose or poetry. Words are defined as single contiguous groups of letters separated by spaces (ignoring the *maqqēph*) and counted accordingly. The particles are identified in accordance with the Massoretic writing and scholarly traditions.

Despite every effort at scientific objectivity, certain ambiguities inherent in the text remain. For example, the particle *'ēt* has a homograph in the preposition meaning "with"; while most cases are easily differentiated, some are disputed. The same is true of the definite article, which is identical in form to the vocative particle; it is possible that the prevailing usage varied. So as not to slant the results, ambiguous terms are in almost all cases included in the totals.

The article, however, is not so included when the only sign of its presence is the *dagesh forte* in the next consonant. (It is clear that the Massoretes recognized no distinction between prose and poetry in this respect; they inserted the *dagesh* whenever they believed it belonged according to their grammatical rules. In fact, one should count the cases in which the dagesh occurs in prose and discount those in poetry, but that would be begging the question [See the table on p. 182].) Once the particle counts have been established, individual cases will be examined, the data will be analyzed, and interpretations will be suggested.

With respect to the Song of the Sea (Exod. 15) and the Song of Deborah (Judg. 5), prose narratives dealing with the same events appear in contiguous chapters of the Hebrew Bible: Exod. 14:1-31 and 15:19-21a and Judg. 4:1-24. The poetic and prose accounts will be directly compared in each case with their corresponding particle counts; the actual number of occurrences for each particle and the frequency percentages will be given in order to establish a valid comparison, as the poems and the prose passages are not of equal length.

The four poems of the Oracles of Balaam are embedded in a larger prose narrative extending through Num. 22–24. Here the prose materials provide a framework for the poems rather than running parallel to them. The proximity of the materials and the fact that prose and poetry here deal with the same persons and form a single story make the comparison valid and useful.

Similar comparisons for the other poems must come from contiguous passages before and after the poems; we must rely on the editors and scribes who combined the materials and transmitted the text to have kept it essentially intact once fixed. Deut. 31 and the prose materials in Deut. 33 (vv. 44-52) and 34 establish the prose context and comparison for the Song and Testament of Moses (Deut. 32–33). Gen. 48:1-22 and Gen. 49:28-33 provide the prose passages to compare with the Blessing of Jacob (Gen. 49). In the case of the poems in Samuel, contiguous prose passages are also used: for the Song of Hannah, 1 Sam. 1 and 2:11-36, and for the Lament of David, 1 Sam. 31 and 2 Sam. 1:1-18. For the Psalm of David (2 Sam. 22) and the Testament of David (2 Sam. 23), I have used 2 Sam. 21 and the remainder of ch. 23. Because ch. 23 has peculiar features, I have also examined ch. 24 and have given those figures; the results are much the same. The remainder of 2 Kgs. 19 is used for comparison with the Prayer of Hezekiah.

The following tables contain the summarized results of these comparisons:

	POETRY		PROSE	
	Genesis 49		*Genesis 48–49*	
Words	259		445	
		%		%
'šr	0	0.00	11	2.47
't	1	0.39	34	7.42
h	4	1.54	30	6.74
Total	5	1.93	75	16.82
	Exod. 15		*Exod. 14, 15:19-21a*	
Words	177		510	
		%		%
'šr	0	0.00	4	0.78
't	0	0.00	31	6.08
h	0	0.00	51	10.00
Total	0	0.00	86	16.86
	Num. 23–24		*Num. 22–24*	
Words	253		1049	
		%		%
'šr	1	0.40	22	2.10
't	1	0.40	44	4.19
h	4	1.58	54	5.15
Total	6	2.37	120	11.44
	Deut. 32		*Deut. 31*	
Words	462		553	
		%		%
'šr	1	0.22	18	3.25
't	0	0.00	42	7.59
h	3	0.65	71	12.84
Total	4	0.87	131	23.69
	Deut. 33		*Deut. 32–34*	
Words	304		329	
		%		%
'šr	2	0.66	17	5.17
't	2	0.66	20	6.08
h	3	0.99	36	10.94
Total	7	2.30	73	22.19

Prose Particles in the Poetry of the Primary History

	POETRY		PROSE		
	Pentateuch				
Words	1455		2886		
		%		%	Ratio
ʾšr	4	0.27	72	2.49	× 9.22
ʾt	4	0.27	171	5.93	× 21.96
h	14	0.96	242	8.39	× 8.74
Total	22	1.51	485	16.81	× 11.13

	Judg. 5		*Judg. 4*	
Words	352		422	
		%		%
ʾšr	1	0.28	7	1.66
ʾt	0	0.00	22	5.21
h	8	2.27	26	6.16
Total	9	2.56	55	13.03

	1 Sam. 2		*1 Sam. 1*	
Words	113		415	
		%		%
ʾšr	0	0.00	4	0.96
ʾt	0	0.00	19	4.58
h	0	0.00	23	5.54
Total	0	0.00	46	11.08

	2 Sam. 1		*1 Sam. 31–2 Sam. 1*	
Words	110		459	
		%		%
ʾšr	0	0.00	7	1.53
ʾt	0	0.00	24	5.23
h	7	6.36	40	8.71
Total	7	6.36	71	15.47

	2 Sam. 22		*2 Sam. 21*	
Words	365		419	
		%		%
ʾšr	0	0.00	12	2.86
ʾt	2	0.55	25	5.97
h	7	1.92	32	7.64
Total	9	2.47	69	16.47

	Poetry		Prose		
	2 Sam. 23		*2 Sam. 23*		
Words	86		354		
		%		%	
'šr	0	0.00	4	1.13	
't	0	0.00	7	1.98	
h	1	1.16	50	14.12	
Total	1	1.16	61	17.23	
	Former Prophets (Judges-2 Samuel)				
Words	1026		2069		
		%		%	Ratio
'šr	1	0.10	34	1.64	× 16.4
't	2	0.19	97	4.69	× 24.68
h	23	2.24	171	8.26	× 3.69
Total	26	2.53	302	14.60	× 5.77
	Totals				
Words	2481		4955		
		%		%	Ratio
'šr	5	0.20	106	2.14	× 10.70 (11)
't	6	0.24	268	5.41	× 22.54 (23)
h	37	1.49	413	8.34	× 5.60 (6)
Total	48	1.93	787	15.88	× 8.23 (8)
	2 Kgs. 19		*2 Kgs. 19*		
Words	114		455		
		%		%	
'šr	1	0.88	13	2.86	
't	3	2.63	17	3.74	
h	0	0.00	35	7.70	
Total	4	3.51	65	14.29	
	Former Prophets (Judges-2 Kings)				
Words	1140		2524		
		%		%	Ratio
'šr	2	0.18	47	1.86	× 10.33
't	5	0.44	114	4.52	× 10.27
h	23	2.02	206	8.16	× 4.04
Total	30	2.63	367	14.54	× 5.53

SUMMARY

	Poetry		Prose		Ratio
Words	2595		5410		
		%		%	
'šr	6	0.23	119	2.20	× 9.57 (10)
't	9	0.35	285	5.27	× 15.06 (15)
h	37	1.43	448	8.28	× 5.79 (6)
Total	52	2.00	852	15.75	× 7.88 (8)

On the basis of the samples given, the ratio of particle frequency between prose and poetry in the Primary History is 8:1. That is, the particles occur eight times as often in prose as in poetry. When the particles are considered separately, the ratio is 10:1 for *'šr,* 15:1 for *'t,* and 6:1 for *h.* Without 2 Kgs. 19, the figures vary as follows: *'šr* 11:1, *'t* 23:1, *h* 6:1. There is a wide variation in specific matchups, but probably this is only a random effect, as individual samples are small.

Except in the rarest circumstances the range for occurrence of particles in poetry and prose in given categories does not overlap; 2 Kgs. 19 is a special case, but this poem belongs to a later age and may reflect a gradual blurring of the distinction between poetry and prose in the use of the particles. Overall there is a marked gap: the range for poetry is 0.00 to 6.36, while for prose it is 11.08 to 23.69. Only two poems have a ratio exceeding 2.56 — 2 Kgs. 19 at 3.51 and the Lament of David at 6.36. The high count of the latter results entirely from cases of the definite article. In its total lack of *'šr* and *'t* the poem conforms to the general poetic pattern and specifically matches three other poems, including two from the same early period of the monarchy (2 Sam. 1 and 2 Sam. 23); Exod. 15 is the other poem in which *'šr* and *'t* do not occur. Gen. 49, Deut. 32, and Judg. 5 have only a single instance of either *'šr* or *'t,* while 2 Sam. 22 and Num. 23–24 have two.

Excluding the poem in 2 Kings from the examination of a fairly homogeneous corpus of poems from the early period of Israel (12th to 10th or 9th century), we note the extreme paucity of occurrences of *'šr* and *'t.* Separation of the five poems in the Pentateuch from the five in the Former Prophets yields the following figures:

	Words	*'šr*		*'t*	
			%		%
Pentateuch	1455	4	0.27	4	0.27
Former Prophets	1026	1	0.10	2	0.19

As this chart shows, these particles occur even more rarely in the Former Prophets than in the Pentateuch; examination of the individual examples should produce additional important information.

In the five poems of the Former Prophets the single example of *'šr* occurs in the

Song of Deborah (Judg. 5:27), one of the oldest poems in the Bible. The circumstances of and comparative data from this poem immediately cast doubt upon the authenticity of the occurrence of *ʾšr.* The most important consideration is the use of a different relative pronoun in the poem, *ʾša-* twice in v. 7. Apparently *ʾšr* is a secondary insertion here. If it is original, however, it should be interpreted not as the relative pronoun, but as the underlying noun, meaning "place." Hence the rendering: "in the place where he fell. . . ." In either case *ʾšr* may be dropped as an instance of the relative pronoun in any of the five poems in the Former Prophets.

The two cases of *ʾt* may be considered next. Both occur in 2 Sam. 22 (vv. 20, 28), there being none in any of the other four poems. Comparing this poem with Ps. 18 (the parallel and equivalent poem) shows up the dubious nature of both examples. First, Ps. 18 does not contain *ʾt* at all. The verse containing the first instance, 2 Sam. 22:20, parallels Ps. 18:20. Both verses contain a verb with suffix, but Ps. 18 attaches the pronominal suffix directly to the verb *(wayyôṣîʾēnî),* while 2 Sam. 22:20 uses the particle *ʾt (wayyōṣēʾ . . . ʾōtî).* Although both uses are well attested, the weight of the evidence from the five poems of the Former Prophets and the particular example of Ps. 18 show that *ʾty* is secondary in 2 Samuel. In the second instance (2 Sam. 2:25 = Ps. 18:28), the word *ʾt* in 2 Samuel is written *ʾattâ* in Ps. 18 and vocalized as the 2nd masc. sg. pronoun, undoubtedly the correct original reading. The word is the same in 2 Samuel but, having been written defectively, was misunderstood by the Massoretes.

The five poems in the Former Prophets, then, contain not one well-attested and confirmed example of either particle, *ʾšr* or *ʾt.* These particles were not used at all in such poetry. If that seems to be a radical or extreme judgment, it is only necessary to examine the data. From a statistical point of view it is of no consequence whether we retain or remove these few examples; the evidence is overwhelming. Three of the five poems make no use of either particle, and four of the five use only one or the other. The conclusion is inescapable: in this group of poems the use of the two particles is practically zero, and the few exceptions can and should be explained as intrusions.

The poems in the Pentateuch present much the same picture, despite a few more instances of each particle: the texts as preserved contain four examples of each, twice as many as in the Former Prophets. However, the percentage is still very low, 0.56%, or about 1/2 of 1%. Examination of the specific instances indicates that either the reliability of the text or the originality of the reading may be questioned. One poem, Exod. 15, has neither particle; a second poem, Gen. 49, has no instance of *ʾšr,* and Deut. 32 makes no use of *ʾt.* The four instances of *ʾšr* are distributed among Num. 23–24 (1), Deut. 32 (1), and Deut. 33 (2). The *ʾšr* in Num. 24:4 is clearly secondary: comparison with 24:16 (where *ʾšr* does not occur, although the texts are virtually identical) makes it clear that a colon has fallen out in 24:4 *(wydʿ dʿt ʿlywn),* and in its place this dubious relative pronoun has surfaced. The occurrence in Deut. 32:38 poses no particular textual or grammatical problem. It might, however, be questioned on metrical grounds, since it unbalances the bicolon in v. 38a.

The two occurrences in Deut. 33:8 and 29 are more difficult. Questions about the originality of vv. 8b-9a have arisen for a variety of reasons, reinforced by the occurrence of *'šr* once and *'t* twice in these three bicola, the highest concentration of these particles in the whole corpus under consideration. In the immediately surrounding materials (vv. 8a and 9b-10a) *'t* is not used, although there would be reason to use it as many as six times with definite direct objects (*tmyk, w'wryk* after *hābû ləlēwî,* which must be supplied to MT on the basis of Q and LXX, *'mrtk wbrytk, mšpṭyk, wtwrtk*). Vv. 8b-9a seem to be a secondary insertion betraying signs of later composition.

The occurrence of *'šr* in v. 29 is also anomalous. It is the only instance of *'šr* (or *'t*) in the Prologue and Epilogue or in the body of the Blessing apart from vv. 8b-9a, and it disturbs the symmetry of the passage. While it is grammatically appropriate in the passage, it should be matched by *'šr* before *mgn ʿzrk // ḥrb g'wtk.* Its absence in the first phrase suggests that it was originally also absent in the second phrase.

In the Pentateuch poems *'t* does not occur at all in Exod. 15 or Deut. 32. It occurs twice in Deut. 33, both times in v. 9, but both cases raise questions. The other examples of *'t* in these poems are in Gen. 49:15 (*'et-hā'āreṣ,* a common and unexceptionable but clearly prosaic expression) and Num. 23:10 (*'et-rōbaʿ yiśrā'ēl,* a problem, but not for grammatical or syntactic reasons).

Of the eleven examples of *'šr* (5) and *'t* (6) preserved in the ten poems under consideration, the following cases are doubtful:

'šr: two in Num. 24:4 (on the basis of parallel usage) and Judg. 5:27 (on the basis of internal evidence). The three remaining cases, in Deut. 32:38 and Deut. 33:8 and 29, can only be challenged on metrical and symmetrical grounds, and while there may be a case, the point need not be pressed here.

't: Of the six occurrences, the two instances in 2 Sam. 22:20 and 28 may be challenged on the basis of the parallel passages in Ps. 18. As for the others, there is no compelling reason to doubt the readings in Gen. 49:15 and Num. 23:19. In Deut. 33:9 there appears to be a problem with the whole passage vv. 8b-9a, but not with the two occurrences of *'t.* Of the five occurrences of *'šr,* then, two may effectively be eliminated; of the six occurrences of *'t* two may be dropped.

The percentages of the eleven examples of *'šr* and *'t* in the poems from the Pentateuch are shown below:

Total Words	2481		1481	
		%		%
'šr	5	0.20	3	0.12
't	6	0.24	4	0.16
Total	11	0.44	7	0.28

The difference is substantial, although the conclusion is the same and inescapable. For all practical purposes, neither *'šr* nor *'t* was used in early Hebrew poetry, certainly not in the poems preserved in the Primary History. The few surviving examples resulted either from error or false correction (two of each); all others slipped in through scribal inadvertence in the long process of transmission.

The very rarity of these accidents is surprising; the scribes' faithful preservation of this peculiarity of Hebrew poetry is quite remarkable. One or two instances of *'šr* and *'t* may be part of the original composition, as was doubtless the case in the composition of some later Hebrew poetry, e.g., 2 Kgs. 19, but originality would be difficult to demonstrate in any particular instance.

The thirty-seven examples of the use of *he* as the definite article remain. While a few of these may be questioned, such as the misdivision in Num. 24:3, 15, which produced an article not original to the text (read *šᵉtummâ ʿāyin* for MT *šᵉtūm hāʿāyin)* and may on reasonable grounds be excluded, a sufficient number remain to require recognition as part of the armory of the poet and intrinsic to poetry even of the earliest Israelite period.

Among the rest, at least two categories of usage should be noted, as they imply a use of the article apparently antedating the general use of the definite article *he* and relatively independent of it:

1) Its use with participles to form the equivalent of a relative clause, as "the one who clothed you" (2 Sam. 1:24). Examples of this usage appear in several poems, in David's Lament (4: vv. 23-24), Deborah (1: v. 9), Gen. 49 (2: vv. 17, 21), 2 Sam. 22 (David's Hymn, 2: vv. 31, 33), nine occurrences in all.

2) Its use as an attenuated demonstrative, especially in stereotyped phrases, e.g., *nᵉ'ūm haggeber* = "oracle of *that* man" (Num. 24:3, 15; 2 Sam. 23:1). This expression occurs three times in the corpus, always with the article (especially striking in 2 Sam. 23:1, where otherwise not a single instance of any of the particles here discussed appears). The expression *byn hmšptym* occurs twice, both times with the article (Gen. 49:14; Judg. 5:16). The article appears repeatedly with El in Deut. 32 and 2 Sam. 22 = Ps. 18.

3) Finally, two instances occur in which the prefixed *he* may be the vocative particle rather than the definite article: Deut. 32:1 and perhaps 2 Sam. 1:19.

Those remaining may be regarded as belonging to the original poems. As the ratio of prose particles in the text preserved by the Massoretes may be set at slightly less than 2%, the case is already firm, especially when the ratio is compared with that in standard prose, where it is about 15%. With the removal of the most glaring examples of forced entry, the percentage total may be reduced to somewhere between 1 and 1.5%. The evidence could hardly be more clear.

The earliest biblical poetry characteristically does not include these particles. To be more precise, the particles *'šr* and *'t* are so uncommon in this material (eleven occurrences in 2470 words) that all surviving examples may be regarded as secondary. As for the more numerous instances of the definite article, some appear to be secondary, while others have specialized functions or meanings (as relative pronouns, attenuated demonstratives, or vocatives); only a handful can be seen as simple definite articles. Early poets seem by and large to have shunned these particles, making use only of the preformative *he* to any extent.

As the present text of the poems in the Primary History has an overall percentage of less than 2% use of these particles, the original poetry can be assumed to have shown an even lower figure, perhaps 1.0 to 1.5%. Several poems fall within a narrow range, from just under 1% to just over 2.5%. Two poems have no prose particles at all (Exod. 15 and 1 Sam. 2), while one is remarkable for the large number of such particles included (David's Lament in 2 Sam. 1:19-27). The anomaly of this poem is difficult to explain, for the text is generally in good order and the early date of the poem (ca. 1000 B.C.E.) is assured. It may clarify the puzzle to note that neither *'šr* nor *'t* occurs in the poem, in accord with the best classical usage, while the definite article occurs in 7 of 110 words. Of these, 4 are attached to participles (vv. 23-24), seeming to reflect a specialized function requiring their use in poetry as well as in prose. A fifth instance is attached to the first word, *hṣby,* and this may be an example of the vocative *he* rather than the article: "O Gazelle of Israel!" rather than "The Gazelle, O Israel, is slain. . . ." That reading would leave two fairly normal occurrences of the article in the poem (vv. 20, 25); the total particle count, noting the absence of *'šr* and *'t,* would then be less than 2% of the total number of words, in conformity with the other poems.

The conclusion of the matter is that classic Hebrew poetry is easily distinguished from Hebrew prose by the criterion proposed, namely, the relative frequency with which the three common particles — *'šr, 't,* and *h* — occur in the two forms of discourse. The virtual absence of the first two even in the current Massoretic text confirms that they were simply not used by ancient Hebrew poets. The case with the definite article is somewhat different. The occasional occurrence of this particle in the surviving text indicates that some limited use of it was permitted and practiced by classic Hebrew poets. In spite of this qualification, *h* is still used markedly less frequently than in prose. Overall, the contrast between the frequencies in prose and poetry is so great (eight times on the average) that we may regard the criterion as firmly validated by the evidence.

The following table shows the frequency with which the definite article is indicated by the *dagesh* alone in the poetry and prose samples, e.g., *baggôyīm* (Num. 23:9):

Poem	words	dagesh %	Prose	words	dagesh %
1) Gen. 49	259	6	1) Gen. 48	445	3
2) Exod. 15	177	9	2) Exod. 14–15	510	11
3) Num. 23–24	253	2	3) Num. 22–24	1049	16
4) Deut. 32	462	3	4) Deut. 31	553	6
5) Deut. 33	304	1	5) Deut. 32, 34	329	3
6) Judg. 5	352	7	6) Judg. 4	422	5
7) 1 Sam. 2	113	3	7) 1 Sam. 1	415	1
8) 2 Sam. 1	110	2	8) 1 Sam. 31–2 Sam. 1	459	4
9) 2 Sam. 22	365	5	9) 2 Sam. 21	419	7
10) 2 Sam. 23	86	3	10) 2 Sam. 23	354	11
Total	2481	41 (1.7%)	Total	4955	67 (1.4%)
11) 2 Kgs.19	114	1	11) 2 Kgs. 19	455	11
Total	2595	42 (1.6%)	Total	5410	78 (1.4%)

It is evident that there is no significant difference between the two columns insofar as the frequency of this form of the definite article is concerned. What it shows is that the Massoretes made no distinction between poetry and prose when it came to marking the presence of the definite article by the appropriate punctuation. The difference between this set of statistics and the data for the use of the article as indicated by the prefixed letter *h* is so striking as to constitute a *prima facie* case for the actual difference in biblical prose and poetic usage, or for the indifference of the Massoretes to this phenomenon.

Bibliography

Andersen, F. I., and A. D. Forbes

1983 " 'Prose Particle' Counts of the Hebrew Bible." *The Word of the Lord Shall Go Forth,* ed. C. L. Meyers and M. O'Connor. Winona Lake: Eisenbrauns/American Schools of Oriental Research, 165-183.

———, and D. N. Freedman

1980 *Hosea.* AB 24. Garden City: Doubleday.

Freedman, D. N.

1977 "Pottery, Poetry, and Prophecy: An Essay in Biblical Poetry." *JBL* 96:5-26. Repr. in D. N. Freedman, *Pottery, Poetry, and Prophecy.* Winona Lake: Eisenbrauns, 1980, 1-22.

1976 "Divine Names and Titles in Early Hebrew Poetry." *Magnalia Dei: The Mighty Acts of God,* ed. F. M. Cross, W. E. Lemke, and P. D. Miller. Garden City: Doubleday, 55-107. Repr. in Freedman, *Pottery, Poetry, and Prophecy,* 77-129.

14

Acrostic Poems in the Hebrew Bible: Alphabetic and Otherwise

The purpose of this paper is to extend and expand an earlier study of the metrical structure of a number of alphabetic acrostic poems in the Hebrew Bible.[1] In that investigation a general description and analysis of all five chapters of the book of Lamentations were given, along with a more cursory examination of nine or ten other alphabetic acrostic poems in the books of Psalms and Proverbs. Briefly put, two different metrical or rhythmic patterns were identified in the corpus under consideration. One, concentrated in the first four chapters of Lamentations, consisted of lines averaging about 13 syllables each, while the other, with lines averaging 16 syllables in length, was reflected in most of the other poems, including Lam. 5.[2]

The difference between the two groups in terms of line length is maintained consistently throughout the corpus, although there is a wide range of variation within each group, and in individual cases there can be considerable overlapping (thus lines of the same length and structure can be found in both groups, but the predominant patterns are quite distinct). We must, therefore, focus attention on means and averages, and increasingly on norms and standards. The bulk of the material will conform to the standards or approximate them, but a number of individual lines will vary or deviate substantially from the norms, thus posing important problems for scholars but at the same time pointing toward a resolution of fundamental issues concerning biblical poetics. In other words, what has hitherto been regarded as part of a serious problem in dealing with Hebrew poetry, may in fact be part of the solution, viz., a range of deviation and abnormality that is a deliberate or intended element in the composition of such poetry.

1. D. N. Freedman, "Acrostics and Metrics in Hebrew Poetry," *HTR* 65 (1972): 367-392.

2. For a statistical profile of Lam. 1–4 demonstrating the 13-syllable line see the charts in Freedman, *HTR* 65 (1972): 370-77. Charts illustrating the 16-syllable line found in Lam. 5; Prov. 31; and Pss. 25, 34, 111, 112, 119, and 145 can be found on pp. 385-392.

We can also correlate these findings with the more traditional and generally accepted accentual or stress-system of describing Hebrew poetry. Thus the 13-syllable line generally has five accents or stresses, and these divide unevenly after the third stress producing the familiar 3:2 pattern, which prevails in Lam. 1-4, and which has been characterized as qina meter or rhythm by K. Budde.[3] For the most part, our independent syllable-counting procedure supports and confirms Budde's analysis, although there are numerous exceptions and deviations. It is important to emphasize that the deviations and irregularities are part of the larger pattern, and not aberrations to be corrected or emended away; at the same time it has to be recognized that errors, scribal and other, would produce similar-looking departures from the norm. The essential problem or challenge to the scholar is to distinguish the one from the other, and neither to emend away a subtle and intentional variation from the norm worked into the poem by the author, nor to preserve and retain a deviant reading, which actually is a mistake accidentally perpetrated in the course of transmission. There are other possibilities, but these are the principal categories that will concern us in what follows:

The bulk of the lines in chs. 1–4 of Lamentations divide naturally after the third stress in the line, in this way producing the characteristic falling rhythm of the so-called qina poems (reflected in the notation 3:2 for stresses). The syllable counts correspond broadly with many of the lines dividing 8:5 or 7:6, along with many variations. A more detailed study of Lamentations than that previously published is under way, and will be presented in due course as part of a monograph on line and verse structure in biblical poetry.

The metrical scheme for most of the alphabetic acrostic poems in the Bible is the much more common 3:3 pattern, with the total syllable count averaging 16. These lines typically have six stresses or accents, and tend to divide at the midpoint. Thus the syllable-count corresponding to the stress-count of 3:3 is 8:8. Since this pattern is by far the most widespread and general in the poetry of the Hebrew Bible (including most of the books of Proverbs and Job, as well as many of the Psalms and other formal poems in the Primary History and the Prophetic Corpus), it can be suggested that the so-called qina rhythm or pattern is derived from the basic pattern by the expedient of dropping the final accent or stress with its corresponding unaccented syllables. In this way we could derive from the standard Hebrew meter, 3:3 (= 8:8 syllables), the qina rhythm of 3:2 (= 8:5). We are speaking conceptually, since in practice the five-stress line divides in a slightly different way, and the actual origin of the qina rhythm may have a different explanation. That much of the poetry of the Hebrew Bible was composed in this meter has been widely recognized for a long time, but now we wish to add to that criterion the equivalent in syllable-counting: the 16-syllable line divided

3. K. Budde, "Das hebräische Klagelied," *ZAW* 2 (1882): 1-52. For a brief discussion of Budde and the ensuing critique of his work, see D. R. Hillers, *Lamentations*. AB 7A (Garden City: Doubleday, 1972, rev. ed. 1992), xxx-xxxiii.

in the middle, or 8:8. We wish also to add the element that the system works with statistical averages and means, and to emphasize that widespread variations of greater or lesser proportions are built into the system (and only a small portion of these can be explained or emended away as the result of errors). The range and rate of deviation can be plotted and graphed for the poems, and it will be seen that they conform to a standard pattern, roughly that of the familiar bell-shaped curve (or the so-called random distribution curve). The phenomenon we are considering, however, is anything but random. Each system has its characteristic distribution pattern: thus the 16-syllable line (and its close relatives with 15 and 17 syllables each) is very common, even normative for the poems in standard meter, while 13-syllable lines (and those immediately adjacent to them, with 12 or 14 syllables) are much rarer, relatively speaking. When it comes to poems in the qina meter (e.g., Lam. 1–4), the opposite is true. The difference when we move from Lam. 1–4 to Lam. 5 is very striking, and the fact that we are in a different milieu in terms of structure, in short a different poetic pattern, is patent and incontestable. Our position with regard to the metrics of Hebrew poetry differs markedly from those, and the number seems to be increasing, who contend that there is no meter, no regularity of structure or pattern in biblical verse. We distance ourselves equally from those who insist on the opposite view that there is a metrical structure and impose a rigid regularity on the surviving material, regarding deviations and variations from the established norms as errors to be corrected by addition, subtraction, or other alterations. While recognizing the value and partial validity of both of these approaches, we try to combine them in a single system, normative yet flexible, conforming to fixed standards and yet diverging in a variety of ways. Thus we accept the use of occasional (and sometimes rather frequent) tricola in the midst (or at the end) of the usual and almost endless parade of bicola. We note the presence of four-stress and two-stress cola as substitutes or alternates to the standard three-stress cola in both the initial and second positions in the lines of poetry. Often these are equivalent in syllable length (normal range from 7-9 syllables), confirming that they are stylistic variants rather than substantive alterations. But there are also examples in which syllable length varies markedly along with the stress-count, so we must face the possibility of a deliberate and often jolting change in the basic rhythm. Error is always a possibility in such cases, but deliberate alteration must also be considered, especially if such changes themselves form a repeated pattern, or contribute in some determinable or calculable way to a symmetrical overall picture (i.e., if a deliberate shortening occurs at one point and a corresponding lengthening at another corresponding point, then both changes from the standard pattern, by balancing each other, become part of an even larger pattern).

With regard to counting stresses or accents, we follow generally accepted procedures. Content words regularly receive one accent, although there may be cases of combinations or construct chains where the two words together should have only one accent: e.g., the sequence *yôm yôm* or *dôr (wā)dôr.* When it comes to particles, including prepositions, exclamations, pronouns, and the like, these may or may not bear the accent, although there are two rules or guidelines which may be of help: one-syllable words generally do not have a separate stress, while those with two or more syllables often do; independent pronouns bear the accent, as do compound prepositions. There is a group that may take the accent in some lines and not in others. On the whole, when there is doubt it is permissible and perhaps desirable to count in the direction of the norm. If the overall pattern is 3:3, then if there is doubt whether a particular colon is 2 or 3, or 3 or 4, I would opt for 3. I would also find it very difficult to emend the text by adding or subtracting a word solely on the basis of the metrical pattern. If, however, there is significant textual evidence, or some other compelling or supporting reason, then the metrical argument can be used.

With regard to counting syllables, we continue to espouse the system used over the years by a number of scholars. The point of origin and departure has to be MT, but it also has to be noted that while the Massoretes faithfully reproduced the biblical text and traditional pronunciation of their day, their system of vocalization includes some postbiblical changes and nonbiblical forms, which do not correctly reflect the actual morphology and phonology of the biblical period. Thus we must modify the received vocalization in accordance with actual information about Biblical Hebrew in the historic period, since our objective is to recover and reproduce so far as possible both the poetry and the meter of classical times. Thus we treat segolate formations as single syllables, and do not count secondary vowels, especially the *ḥatefs* associated with laryngeals (including the so-called *pataḥ* furtive). One area of uncertainty concerns the proper way to count the syllables of pronominal suffixes, in particular those of the 2nd masc. sg. and the 3rd fem. sg.: *-tā, -kā,* and *-hā.* There are actually two different forms, one long, ending in a vowel, and the other short, ending in the appropriate consonant. In MT, however, these have been commingled for the most part, so that the "kethib" most often has the short form (with only the consonant), while the "qere" represents the long form, resulting in the anomalous forms given above. There are enough examples of the long form written out with the final vowel letter, e.g., *-kh, -th,* to confirm that such forms existed in the language, and this is confirmed by the predominance of the long form in many Qumran MSS, including the great Isaiah scroll and others. At the same time, there are enough instances of a vocalization conforming to the short form, especially in pausal positions, to establish the short reading as also legitimate. Whenever the vocalization and the spelling are in conformity with each other, we follow suit, but when, as in the large majority of cases, the reading is mixed, then it is difficult to decide what the original vocalization was or what the poet intended. It is perfectly legitimate to suppose that the poet used both forms, since MT does, and that the choice may have been influenced by a sense of euphony or rhythm. In the calculations that follow, I have included both counts, and presume that the poet's intention lies somewhere between the extremes or at one end or the other. The extent of the range depends upon the frequency of the pronouns in the poem, as well as other terms which have long and short forms not always clearly distinguished in MT; but the uncertainty will also reflect the fact that in the end we cannot be entirely sure of the actual vocalization of the words and lines of an ancient poem. We must allow for contraction and elision in the actual presentation, a situation which we recognize in the adaptation of poems to rhythmic and musical settings, but which would not be represented in the spelling of the words in a written text. Thus a variation in the count of a syllable, or even two, per line would not be unusual, even when the lines were intended to be and were considered to be equivalent. We must not press the counting too far, although what remains surprising is how remarkably balanced and precise the figures come out without appealing to these qualifying factors. It should be pointed out that the low number in the figures which follow can also be considered a minimum count and the base upon which further calculations or adjustments can be made. In addition, we can speak of a norm or standard against which to compare the empirical results derived from the surviving texts.[4]

Counting syllables is one thing, measuring or weighing them is another and more difficult matter. Doubtless, an accurate count should reflect at least the difference between long and short vowels, a distinction which is not only justified on theoretical grounds, but can be verified at least in part from contemporary inscriptions. It is well known that vowel letters, whether in final or medial positions, systematically represent long vowels, and from the time of their introduction, perhaps as early as the 10th century B.C.E. and their expanded use in later times, the purpose was to represent long vowels, and long vowels only. Certainly by the time the Hebrew Bible reached anything like its permanent form, vowel letters were used regularly and throughout the text, more in later parts of the Bible, fewer in earlier parts. MT therefore reflects faithfully and reliably the system of consonants and vowel letters adopted in the postexilic period, and it would be beneficial to incorporate a vowel-weighting program in our syllable-counting system, at least to distinguish long vowels from short ones.[5]

A serious attempt at quantifying and weighting the syllable count of Hebrew poetry has been undertaken by Duane Christensen in his revival of the old system of

4. The charts in Freedman, *HTR* 65 (1973): 367-392, of the syllable counts of the poems in Proverbs and Psalms use the figures including the pronominal endings (corresponding to Col. B of the Lamentations counts). Considering the existence of a norm, the lower or minimal count may have been preferable.

5. For a detailed discussion of this complex problem, see F. I. Andersen and A. D. Forbes, *Spelling in the Hebrew Bible,* forthcoming as vol. 1 in the Dahood Memorial Lecture series to be published by the Pontifical Biblical Institute. [Biblica et Orientalia 41 (1986)] Of special interest is the evidence of early vowel letters in the 10th century from Tell Fekheyre. [See now Andersen and Freedman, "The Orthography of the Aramaic Portion of the Tell Fekheyre B1-lingual." Pp. 9-49 in *Text and Context,* ed. W. Claassen. JSOT Sup 48 (Sheffield: Sheffield Academic Press, 1988)]

counting "morae," and due credit should be given to him for this laborious effort.[6] Nevertheless, and even though the results so far achieved seem to confirm the less precise systems being used here, whether of stresses or syllables generally, even when carried out with minute precision, the *morae* system remains questionable, if it is not actually defective. In his usage, the system depends entirely upon the Massoretic vocalization of the text, itself a valiant effort on the part of the scribes to preserve and reproduce the exact quality and quantity of the vowels (not to speak of the consonants) of the Hebrew Bible. While they may have succeeded to a considerable degree in identifying and isolating the different vowel sounds and also their length or duration, at the same time their efforts, which were intended to elucidate and expand the vowel-letter system which had been incorporated into the text, occasionally if not more frequently, had the effect of disturbing and distorting the older system. Just as the use of vowel letters indicated vowel quantity more reliably, if not consistently, than vowel quality, so the Massoretic vocalization served better to indicate quality rather than quantity. Most, if not quite all, of the vocalic signs could be used for short as well as long vowels, with the distinction made certain only when the vowel points were used in conjunction with the vowel letters. In the absence of the latter, analogy with more fully written forms or argument from linguistic analysis and date could be used to make such a determination. Even assuming that all the problems associated with Massoretic vocalization could be resolved and we could recover and reproduce the system in full, with reference both to quantity and quality, would we thereby have an accurate portrayal or profile of the classical language? Probably not!

In any event, the *morae* system does not faithfully reflect the tripartite quantitative system of the Massoretes, who used not only long and short vowels, but also a partial series of very short vowels (i.e., *shewa* and the several *ḥatef*s). This last group should be distinguished from full vowels, whether long or short, and should be given a value markedly different from that of a short full vowel. The fact that the Massoretes used the same sign to indicate both a slight vocal sound and no sound at all (i.e., vocal and silent shewa) indicates both how slight the sound may have been and the distance between such a sound and a full vowel, however short. At the same time, the *ḥatef* vowels show that there was a real sound, and that this extremely short vowel could be distinguished both by quality and sound.

At the other end of the scale, the *morae* system hardly reflects the realities of vowel quantity in classical Biblical Hebrew. To recapture or reconstruct Biblical Hebrew is a major challenge and perhaps ultimately an insoluble problem. Even making a reasonable stab at a solution requires extraordinary effort and inspired application to detail. Here we may limit ourselves to the simpler differentiation between long vowels and short vowels, and insofar as possible follow the lead of

6. D. L. Christensen, "Two Stanzas of a Hymn in Deuteronomy 33," *Bibl* 65 (1984): 382-89; and "The Song of Jonah: A Metrical Analysis," *JBL* 104 (1985): 217-231.

the ancient scribes in their judicious but somewhat limited use of vowel letters. It is not clear, however, that even if the undertaking were generally or partially successful and we were able to vocalize the text correctly and count and weigh the syllables accurately, that the results would justify the time, trouble, and effort involved, or that they would be materially affected by a more precise counting of the syllables as distinguished from the admittedly less precise and somewhat cruder systems of syllable and stress counting now employed. It is possible that more exact quantification of the syllable-count would produce interesting and significant results, and that intimations of symmetry and other complex configurations implied by the use of present methods would be confirmed and enhanced by closer evaluation of the data, especially in terms of quantity. On the other hand, greater precision in measurement might point to greater differentiation and more confusion in evaluation and interpretation of the evidence, but until a serious, sophisticated endeavor at legitimate quantification is made we can only guess at the outcome. In the meantime we have to operate on the premise or assumption that the differences in vowel length, which admittedly are part of the data base, will cancel out, if not between cola or lines, then over larger units and especially whole poems. It is unlikely that an exact correlation of long and short vowels exists, or if they are measured in equivalences (hypothetically at any rate it is assumed that long vowels have double the value of short ones), that such equivalences will be maintained colon by colon or line by line. If the counts and accounts balance out, it will probably be with respect to larger units and whole poems, as in fact is the case now with general syllable counting. At most we could expect a refinement in the system to produce more detailed information than previously, but it is difficult to imagine that the picture as a whole will change very much.

Turning now to Lam. 5, we may examine it more closely with respect to structure and meter than was the case in the article already alluded to. In addition to basic information about line-length — averages and related data — already provided in the earlier article, we will include a more detailed analysis of the internal structure of the lines, the position of the caesura or major pause, the number and distribution of the stresses or accents, and other items. It has already been noted that Lam. 5 is modeled on alphabetic acrostic poems, although it lacks the most obvious identifying feature of one: the use of the alphabet sequence with the 22 lines of the poem. Lam. 1–4 were all composed as alphabetic acrostics, although the structures vary somewhat. The first three chapters have 22 three-line stanzas each (there are exceptional four-line stanzas in chs. 1 and 2), while ch. 4 has 22 two-line stanzas. Ch. 5 has 22 one-line units and, except for the absence of the alphabetic feature, is very much like the acrostic poems in Prov. 31:10-31 and Pss. 25, 34, and others, in which the device figures prominently. The restriction to 22 units (or 23 in some instances) shows that the alphabetic acrostics reflect the original pattern and intent of such poems, while the omission of the alphabetic feature represents a modification, a slight sophistication, of the original arrangement, and not the other way around. Comparing Lam. 5 with other poems sharing the same structure, including not only the alphabetic acrostics mentioned above but also a number of other poems that share the same features, but like Lam. 5, do not use the alphabetic device (for want of some better designation, I call these latter [including Lam. 5] nonalphabetic acrostics in order to emphasize how much alike they are in all other respects), we come up with the following basic description or standard for such poems:

1. Twenty-two lines or units of more or less than 1 line (corresponding to the half-line acrostic Pss. 111 and 112; Ps. 37 has a two-line stanza form, while Ps. 119, the longest poem in the Psalter, has eight-line stanzas in the same pattern).

a. A variant poem has 23 lines or units in contrast with the basic model, which has only 22, corresponding to the letters of the alphabet. The 23rd line or unit serves to complete the poem in an interesting way. Thus in Pss. 25 and 34 there is a 23rd line. In both instances the line begins with the letter *pe*. For an ingenious and persuasive explanation of this phenomenon as an integral part of the poem, see the comments of P. W. Skehan.[7] There are nonalphabetic examples of the 23-unit type of poem as well. Just as the other lines have no alphabetic sequence, there seems to be no preference for the letter *pe* in the 23rd line of these poems.

b. A second variation involves the occurrence of at least one tricolon in the midst or at the end of what would normally be a steady procession of bicola. While the appearance of a third colon in a series of bicola still meets with skepticism on the part of modern scholars and editors, it seems clear that such additions are not always and invariably the result of scribal or editorial error, and that occasionally at least it should be regarded as a deliberate modification of the normal pattern. The combination of the addition of a 23rd line and the use of a tricolon instead of the ordinary bicolon to close off the poem has a pleasing effect, and this combined feature can be seen in a nonalphabetic acrostic poem in Ps. 94, which will be examined later on.

2. The standard line consists of a 16-syllable hexameter with the caesura or major pause in the middle of the line, thus producing the familiar 3:3 stress pattern (which is equivalent to 8:8 in syllables). In general, the bulk of the lines or at least the largest single group will conform to this pattern, having six stresses divided evenly between the two cola, or having 16 syllables divided in the middle, or both. Slight variations in the syllable count are fairly common as well. A shift of one

7. P. W. Skehan, "The Structure of the Song of Moses in Dt 32,1-43," *CBQ* 13 (1951): 153-163; repr. *Studies in Israelite Poetry and Wisdom.* CBQ Monograph 1 (Washington: Catholic Biblical Association, 1971). On pp. 74-75 Skehan points out that the addition of a *pe* line as the 23rd line of the acrostic makes *lamedh* the middle letter of the acrostic, and thus the first, middle, and last letters of the acrostic together spell *aleph* — summing up the whole alphabet in the first letter.

syllable in either direction should not be regarded as significant, since we can hardly claim so much precision or exactness in making our counts. Greater variation is sufficiently common or frequent to require further explanation, especially when these involve differences in stress-counting as well as the syllable-count. This is the area in which we find deliberate patterns of deviation from the norm, but these more serious variations typically balance out so that unusually short lines are matched by unusually long ones, with the result that the norm, mean, or average is not seriously affected. While the average or mean is calculated from all the data, we have an additional control in a theoretical norm, which has been arrived at without reference to the particular lines under investigation. Thus the poet is able to achieve variety and diversity in his work without significantly departing from the norms or standards for poems of this kind. This combination of overall regularity and extensive internal variation and freedom is quite unusual, especially when we compare Hebrew poetry with that of other languages and cultures, and all too often scholars in our field have failed to observe and acknowledge either the regularity or the freedom, or the relationship between them. That is hardly surprising in view of the fact that it is difficult to find comparable phenomena in the cultures and languages with which we are familiar; but since the same combination of features keeps turning up in the poetry of the Hebrew Bible wherever we look at the poems — i.e., overarching unity, structure, and regularity along with a considerable degree of freedom in varying from norms and departing from conventions — we should be prepared to recognize that it is precisely the combination that is the essential and integral feature of Hebrew poetry, and not merely one of them to the exclusion of the other in specific poems.

In the following tables we will give the stress count and the syllable count for each unit, and then offer comments about individual cola and lines and the poem as a whole. We will also provide a profile of the poem in terms of line-length and the distribution of lines throughout the poem. We will then tabulate the data for other poems with the same or similar structures. Finally, we will summarize and compare the findings. In the tables Column A will give the minimum count, while Column B will incorporate an alternate (and higher) count based upon variations in readings and vocalizations.

Lamentations 5

Verse	Stress Count	Syllable Count (A)	Syllable Count (B)
1	4 + 3 = 7	9 + 10 = 19	9 + 11 = 20
2	3 + 2 = 5	10 + 6 = 16	10 + 6 = 16
3	3 + 2 = 5	8 + 8 = 16	9 + 8 = 17
4	3 + 3 = 6	8 + 8 = 16	8 + 8 = 16
	13 + 10 = 23	35 + 32 = 67	36 + 33 = 69

Verse	Stress Count	Syllable Count (A)	Syllable Count (B)
5	3 + 3 = 6	8 + 8 = 16	8 + 9 = 17
6	3 + 3 = 6	6 + 5 = 11	6 + 5 = 11
7	3 + 3 = 6	9 + 11 = 20	10 + 12 = 22
8	3 + 3 = 6	8 + 6 = 14	8 + 6 = 14
	12 + 12 = 24	31+ 30 = 61	32 + 32 = 64
9	3 + 3 = 6	9 + 7 = 16	9 + 7 = 16
10	3 + 3 = 6	9 + 8 = 17	9 + 8 = 17
11	3 + 3 = 6	7 + 9 = 16	7 + 9 = 16
12	3 + 3 = 6	7 + 9 = 16	7 + 9 = 16
13	3 + 3 = 6	8 + 9 =17	8 + 9 = 17
14	3 + 2 = 5	8 + 8 = 16	8 + 8 = 16
	18 + 17 = 35	48 + 50 = 9	88 + 50 = 98
15	3 + 3 = 6	7 + 8 = 15	7 + 8 = 15
16	3 + 3 = 6	8 + 8 = 16	8 + 8 = 16
17	4 + 3 = 7	9 + 9 = 18	9 + 9 = 18
18	3 + 2 = 5	7 + 7 = 14	7 + 7 = 14
	13 + 11 = 24	31 + 32 = 63	31 + 32 = 63
19	4 + 3 = 7	9 + 6 = 15	9 + 7 = 16
20	3 + 3 = 6	8 + 8 = 16	8 + 8 = 16
21	4 + 3 = 7	11 + 7 = 18	13 + 7 = 20
22	3 + 3 = 6	8 + 8 = 16	8 + 9 = 17
	14 + 12 = 26	36 + 29 = 65	38 + 31 = 69
Totals	70 + 62 = 132	181 + 173 = 354	185 + 178 = 363

Distribution

	Stresses or Accents	
Balanced Bicola	3 + 3	(14)
Unbalanced	4 + 3	(4)
	3 + 2	(4)

Of the 44 cola in the poem, 36 have 3 stresses while 4 have 4 stresses, and 4 have 2 stresses. The total of 132 stresses or accents is equal to the norm of 6 stresses in each of the 22 lines of the poem.

Syllables

Cola

	A		B
5)	1	=	5
6)	3	=	18
7)	8	=	56
8)	15	=	126
9)	12	=	108
10)	2	=	20
11)	1	=	11
12)	1	=	12
13)	1	=	13
	44	=	363

Bicola

	A			B		
11)	1	=	11	1	=	11
12)	0	=	0	0	=	0
13)	0	=	0	0	=	0
14)	2	=	28	2	=	28
15)	2	=	30	1	=	15
16)	11	=	176	9	=	144
17)	2	=	34	5	=	85
18)	2	=	36	1	=	18
19)	1	=	19	0	=	0
20)	1	=	20	2	=	40
21)				0	=	0
22)				1	=	22
	22	=	354	22	=	363

Notes

When comparing the total figures for Columns A and B, we note that B has 9 added syllables. In six instances, the qere adds a syllable to kethib: four of these involve the addition of the conjunction *(w),* about which we will say something later; the other two involve the so-called emphatic ending which is added to the imperative form of the verb in v. 1 and forms the cohortative ending of the first person verb in v. 21. The remaining three instances involve the 2nd person masc. sg. suffix *-tā* attached to the verb in v. 22, and *-kā* attached as the pronominal suffix to a noun in v. 19 and a preposition in v. 21. While the readings in these cases in A and B are semantically equivalent and both merit consideration, we observe that the norm for this poem is 352 syllables, i.e., 22 lines at 16 syllables each, and that Column A is much closer to the norm than Column B. With a single exception to be discussed later, we would reject the longer readings as secondary and hold to the shorter text of Column A. We would observe further that the poem as a whole contains only two "prose particles," which is rather remarkable considering the lateness of composition (6th century B.C.E.) and the transmission history of the text.[8] These are respectively the sign of the definite direct object in v. 1 *('t-ḥrptynw)*

8. See F. I. Andersen and A. Dean Forbes, " 'Prose Particle' Counts of the Hebrew Bible," *The Word of the Lord Shall Go Forth,* ed. C. L. Meyers and M. O'Connor (Winona Lake: Eisenbrauns/American Schools of Oriental Research, 1983), 165-183.

and the definite article in v. 9 *(hmdbr).* Of the two, the *nota accusativi* is the more suspect, since that particle is extremely rare in poetry throughout the Bible, and a single occurrence in an entire poem is unusual, to say the least. The definite article is more common in poetry, though still rare as compared with prose, and it plays a significant role in certain poems, so the matter here must remain open. Excluding the prose particles would produce the desired norm in the figures from Column A, and we could rest the case at that point.

Looking at the statistics overall, we can say without question that the dominant meter of the poem is 3:3 when it comes to accents, and 16 syllables for the line or bicolon, while the single colon has a norm of 8 syllables. All of these data are derived empirically from the poem, but the norms, which are exactly the same, are derived from theoretical considerations and from the evidence of numerous other poems. The pattern 3:3 occurs in fourteen of the twenty-two verses, while the three-stress colon occurs in thirty-six cola out of forty-four. The four-stress and two-stress cola occur only four times each. Similarly, the 16-syllable bicolon occurs eleven times in 22 lines, but no other bicolon with a different count (whether 15 or 17, 14, or 18) occurs more than twice. The 8-syllable colon occurs eighteen times, which is almost twice as many as any other single colon (the 9-syllable colon occurs ten times, and the 7-syllable colon seven times). The three together constitute an overwhelming majority of all cases. To summarize, out of 22 lines, fourteen have the stress pattern 3:3, while eleven have a syllable count of 16. They overlap in eight instances, while in five cases the matchup is exact: 3:3 and in syllables 8:8. In all, 17 lines have either a 3:3 stress count or a 16-syllable count, or both. Thus 8 lines have both 3:3 and 16 syllables, while in six cases we have the 3:3 stress pattern but not 16 syllables, and in three cases we have a 16-syllable count but a different stress count.

There are 8 lines with an apparently different metrical pattern: four of them have a stress pattern of 4:3, and four others have a 3:2 pattern:

The pattern 4:3 occurs in vv. 1, 17, 19, 21. In the first three instances the number of syllables is 9, which is not excessive for a three-stress colon, as shown in vv. 7a, 9a, and 10a. Thus the poet was able to incorporate an additional stress in the colon without disturbing the underlying metrical pattern unduly. In the fourth instance (v. 21) the first colon is substantially longer than the normal three-stress unit, and clearly belongs in the normal pattern for four-stress cola or half-lines. With 11 syllables (13 in Column B) it is easily the longest first colon in the poem. In this case, the poet moved out of the normal range of his standard formula for cola in this poem. We might suspect that the text is not intact at this point, and that possibility must be taken into consideration; but it may serve our purposes better to look elsewhere in the poem for a compensating omission or diminution to balance the excess in this line. To that point we will return, but in the meantime we want to point out that every colon with four stresses comes in the first half of the line or bicolon. Thus the lines in question are all overbalanced in the first half-line, giving at least the impression of a falling rhythm, which is standard fare in the first four chapters of Lamentations (3:2 meter is the norm in those poems). Supporting this maneuver is the corresponding reduction in the number of stresses in the second colon, also in four instances. In no case do we have the two-stress second colon after a four-stress first colon, but the cumulative effect is to add four stresses to the first half-line and to reduce the second half-line by the same number, with the result that the first colon throughout the poem has a total for eight more stresses than the second colon, thus deliberately unbalancing the otherwise apparent equilibrium of a metrical scheme with cola of equal length in each line. In this subtle fashion, the poet, while using a standard rhythm (in fact, the standard meter for the whole Bible), nevertheless has modified it sufficiently to give the impression and tone of the falling rhythm of a lament. The basic pattern remains essentially intact, but the sensitive reader or hearer can detect the mood and character of the falling rhythm associated with laments.

We may now look at the four two-stress cola in the poem, all of which occur in the second half-line of the verse as opposed to the four-stress cola, all of which occur in the first half-line; vv. 2, 3, 14, 18. Of the four, two have eight syllables each (vv. 3, 14), while a third has 7. All of these qualify for inclusion in the normal range of the three-stress colon, just as three of the four four-stress cola also qualified (with 9 syllables each). In other words, these understressed cola do not disrupt the basic metrical pattern any more than the overstressed cola do. Thus the poet remains within the dominant pattern, while shifting the weight of accentuation from a balanced system to one that is tipped significantly in favor of the first colon as over against the second one. The remaining two-stress colon, however, is clearly short of the norm, having only 6 syllables (v. 2b); and with this one, the poet has broken through the normal limits of his metrical scheme. In three of the four cases he stayed within the limits of a three-stress line, and that is also the case with the four-stress cola. In one instance of the latter, he exceeded the normal limits and came up with an 11-syllable colon, whereas here he has fallen short with a 6-syllable colon. Needless to say, they balance nicely against each other, and the syllables he took away in v. 2 he restores (with small interest) in v. 21. That the two verses are equidistant from the ends and middle of the poem will not have escaped the attentive student of the subject of Hebrew poetry.

It may be asked why we do not take into consideration the very short bicolon in v. 6, where we have cola of 6 and 5 syllables for a total of 11 for the bicolon, no more than the single colon in v. 21a. But in v. 6, the case is quite different. In spite of the severe shortness of the cola, they both have three stresses, and hence qualify for the standard pattern, although such brevity in syllable count is very unusual. This extreme example of a 3:3 pattern is matched in the very next verse (v. 7), where we find the longest line in the poem, but also with a 3:3 stress count. The two represent rare extremes, and probably demonstrate the versatility of the poet. They also balance each other remarkably well, and if we combine them, as in fact they are adjoining in the poem, the total for the two bicola or two lines is practically on target (31 syllables against the normative 32, while the stress count at twelve is exactly right). Adding the lines and averaging out produces an almost perfect approximation to our norm: first cola — 3:3 (stresses) and 6 + 9 = 15 (syllables); second cola — 3:3 (stresses) and 5 + 11 = 16 (syllables). If we were to accept the qere of v. 7a as more original than the kethib, i.e., *wᵉʾênām* for *ʾênām,* then the matchups would be perfect indeed: 6 + 10 = 16 (for the first cola) and 5 + 11 = 16 (for the second cola), with the total for the double bicolon at 32. The omission of the conjunction in kethib can be explained as the result of haplography, i.e., the loss of *waw* at the beginning of *wʾynm* through a scribal lapse owing to the *waw* at the end of the preceding word, *ḥṭʾw.* Nevertheless, we prefer kethib to qere at the beginning of the second colon of v. 7, where kethib has *ʾᵃnaḥnû* while qere adds the conjunction at the beginning of the word: *wʾnḥnw.* Stylistically, kethib is superior, even though it was customary to introduce second cola with the conjunction, and this is quite common in the mass of Hebrew poetry. Nevertheless, in the earliest poetry and in the best tradition the conjunction was not used at the beginning of cola. In this poem, of 22 lines, only one second colon is introduced by the conjunction *waw,* v. 13b. All the others, from v. 1 through v. 22, lack the conjunction at the beginning of the second colon, and that is sufficient evidence to show the poet's preference and his/her idea of high style. This evidence is so preponderant that we can vote with kethib against qere at the beginning of v. 7b and leave out the conjunctions, even if we add it in v. 7a. In fact, we can raise the question as to the originality, apart from the propriety, of the conjunction in v. 13b, where we would hardly have expected to find it. Apart from the fact that it is the only example in the whole poem of this practice, it is placed very oddly in a series of nouns with which the unit of four bicola is composed. Thus in vv. 11-14 we have a series of nouns describing groups or classes in society, and in every other case, no conjunction is used: *nšym // btlt* (v. 11), *śrym // (pny) zknym* (v. 12), *zknym // bḥwrym* (v. 14). We would have expected in v. 13 the sequence *bḥwrym // nʿrym* rather than *wnʿrym.* In fact, the presence of the unwanted *waw* in MT can be explained as a case of dittography deriving from the *waw* at the end of the preceding word *nśʾw,* the scribe committing the opposite error of the one we charged him with in v. 7a. Unconscious compensation is not unknown in the arcane world of scribal lapses, and in these cases both changes make reasonable sense. And given the sequence of four pairs of nouns in vv. 11-14, it is very strange that in only one of them, and that one in the middle of the series, we have the conjunction with the second colon. Finally we observe that each of the four bicola has 16 syllables (our norm), with the single exception of v. 13, which in its present form has 17 syllables. Without it, the bicolon would conform to the pattern established for the poem as a whole, and specifically for this group of four verses. The group can be charted as follows (with the emendation):

7 + 9 = 16 (v. 11)	8 + 8* = 16 (v. 13)
7 + 9 = 16 (v. 12)	8 + 8 = 16 (v. 14)

But after all is said and done, it is possible that the deviation in MT at v. 13 was a deliberate decision on the part of the poet, if only to show that he was not a slave to any pattern, no matter how aesthetically satisfying. There should be at least one exception to every rule in a poem by an artist, so we may be compelled to leave the *waw* in v. 13b. But there is no reason for a second one, so we will not add it in v. 7b.

Before leaving Lam. 5, we wish to point out that the name Yahweh occurs only three times in the poem, once at the beginning (v. 1) and twice more toward the end of the poem (vv. 19, 21); the use of the name YHWH as an echoing device in Hebrew poetry (i.e., at the beginning and end of poems) is well known (e.g., Ps. 23 for a good example). What is less obvious in this instance is the fact that all of the examples of the name Yahweh occur in four-stress cola (three out of four of the latter have the name Yahweh, and these are the only places where the name occurs). In a poem that has an overwhelming number of three-stress cola, this selectivity is rather remarkable and can hardly be the result of chance distribution. The effect is to give added weight to the use of the divine name and to call attention to it. This circumstance might be regarded as a mildly interesting phenomenon in the current poem, but it occurs elsewhere, showing that the technique was used to advantage by other poets as well. Thus the same sort of overbalancing of lines in which the name Yahweh is present occurs in Pss. 33, 34, and 94, although the details vary from poem to poem. What they all have in common is that they are acrostics, Ps. 34 an alphabetic acrostic with an added line (although one of the regular lines has been lost through accident, no doubt), while Pss. 33 and 94 are acrostics of the same type as Lam. 5, i.e., without the alphabetic device.

We turn briefly to Pss. 33 and 94, since they are nonalphabetic acrostics of the same basic type as Lam. 5, in order to show that all of them have essentially the same structure, although the accidents and ornaments differ. The analogy with automobile manufacturers is appropriate in the sense that the great variety of automobiles produced by General Motors, e.g., are built upon a very limited number of basic chassis types, with a bewildering number of options in all peripheral and superficial features.

Ps. 33 has the same basic structure as Lam. 5, while Ps. 94, also nonalphabetic, resembles Pss. 25 and 34 in having an added 23rd line. In addition, the added line is a tricolon, a fitting conclusion to such a work. Such a variation, i.e., closing with a tricolon, is also known in biblical poetry. Several of the acrostic poems, alphabetic and nonalphabetic, have tricola somewhere in the course of the normal bicola, and such additions are to be regarded as optional equipment. Since space forbids a detailed analysis of the poems under consideration, we will limit ourselves to suitable charts and tables to show that the poets all used the same basic metrical pattern to produce their works of art: essentially it is a 3:3 stress-count system with a corresponding 8 + 8 = 16 syllable-count, along with the usual range of variation and ornamentation.

Psalm 33

Verse	Stress Count	Syllable Count (A)	Syllable Count (B)
1	3 + 3 = 6	9 + 9 = 18	9 + 9 = 18
2	3 + 3 = 6	8 + 8 = 16	8 + 8 = 16
3	3 + 3 = 6	6 + 8 = 14	6 + 8 = 14
4	3 + 3 = 6	7 + 9 = 16	7 + 9 = 16
5	3 + 4 = 7	8 + 8 = 16	8 + 8 = 16
6	4 + 3 = 7	8 + 8 = 16	8 + 8 = 16
7	3 + 3 = 6	7 + 9 = 16	7 + 9 = 16
	22 + 22 = 44	53 + 59 = 112	53 + 59 = 112
8	3 + 4 = 7	9 + 12 = 21	9 + 12 = 21
9	3 + 3 = 6	7 + 6 = 13	7 + 6 = 13
10	4 + 3 = 7	8 + 7 = 15	8 + 7 = 15
11	4 + 4 = 8	9 + 9 = 18	9 + 9 = 18
	14 + 14 = 28	33 + 23 = 67	33 + 34 = 67
12	*4 + 3 = 7	*10 + 8 = 18	10 + 8 = 18
13	3 + 3 = 6	7 + 8 = 15	7 + 8 = 15
14	3 + 3 = 6	7 + 7 = 14	7 + 7 = 14
15	3 + 3 = 6	6 + 8 = 14	6 + 8 = 14
	13 + 12 = 25	30 + 31 = 61	30 + 31 = 61
16	3 + 3 = 6	8 + 9 = 17	8 + 9 = 17
17	3 + 3 = 6	6 + 9 = 15	6 + 9 = 15
18	4 + 2 = 6	9 + 8 = 17	9 + 8 = 17
19	3 + 2 = 5	7 + 8 = 15	7 + 8 = 15
20	3 + 3 = 6	9 + 9 = 18	9 + 9 = 18
21	3 + 3 = 6	7 + 8 = 15	7 + 8 = 15
22	4 + 3 = 7	9 + 7 = 16	10 + 7 = 17
23	23 + 19 = 42	55 + 58 = 113	56 + 58 = 114
Totals	72 + 67 = 139	171 + 182 = 353	172 + 182 = 354

*The only emendation we make in the text is to substitute *še-* for *ʾ^{a}šer* in v. 12 on the basis of the reading in a few MSS. The particle *ʾšr* is extremely rare in poetry (but cf. *kaʾ^{a}šer* in v. 22, which seems to be original) and clearly disturbs the meter with regard to both stress-count and syllable-count. The reading with *še-* may be questioned as well, although it is used in poetry and is superior to *ʾšr*. The relative pronoun is often omitted in poetry, and that may have been the original reading, thereby reducing the syllable count for 12a to 9.

Distribution

	Stresses or Accents	
Balanced Bicola	3 + 3	(13)
	4 + 4	(1)
Unbalanced	4 + 3	(4)
	3 + 4	(2)
	4 + 2	(1)
	3 + 2	(1)

Of the 44 cola in the poem, 33 have three stresses, while 9 have four stresses, and 2 have two stresses. The total of 139 stresses or accents is somewhat higher than the norm of 132 representing 22 lines with six stresses each. The poem is overbalanced with more stresses in the first cola than in the second (72 to 67), as was the case with Lam. 5. Six of the first cola (out of 22) have four stresses each, and in every one of them the name Yahweh appears (cf. the discussion of this phenomenon in Lam. 5). There are six other occurrences of the name YHWH in first cola, all of which have three stresses only. The lone appearance of YHWH in a second colon occurs in v. 5b, which also has four stresses.

***Syllables**

Cola			Bicola		
6)	4 =	24	13)	1 =	13
7)	10 =	70	14)	3 =	42
8)	15 =	120	15)	5 =	75
9)	13 =	117	16)	6 =	96
10)	1 =	10	17)	2 =	34
11)	0 =	0	18)	4 =	72
12)	1 =	12	19)	0 =	0
	44 =	353	20)	0 =	0
			21)	1 =	21
				22 =	353

*Since only one figure in the entire list is different for Column B, it seemed pointless to make a separate listing of the numbers in that column. The overall picture would not be affected. It only remains to be noted that with the omission of *ʾᵃšer* in v. 12a, we would not only restore metrical harmony in that colon (we will also omit *še-* as a secondary intrusion) but also reduce the overall figure for the poem to 352, which would correspond exactly with the presumed norm for poems of this kind: 22 lines at 16 syllables each equals 352. If we leave *ʾᵃšer* alone, then the total would be 354 (Column A), which would correspond exactly with the figure for Column A of Lam. 5. In both poems the added numbers seem to derive from unnecessary prose particles.

Psalm 94

Verse	Stress Count	Syllable Count (A)	Syllable Count (B)
1	3 + 3 = 6	6 + 6 = 12	6 + 6 = 12
2	3 + 3 = 6	7 + 7 = 14	7 + 7 = 14
3	3 + 3 = 6	8 + 9 = 17	8 + 9 = 17
4	3 + 3 = 6	9 + 9 = 18	9 + 9 = 18
5	3 + 2 = 5	8 + 7 = 15	9 + 8 = 17
6	3 + 2 = 5	8 + 7 = 15	8 + 7 = 15
7	3 + 3 = 6	8 + 9 = 17	8 + 9 = 17
	21 + 19 = 40	54 + 54 = 108	55 + 55 = 110
8	3 + 3 = 6	7 + 9 = 16	7 + 9 = 16
9	4 + 4 = 8	8 + 8 = 16	8 + 8 = 16
10	3 + 3 = 6	9 + 7 = 16	9 + 7 = 16
11	4 + 2 = 6	9 + 4 = 13	9 + 4 = 13
	14 + 12 = 26	33 + 28 = 61	33 + 28 = 61
12	*4 + 2 = 6	*10 + 10 = 20	10 + 11 = 21
13	3 + 3 = 6	7 + 8 = 15	7 + 8 = 15
14	3 + 2 = 5	8 + 7 = 15	8 + 7 = 15
15	3 + 3 = 6	7 + 7 = 14	7 + 7 = 14
	13 +10 = 23	32 + 32 = 64	32 + 33 = 65
16	3 + 4 = 7	8 + 10 = 18	8 + 10 = 18
17	3 + 4 = 7	8 + 9 = 17	8 + 9 = 17
18	3 + 3 = 6	8 + 8 = 16	8 + 9 = 17
19	3 + 3 = 6	8 + 9 = 17	8 + 10 = 18
20	3 + 3 = 6	8 + 7 = 15	9 + 7 = 16
21	3 + 3 = 6	7 + 7 = 14	7 + 7 = 14
22	3 + 3 = 6	9 + 7 = 16	9 + 7 = 16
	21 + 23 = 44	56 + 57 = 113	57 + 59 = 116
Totals	69 + 64 = 133	175 + 171 = 346	177 + 175 = 352
23	3 + 2 + 3 = 8	9 + 8 + 9 = 26	9 + 8 + 9 = 26
Totals	72 + 66 + 3 = 141	184 + 179 + 9 = 372	186 + 183 + 9 = 378

*Once again we omit the relative pronoun *ʾašer* on the basis of its omission in two MSS (cf. discussion of the same verse in Ps. 33). V. 12 in both Psalms has a similar structure, and in both cases there is an intrusive *ʾšr.* The omission in MSS for this Psalm strengthens the case for omission in Ps. 33 (instead of substitution). The counts for the first 22 lines (= verses) are given for comparison with the two preceding poems. The figures for the closing tricolon are given separately and then the totals for the whole poem are given.

Distribution

	Stresses or Accents	
Balanced Bicola	3 + 3	(14)
	4 + 4	(1)
Unbalanced	3 + 2	(3)
	4 + 2	(2)
	3 + 4	(2)
	3 + 2 + 3	(1)

Of the 44 cola in the main body of the poem (first 22 lines), 33 have three stresses, while 6 have four stresses and 5 have two stresses. If we add the figures for the closing tricolon, we have 35 cola with three stresses, and 6 each with four and two stresses. For the first 22 lines, the total number of stresses is 133, very close to the norm of 132, with a slight preponderance in the first cola as compared with the second cola (69 to 64 stresses). For the whole poem the total number of stresses is 141, which is exactly in accord with the norm for 47 cola (x 3 = 141) or 23 lines (plus an added colon = 23½ lines).

Syllables

	Cola			Bicola	
	A	B		A	B
4)	1 = 4	1 = 4	12)	1 = 12	1 = 12
5)	0 = 0	0 = 0	13)	1 = 13	1 = 13
6)	2 = 12	2 = 12	14)	3 = 42	3 = 42
7)	14 = 98	13 = 91	15)	5 = 75	3 = 45
8)	14 = 112	12 = 96	16)	5 = 80	5 = 80
9)	10 = 90	12 = 108	17)	4 = 68	5 = 85
10)	3 = 30	3 = 30	18)	2 = 36	3 = 54
11)	0 = 0	1 = 11	19)	0 = 0	0 = 0
	44 = 346	44 = 352	20)	1 = 20	0 = 0
8)	1 = 8	1 = 8	21)	0 = 0	1 = 21
9)	2 = 18	2 = 18		22 = 346	22 = 352
	3 = 26	3 = 26	26)	1 = 26	1 = 26
	47 = 372	47 = 378		23.5 = 372	23.5 = 378

For the first 22 lines (equivalent to the other two poems under consideration), the syllable count for Column A is slightly below the norm of 352 syllables, while the figure for Column B is exactly on target (352). We could infer from this circumstance that the long form of the pronominal suffixes was intended by the poet (cf. vv. 5, 12b, 18b, 19b, and 20a). When we add v. 23, the total for Column A is 4 under the norm of 376, while for Column B it is 2 over. As in the case of the other poems, this one is very close to the norm for syllables and stress counts. The findings for the three poems under consideration can be summarized in the following chart:

	Lam. 5	Ps. 33	Ps. 94
Stresses:	70 + 62 = 132	72 + 67 = 139	69 + 64 = 133 (22 lines)
Syllables:	181 + 173 = 354	171 + 182 = 353	177 + 175 = 352 (Col. B)

Distribution: Stresses

Balanced Cola:			
3 + 3:	14	13	14
4 + 4:	0	1	1
Unbalanced Cola:			
4 + 3	4	4	0
3 + 2	4	1	3
4 + 2	0	1	2
3 + 4	0	2	2
Tricolon:	0	0	1

Syllables:

		Cola	
4)	0 = 0	0 = 0	1 = 4
5)	1 = 5	0 = 0	0 = 0
6)	4 = 24	4 = 24	2 = 12
7)	7 = 49	10 = 70	13 = 91
8)	18 = 144	15 = 120	12 = 96
9)	10 = 90	13 = 117	12 = 108
10)	2 = 20	1 = 10	3 = 30
11)	2 = 22	0 = 0	1 = 11
12)	0 = 0	1 = 12	0 = 0
Totals:	44 = 354	44 = 353	44 = 352

	Lam. 5	Ps. 33 *Bicola*	Ps. 94
11)	1 = 11	0 = 0	0 = 0
12)	0 = 0	0 = 0	1 = 12
13)	0 = 0	1 = 13	1 = 13
14)	2 = 28	3 = 42	3 = 42
15)	2 = 30	5 = 75	3 = 45
16)	11 = 176	6 = 96	5 = 80
17)	2 = 34	2 = 34	5 = 85
18)	2 = 36	4 = 72	3 = 54
19)	1 = 19	0 = 0	0 = 0
20)	1 = 20	0 = 0	0 = 0
21)	0 = 0	1 = 21	1 = 21
	22 = 354	22 = 353	22 = 352

Conclusion

It has been a commonplace of research in biblical poetry that the alphabetic acrostic poems share a standard structure and present a fairly uniform profile. The great majority have lines that average out around 16 syllables (or range between 15-1/2 and 16-1/2 syllables); there are usually three stresses or accents in each half-line, with a major pause around the middle of the line. All of the poems we have examined in this study and most of the alphabetic acrostic poems meet these requirements. Exceptional in this respect are the first four chapters of the book of Lamentations, in which the prevailing accentual pattern is 3:2 and the syllable count averages out between 13 and 13-1/2 syllables.

The purpose of the present paper was to extend the area of research to include a group of poems that share many of the features of the standard alphabetic acrostic poems, but lack the most immediate and obvious characteristic, namely, the alphabetic factor. It has never been doubted that Lam. 5 belonged to this category, and increasingly in recent years numerous other poems have been identified as members of the nonalphabetic acrostic group. Among many available for study, we selected a couple of Psalms (33 and 94) for analysis, and might have included several chapters from the book of Proverbs (especially from the first unit, chs. 1–9, which include acrostic poems [nonalphabetic] in chs. 2, 5, and 8:32-36 plus 9:1-18; ch. 1 has a more complex arrangement of similar elements, while 8:1-31 consists of three half-line acrostics in sequence (vv. 1-11, 12-21, and 22-31).[9] In structural terms, they are practically indistinguishable from the alphabetic acrostics. All of them build on the basic 22-line or unit foundation, which they all have in common. Other features are less constant, but turn up in a number of the poems: the 23rd line summation or conclusion and the occasional third colon, which interrupts the otherwise undeviating bicolon continuity. Rarely an equivalent pattern of 2:2:2 stresses varies the normal 3:3 (we incorporate it into the bicolon structure as 4:2 or theoretically 2:4). Other variations are relatively frequent, such as 4:3 and 3:2, but for the most part these are woven into the existing syllabic structure so that most lines come close to the norm. When lines of unusual length appear (whether excessively long or short), they often balance out against each other, thus confirming the deliberate construction of the author, rather than pointing to a scribal lapse or editorial intrusion. It is not always easy to tell the difference.

Curious, but also significant, is the apparent affinity of the sacred name, YHWH, for cola with four stresses or accents instead of the normal three. These occur most often in the first colon of a bicolon (although a striking exception was noted) and thus help to tip the balance in favor of the first colon when measured against the second. By combining a stress-counting with a syllable-counting technique, we can reach a more exact description of the poetic units and a better basis for comparing them. The major result of the investigation thus far is to show that these poems, which constitute a much

9. R. B. Y. Scott, *Proverbs–Ecclesiastes*. AB 18 (Garden City: Doubleday, 1965), 71.

larger group than previously thought, especially when we link the known alphabetic acrostics with the emerging collection of nonalphabetic acrostics, use the standard meter of Hebrew poetry, which we may define in the words of the 4th-century Church Father Eusebius of Caesarea as a hexameter of 16 syllables.[10] Many of the lines conform exactly to this model, while others vary only marginally from the norm. Still others deviate more widely, but they can be regarded as part of the system, which had a definite structure but also permitted degrees of freedom.

Other studies showing in detail how such poems are constructed and organized will follow, including the special group in Lam. 1–4. In addition, there are more examples of the nonalphabetic acrostic type in the so-called Wisdom books of the Bible, among them a number of Psalms, more chapters and units of Proverbs, and several speeches and parts of speeches in the book of Job. Along with these we must not omit the Wisdom of Ben Sira. The author made extensive use of this poetic form, as has been pointed out by various scholars, conveniently summarized by A. A. Di Lella in the forthcoming Anchor Bible commentary on that book.[11] It may be noted, in passing, that just as the book of Proverbs begins with several nonalphabetic acrostic poems and closes with a clearly defined alphabetic acrostic poem on "The Magnificent Woman" (31:10-31), so Ben Sira begins and ends in similar fashion. The opening chapters consist of nonalphabetic acrostic poems, while the last chapter, 51, has been confirmed as an alphabetic acrostic in the original Hebrew by the discovery of the Psalms Scroll from Cave 11 at Qumran. That scroll includes ch. 51 of Ben Sira or at least half of it, and the alphabetic device shines forth quite clearly.[12]

It is further our belief that the 16-syllable line, with six stresses divided in the middle by the caesura or major pause, was the standard or common meter of extant Hebrew poetry, and that it was used by the poets of the Bible regularly and more frequently than any other meter or even combination of meters. There are many modifications, deviations, and departures from the norm, also deliberate alterations and adjustments, but the basic meter is a constant throughout the books of Proverbs and Job, and was used frequently in the composition of the Psalter; it is also found throughout the prophetic literature and underlies much of the poetry of the Pentateuch and Former Prophets.

10. Eusebius, *Praeparatio Evangelica* ix.5.

11. P. W. Skehan and A. A. Di Lella, *The Wisdom of Ben Sira.* AB 39 (Garden City: Doubleday, 1987).

12. J. A. Sanders, *The Psalms Scroll of Qumrân Cave 11 (11QPs[a]).* DJD 4 (Oxford: Clarendon, 1965), 79-85. See p. 80 for the Hebrew of the Qumran text and Plate XIII for the photograph.

15

Deliberate Deviation from an Established Pattern of Repetition in Hebrew Poetry as a Rhetorical Device

Repetition is a well-known and often used rhetorical device in all of literature, and the phenomenon is widely recorded and represented in the Hebrew Bible. What is not as clearly or unanimously recognized is the occurrence of modifications or departures from an established pattern of repetition. Such deviations in the preserved text of the Hebrew Bible are often regarded as unintended errors, and we must allow for that possibility always. But when such deviations recur in a variety of places, and develop their own patterns, then it is important to stop, reflect, and consider whether they are not part of the arsenal or equipment of the poet in his/her effort to express or communicate in some significant and personal manner. Instead of deleting the phenomenon or dismissing these curious departures or defections from determinable norms, it may be well for us to take note of them and analyze their characteristics and possible function or purpose. Even if no discernible intention can be discovered, and even if they are purely ornamental or aesthetic adaptations, they will tell us something about the literary tastes and attainments of the author/editor and we will gain a new and heightened respect for Biblical Hebrew literature.

Let us look at some examples of the phenomenon in question: the essential requirements are first a clearly established pattern of repetition, and second, an equally obvious or explicit departure from the norm.

In the well-known oracle at the beginning of the book of Amos (1:3–2:8), there is a series of denunciations or pronouncements of judgments on eight nations. There is a common framework for these utterances, in which a number of elements are repeated, including the opening words, and also the words describing the punishment to be inflicted. The latter is repeated seven times, once for each of the first seven nations listed. The clause which concerns us reads as follows:

w^{e}šillaḥtî 'ēš b^{e}-	and I will send fire against

The expression occurs in the following places:

1:4	(Aram)	12	(Edom)
7	(Philistia)	2:2	(Moab)
10	(Tyre)	5	(Judah)

In these six occurrences the wording is the same, thus establishing the pattern of repetition beyond question. There is a seventh instance, in the oracle on the Ammonites, but the wording in 1:14 is different:

w^{e}hiṣṣattî 'ēš b^{e}

A different, less common, verb has been substituted for the familiar, repeated, *šillaḥtî,* but there is no detectable difference in meaning or intention. It is a deviation, but so far as we can tell purely stylistic in character. The deviation is sufficiently jarring for one of our most eminent commentators, the dean and doyen of commentators, to impel him to declare that the text is corrupt, and that therefore it is incumbent on us to repair the damage caused by the ubiquitous Deuteronomic editor (who leaves his clumsy fingerprints in selected nooks and crannies of the Bible so as to call attention to his presence) and restore the obviously original *w^{e}šillaḥtî* in that passage. Then we will have the full complement of seven repetitions, without departure or deviation from the straight and narrow path.

We must in fact demur and insist that barring compelling and convincing evidence to the contrary the text be retained with its deviation. (On the face of it, textual corruption would move in the opposite direction.) Editors and scribes would be more likely to substitute the established and endlessly repeated *w^{e}šillaḥtî* for an unusual and pattern-breaking *w^{e}hiṣṣattî* and bring everything into uniformity than the other way around. The danger for modern scholars is that they are like ancient ones and prefer everything to be neat and orderly. But poets and prophets are made of different stuff, cut from different cloth.

For the present, we note the sequence of repetitions and the alteration in midcourse, or more precisely at the fifth member of a series of seven. We proceed now to a similar phenomenon in ch. 6 of the same book of Amos. In 6:1-6, we have another series of seven pronouncements introduced by the word *hôy* for "Woe!" The woes consist grammatically of a series of addresses to various groups which are identified as verbal nouns (i.e., participles or roughly equivalent terms), e.g., *hašš^{a}'anannîm* in v. 1 is not a participle but an equivalent verbal noun. What these terms have in common is that most of them are preceded by the definite article: *ha.* Thus we have:

6:1 *hašša'^{a}nannîm*	Those who luxuriate
1 *w^{e}habbōṭ^{e}ḥîm*	and those who feel secure
3 *ham^{e}naddîm*	those who rush along[?]

4 *haššok*e*bîm*	those who lie down
5 *happor*e*ṭîm*	those who strum or hum
6 *haššōṯîm*	those who drink

We note that six of the total of seven conform to this usage, thus establishing a consistent pattern of repetition. The remaining term in the list is to be found in v. 4, and it is:

6:4 *w*e*'ōk*e*lîm*	and those who eat

It seems evident that the omission of the definite article does not affect the meaning of the term or its definiteness — it is just as definite as those with the definite article (which serves more as a relative pronoun than simply as the definite article) or as indefinite. The point is that there is a specific and observable deviation from an established norm. Curiously enough, the deviant member of the series is the fifth out of seven, just as in the case of the series in chs. 1–2.

We turn to a third case in the book of Amos: 4:4-5. Here we have a series of verbs, seven in all, and most of them clearly marked as 2nd masc. pl. imperative forms:

4:4 *bō'û*	Come to
ûpiš'û	and transgress
harbû (lipšōa')	multiply (to transgress)
*w*e*hābî'û*	and bring
4:5 *w*e*qir'û*	and proclaim
hašmî'û	make heard

In all six cases we have a 2nd masc. pl. form of the verb. In the remaining instance, in v. 5, there is an additional verb, which is expected, but its form is noticeably different from the others:

4:5 *w*e*qaṭṭēr*	and burn as a sacrifice

Clearly the form is not a 2nd masc. pl. imperative like the others, and we are instructed in the latest edition of the Kittel Bible (BHS), as in earlier editions, to read *qaṭṭ*e*rû* to make the form the same as in the other six verbs.

But is such an emendation either necessary or desirable? Usually the surviving form is taken to be the imperative singular, and hence out of phase with the overwhelming majority of plural forms. It is much more likely, however, that the form is the piel infinitive absolute, which is indeclinably singular, here substituted for the 2nd masc. pl. forms which predominate and establish the pattern. While the infinitive absolute is not used often in this way, it is established usage and occurs more frequently than the grammars recognize or acknowledge. In this instance, as also in the Decalogue (*šāmôr* and *zākôr* in the commandment concerning the

Sabbath; cf. Deut. 5:12 and Exod. 20:8), the infinitive absolute stands for the fuller expression: *zākôr tizkᵉrû* or *šāmôr tišmᵉrû* — "you shall surely remember" or "you shall surely observe." Whether or not that is the rationale behind the appearance of the infinitive absolute in a series of imperatives, the form serves effectively as a substitute for the normal forms with the full force of the imperative.

Once again we have a marked and visible deviation from an established norm. Without pressing the point, we wish to observe that the unusual form is once again the fifth in a series of seven.

Turning now to other examples of this unusual phenomenon, we look at the oracle on Joseph in the Blessing of Jacob (Gen. 49) and compare it with the corresponding utterance in the Blessing of Moses (Deut. 33). In Gen. 49:25-26 we have a series of blessings on Joseph, each one beginning, appropriately enough, with the word *birkōt,* "blessings." There are six such specified blessings, and five of them begin with the word *birkōt:*

> 49:25 *birkōt šāmayim mēʿāl*
> *birkōt tᵉhôm rōbeṣet tāḥat*
> *birkōt šādayîm wāraḥam*
> 26 *birkōt ʾābîkā gābᵉrû ʿal-*
> *birkōt hôray ʿad*

The sixth and last entry in this sequence begins with the word *taʾᵃwat* rather than *birkōt;* while they are hardly synonymous terms it is clear from the context that they share a common meaning and force. The sequence is arranged in pairs, with the first pair describing blessings from the heavens above and the subterranean sea below, the second pair referring apparently to female fecundity and male might (perhaps an echo of the ruling deities of the Canaanite pantheon). The third pair refers to the everlasting mountains//eternal hills, a familiar cliche, while the terms *brkt* and *tʾwt* can be taken as a complementary combination: blessings consisting of desirable things.

For our purposes the important point is that there is a clear pattern of repetition and an equally clear deviation from that pattern. There are six components in the sequence: five have *birkōt* while the sixth has *tʾwt,* a deviation from the pattern of repetition.

If we compare the two blessings of Joseph, we find a similar phenomenon in the Blessing of Moses. In Deut. 33:13-16 we have a comparable series of blessings bestowed on Joseph. In this sequence the operative word is *mimmeged,* which is rendered "choicest gifts" or the like in RSV, and that will suffice here. There are six such blessings in these verses, and five of them are introduced by this term *mmgd:*

> 33:13 *mimmeged šāmayîm miṭṭāl*
> *ûmittᵉhôm rōbeṣet tāhat*

14 *ûmimmeged t^{e}bû'ōt šāmeš*
ûmimmeged gereš y^{e}rāḥîm
15 *ûmēro'š har^{e}rê-qedem*
ûmimmeged gib'ôt 'ôlām
16 *ûmimmeged 'ereṣ ûm^{e}lō'āh*
ûr^{e}ṣôn šōk^{e}nî s^{e}neh

In the list of blessings here, there are four pairs (not counting the opening clause, which corresponds to Gen. 49:25a), two of which correspond closely with the first two pairs in the Blessing of Jacob. In v. 13 a metrical anomaly is resolved by omitting *mmgd* before the second clause (unlike Gen. 49, where *brkt* is repeated in spite of the longer second colon). In v. 15, where the parallel phrases, including the everlasting mountains and the eternal hills (in the same order as Gen. 49:26), occur as in Gen. 49, we also have the alteration in the key word. Where Gen. 49 has the order *brkt//t'wt,* this passage has *mr'š//mmged,* reversing the order of the deviation. How *mr'š* fits into the sequence and context is not altogether clear, but the fact that the primary deviation occurs in the same bicolon here as in Gen. 49 should caution against the temptation to emend and restore the text. While *mr'š* is no synonym of *mmgd,* and while it may be a mistake for something else, it is unlikely that the word to be restored here is *mmgd.* As in Gen. 49, we have five instances of the key word, and one instance of a deviant term. That expression should form a combination with *mmgd,* and perhaps it signifies the best or most valued of these choice gifts, similar to the combination formed by *t'wt* and *brkt* ("the most desirable blessings") — so here the best of the gifts, the choicest of presents.

It is clear that the pattern of repetition in Deut. 33 exhibits further modifications and alterations than the passage in Gen. 49. What they have in common is the five fixed repetitions of the key term *brkt* in Gen. 49 and *mmgd* in Deut. 33. In the passage relating to the everlasting mountains//eternal hills we find a departure from the pattern on both poems: *brkt//t'wt* and *mr'š//mmgd.* In addition, in Deut. 33 the last bicolon apparently has another deviant feature in which *mmgd* is parallel to *wrṣwn.* At the same time it may be noted that the unique phrase *škny snh* qualifies *yhwh* at the beginning of the verse (13), and together the two cola form an envelope around the list of blessings or rich gifts:

m^{e}bōreket yhwh 'arṣô
. . . *ûr^{e}ṣôn šōk^{e}nî s^{e}neh*

Blessed of Yahweh be his land
. . . and the good will of the dweller
of the Seneh (bush).

Compare the parallels of *rṣwn* and *brkt* (in chiastic order) in the same poem, in the blessing of Naphtali (33:23).

In the end, therefore, we probably have the same basic collocation in which there are six elements in the series, the key term being *mmgd;* there is in addition a deviant expression *mr'š,* which occurs in the fourth position rather than the sixth as in Gen. 49.

In Jer. 51:20-23, we have a series of ten clauses, in which the key expression is *w^{e}nippaṣtî b^{e}kā.* The clause *wnpṣty bk* occurs nine times, which establishes the basic pattern by exact and frequent repetition, but there is an exception. The second clause in the series has *w^{e}hišḥattî b^{e}kā,* which has essentially the same meaning but is visibly different, and can be considered a formal and deliberate deviation from the standard pattern. In this case the deviation occurs very early in the sequence (second out of ten), but there can be no question that the same phenomenon is involved.

A somewhat more complicated example is to be found in Mic. 5:9-13, where we have a series of bicola dealing with the theme of destruction "in that day." In this instance the key verb is found at the beginning of each bicolon, and it is marked by a parallel verb in the second bicolon. The key verb is repeated while the parallel expressions varies. There are four cases of repetition, as indicated in the following table:

5:9	*w^{e}hikrattî . . .*	and I will cut off
	w^{e}ha'^{a}badtî	and I will cause to perish
10	*w^{e}hikrattî*	and I will cut off
	w^{e}hārastî	and I will destroy
11	*w^{e}hikrattî*	and I will cut off
	lō' yihyû-lāk	they shall not belong to you
5:12	*w^{e}hikrattî . . .*	and I will cut off
	w^{e}lō'-tištaḥ^{a}weh	and you shall not worship
13	*w^{e}nātaštî . . .*	and I will pluck up
	w^{e}hišmadtî	and I will destroy

Out of ten clauses only five show a pattern of repetition, but these are advantageously placed at the beginning of the first four bicola of the oracle. The key word therefore occurs four times in sequence. The deviation comes with the fifth — *w^{e}nātaštî,* a suitable parallel for the repeated *w^{e}hikrattî.* There are other patterns and sequences in this oracle — the rhyme scheme with the constant repetition of the 2nd masc. sg. suffix, and the rhythmic or metrical pattern of matching cola, with the exception of the fourth unit in the series, which is almost double the length of the others. Thus we recognize that the device of variation or deviation from an established pattern occurs in many different forms. A fixed pattern with specific variation along with wide-ranging flexibility seems to characterize Hebrew literary compositions.

We turn to the oracles of Balaam for a slightly different version of this phenomenon. In the oracles as a group the pair Jacob//Israel occurs frequently, in fact seven times in the four poems as follows:

I Num. 23:7-10
1) 23:7
2) 23:10

II Num. 23:18-24
3) 23:21
4) 23:23a
5) 23:23b

III Num. 24:3-9
6) 24:5

IV Num. 24:15-19
7) 24:17

This would seem to be a fairly well-established pattern, and in fact is very common in the Bible. In the great majority of cases, Jacob is the A word and Israel the B word, meaning that Jacob regularly precedes Israel in the common pairing of these words. There are some exceptions, to be sure, and these are to be expected. It is therefore only partially a surprise to discover that in vv. 18-19 of Num. 24 there is one more instance of this pair, only this time the order is Israel//Jacob. True, the order is often reversed by modern scholars, but in this case I think it is better to let the exception stand.

In the eight instances of the pair Jacob//Israel the first seven are found in the standard order, thus establishing a pattern of repetition. But in the eighth and last case the order is reversed. I think it is a reasonable example of a significant and visible deviation from an established norm.

We return to the book of Amos to illustrate another facet of this phenomenon, namely the deviation from the regularity of an established pattern of repetition. We may call it a deviation from the deviation.

In the oracle of judgment in chs. 1–2 of Amos with which we opened the subject, we noted that a formal framework was provided in which the opening lines as well as certain others were repeated. The threat of destruction was our first example and involved the repetition of the formula *w*ᵉ*šillaḥtî 'ēš* six times, while the variant *w*ᵉ*hiṣṣatî 'ēš* occurred once.

Now we wish to look at the opening formula, the framework of which has the following pattern:

*'al-š*ᵉ*lōšâ piš'ê —*	For three transgressions, of . . .
*w*ᵉ*'al-'arbā'â*	even for four
*lō'-'*ᵃ*šîbennû*	I will not reverse it

In each case the blank is filled in with the name of the targeted city or nation. This opening bicolon occurs eight times in the oracle, once for each of the eight nations addressed:

1:3, 6, 9, 11, 13; 2:1, 4, 6

In every case the formula is the same. There is no change whatever. What that means is that while the poet-prophet was free to vary from any repeated pattern, he was also free to stick with it without variation.

Another example of a repeated formula is to be found in Amos 4:6-11, where the closing refrain is as follows:

wᵉlōʾ-šabtem ʿāday	But you did not return to me.

This refrain occurs five times, at 4:6, 8, 9, 10, 11. It is always the same; there is no change. That is the variation from the principle of deviation. How do we know which way he decided to go? We are dependent on the texts which have come down to us and the reliability of editors and scribes since there is no way to predict in advance which way the prophet-poet went. In the book of Amos we have seen several examples of deviation from an established pattern of repetition and more than one where the deviation from the deviation resulted in holding fast to the pattern of repetition. We still have a lot to learn about prophets and poets in ancient Israel.

16

Another Look at Biblical Hebrew Poetry

The purpose of this presentation is to establish two points or theses about Biblical Hebrew poetry. Neither is exactly new, and both have been regarded as plausible if not probable. In recent years, however, a plethora of data, many of them statistical, has become available, and these data have provided both the evidence and the stimulus for reformulating and refining the points under discussion.

Briefly these points may be stated as follows:

1. The long-standing recognition that certain particles are typical of and commonly used in Hebrew prose, but not (or not as frequently) in Hebrew poetry, can be converted into a criterion for separating passages of prose from those of poetry throughout the Hebrew Bible. The so-called prose particles are the definite article h-, the relative pronoun !ašer, and the sign of the definite object !et. For a discussion see Andersen-Forbes 1983:165-68 and Freedman 1977:6-8.
2. The question of meter (or more properly, quantity) has been much debated and discussed, with opinions ranging from the conviction that there is no meter or measurable quantity in Hebrew poetry, to the equally strong conviction that Hebrew poetry can be quantified in a very precise manner, comparable to the poetry of Greece or Rome, or at least to that of France or England. Unfortunately, much of the work of scholars in recent decades has had a tendency to impose a meter or rhythm on a text by altering the text to suit the presumed rhythm, an ultimately self-defeating procedure. Now it can be affirmed that certain kinds of Hebrew poetry are quantifiable, and a demonstration can be made as to the nature of the meter or measure so employed and how it produces closely similar if not identical results in a series of poems. For it is one thing to find some sort of rhythmic pattern in a poem, but a much more important matter to show that the results are duplicated or repeated in other pieces. In the process we will see that quantity

> in Hebrew poetry, where it has been observed, is quite unlike that in other languages and literature, since there are opposing processes at work: a centralizing or regularizing one which defines the average, mean, or total length of a line or half-line, and a random effect which incorporates lines of variable length, or pronounced deviations from a norm. But even these deviations can be plotted so that in the end we can say of a certain group of poems at least, that their pattern and totality are predictable (within limits) and meet appropriate aesthetic requirements.

The conclusion I wish to draw is that on the basis of these points, it should be possible to tackle the great bulk of biblical literature and, on the one hand, divide between poetry and prose, identifying the former and even isolating that intermediate group that lies between the two classes and, on the other hand, determine the real quantity or metrical character of Hebrew poetry, recognizing both its regularity, or normality, and its random aspects, or its freedom, at the same time. These two main points raise two basic questions about biblical poetry. First, how does one distinguish poetry from prose? That question may seem simplistic, but a simple mechanical text could do wonders in clearing the air, in view of all the complexities involved in formulating a definition or articulating a philosophy. Second, how does one decide whether there is anything like quantity in Hebrew poetry? This question involves matters of rhythm and meter, but is really an attempt to deal with another basic question, and to give it an answer.

Dealing with the first question begins with the so-called prose particles and what they can indicate if not determine; my comments are based on statistics cited in Andersen-Forbes 1983. The investigation raises implications as to the possible evolution of poetic canons. There is some evidence to show that the so-called prose particles are almost entirely absent from the earliest poetry, while they increase in number in late poetry. This observation has to be made carefully, because while there is a considerable amount of late poetry which has very low particle counts, the reverse is not true. No early poetry has a high count.

Using Andersen-Forbes's table 0 (Andersen-Forbes 1983:170), we note that the data are clearly decisive, even though we must always bear in mind the important qualification that their counts and percentages and the like are all based on the chapter as a unit. Thus, Psalm headings (obviously prose) are mixed in with the psalms themselves; and the same is true of other mixtures of poetry and prose, e.g., Exod. 15, which is listed at 5.6%, fairly high for old poetry, although very low for prose. In this case, the percentage shown in the table is relatively meaningless, because the chapter consists of a clearly marked poem embedded in surrounding prose. The poem itself, vv. 1-18 and 21, has no prose particles at all, and is an outstanding example of early Hebrew poetry, indeed of poetry in general, as everyone would agree. The surrounding material is clearly straightforward prose. The prose particle count can be calculated easily, since there are 18 such particles in that material, while the number of words in the prose section is the total for the chapter, 321, minus the number in the poem, 177, for a net of 144 words. The prose particle percentage is 12.5%, so the chapter figure of 5.6% conceals a really impressive contrast between the poem, which is 0.0%, and the rest of the chapter, which has a count of 18 for 12.5%. In spite of such roughness, the figures are nevertheless impressive and convincing, as the following summary and comparison will show.

On the basis of the data presented, we can say that practically everything with a reading of 5% or less will be poetry, whereas practically everything with a reading above 15% will be prose. If we consider only the books which are commonly regarded as poetic, in comparison with books regarded as prose (taking Andersen-Forbes's first column and comparing it with a combination of columns 3 and 4, Torah and History), then for 5% or under we have 186 chapters of poetry and seven chapters of prose. But four of the prose chapters are in fact poems, as we know; so there are only three chapters of prose writing which come in under 5%, and in every case an explanation can be given. After all, there is nothing intrinsic in prose that requires that there be these particles, and in some situations they would be scarce.

Contrariwise, in the case of readings of 15% and up, one counts 248 chapters of prose, against four of poetry. While in view of the data and the method we could hardly expect the compartments to be airtight, the shift from one end of the spectrum to the other corresponds precisely to the shift from prose to poetry and vice versa. There can be little question that the proposed criterion works; it not only reflects the traditional divisions between poetry and prose, but also can be used to identify poetry and prose respectively, by the counts and proportions.

We can sort out the intermediate range by drawing the line at 10% and suggest that under that figure we would be inclined to see poetry, while over it we would see prose. The figures generally support this conclusion, but the distinction is not so sharply drawn as the larger numbers show: we would have 216 chapters of poetry under 10% and only nine over that number; we would have fifty-two chapters of prose under 10% (of which some are demonstrably poems hiding out in prose books), with 389 over 10%. If we look at the nine poems over 10%, we find that they are all Psalms, and all belong to the last or fifth book of the Psalter. While these are generally considered late Psalms, we can hardly date them exactly. They include, however, Ps. 137, which cannot be earlier than the middle of the 6th century, hence almost by definition a late poem. The fact that all of the Psalms over 10% are to be found in the single book of the Psalter is an indication of an inner development in poetry, whereby the use of such prose particles gradually became possible or acceptable. More than half of the same collection of the Psalter remains well below 10%, so it is clear that it was possible and acceptable to compose poems in the old manner, with few if any prose particles. It is also possible that low counts indicate an earlier date for those poems, since there is no way to decide the date of each poem in the collection. For example, we have poetry of the 6th century with very low counts, such as 2 Isaiah generally (beginning with ch. 40 we have percentages of 5.0, 5.4, 4.2, 3.2, 1.5, 3.3, 3.3, 2.6, 3.9, 2.8, 6.9, 5.4, 4.2, 2.3, 9.7, 6.7, 6.2, 1.4, 2.5, 4.7, 2.4, 7.9, 2.9, 2.3), but for chs. 65–66 we have 11.1 and 12.4 (a point made by M. Pope many years ago), and for Lamentations we have 2.9, 2.6, 2.6, 4.2, and 1.4. And Ezekiel, normally written in dense prose, has a number of chapters in the poetic range, including especially ch. 19, regarded by all as a poem and having a prose particle percentage of 0.6.

What remains to be examined is the large group of books generally listed as prophecy. Here the distribution falls roughly between the poetic and the prose books, with a relatively even apportionment among all the percentages from zero to over 20%. Once again we must bear in mind the nature of the analysis, which runs according to chapters — however heterogeneous the chapters may be in containing both prose and poetry. Thus, it would be important to sort the parts out more carefully in order to gain a truer picture of the prose-poetry ratios in the prophets. But even on the basis of the rather crude data we have, some judgments can be made. First of all, there is considerable straight poetry in the prophetic collection, including fifty-two chapters that have percentages under 5%. Most, if not all, of these would be classified as poetry. At the other end, we have fifty-six chapters over 15%: most of these would be reckoned as prose, especially the large sections of Jeremiah and Ezekiel that are obviously prose by any standard. Then there are roughly equivalent segments in the 5 to 10% bracket (seventy-two chapters), and another fifty-four chapters in the range from 10 to 15%. Discounting mixed chapters, of which there are clearly a number, we could divide roughly at 10% and say that 124 chapters of the prophets are below 10%, and hence more likely to be poetry than prose, and another 110 chapters are over 10%, and are more likely to be prose than poetry.

Nevertheless, and especially with regard to prophecy, there is another possibility to consider. One might establish a third category, which is neither prose nor poetry, but shares features with each and could tentatively be called *prophetic discourse.* As we know from other languages and literatures, there are few if any sharp lines between prose and poetry, and there are various stages between pure poetry and pure prose which can be categorized as prose-poetry, or poetic prose, or prosaic poetry. [For a similar proposal for ancient Egyptian, see M. Lichtheim, *A Book of Readings* (Berkeley: University of California, n.d.), 1:11] It is in the middle range that we should look for this phenomenon, which seems to be reflected in the prophetic category, although we should not exclude it from the other groups of books. It is important to exclude accidental combinations of prose and poetry in the same and succeeding chapters, where the resulting average falls in between those for poetry and those for prose. Frank Andersen and I suggested as much in our analysis of the prosody of Hosea, but were still uncertain as to how to classify or categorize such material (Andersen-Freedman 1980). Similar phenomena have turned up in the book of Amos, so it seems likely that a third or middle category should be identified, with a range between 5% and 15% for the prose particle count. It will be noted that a majority of the chapters in the prophetic corpus falls between these limits (126, in contrast to 108, either lower or higher), and that almost half of all the chapters found in the 5% to 10% range come from the prophetic corpus (72 out of a total of 147). While it is too early to make a definite statement about this situation, the overall data and a preliminary analysis suggest that the biblical divisions (modified as indicated by Andersen-Forbes in their notes) have a strong correlation with prose-particle counts. It is possible to summarize the findings of this line of inquiry in the following fashion:

1. The so-called poetic books are predominantly poetic in fact, and the great bulk of the chapters have counts under 5%, with a substantial but smaller group in the next bracket (5%-10%), and only a handful above 10%.
2. The predominantly prose books (Torah and History categories) are predominantly prose, with the majority of chapters (248) above 15%, while a substantial minority (141) are between 10% and 15%. A much smaller group is in the 5%-10% range (45), and there are practically none below 5% (7, but several of these are clearly poems embedded in the prose text).
3. The prophetic corpus has an entirely different profile, and overall is spread out fairly evenly over the whole range. We posit, however, that the chapters below 5% constitute poetry, and those over 15% are clearly prose. The remainder may to a substantial degree constitute a third category of elevated speech, which we call prophetic discourse. In any event, the question of a third category is worthy of further investigation.

The prose particle counts confirm the traditional division of the Hebrew Bible to a remarkable extent, and show that the Massoretic Text reflects and preserves those distinctions. The poetic books, with their distinctive arrangements and cantillation, are overwhelmingly poetic in terms of the prose particle counts, while the prose books are overwhelmingly prosaic. Exceptional are certain poems which are arranged as poems in the prose books, although there are several other poems which are written as prose, but the prose particle counts are a better indicator of what is prose and what is poetry.

The prose particle count, overall, is an excellent indicator and discriminator in separating prose from poetry, and also in indicating the possible middle category, especially for the prophetic corpus. Discounting mixed chapters of prose and poetry, we can suggest the following:

1. Anything with a count under 5% is almost certainly to be regarded as poetry.
2. Anything with a count over 15% is almost certainly to be regarded as prose.
3. Anything with a count between 5% and 10% is more likely to be poetry than prose, but I think that many of these units will turn out to be prophetic discourse or some form of poetic speech.

4. Anything between 10% and 15% is more likely to be prose than poetry, but may share some of the qualities of the adjacent category (between 5% and 10%), having some poetic elements in it.

The chief value of this method is that it is simply applied, is purely mechanical (with some slight interpretative requirements), and obviously works in the great majority of cases. It identifies as poetry what most scholars would agree was poetry, and as prose what most scholars would agree was prose. Hence it is likely that it will work in areas and passages where there is disagreement among scholars.

We can test the system in a provisional way against the book of Ezekiel, which, as is well known, poses severe problems of analysis and identification in terms of what is prose and what is poetry in the text. First, it is clear from every point of view that much of Ezekiel is straight prose. There are fourteen chapters over 15%, while another eighteen are in the range between 10% and 15%. The remaining sixteen chapters are under 10%; of these, twelve are in the range 5% and 10%, while four are below 5% (chs. 19, 21, 27, 28). These latter would be the obvious targets for identification as poetry, and the printed versions tend to reflect and confirm this identification. We will use Kittel's Biblia Hebraica (BHK) and the Stuttgart Biblia Hebraica (BHS) for comparison. Thus ch. 19 in both BHK and BHS is printed as poetry in full; the prose particle count is 0.641%, which would be decisive in any case. Ch. 21 has a count of 4.9% and is printed partly as poetry and partly as prose in both BHK (vv. 13-22 as poetry, the rest as prose) and BHS (same). In chs. 27 and 28, the prose particle count is 3.2% and 3.7% according to Andersen-Forbes, and again BHK and BHS render the material partly as poetry and partly as prose. It may be noted that BHS renders ch. 28 entirely as prose, but this seems to be an arbitrary decision in view of the prose particle count.

If we look at a pair of controversial or questionable chapters in BHK and BHS, we may find a comparison of the prose particle counts useful. Thus in BHK, ch. 7 is printed entirely as prose, while ch. 15 is printed as a poem. In BHS, ch. 7 is printed entirely as poetry, while ch. 15 is printed exclusively as prose. The prose particle count for ch. 7 is 11.95%, while for ch. 15 it is 16.5%. On the basis of the prose particle counts we would judge that ch. 15 is certainly a piece of prose, and that the same is probably true of ch. 7, although the categorization is slightly less certain. Reexamination of both chapters reinforces the conclusion that both chapters are pieces of Ezekielian prose; so BHK and BHS are each half right.

We must turn now to the other major point to be made about Hebrew poetry, and that concerns the question of meter and rhythm, or as I prefer to speak of it, the question of quantity. Here we rely mainly on the study of the five chapters of Lamentations, which I published in *The Harvard Theological Review* in 1972 (Freedman 1972). I used syllable-counting in order to establish a basis of comparison between the poems in terms of length. As I have noted in this chapter, an equivalent is to count words, since they show the same correlations, and it is possible to argue that ancient Israelites could have counted words rather easily since they generally wrote using word dividers. The main point I wish to make here is that there really is quantity in Hebrew poetry, and that we can prove it, and that it cannot therefore be ignored in any overall estimate of the nature, quality, or character of Hebrew poetry. While the examples I have used in the article cited are all acrostic poems (or modelled on them), I have no doubt that the same principles apply to Hebrew poetry generally, and that there will be many other examples that can be classified and quantified in the same or similar ways. The advantage of acrostics is that they provide us with stanza and (occasionally) line limits, so that we can be relatively sure where such units begin and end.

The nature of quantification in Hebrew poetry has to be defined carefully, since it is different from what we regard as quantity or meter in other kinds of poetry. In Hebrew poetry, or at least in the sample examined in my chapter, the regulation or control of quantity refers to the whole poem rather than to its discrete parts. We have an apparently anomalous situation in which the poems or chapters are almost identical in length (with a range of 1%) or proportionately so: i.e., ch. 4 of Lamentations is 2/3 as long as chs. 1–3, since it consists of two-line stanzas instead of three-line stanzas. The same principle applies to the 16-syllable acrostics, including Lam. 5 (special case), and the different Psalms listed in the paper. Strangely enough, the range in length between the whole poems is less or not more than it is between lines and stanzas of the same poems. While the average length of line in each of the first three chapters of Lamentations is 13 syllables, the lines may vary from as few as 9 or 10 syllables to as many as 16 or 17. The same is true proportionately of stanzas. But the overall length of the poems is the same, or only negligibly different, as the charts show.

We may contrast this phenomenon with an example drawn from English poetry. We are confident, for example, that English sonnets, especially of the Shakespearean variety, will have a total length of 140 syllables, plus or minus one or two. We can be sure of this, because the rule for such sonnets is that they consist of 14 lines of iambic pentameter, and thus will come out as indicated. Some slight variations are allowed, but the reason for the regularity in the total is that each line is roughly the same length as the other lines. In other words, the regulating feature is the length of each line; adding them up, we get a predictable total. What is different about Hebrew poetry is that, while the sum-total is predictable within a very narrow range, the total is not based upon the repetition of lines of the same length, as in the case of the English sonnet. Unless we engage in wholesale emendation and improvement of the text, we must recognize it as a basic fact of Hebrew poetry that individual lines (and stanzas) vary considerably in length. Nevertheless — and this is all the more remarkable — the length of the whole poem is fixed. We have poems which vary widely in line and stanza length, but which come out with the same total length. That this is no accident, but the result of careful planning and deliberate decisions throughout the poem, is clear from the statistical tables and the theoretical considerations in determining the difference between deliberate and chance arrangements. While the distribution of lines and stanzas according to their lengths follows the pattern of the familiar bell-shaped curve (reflecting random distribution), there can be little question that these cases reflect conscious artistic choices and decisions.

When we look at Frank Cross's reconstruction of ch. 1 of Lamentations on the basis of a 4Q manuscript (Cross 1983), we note that there are many differences from MT, and that few if any of the lines are the same in the two versions. But amazingly enough, his total length for the poem (838 syllables, on the basis of his counts, verse by verse) is exactly the same as one of my counts for the same chapter. (I refer to it as type "A" in ch. 1, although the basis for counting is quite different.) The point is that a set of controls is at work in these poems which constrains not only the original poet, but any scholarly reconstructor, whether that person is aware of it or not. There are different hypothetical ways in which the poet could control the overall length of the poem while allowing himself freedom in dealing with individual lines and stanzas. But the point is that the control is there, and that quantity cannot be disregarded as an element in the construction of poems. How to count it is almost immaterial, and I have opted for syllables because there are a lot of them, and hence a disagreement about a few of them will not make much difference. I steer a middle course between counting words, which will work but may be a little too crude, and counting morae, which may be more precise but seems overly fussy and produces more detailed information than is necessary or desirable. But so long as a system is applied consistently, it should work reasonably well and tell us what we want to know — namely, how long a line, a stanza, or a poem is.

What do we learn from this investigation of quantity? Chiefly, that the Israelite poets counted something, and made their poems come out according to a predetermined scheme. At the same time, they allowed themselves a freedom in composing individual lines and stanzas, which has been a source of confusion and misunderstanding about Hebrew poetry since Day One. Scholars have gone in two directions. One group began by assuming that Hebrew poetry was severely metrical; but when they discovered that lines and stanzas do not conform to any strictly metrical system, they either gave up, or went ahead to reconstruct the poem so as to conform to the meter they had already established for the poem. The other group decided that lines and stanzas are irregular, and hence that there is no meter in Hebrew poetry. Both sides are right in their way, and wrong in another. The specifically Hebrew phenomenon has not been recognized for what it is: it is quantitative, but with a degree of freedom rarely seen in metrical poetry. The result is that we should recognize the phenomenon for what it is, and we should also recognize our limitations in dealing with Hebrew poetry.

Perhaps it is best to start on the negative side, that is, what the quantitative factor will *not* do for us in dealing with Hebrew poetry. It won't allow or encourage us to emend the text. What that means is that the degree of freedom allowable in lines and stanzas will make it impossible to demonstrate any emendation on the basis of meter or rhythm. Adding or subtracting a word would not be permissible in this situation, unless there were some other indication of excessive line length (or the reverse). While the bulk of the lines hover around the 13-syllable mark in chs. 1–3, there are many, too many, which vary widely from the norm, to indicate that there is some ultimate limit below or above which we cannot go. The same is true of stanzas. We have in chs. 1 and 2 two stanzas (one each), with 4 lines instead of the standard 3. I don't believe that there is any way to decide the question whether the fourth line is part of the original composition or an editorial or scribal addition which should be removed, on the basis of quantitative considerations. In fact, the presence of the extra line in those poems brings their totals in closer harmony with ch. 3, which has 22 three-line stanzas. But the difference is too slight to ensure that the longer count in chs. 1 and 2 is better than a shorter count.

I consider this sort of variation to be an instance of a larger phenomenon, namely, general deviation or variation from a norm to avoid monotony or to demonstrate versatility and virtuosity. The fact that lines and stanzas vary so considerably in the poems we have (and be it noted that except for making all the stanzas consist of 3 lines, and other sporadic efforts at conformity to a preconsidered plan, Cross's reconstruction has the same wide variation in individual line length and also in stanza length) suggests that the poet exercised sovereign freedom in all respects except for the total length of the poem. Whether the different chapters of Lamentations were written by one or several poets, the result is the same. The constraints are too sharply drawn and specific to be regarded as mere happenstance or accident. Although we may not be able to describe the mechanism by which Israelite poets achieved such precision in total length while at the same time exercising considerable freedom in the case of individual lines and stanzas, we must face the fact that they did this quite consciously, and it must enter into our judgment about the quantitative factor in Hebrew poetry.

On the basis of the data secured in the research into Lamentations and other acrostics, we can make additional inferences and suggest some ideas about the way in which Hebrew poets worked. We have noted that the standard acrostic poem in the Bible (i.e., Prov. 31 and several Psalms, especially Ps. 119) has lines that average 16 syllables in length, and that these lines are divided generally in the middle. They are bicola of 16 syllables, generally with the pause in the middle, so that each colon has 8 syllables. This is equivalent to the familiar 3:3 pattern of stress or accent-counting systems. The same rules apply: overall length, averages, and means all come out strictly according to preplanned construction, but there is considerable range in individual length of lines and stanzas. Ch. 5 of Lamentations, which as we all know lacks the alphabetic element in the acrostic (although there may be a hidden system or cipher which has not yet been elucidated), nevertheless conforms admirably to the 16-syllable pattern, evenly divided. This stands in marked contrast to the other four chapters, in which the line length is 3 syllables shorter, and comes out in average and mean at 13 syllables with the usual variations. The difference is certain, and certainly deliberate and marked. While there are 13-syllable lines in the 16-syllable poems, and 16-syllable lines in the 13-syllable poems, there is no question about the general pattern or the role of the shorter or longer lines in the different configurations. These poems are not accidentally different, but deliberately so.

Furthermore, the pattern in chs. 1–4 is clearly different in another respect as well. We can confirm the Budde hypothesis about Qina-meter or falling rhythm, on the basis of the data. Statistically, Budde is right about the 3:2 pattern (using the old stress system): the lines are divided unevenly for the most part, and especially in chs. 2–3 (but also 4) the falling rhythm is nearly universal. There are nevertheless variations, so that some lines balance out evenly, and others are in reverse order. But the great majority are in a 3:2 pattern, or if we use syllables, then the major group is in the 7:6 or 8:5 pattern, or somewhere in between, depending upon the total number of syllables in the line. So, not only do we have a different average line length in chs. 1–4, but also a distinctive pausal arrangement: that the first colon is regularly longer than the second, although not always so. There is too much freedom to justify emendation on the basis of so-called meter, but there is more than enough regularity to show that these acrostic poems (Lam. 1–4) are quantitatively different from the other acrostics, while in and among themselves they are absolutely regular in terms of overall length, but nevertheless exhibit wide variation in individual lines and stanzas. The same is true of the 16-syllable group.

Perhaps this presentation will suffice to show that the phenomenon of quantity is clearly demonstrable in Hebrew poetry, at least of a certain kind, and that it must be taken into consideration in any discussion of Hebrew poetry or the way in which Israelite poets constructed their poems. At the same time, the facts in the case discourage manipulation or emendation of the text in order to produce a certain narrow conformity to a standard or pattern, which is itself only an average or a norm, and from which deviation was expected and taken for granted. I think that this is the best way to describe a curious phenomenon, with which we are generally not acquainted from experience with other poetry in the ancient world (or modern one): i.e., quantity in terms of the large or overall constructions, and freedom at the level of smaller units. Another way of looking at the phenomenon is that the poet had a model or structure in mind which would cover the whole poem (e.g., my treatments of Ps. 23 [Freedman 1976] and Ps. 137 [Freedman 1971]), and then while following it generally and on the average, he deliberately varied or deviated from it at specific points. So we are justified in the first place in trying to determine the overall pattern, and then in the second in recognizing deviations and variations as part of the deliberate activity of the poet rather than the mistaken activity of the editor or accidental alteration on the part of the scribe. I should add that in all this I do not want to appear to be a defender of the MT or any other text against all emendations. On the contrary, I believe that there is a very important place for textual reconstruction on the basis of other texts and versions, and that there is a place for conjectural emendation as well (as a last but very important resort nonetheless). What I object to is conjectural emendation on the basis of supposed meter or rhythm. Even this is possible in a general way, and it might be argued that we have a right to move in the direction of the norm or average: but it is very risky, often overdone, and therefore on the whole to be avoided.

Before drawing a few conclusions from this survey, I want to mention some of the implications and ramifications of these two main points. First, there is the matter of the difference between prose and poetry related to the so-called prose particles. I want first of all to apologize for the use of the term "prose" particles, since this seems to prejudge the case. The exercise is entirely inductive, and we have simply recorded the occurrence of certain particles, and then only on the basis of distribution and frequency have come to the conclusion that they are characteristic of prose and unusual in poetry, the two categories (prose and poetry) having been defined and the examples chosen on the basis of other criteria entirely. But the terms were called prose particles long before this exercise was undertaken, and it was simply a convenient way to label them. In view of the results, the label is appropriate, and so the technique can be used diagnostically in dealing with difficult passages. One obvious implication of their usage or non-usage is that poetry tends to be shorter and more elliptical, or more parsimonious in the use of particles and other terms. Thus ellipsis generally is a phenomenon more common in poetry than in prose. And to be more specific, there are other particles which are in shorter supply in poetry than in prose. We have used as the most striking and flagrant examples the three particles mentioned.

But the investigation could be extended, and should be, to include particles such as conjunctions and prepositions. I believe that the distribution of the basic conjunction is quite different in poetry from what it is in prose, but the statistics are not easy to come by, and we are working on a program that will sort out the conjunctions in poetry. What we are interested in is the use of conjunctions at the beginning of cola. And we would want to screen out simply coordinating conjunctions between nouns and other parts of speech. The impression I have is that for standard Hebrew poetry, the conjunction is not used at the beginning of the first colon, but is used before the second and third. The oldest poetry may have been still more sparing in their use, while later poetry may have used them even at the beginning of first cola. In any case, the usage is probably considerably below that of prose, although the difference may not be as striking as what we have seen in the case of the three particles selected so far.

Prepositions are another matter entirely, although the same pattern may obtain. In the case of prepositions, meaning is significantly involved, especially if the Hebrew poets made a habit of omitting prepositions where they should be understood. Once again, the overall statistics are not easy to arrive at, but we have the impression that fewer prepositions are used in poetry than in prose. What this means for understanding and interpreting Hebrew poetry is not altogether clear, but we can suggest a rationale. From time immemorial, at least in inflected languages, it has been possible to express various relations between verbs and nouns and nouns and nouns either by use of various case-endings or by the use of prepositions. There is no reason to suppose that these possibilities did not exist side by side. Once the inflections were lost, however, then inevitably prepositions as well as other parts of speech were called upon to bear a larger share of the burden in sentence constructions. What we suggest is that originally Hebrew, like other Semitic languages, was inflected and that prepositions were used alongside of case-endings. When the case-endings were lost, then the use of prepositions was increased. That is what happened in prose in the normal development of the language. In poetry, however, the older pattern was preserved, with partial use of prepositions and partial use of inflections. When the inflections were lost (and most of the few surviving ones are in the poetry), then poetry persisted without them, but also without adding prepositions, or supplying them in smaller number. This left a number of cases in which the meaning would have been clear if the case-endings had been preserved, but without them the absence of a preposition is or poses a difficulty in interpretation.

We do not wish to pursue this point further, but simply to point out that the shortage of prepositions is a characteristic feature of Hebrew poetry as compared with prose, and that it has implications for the interpretation of Hebrew poetry. In some cases, it may belong to the pattern of so-called double-duty particles, in which one preposition does duty for more than one noun or phrase. A striking example is to be found in Amos 6:5, where it would be appropriate to apply the preposition *ʿal* to both cola, and thus interpret the second colon as referring to the devising or composing of songs *on* instruments of music, rather than the anomalous (but persistent) interpretation that Amos is referring to the invention of new instruments. In another case, we can supply the preposition on the basis of a parallel passage. In this situation, the meaning is clear in one passage where the preposition is used, and less clear where it fails to put in an appearance. Thus, in Amos 2:7, the words are normally interpreted as a verb plus a construct chain and rendered: "They turn aside the way of the afflicted." The related passage is in Job 24:4, where the same or synonymous words are used, but we have the preposition *min* before the word for "way" *(drk).* The meaning there is plain: "They push the poor out of the road." That that is what Amos intended seems clear from the passage and its parallel in Amos 2:7, namely, that a violent physical action is presumed. That the preposition was omitted is the all-important element in the picture. We can suppose that the original reading was based upon usage at a time when case-endings were in vogue, and that the judicious use of these would have shown that no construct chain was intended, and hence the phrase *derek ʿanāwim* was not meant as a construct chain. Had that been the situation, then the word *drk* would have been vocalized as an accusative: *darka.* With the sense derived from the Job passage, the reading would have been *darki,* the oblique case to be interpreted in context as spatial.

With regard to the question of quantity, there are implications for further study, namely, that we should look more closely at large structures, expecting to find rigid constraints and nearly equal counts of length for major parts and complete poems. We have been able to determine the existence of such gross structures for poems widely scattered in the Bible; so it stands to reason that the same is true of other poems in the Bible, although it may be more difficult to determine these because they lack the obvious markers which acrostic poems provide. With regard to lines and verses and small structures, the message seems to be both sharp and certain: there is too much freedom and variation to discern any but statistical patterns, and it is time to turn attention more to large configurations and units, including whole poems. It seems likely that a handful of such patterns will merge, and we will begin to gather clues and form opinions as to desirable length and the constraints that produced the variety of poems that we have in the Bible.

The following are some provisional conclusions about Hebrew poetry:

1. Out of the welter of debate and discussion I wish to draw attention to certain objective data, which should play a significant role in future research. The first is both basic and obvious: the determination of what is poetry and what is not. The new technique, which is simply the formulation and application of an old impression, has proved to be basically right. It consistently supports the older tradition about what was prose and what was poetry (although with refinements), and offers the possibility of clearing up disputed and debated compositions. It also points the way to clarifying and perhaps resolving a question that has surrounded the prophetic corpus since scholars first began to identify poetic materials in this body of literature. It may be that in addition to prose and poetry in the corpus as we have elsewhere, there is also a *tertium quid,* which needs to be defined and described more accurately, but which lies between the extremes indicated by the other categories. Analysis of this category might also help to explain why, in the tradition, prophecy was not transmitted simply as poetry, as books such as Proverbs, Psalms, and Job were, along with some poems in the Primary History.
2. I wish to make a second point which has to do with the scansion of Hebrew poetry. I think it is clear now that both sides of the debate as to whether there is quantity, definable and countable, in Hebrew poetry were partly right and partly wrong. There is quantity, but there isn't meter in the usual sense of the word. Quantity can only be determined and calculated for large structures, whole poems, or large units; whereas there is considerable freedom and irregularity in small units, especially lines and cola. Both sets of facts seem indisputable, and therefore both elements must be considered when talking about poetry. There are other factors as well, but we must include quantity as a basic fact, along with freedom. The method of counting seems to be less important, although the case should be made for the most objective and

mechanical system possible, so as to avoid argument and debate about injecting interpretive criteria and conclusions in the statistical analysis and actual counting. I have opted for syllables, but word counting would probably serve almost as well, and counting morae (if the rules were set down carefully so as to decide the question of which vowels are really long and which are artificially so in the Massoretic system) might be even better. But there is no doubt that syllable counting gives a very reliable picture of comparable length, which is the essential purpose of the analysis. That Israelite poets had a system for counting seems both clear and inescapable, since otherwise it is impossible to explain how they produced poems of exactly equal length. No doubt music played a role, but that is an investigation in and of itself.

Bibliography

Andersen, F. I., and A. D. Forbes

1983 " 'Prose Particle' Counts of the Hebrew Bible." *The Word of the Lord Shall Go Forth,* ed. C. L. Meyers and M. O'Connor. Winona Lake: Eisenbrauns/American Schools of Oriental Research, 165-183.

———, and D. N. Freedman

1980 *Hosea.* AB 24. Garden City: Doubleday.

Cross, F. M.

1983 "Studies in the Structure of Hebrew Verse: The Prosody of Lamentations 1:1-22." *The Word of the Lord Shall Go Forth,* 129-155.

Freedman, D. N.

1971 "The Structure of Psalm 137." *Near Eastern Studies in Honor of William Foxwell Albright,* ed. Hans Goedicke. Baltimore: Johns Hopkins University Press, 187-205. Repr. in Freedman 1980, 303-321.

1972 "Acrostics and Metrics in Hebrew Poetry." *HTR* 65:367-392. Repr. in Freedman 1980, 51-76.

1976 "The Twenty-Third Psalm." *Michigan Oriental Studies in Honor of George G. Cameron,* ed. Louis L. Orlin, et al. Ann Arbor: University of Michigan, Department of Near Eastern Studies, 139-166. Repr. in Freedman 1980, 275-302.

1977 "Pottery, Poetry and Prophecy: An Essay on Biblical Poetry." *JBL* 96:5-26. Repr. in Freedman 1980, 1-22.

1980 *Pottery, Poetry and Prophecy: Studies in Early Hebrew Poetry.* Winona Lake: Eisenbrauns.

17

On the Death of Abiner

David's dirge over Abiner, the commander-in-chief of the armies of Israel (2 Sam. 3:33-34), has been overshadowed by the more famous elegy for Saul and Jonathan (2 Sam. 1:19-27), but it is deserving of study and appreciation of its literary merit and artistic features. Thanks to the recent publication of prime textual data from Qumran (4QSam^{a} in particular) in the *Biblica Hebraica Stuttgartensia,* it is possible to restore the poem to a more original and complete state than what is preserved in MT or LXX.[1] What has survived in any case is very brief, perhaps only an excerpt or stanza of a much longer work. If we compare it with the Lament over Saul and Jonathan, we note that the latter consists of 110 words, whereas the former has only 16 (MT) or 17 (4Q). The preserved portion, whether the entire elegy or only a fraction of it, is itself a carefully constructed entity, which can be examined and evaluated apart from the question of its completeness.

In what follows, we offer a reconstruction of the text; the vocalization is in accordance with MT except where otherwise indicated. Explanations and arguments will be appended.

hakk^{e}môt nābāl yāmût ʾ^{a}bīnēr	(Line A)	As the dying of a scoundrel, did Abiner die?
ʾ^{a}sūrôt yādêk lōʾ b^{e}ziqqîm	(Line B)	Bound were your hands not in manacles;
raglêk lōʾ binḥuštaym huggāšû	(Line C)	Your feet not into fetters were thrust;
kinpôl lipnê b^{e}nê ʿawlâ nāpālt	(Line D)	As a falling before criminals did you fall?!

1. The idea for this paper and the approach were stimulated by the excellent studies of 1 and 2 Samuel by P. Kyle McCarter, Jr., in his published and unpublished works on those books. All the textual information used in this article, however, is to be found in the apparatus of BHS.

Notes

Line A: That the name is correctly vocalized *'ᵃbīnēr* is shown by the spelling in 1 Sam. 14:30 *('bynr)*. Throughout MT the older spelling, as here, *'bnr,* is preserved, and it has affected the vocalization, so that MT regularly reads *'abnēr* (cf. P. Kyle McCarter, *I Samuel.* AB 8 [Garden City: Doubleday, 1980], 254).

Line B: MT *ydk,* if correctly interpreted as singular, must be adjusted in the light of the context and sense to the plural, as with many MSS and the versions. For the whole line I have adopted the apparent and reconstructed reading of 4Q, with the changed order of words, and the addition of the phrase *bzqym,* "in manacles." Whether this word is a plus in 4Q, or a minus in MT and LXX, is not easy to determine, but the following arguments may be presented in support of the view that *bzqym* is an integral part of the text, and belongs to an earlier form of the poem than what was preserved in MT and LXX:

1. The phrase *bzqym* is a very suitable parallel for *lnḥštym* (so MT; 4Q has *bnḥš.m),* a noticeable lack in the standard text. Nevertheless, in view of the formidable textual evidence against this expression, along with a normal preference for the shorter text, as well as the absence of a rationale for its omission through scribal error, it could be argued that *bzqym* was added by a conscientious and poetically sensitive editor under the influence of *bnḥštym* in the next colon. That analysis has a certain appeal, but it does seem odd to attribute greater sensitivity to prosodic and rhetorical factors to an editor or scribe, rather than to the poet himself. Furthermore, in spite of the obvious connection between *zqym* and *nḥštym,* they are not found together in any other passage in the Bible; that is a strong indication that the presence of *nḥštym* would not naturally or automatically suggest *zqym* to an inattentive scribe. In other words, it is not only not a common word-pair in Biblical Hebrew, but until the present discovery not even known to exist in that language. In addition, in this poem practically every word is balanced by a corresponding term. The glaring exception is *nḥštym,* that is, in MT. Please note the following pairs: a. *kmwt* and *ymwt* (A) and *knpwl* and *nplt* (D); the two pairs also balance each other; b. there is a matchup between *nbl* and *'bnr* in A, but there is a more important association between *nbl* (A) and *bny 'wlh* (D); c. *ydyk* (B) and *rglyk* (C); d. *'srwt* (B) and *hgšw* (C); e. even *l'* (B) is matched with *l'* (C). The only elements without a direct matchup are the interrogative *he* at the beginning of A, and the compound preposition *lpny* in D. The implication of this steadfast pairing is that originally there was a parallel term for *nḥštym,* and that it was lost in the process of transmission. While it would be temerarious to supply one, we may take a more positive view of the one preserved in 4Q.

2. It has been observed that the order of the words in lines B and C is different in 4Q when compared with MT or LXX; furthermore, the order in 4Q preserves an excellent example of chiasm, which is largely lost in MT, and therefore 4Q may be regarded as more original than MT in this respect. The chiasm in lines B-C is

to be seen in the placement of the parallel verb forms: *'srwt* at the beginning of line B is balanced by *hgyš* at the end of line C. This is not the case in MT, where the verb forms are in parallel pattern: *'srwt* at the end of line B, and *hgšw* at the end of line C. This circumstance in 4Q might be regarded as trivial and possibly accidental, but the latter is not likely, especially since there are several other elements in the poem which support the view that the chiasm is deliberate and an integral element in the structure. Lines A and D are closely related in the selection and order of words, as well as in their content. They form an envelope around lines B and C, and provide the basic theme of the dirge: Did Abiner die as a scoundrel dies? On the contrary, he was the innocent victim of people like that, criminals. The envelope construction is an important ingredient in the overall pattern of chiasm. The chiasm or cross-over occurs at the very center of the poem, in this case in lines B-C. This emerges more clearly in 4Q than in MT or LXX, with the placement of the verbs at opposite ends of the bicolon. We infer, then, that 4Q preserves an earlier form of the text, which includes *bzqym*. Hence that term belongs to the older stratum, while its loss is reflected in a later tradition (i.e., MT and LXX).

Line C: Through a comparison of texts preserved in MT, 4Q, and different versions of LXX, we can recover two variant and competing texts of this line:

1. *raglêk lō' linḥuštaym huggāšû*
2. *w^eraglêk binḥuštaym lō' higgîš*

The first is based mainly on the existing MT; the initial conjunction is not found in LXX, and may therefore be omitted. The second is based mainly on 4Q; the final hiphil form of the verb is supported in all likelihood by the major witnesses of LXX. Very likely these two versions are old and derive from the process of oral transmission. Nevertheless it may be possible to establish priority for one rather than the other on the basis of poetic factors. In trying to choose between the hophal 3rd masc. pl. verb and the hiphil 3rd masc. sg., we note that passive verb forms are less common in Biblical Hebrew than active ones, and therefore that the hophal is likely to be more original than the hiphil. An added point is that when we compare the chiastic verb forms in lines B and C, we note that *'^asūrôt* has the vowels "a" and "u" in that order, while *huggāšû* has the same vowels in the opposite order ("u" and "a" from the beginning of the word, as in the case of *'srwt*). Needless to say, such refinements vanish from the scene if the hiphil reading *higgîš* is adopted.

In choosing between the colon with initial *waw* (as conjunction) and the one without, we must consider the general pattern of usage. On the whole, there is a tendency to omit the conjunction at the beginning of opening cola (e.g., line B) and to include it at the beginning of second cola (e.g., line C) in balanced constructions. To what extent the transmission of poetic texts has been influenced by normal prose usage (with its endless proliferation of clause-initial conjunctions) and therefore how many of these conjunctions at the beginning of second cola have been introduced secondarily is difficult to say, but other texts indicate that there has been relatively little contamination of poetic texts. In this case, therefore, we might expect the conjunction before *rglyk* to be original, but the evidence of the LXX, which omits the conjunction, and the syllable count for parallel cola (lines B and C) tips the scale in favor of deletion.

We must still deal with the question of *bzqym*. If it was part of the original poem, then how did it disappear from the mainstream of the textual tradition, i.e., MT and LXX? In order to explain this serious omission, we require evidence pointing to one of the more familiar scribal lapses, namely, haplography. An examination of the texts preserved in MT and LXX gives no such indication, and while it is not necessary to explain every vagary of the human actor, especially a scribe, the lack of a rationale may undermine the case for the originality of *bzqym*. So we wish to propose a hypothetical case, an unattested stage in the history of transmission, but which would provide a plausible occasion for the desired scribal error. The existence of this stage can also be defended on grounds other than its suitability for scribal errors. We have already noted the classic instance of chiasm in the 4Q version of lines B-C. That, however, is a single or partial chiasm, the remaining words being in parallel order. Since the three texts MT, LXX, and 4Q reflect a variety in the order of the words in lines B-C, we suggest still another order, more original perhaps than any extant. This would involve complete or perfect chiasm, in which each term balances its correlate in verse order. For line C that would produce a sequence such as this:

bnḥštym rglyk l' hgyš

Thus in addition to the verb pair already matched at the beginning of B and the end of C, we have matching nouns (*ydyk* and *rglyk*) in the middle of each colon, and the prepositional phrases (*bzqym* and *bnḥštym*) at the end of B and the beginning of C. These two words would be in direct sequence, and an explanation of the apparent haplography is at hand: *bzqym bnḥštym*. In this case, the scribe's eye would have skipped from the first *b* to the second *b* and in the process the word *zqym* would have disappeared from the text. While we have disposed of the cumbersome *zqym* we must still explain the shift from the presumed original preposition *b* to *l* before the second term, *nḥštym*. This looks like an example of the substitution of the common or normal preposition *l* with the H-stem of *ngš*, in contrast to the unusual instance of *b*, which does not occur anywhere else in the Bible with the H-stem of *ngš*.

Line D: The pattern of verb forms, *knpwl . . . nplt* is deliberate and matches the similar pair in line A: *kmwt . . . ymwt*. In each case the infinitive form of the verb is preceded by the preposition *k*, and followed by the finite form of the verb; imperfect (prefix) in the first case *(ymwt)* and perfect (suffix) in the second case *(nplt).* The alternation of prefix and suffix forms of the finite verb is an important feature of classic Canaanite and Hebrew poetry and should be regarded as part of the basic plan of the poet. As in so many other cases, it is altogether likely that they share the same tense and aspect, and hence should be translated in the same fashion: "Did Abiner die?" and "Did you fall." While the context implies that the last line (D) is a response to the question in the first line (A), I wonder whether the poet may have intended to place both possibilities before the audience, and leave the issues unsettled. In that case the force of the initial interrogative *he* would carry over to the second infinitive *(knpwl).*

In line D there is extensive use of sound effects. We wish to call attention to repeated instances of the consonants n-p-l: *knpwl lpny . . . nplt,* with reversal or chiasm *(npl-lpn-npl).* In addition, the consonants *bn* and *l* appear in the compound noun *b^{e}nê ʿawlâ;* the only difference is the substitution of the sonant stop *b* for the voiceless stop *p.* This last term, however, has a more significant link with *nābāl* in line A, which shares exactly the same consonants. As previously noted, lines A and D balance each other, and the terms *nābāl* and *b^{e}nê ʿawlâ* perform parallel functions in their respective clauses. In addition, the letters *bn* appear in the name *ʾbnr* (Abiner) in line A. While we may dismiss the last collocation as a coincidence, there is no doubt that the repetition of sounds plays a definite and important role in the art of poetic composition; the association of *nbl* and *ʾbnr* in the mind of the poet may have arisen in part from the similarity of sounds.

Now we wish to turn to the metrical structure of the poem. On the basis of the proposed restoration we secure the following syllable count:

hakk^{e}môt nābāl yāmût ʾ^{a}bīnēr	(A)	3 + 2 + 2 + 3	= 10
ʾ^{a}sūrôt yādêk lōʾ b^{e}ziqqîm	(B)	3 + 2 + 1 + 3	= 9
raglêk lōʾ binḥuštaym huggāšû	(C)	2 + 1 + 3 + 3	= 9
kinpôl lipnê b^{e}nê ʿawlâ nāpālt	(D)	2 + 2 + 2 + 2 + 2	= 10

I have used the short form of the 2nd masc. sg. perfect form of the verb (*nāpālt* for *nāpaltā*) and of the 2nd masc. sg. pronominal suffixes (*yādêk* and *raglêk*), based upon the written text (the Kethib). It is quite possible that the long forms were used by the poet, in which case we must add a syllable to each of the last three lines (10-10-10-11). There is no great difference, but perhaps some weight should be given to the precise symmetry produced by counting the short forms.

This analysis produces a perfectly balanced metrical pattern reflecting the chiastic structure of the poem already described. Thus lines A and D match each other metrically as well as in form and content and sound effects, while the same is true of lines B and C. Needless to say, the omission (or loss) of *bzqym* distorts the chiasm and demolishes the metrical symmetry. We can be permanently grateful to the unknown scribe at Qumran for transmitting to us a more exact version of David's elegy for General Abiner, thus confirming to a substantial degree the artistry and reputation of the great royal poet. This dirge is a model of exquisite craftsmanship.

18

The Structure of Isaiah 40:1-11*

The present chapter is intended to shed some light upon the meaning and import of one of the most familiar and famous passages in the Hebrew Bible through a detailed analysis of its structure. While it is certainly risky and may be foolhardy to undertake a fresh treatment of a text that has been enshrined in the inspired translation of our language (the King James Version) and further hallowed by an equally extraordinary music arrangement (*Messiah* by Handel), let me assure scholars and readers alike that my intention is to take nothing from the traditional values associated with this magnificent piece of prophetic poetry, or to challenge established renderings and interpretations, which have been built up over the centuries, but rather to add something to the insights of others, and to uncover or better recover elements in the composition, which have hitherto escaped notice.[1]

1. For general orientation about the poem in Isa 40:1-11, the reader may consult the following: J. Muilenburg, "The Book of Isaiah, Chapters 40-66." *IB* 5 (1956), 381-773; C. R. North, *The Second Isaiah: Introduction, Translation and Commentary to Chapters XL-LV* (Oxford: Clarendon, 1964); J. L. McKenzie, *Second Isaiah.* AB 20 (Garden City: Doubleday, 1968); C. Westermann, *Isaiah 40-66.* OTL (Philadelphia: Westminster, 1969), translated from the German: *Das Buch Jesaja, Kapitel 40-66.* ATD 19 (Göttingen: Vandenhoeck und Ruprecht, 1966). [See also R. Melugin, *The Formation of Isaiah 40–55.* BZAW 41 (Berlin/New York: Walter de Gruyter), 1976]

*This chapter was originally written as a contribution to a volume honoring Professor F. I. Andersen on the occasion of his sixtieth birthday. It has come to my attention that Professor Andersen has recently completed a commentary on the book of Isaiah [unpublished, Ed.] including extensive notes and comments on the passage which I have treated in this article. Since we have worked closely for many years on many parts of the Bible, including especially the Prophets, it is altogether likely that some or many of the points made in this chapter have been made by Andersen in his volume. The volume has not yet been published, and I have not seen the manuscript. So far as I am aware, I have arrived at the positions and statements in this chapter independently, but I may have been influenced by communications and comments from my colleague. So any resemblances between our studies should be credited to him since his manuscript was finished before this chapter was written; and I can be blamed for divergences and differences.

Happily for our purposes the text is essentially sound and the meaning of words and phrases is quite clear and generally not in dispute. There is therefore no need to take and waste time with drastic or dramatic emendations or rearrangements of various parts of the poem. We can proceed directly to the structural analysis, noting here and there a variant reading or a different meaning as to which a preference or a choice can be expressed, but more often a recognition of multiple values and levels of significance. In the course of the study, I will propose a possible solution to the problem, which arises at the very beginning of the piece. The opening words *naḥᵃmû naḥᵃmû* ("comfort, comfort") are analyzed as masculine plural forms of the piel imperative of the root *nḥm;* the question is who or what constitutes the subject being addressed through these words. The verse in its entirety reads as follows: "Comfort, comfort my people, says your God" (Isa. 40:1, RSV). The message originates with "your God." The object of the verbs is clearly "my people." What God is commanding is that some group (N.B., the verbs are plural) comfort his people. Just who are those being ordered to carry out this function? A number of proposals have been made, and among them may well be the correct answer to the question, but it seems to me that the matter is still open, partly at least because a grammatical subject has not yet been located in the text of Exilic Isaiah. It has been my hope and is my belief that patient search, even at some distance from the verse itself, may turn up the missing element and thus resolve the issue out of the work itself.[2]

The poetic composition (vv. 1-11) consists of four parts, which can be separated out on the basis of content and form, and the presence of certain identifiable tokens or terms in the piece. These parts are of roughly equal length (whether we count words or syllables does not make much difference), except that the last part is just about double the length of any of the others. Actually, the last part constitutes a double unit in which the latter section is an extension, an elaborate figure of speech, i.e., of the good shepherd leading his flock. The first section of the last part is a necessary and integral element in the structure of the poem, whereas the second is less integral and more ornamental, a kind of coda, entirely appropriate as a conclusion to the piece.

That it is a piece of poetry is beyond question. What is less obvious is that although it is a postexilic composition, it is composed in the classic tradition of the older poetry of the Bible. In accordance with that tradition, it makes very sparing use of the so-called prose particles. There is not a single instance of either *'ᵃšer* or *'et* (the chief characteristics of old poetry), and there is very limited but deliberate use of the definite article (also a feature of early poems such as the Song of Deborah and the Lament of David over Saul and Jonathan). There are

2. See the discussion of the identity of those addressed in the various commentaries, esp. Muilenburg. Cf. F. M. Cross, Jr., "The Council of Yahweh in Second Isaiah," *JNES* 12 (1953): 274-77.

Table 1

	Words	Syllables
1. Part I (vv. 1-2)	24	56
2. Part II (vv. 3-4)	22	56
Central Divider (vv. 5-6a)	17	32
3. Part III (vv. 6b-8)	27	55
4. Part IV (vv. 9-11)		
A. First Section (vv. 9-10a_1)	23	45
B. Second Section (vv. 10a_2-11)	20	55
Totals	133	308

only five occurrences of the definite article out of 133 words in the piece as a whole, giving a 3.8% rating, which is well within the usual limits for biblical poetry (i.e., anything under 5%).[3]

The organization of the poem may be diagrammed as in Table 1.

The division of the poem into its main parts follows the traditional paragraphing of the Massoretic Text (i.e., closed sections are marked at the end of vv. 2, 5, 8) and of contemporary scholarship (e.g., RSV with the same paragraphing).[4] There are only two minor modifications in the arrangement I propose: 1) I separate v. 5 from the second unit because it is independent of its immediate context, and is in fact the centerpiece and culmination of the poem as a whole; 2) in the subdivision of Part IV, I mark the separation, not between vv. 9 and 10, but after the first colon of v. 10, which provides us with the logical parallel to the last colon of v. 9:

hinnēh ʾelōhêkem (v. 9)	Behold your God!
hinnēh ʾadōnāy yhwh (v. 10)	Behold my Lord Yahweh!

The proposed arrangement can be supported by other considerations, and these will be discussed further on in the chapter. At the same time, the two phrases serve as a transition between the two subsections (A and B), and what follows in vv. 10-11 is dependent upon the nouns at the beginning of v. 10.[5]

3. See the discussion by F. I. Andersen and A. D. Forbes, " 'Prose Particle' Counts of the Hebrew Bible," *The Word of the Lord Shall Go Forth,* ed. C. L. Meyers and M. O'Connor (Winona Lake: Eisenbrauns, 1983), 165-183.

4. The Aleppo Codex has the same paragraphing, and so does the great Isaiah Scroll from Qumran Cave 1.

5. There is a third modification which should be mentioned. The opening line of Part III, v. 6a, is really a distinctive element, although it leads into the main section, vv. 6b-8. I have generally treated it as belonging to Part III, but it is also separate from it. I consider v. 6a as the logical or chronological starting point of the poem, and v. 5 as its conclusion. It is no accident that they are grouped together in the center of the poem.

Critical to the structural analysis of the poem, in addition to the grammatical and syntactic features and considerations of symmetry (approximately equal length of the parts), is the distribution of the numerous divine names and titles. There are essentially three of these: *yhwh,* which occurs six times; *'lhym,* which occurs in two forms — *'ᵉlōhêkem* twice, and *'ᵉlōhênû* twice, for a total of four times; and *'dny,* which is purely ornamental and is attached to the last occurrence of *yhwh* as a flourish, to vary from constant repetition. The author has achieved his objectives in distributing the names throughout the piece by breaking up a very common phrase that is used with great frequency in the Bible: *yhwh* + *'lhy* + pronominal suffix (in this piece only the second masculine plural and first plural forms). The poet has taken apart these traditional and commonplace phrases and distributed the components in an imaginative and symmetrical fashion throughout the poem. In no case has the basic phrase been left intact, but the components have been arranged in such a way that the order is sequential in the four parts we have identified. That means that in each of the four major sections or parts, we have a single instance of each name or title, so that together they make up the traditional expression; but they are always separated, and the order varies so that in Part I the normal order is inverted, whereas in Part II the sequence is regular, and also in Part III; in Part IV it is inverted again. The total effect is both symmetrical and chiastic, kaleidoscopic perhaps, as the poet exploits the possibilities and opportunities stemming from the simple procedure of breaking up a traditional expression. It should be added that in v. 5, which we have isolated as a separate and climactic element in the poem, the name *yhwh* is used twice without the other element at all, thus emphasizing the centrality and incomparability of this sole and unique deity. We note that the same device of balancing the name *yhwh* with itself, rather than some parallel term, is already present in the oldest poem in the Hebrew Bible, the Song of the Sea (cf. Exod. 15:3, 6). We show the distribution of the names and titles in Table 2 (on p. 236).

It will be noted that the selection and arrangement of the names is both symmetrical and chiastic. Thus the first half (Parts I and II) has a sequence beginning with *'lhykm* and ending with *'lhynw,* while there are two instances of *yhwh* between them. In the second half (Parts III and IV) the sequence opens and closes with *yhwh,* while between them we have *'lhynw* and *'lhykm,* which are in reverse order compared to that in the first half.

Two features of chiastic structures are present in our poem, and they deserve notice: 1) In chiastic patterns attention is normally focused on the center of the composition, the point of crossover. We have already observed that v. 5, which is at the midpoint of the poem, serves in this capacity and is distinctive in other ways as well. 2) The two ends of the poem are often linked to form an envelope around the body of the poem. Regarding the second point, we are led to look for positive links between Parts I and IV of the poem, and we note that the sequence of divine names is the same in the two parts, just as it is in Parts II and III. In both Part I and Part IV we have the sequence *'lhykm . . . yhwh* (the *'dny* prefixed to *yhwh* in

Table 2

Part I: vv. 1-2	
	v. 1 *'elōhêkem*
	v. 2 *yhwh*
Part II: vv. 3-4	
	v. 3 *yhwh*
	v. 3 *'elōhênû*
Centerpiece: v. 5	
	v. 5 *yhwh*
	v. 5 *yhwh*
Part III: vv. 6-8	
	v. 7 *yhwh*
	v. 8 *'elōhênû*
Part IV: vv. 9-11	
	v. 9 *'elōhêkem*
	v. 10 *'dny yhwh*

v. 10 is the closing flourish of which we have spoken and does not affect or undermine the underlying pattern), whereas in Parts II and III we have *yhwh . . . 'lhynw.* This leads us to further inquiry for points of contact between the opening and closing sections. We note the repetition of the proper noun Jerusalem (which does not otherwise occur in the poem). Closer inspection will show that the linkage is more organic (i.e., grammatical and syntactical) and dramatic (there is a sequence of speeches), and that it provides important clues to a radically different understanding of the relationships of the parts with respect to both time and place.

Thus in v. 2, the same subjects of the verbs in v. 1 are instructed or rather commanded to speak to Jerusalem and cry out to her. There are two more masculine plural imperative verbs here *(dabberû . . . weqir'û)* to go with the pair in v. 1. The question then arises as to just what this unnamed group is to say to Jerusalem. It has been the universal assumption, reflected in all known translations and commentaries, that what follows in v. 2 is the content of the message to be delivered by the subjects of the verbs in v. 2, i.e., the three clauses, introduced by the particle *kî* to the end of the verse. So far as I am aware, no one has ever questioned this quite natural assumption, but, strictly speaking, what follows in v. 2 cannot be the message commanded the subjects of the verbs in vv. 1-2. The three clauses in v. $2a_2$-2b are in the third person, not the second person, and hence are not direct address but at best indirect address. That would mean that they contain the content of the message if not the message itself. The speakers would then put the message in direct speech to Jerusalem. It is questionable, however, whether the clauses are intended as indirect address, i.e., to communicate information to Jerusalem. Rather, they are qualifying clauses used to explain to the unnamed messengers the reasons for the commands they have been given. These clauses explain to the messengers and the readers that circumstances have changed and are now propitious for a new message to be given to Jerusalem. The time of servitude has ended and a new age is about to begin. What is expected therefore is a direct address to Jerusalem using appropriate second person verbal forms. As already noted, nothing of the kind is to be found in Part I, but it turns out that the direct address to Jerusalem, which we look for after the imperatives of v. 2, is present and quite prominent in Part IV. There are no fewer than five 2nd fem. sg. verb forms in v. 9, all addressed directly to Zion/Jerusalem. Here in Part IV is the sequel to the imperative verbs of v. 2. The message itself, carried by verbs which are also imperatives, is essentially a command to Jerusalem to assume the role of messenger and deliver it to her sister cities in Judah. That is the first part of the message, namely to act as a messenger, and the second part is the message itself, briefly, "Behold your God!" In other words, Jerusalem is one in a series of messengers who transmit the word of Yahweh until it reaches its final destination, which in this case is the cities of Judah. Only then, at the end of the series and of the poem, is the message itself revealed (the content is given in the last two words of v. 9 and the whole of vv. 10-11).

In Parts I and IV of the poem we can identify at least four stages in the transmission of the message until its final articulation in vv. 9-11. Just as the last stage of the transmission, i.e., the statement of the message itself, is characterized by the words *hinnēh 'ᵉlōhêkem,* so the first stage is characterized by the corresponding words in v. 1, *yō'mar 'ᵉlōhêkem* (these are the only two occurrences of *'lhykm* in the poem). Since Yahweh does not speak directly in the poem (i.e., using the first person in his speech), but is quoted, cited, or spoken about, we must assume that his words were spoken to others (i.e., angels) and that they reached the prophet through their agency. The prophet in turn must convey the double message to the subjects of the verbs in vv. 1-2. The two parts of the message are respectively the instruction to be a messenger in turn, and then the content of the message itself. These subjects of the verbs in vv. 1-2 are to bring the message to Jerusalem (vv. 2, 9-11), and Jerusalem for its part must then bring the message to "the cities of Judah" (v. 9). At that point the message itself is to be announced in a loud, clear voice and the chain of transmission comes to an end.

We may summarize the findings thus far with respect to Parts I and IV of the poem:

1) The divine names *'lhykm* and *yhwh* are found in both parts. More particularly the expressions *y'mr 'lhykm* and *hnh 'lhykm* form a combination indicating the origin and culmination in the stages of transmission of the key message of the poem, namely that Yahweh your God is coming back to his land with his people, leading them as a shepherd leads his flock.

2) The words *'ammî,* "my people," *yᵉrûšālayim,* "Jerusalem," and the 3rd fem. sg. pronominal suffix in *'ēleyhā,* "unto her" (vv. 1-2), form a chiastic pattern

with the corresponding terms in v. 9: *ṣiyyôn,* "Zion"; *yᵉrûšālāyim,* "Jerusalem"; and *ʿārê yᵉhûdâ,* "the cities of Judah." In both lists the word Jerusalem is the middle term, whereas the feminine pronominal suffix, ostensibly a reference back to Jerusalem, also corresponds to the alternate term for the holy city, Zion. The remaining terms, *ʿmy* and *ʿry yhwdh,* constitute a combination: "my people who are in the cities of Judah"; we would interpret the expression inclusively so that the people of Jerusalem would not only be reckoned as part of the larger group, but also the first to receive the message, which they are to deliver to the others. In this way also we find a suitable masculine noun for the masculine plural pronominal suffix with *'lhykm* at the end of v. 9. (We may note that the word *ʿammî* in Exilic Isaiah is regularly construed in the plural, e.g., 47:6; 51:4; 58:1; 63:8; 65:10; it is construed as a singular in 51:16 and 52:4-6.)

3) There are four 2nd masc. pl. imperative verbs in vv. 1-2 *(nḥmw, nḥmw, dbrw, qr'w),* balanced by four imperative 2nd fem. sg. verbs in v. 9 *(ʿly, hrymy, hrymy, 'mry)* plus the equivalent of a negative imperative *('l-tyr'y).* It will be noted as well that in each group one of the verbs is repeated.

4) The three clauses beginning with the particle *ky* in v. 2 are balanced by the three *hnh* clusters in vv. 9-10.

The coming of Yahweh with his exiled people back to his land and his city, to be welcomed by the inhabitants left behind during the Babylonian Captivity, is the fulfillment of the message transmitted through and by the poem. The final act in the drama, which occurs at the same time, is the manifestation of the glory of the God of Israel to the whole world, which is announced in v. 5:

> And the glory of Yahweh shall be revealed
> And all flesh shall see it together
> For the mouth of Yahweh has spoken.

These words at the center of the poem constitute the prophetic comment on or summation of the activity initiated, generated, and consummated by the word of Yahweh. The original utterance of the deity (not actually presented or quoted but referred to in v. 1 by the expression *y'mr 'lhykm*) is now confirmed by the statement at the end of v. 5, the third colon of this unit, when the revelation of the glory of Yahweh has taken place in the context of the holy city and the holy land, with Yahweh in the midst of his reunited and restored people. The two clauses in vv. 1 and 5 form a compact unit combining the central and essential elements of the entire piece:

> *yō'mar 'ᵉlōhêkem*
> *kî pî yhwh dibbēr*

The arrangement is chiastic, and the nouns and verbs balance and complement each other: *y'mr // dbr* (note the alternation of imperfect and perfect, a classic pattern in old Hebrew poetry, whereas in this case the tenses are the same) and *'lhykm //*

yhwh (which form a traditional phrase). The poem is dominated by the theme of "the word of Yahweh" (cf. v. 8) from the initial utterance, its transmission through a series of agents, and its ultimate arrival among the people of the cities of Judah, in time for the coming of Yahweh with his exiles and the manifestation of his glory from his holy city. Not only the people of Judah and the returned exiles, but the whole world will behold his glory.

If we have analyzed correctly the interconnection between vv. 1-2 and 9-11, then we can trace the latter stages of the transmission of the central message of Yahweh to his people in Jerusalem and the cities of Judah. The sequence can be clarified by juxtaposing Parts I and IV graphically, but this rearrangement is made solely to assist in understanding the intentions and objectives of the poet, not to improve on his work. The organization of the material has a literary focus and dramatic intensity which results from the distinctive pattern of the parts, and like other poetry in the Bible the action is presented in epic style. Thus it opens at a point near the climax of the action, and then retraces its steps back to a point of origin before resuming and continuing the story to its conclusion. In this poem there are other factors and objectives, but the essential story line is as presented. The action begins with the transmission of the message already well advanced, with two stages still to be achieved: the announcement to Jerusalem by the unnamed subjects in vv. 1-2, and then the bringing of the message by Jerusalem to the other cities of Judah (vv. 9-11). But a series of actions and conversations have taken place before the stage described in v. 1 has been reached, and these are dealt with in the middle sections of the poem, vv. 3-4 and 6-8.

The arrangement proposed in Table 3 (on p. 240) is designed to show how the different parts of the poem fit together, and are connected logically and chronologically. The poet had other and more compelling reasons for disposing of the parts as he has, and what we are doing has no relation with the common scholarly practice of improving upon the existing order or restoring a supposedly more original one. Our purpose is simply to show how the parts are related linguistically and logically. We will append a few notes on the text and translation and then proceed with the rest of the poem.

In v. 1, I translate the verb *y'mr* in the past tense. The imperfect is often used in this way in poetry, with or without the conjunction, contrary to the normal prose usage, which requires the *waw* consecutive before the verb form. Obviously the future tense will not do, although that is the common meaning of the imperfect, and the standard rendering in the present will not do either. The point is that the prophet or other agent of Yahweh is repeating words that he has already heard from the deity or through a divine emissary. The standard formula uses the perfect form of the verb, *kōh 'āmar yhwh,* "Thus has said Yahweh," which is properly rendered in the past tense. To put it in basic terms, the prophet is a messenger, not a medium. The deity speaks to him, and then he repeats or reports the word he has received. The deity is not speaking when the prophet is speaking. The deity has spoken; the

Table 3

	Text	Words	Syll.	Translation
(1)	*naḥ^{a}mû naḥ^{a}mû ʿammî*	3	8	Comfort, comfort my people
	yōʾmar ʾ^{e}lōhêkem	2	6	your God has said.
(2)	*dabb^{e}rû ʿal-lēb y^{e}rûšālēm*	4	9	Speak to Jerusalem herself
	w^{e}qirʾû ʾēleyhā	2	5/6	and cry out to her
	kî māl^{e}ʾâ ṣ^{e}bāʾāh	3	7	because she has fulfilled her service
	kî nirṣâ ʿ^{a}wōnāh	3	6	because her punishment has been deemed sufficient
	kî lāq^{e}ḥâ miyyad yhwh	4	8	because she has received from Yahweh's hand
	kiplayim b^{e}kol-ḥaṭṭōʾteyhā	3	7/8	double for all her sins.
(9)	*ʿal har-gābōah ʿ^{a}lî-lāk*	5	7	"Upon a high mountain, climb up for yourself
	m^{e}baśśeret ṣiyyôn	2	5	O herald Zion
	hārîmî bakkōaḥ qôlēk	3	7	Raise with power your voice!
	m^{e}baśśeret y^{e}rûšālēm	2	7	O herald Jerusalem
	hārîmî ʾal-tîrāʾî	3	7	Raise it! Be not afraid!
	ʾimrî l^{e}ʿārê y^{e}hûdâ	3	8	Say to the cities of Judah:
	hinnēh ʾ^{e}lōhêkem	2	6	'Behold your God!
(10)	*hinnēh ʾ^{a}dōnāy yhwh*	3	7	Behold my Lord Yahweh!
	b^{e}ḥāzāq yābôʾ	2	5	As a mighty one he will come
	ûz^{e}rōʿô mōš^{e}lâ lô	3	8	and his arm will rule for him.
	hinnēh ś^{e}kārô ʾittô	3	7	Behold, his payment is with him
	ûp^{e}ʿullātô l^{e}pānāyw	2	8	and what he worked for is in front of him.
(11)	*k^{e}rōʿeh ʿedrô yirʿeh*	3	7	As a shepherd, who feeds his flock
	bizrōʿô y^{e}qabbēṣ ṭ^{e}lāʾîm	3	9	who gathers with his arm the lambs
	ûb^{e}ḥêqô yiśśāʾ	2	6	and who carries them in his bosom
	ʿālôt y^{e}nahēl	2	5	who guides the nursing ewes.' "
(5)	*w^{e}niglâ k^{e}bôd yhwh*	3	7	And the glory of Yahweh will be revealed
	w^{e}rāʾû kol-bāśār yaḥdāw	4	8	and all flesh will see (it) together
	kî pî yhwh dibbēr	4	6	For the mouth of Yahweh has spoken!

prophet relays the message. This analysis is confirmed by the statement in v. 5: *ky py yhwh dbr,* "For the mouth of Yahweh has spoken." Cf. Amos 3:8, *ᵓᵃdōnāy yhwh dibber // mî lōᵓ yinnābēᵓ*, "My Lord Yahweh has spoken // Who will not prophesy?"

Turning to v. 2, we note that the verb *mlᵓh* is qal perfect third feminine singular and therefore that *ṣbᵓh,* which is masculine, cannot be construed as the subject of the verb. Nevertheless most translations tacitly emend the text and make the verb masculine so that *ṣbᵓh* can be read as the subject, just as *ʿwnh* is the subject of *nrṣh* (the reason being that while *ʿwnh* is masculine as is *ṣbᵓh,* the verb *nrṣh* is also masculine, although it seems to have a feminine ending): e.g., ". . . that her warfare is ended, that her iniquity is pardoned." Some support for the emendation can be gathered from the great Isaiah scroll from Qumran Cave 1, since it reads *mlᵓ,* i.e., the third masculine singular form of the verb. That reading, however, looks like a correction of the more difficult original, which is preserved in MT. We translate *ṣbᵓh* as the object of the verb *mlᵓh,* and Jerusalem as the subject, just as it is the subject of the third colon in the sequence and of the verb *lqḥh.* We also observe that the first two cola form a combination involving both verbs and both nouns. In order to bring out the meaning and the force of the assemblage of words we paraphrase as follows: "She (Jerusalem) has fulfilled her time of service for her iniquity, and the demands of penal justice have been fully satisfied." As already noted, the three *ky* clauses in v. 2 are all in the third person, are not addressed to Jerusalem but convey information about her, and hence cannot constitute the direct address inherently stipulated in the two imperative verbs in v. 2a: *dabbᵉrû* and *qirᵓû.* For the speech which the masculine plural subjects are directed to say directly to the city of Jerusalem, we must turn to vv. 9-11. It is worth noting that just as there is no direct address in v. 2, in spite of the imperative verbs in that verse which require it, in v. 9 we have no introductory statement about the direct speech, which begins abruptly in that verse. In other words, the speaker or speakers are not identified, while the speech is given. In v. 2, on the contrary, we have the proper introduction but no speech. If it were not for the separation in space between v. 2 and v. 9, we would have no hesitation in connecting the verbs in v. 2 with the speech in vv. 9-11.

In the critical editions, BHK and BHS, v. 9 is divided into seven units, which is quite acceptable, but the organization of the units is clearly lopsided. In the presentation of the text and translation offered above, we have suggested a more symmetrical arrangement. The first six units or cola are balanced in an envelope construction: the first and last of these match and balance each other and form an envelope around the four cola in the middle. These in turn have a strictly parallel structure. The seventh unit is the declaration itself, and belongs with the rest of the quotation which follows in vv. 10-11. To show the close links between the first and sixth units of the verse, we will put them together:

ʿal har-gābōah ʿᵃlî-lāk
ᵓimrî lᵉʿārê yᵉhûdâ

We note the chiastic order of the words, with the prepositional phrases at the beginning of the first colon and the end of the sixth, and the verbs at the end of the first and the beginning of the sixth. The verbs have the same grammatical form, while together they describe the beginning and the end of the action: "Climb up . . . say." The prepositional phrases are likewise complementary, providing the locations of the speakers and the listeners. The four intervening cola are strictly parallel, with alternate cola beginning with the same words:

> *m^{e}baśśeret ṣiyyôn*
>   *hārîmî bakkōaḥ qôlēk*
> *m^{e}baśśeret y^{e}rûšālēm*
>   *hārîmî 'al-tîrā'î*

In v. 10, there is strong support for reading *b^{e}ḥōzeq* instead of MT's *b^{e}ḥāzāq*. The former, which is read by the Versions and also the great Isaiah scroll, would be rendered, "with strength." The latter, which is clearly the more difficult reading, would have to be read with the *bet essentiae,* i.e., "as a strong one." In either case, however, we note the use of two terms, which evoke a longer and more familiar even stereotyped expression, *b^{e}yad ḥ^{a}zāqâ ûbizrōaʿ n^{e}tûyâ,* "with a mighty hand and an outstretched arm." Since the latter is used in connection with the tradition of the Exodus, the evocation is entirely appropriate in a passage such as this with its New Exodus coloring and overtones. However, the expression in Isa. 40 is elliptical and allusive.

In v. 10b, we have another combination, involving the words *śkrw* and *pʿltw.* The reference is to the payment or compensation that one receives for work performed. So we would render "his compensation for his labor"; it is the captives from Babylon who constitute this payment. Having earned the right to claim them by some work performed, Yahweh is now taking them from their place of exile back to their homeland. The prepositional phrases in this verse, "with him" and "before him" (*'ittô* and *l^{e}pānāyw*), anticipate the imagery of the simile which closes the poem. The good shepherd follows his flock, making sure that none stray or are lost.

I take v. 11 as an extended simile, with each of the four verbs forming a relative clause dependent upon the initial noun, *k^{e}rōʿeh:*

> Like a shepherd
>   who feeds his flock
>   who gathers the lambs with his arm
>   who carries (them) in his bosom
>   who guides the nursing ewes.

In addition, we can identify two other parallel pairs: *bzrʿw* and *wbḥyqw,* "with his arm" and "and in his bosom" as well as *ṭl'ym* and *ʿlwt,* "lambs" and "nursing ewes." In both pairs we have complementary terms, not synonymous ones, although they pair up in different ways. In spite of all the related terms and symmetrical numbers (e.g., 2 and 4), there is considerable difficulty in arranging the text in an appropriate pattern. We suggest the following points: 1) Since the term *ʿdrw,* "his flock," is the general term and includes both the *ṭlʾym* and the *ʿlwt,* and the verb *yrʿh* is also a general term, and since the key noun *krʿh,* "like a shepherd," is present with the others in the first colon, we suggest that it is introductory and stands apart from the rest of the verse. 2) In the remaining words we have a breakdown of the general terms into specific components, in particular the lambs and the ewes, the two elements most in need of special care and consideration on the part of the shepherd. An imbalance occurs because two of the clauses are apparently devoted to the lambs and only one to the ewes. Two different and interlocking structures can be identified in the last three clauses of v. 11:

bizrōʿô yeqabbēṣ	With his arm he gathers
ûbeḥêqô yiśśāʾ	And in his bosom he lifts (= carries).

and

yeqabbēṣ ṭelāʾîm	He gathers the lambs
ʿālôt yenahēl	The nursing-ewes he guides.

In the first pair we find straightforward parallelism, with the terms complementing each other: thus we may say that he gathers with his arm and lifts or carries in his bosom. Or we can cross over and say that he bears in his arms and gathers into his bosom. Probably all the combinations are intended, since this is a picture of the Good Shepherd who has special concern for the lambs, especially those that are separated from their mothers. In the second pair we have a chiastic construction with the animals as the center terms, while the verbs are at the extremes.

Thus far we have traced the transmission of the divine message from its origin in the speech of Yahweh through various stages involving the prophet and the subjects of the imperative verbs in vv. 1-2, then Zion/Jerusalem in vv. 2 and 9, until its final destination, the people in the cities of Judah. These, however, are the later stages in the process of transmission, and for the earlier ones we must look at the center sections (Parts II and III) of the poem. One way to track down the stages of transmission is to look for and at the verbs of speaking and calling used in the text. There are four of these, distributed widely and symmetrically throughout the material (see Table 4 on p. 244). It will be observed that there are no fewer than twelve verbs in the passage devoted to the articulation of the message, which consists of two parts: 1) the instruction to deliver the message to the next agent or agency, and 2) the message itself, which is not revealed until the last stage in the process, but which must have been conveyed from the beginning. Since many of these verbs occur in Parts II and III as in Parts I and IV, we would expect that about half of the stages in the process will be found in that section to match the ones already uncovered in the opening and closing parts.

The first stage of all, the actual utterance of the message by Yahweh, is not contained in the poem, but is presumed to have occurred offstage. It is mentioned

Table 4

Verbs	Parts I & IV	Parts II & III	Total
1. *'mr* (vv. 1, 6, 6, 9)	2	2	4
2. *dbr* (vv. 2, 5)	1	1	2
3. *qr'* (vv. 2, 3, 6, 6)	1	3	4
4. *hrym* (*qwl;* vv. 9, 9)	2	0	2
Totals	6	6	12

in both v. 1 *(y'mr 'lhykm)* and v. 5 *(ky py yhwh dbr)*. The first stage in the transmission which we can observe or hear is to be found in v. 6. On the basis of the distributional pattern in Parts II and III, we believe that v. 6 describes the first stages in the process, while the opening words of v. 3 reflect another part of the same process. We may render the verse as in Table 5 on p. 245. The obvious question about v. 6, which serves as a transition from Parts I and II to Parts III and IV, and especially after the separate concluding element consisting of v. 5, is who is talking to whom. As we investigate the question, it is necessary to consider an important textual variant. The fourth word in the verse is read as *wᵉ'āmar* in MT, the third masculine singular qal perfect with the *waw* conversive, to be translated, "and he will say." The reading in 1QIsa[a] is *w'wmrh,* which is to be vocalized *wā'ômᵉrâ;* while it is slightly anomalous, it is probably to be understood as the qal imperfect first person singular with the *waw* consecutive, and to be translated as "and I said." This reading is supported by the LXX and the Vulgate, and has been adopted in most modern translations and by most scholars. It is certainly a plausible reading and may be original. It would introduce the prophet into the chain of transmission directly and at an early stage, since he would be represented by the first person form. It is true that other prophets speak up in the course of revelatory experiences, and there is an important parallel to this passage in First Isaiah (ch. 6) in which the prophet speaks up and in the first person (Isa. 6:5, 8 for the same first person form of the verb *'mr* as is reflected for this verse in the Versions and the Isaiah scroll). It is also true that no change in the consonantal text would be required for this shift. In the original manuscript, the word would have been written *w'mr,* which could be vocalized as *wᵉ'āmar* (MT), or as *wā'ōmar* (the versions).

Nevertheless, in spite of the evidence and the arguments, I think that MT preserves a more difficult and hence a more original text. In the end, the difference is slight, since I would agree that the prophet is intended here, but he speaks of himself in the third person, since unlike the prophet Isaiah, this prophet is very reclusive and anonymous. He or his editors seem eager to conceal his identity or to hide it behind that of the great prophet of Jerusalem of the 8th century. This one does not speak out in his own person or name (which we do not even know). The scene in which the transmission of the divine word takes place, presumably in the

Table 5

Text	Words	Syll.	Translation
qôl 'ōmēr qᵉrā'	3	5	Hark! Someone says, "Cry out!"
wᵉ'āmar mâ 'eqrā'	3	6	And someone (else) says, "What shall I cry?"

heavenly palace which is also the scene of the divine revelation in Isa. 6, on which this description seems to be modeled, is much more obscure in this passage than in the other.

In ch. 6, the prophet Isaiah plays a prominent role and describes the scene with a remarkable richness of colorful detail. We are presented with a vivid and unforgettable picture of Yahweh enthroned in his heavenly palace, surrounded by his retinue. We are told about *seraphim* in the heavenly court, and discover, for the only time in the Bible, something about their appearance and their function. We also find them chanting and speaking among themselves, but individuals speak too. It is only the last element that appears in our scene; one member of the heavenly court speaks presumably to the prophet, but we are told nothing about who it is, or what kind of creature, whether a *seraph* or a *cherub* or just a member of the general category of *mal'āk* or *rûaḥ*.

As suggested earlier, Yahweh himself is no longer on the scene. His actual speech is the ultimate starting point for the transmission of the message, but that occasion and exactly what was said are not recorded. We draw this conclusion for two reasons: 1) There is no description of Yahweh speaking directly to anyone, whether to an angel or to the prophet. 2) The recorded words of the message in the poem all speak of Yahweh in the third person, whereas elsewhere in this book Yahweh speaks repeatedly in the first person, which is what we would expect in direct address by the deity. The person entrusted with the message, apparently one of the angels, is the first speaker in v. 6. Since we can reasonably identify the prophet himself as the second speaker in the same verse, we must identify the first one as the link between the deity and the prophet. This circumstance points to another difference between our scene and that in Isa. 6. In that scene the prophet is present and exchanges words with Yahweh himself. The same sort of experience is reported generally by the preexilic prophets right down to Ezekiel, but in the case of the latter, angels or spirits play an important role. With the postexilic prophets we find angels acting as intermediaries, especially in the case of Zechariah. In the present scene we assume that the prophet was not present, because he finds it necessary to ask the angel about the content of the message, when he is accosted by the latter.

We may assume therefore that the speaker at the beginning of v. 6 is an angel of the throne room, one who has direct access to the deity and hence is of the first rank. Nevertheless neither he nor any other of the transmitters of the word of Yahweh is identified in any other way, except as a voice. Not until the message reaches its final destinations, Jerusalem and the other cities of Judah, is anyone specified or identified. Even the prophet is hidden in anonymity, as the spotlight and the attention of all are focused on the message itself. The second person mentioned in v. 6, whom we have identified as the prophet partly because of the variant reading of the verb in the first person, might be another angel, say of a lesser rank. There is still another voice in v. 3, who could be another angel. The list could be extended indefinitely in this chain of transmission, but we prefer to keep it to a minimum, and suggest that both of these latter voices (in v. 6 and in v. 3) belong to the prophet. He is the pivotal link in the chain, when the message is transferred from the heavenly to the earthly sphere. He is the one who receives the message from the heavenly agent and then transmits it to earthly ones.

An added argument in favor of this analysis can be derived from an examination of the passage which immediately follows the colloquy between the two voices in v. 6a. In response to the command of the first speaker (the angel), the second speaker (the prophet) naturally asks: "What shall I proclaim?" What follows in vv. 6b-8 is not the message itself, but rather an explanatory discourse on the frailty and perishability of all things human and mundane set in contrast to the permanence and solidarity and utter reliability of "the word of our God." This discourse, which stresses the central and ultimate importance of the word, and thereby enhances the role of the prophet and the significance of the message yet to be delivered, corresponds to the explanatory comments attached to a similar command in v. 2, which we have already discussed. Just as the direct speech commanded and promised in v. 2 is not actually presented until we reach v. 9, so in the direct address, the message the prophet is supposed to deliver is not actually spelled out until we reach vv. 3-4. As the poem is now arranged, the message in vv. 3-4 precedes the dialogue in vv. 6-8, but the temporal order goes the other way. As we understand the sequence, the first speaker in v. 6 is the angel from the throne room who bears the message directly from God. He transmits the word to the second speaker in v. 6, the prophet, and at the same time delivers the discourse in vv. 6b-8. The prophet then (in vv. 3-4) delivers the actual message to an unidentified group. The rest of the message is given by the same speaker to the same group in vv. 1-2 and 9-11, thus completing the chain of transmission.

Some features of Part III deserve a brief discussion (see Table 6 on p. 247). The main unit (vv. 6b-8) consists of a series of three bicola (vv. 6b, $7a_2$-b, 8b) separated by a repeated refrain consisting of an extremely short bicolon (vv. $7a_1$, 8a). The refrain consists of the words *ybš ḥṣyr // nbl ṣyṣ;* it serves not only to set off the sequence of bicola but also as a commentary on their content. The first two bicola nevertheless form an interlocking structure in which the opening line of the first bicolon (v. $6b_1$) links with the second line of the second bicolon (v. 7b) to form an envelope around vv. 6b-7. The units under consideration read as follows:

Table 6

	Text	Words	Syll.	Translation
(6)	*qôl ’ōmēr q^{e}rā’*	3	5	Hark! Someone says, “Cry out!”
	w^{e}’āmar mâ ’eqrā’	3	6	And another says, “What shall I cry out?”
	kol-habbāśār ḥāṣîr	3	6	All flesh is like grass
	w^{e}kol-ḥasdô k^{e}ṣîṣ haśśādeh	4	9	And all of their fidelity is like the flower of the field
(7)	*yābēš ḥāṣîr nābēl ṣîṣ*	4	7	The grass has dried up the flower has faded
	kî rûaḥ yhwh nāš^{e}bâ bô	5	8	Because the breath of Yahweh blew on it.
	’ākēn ḥāṣîr hā‘ām	3	6	Surely the people was like grass.
(8)	*yābēš ḥāṣîr nābēl ṣîṣ*	4	7	The grass has dried up the flower has faded
	ûd^{e}bar-’^{e}lōhênû	2	7	But the word of our God
	yāqûm l^{e}‘ôlām	2	5	shall stand forever.

	Text	Words	Syll.	Translation
(3)	*qôl qôrē’*	2	3	Hark! someone cries out:
	bammidbār pannû derek yhwh	4	8	In the wilderness prepare a road for Yahweh
	yašš^{e}rû bā‘^{a}rābâ	2	7	Make straight in the desert
	m^{e}sillâ lē’lōhênû	2	7	a highway for our God
(4)	*kol-gey’ yinnāśē’*	3	5	Every valley shall be raised
	w^{e}kol-har w^{e}gib‘â yišpālû	4	9	and every mountain and hill *shall be lowered*
	w^{e}hāyâ he‘āqōb l^{e}mîšôr	3	9	and the bumpy ground shall become a plain
	w^{e}hār^{e}kāsîm l^{e}biq‘â	2	8	and the rough places a flatland.

kol-habbāśār ḥāṣîr
’ākēn ḥāṣîr hā‘ām

We have repetition, with the word *ḥṣyr* being repeated in these units and appearing twice in the refrains as well. The words *hbśr* and *h‘m* are in chiastic order, and both bear the definite article in addition, showing their close association. The last bicolon (v. 8b) stands by itself, necessarily and properly, since it is in absolute and striking contrast with all the preceding material. It is nevertheless linked to the earlier statement, not only by contrast, but also by the breakup of a stereotyped expression, the two parts of which are divided between the units: i.e., *yhwh* (v. 7a) and *’lhynw* (v. 8b).

As indicated, the discourse in vv. 6-8 is designed to emphasize the vital importance of the divine message. The climactic statement in this unit is the closing words: "But the word of our God will stand forever." In the course of establishing this undeniable truth and providing a rationale for the elaborate transmission procedure to be followed in bringing the message to its ultimate audience, the angel also discusses the frailty and fragility of the human world, a subject of obvious importance and interest to the prophet. And this is the point at which the message passes from heavenly into human hands. For the message to be transmitted properly it must go from God to the prophet, often through the agency of a heavenly messenger, and from the prophet to the human audience for whom it was intended. For the actual message, we must look to Part II, but before we leave Part III, we wish to call attention to a pair of words which are embedded in the text of vv. 6-7, and have important connections elsewhere in the poem. In describing the perishability of the human species, the speaker refers to "all flesh" *(kol-habbāśār),* which would include all living things, but the predominant interest is in the human species. At the beginning of v. 6b, they are described as being "like grass" (the preposition *ke-* serves the first clause as well as the second, where it is attached to "the flower of the field," a retrospective double-duty or backward-gapping device). In other words, the preposition attached to *ṣîṣ* also serves the noun *ḥāṣîr.* Then at the end of v. 7 we have the word *hāʿām,* "the people," who are also described as being "like grass" (the force of the comparative preposition carries to this point as well). The association between "the people" *(hʿm)* and "all flesh" *(kl-hbśr)* is clear but also complex. "The people" not only share in the general frailty of "all flesh," but they are part of the larger entity; nevertheless they are distinct from it as well. The use of the definite article with both nouns in these verses can hardly be accidental. Both of these terms occur elsewhere in the poem, and doubtless are mentioned here with identifying markers to show that they have related and reciprocal roles in the unfolding drama. Thus "all flesh" will participate in the final revelation of Yahweh; they will see his glory when he returns with his people (v. 5). As for "the people," they can be identified with "my people" *(ʿammî)* in v. 1, and are the object of the imperative verbs in that verse. As we have seen, they are also connected with "the cities of Judah" in v. 9. But who are the persons who are commanded to comfort, i.e., encourage, "my people in the cities of Judah?" I believe that the answer lies in the other expression, "all flesh" *(kl-hbśr).* Just as "the people" (= "my people") are one part of the total group, so there is another part, the other part, namely the rest of humanity, not specifically designated but implied in the structure of the poem. The unspecified persons in vv. 1-3, who are to carry out the commands embedded in the six verbs in the imperative form, are the rest of humankind, the nations, peoples, coastlands, of whom and to whom this prophet speaks in the name of Yahweh on so many occasions.

Before returning to our original point of departure, vv. 1-2, we must deal with Part II, vv. 3-4. At the beginning of v. 3 we find a lone figure, just a voice, making a proclamation. It is becoming clear now that when the message is actually being transmitted the operative verb is *qr'*, "to call, proclaim," whereas other verbs such as *dbr* and *'mr* are used when the discussion is about the transmission of the message, either past or future. Thus Yahweh's original statement is described by *'mr* in v. 1 and *dbr* in v. 5. Similarly, the final stage, when Zion/Jerusalem tells the cities of Judah, is presented by *'mr* (v. 9), but that lies in the future. When the first angel speaks to the prophet (v. 6), the verb *'mr* is used, but he does not tell the prophet the actual words of the message, although he tells the prophet that he is to proclaim it *(qr')*. The prophet speaks to the angel using the same verb *('mr)*, but confirms that when he gives the message it will be with the verb *qr'* ("What shall I proclaim?"). When the message is actually given in vv. 3-4, it is introduced by the verb *qr'*. The same person utters the message in v. 1, which is addressed to the same people as vv. 3-4; we note also that the verb *qr'* is used to describe the message that Jerusalem is to deliver to the cities of Judah. We conclude that the anonymous speaker in v. 3 is the prophet himself, who has been apprised of the message, and is actually delivering it. It is entirely in keeping with the prophet's passion for anonymity that he is identified only as a voice. That practice, which typifies the poem and the rest of the book, is the result in all likelihood not of a political but rather a theological decision. Nothing must be allowed to share the limelight with or interfere with the full impact of the Word of Yahweh. In this poem that is the only thing that counts.

In vv. 3-4, both messenger and message appear on the scene, and the latter is articulated. Neither the speaker nor the audience is specifically identified here or elsewhere in the poem, with two exceptions, one at each end of the line of transmission. It is clear that the message originates with Yahweh, a point made twice: *y'mr 'lhykm* (v. 1) and *ky py yhwh dbr* (v. 5). The last messenger is also identified — *mbśrt ṣywn // mbśrt yrwšlm* ("herald Zion // herald Jerusalem") — also with a compound title, and also with two verbs *(hrymy qwlk* and *'mry*, all in v. 9). All of the other links in the chain are anonymous figures, including at least the following: the throne angel of v. 6, the prophet in v. 6 and v. 3, and the other peoples in vv. 1-4. The contrast with Isa. 6 where a similar scene is described is striking. In the earlier scene, the prophet identifies all the participants either by name or appearance and function, and describes clearly how the message originates and how it is transmitted from heavenly to earthly beings. In ch. 40, everything between the first and last stages is cloaked in obscurity and anonymity.

The prophet, having heard the message from the angel mentioned in v. 6, is now prepared to deliver it. In the interests of economy, the message is not repeated, but given once at the point of final delivery. It is contained in vv. 3-4, and contains orders for the group we have tentatively identified with the balance of humanity to prepare a roadway for Yahweh. Whether the colorful and perhaps hyperbolic imagery is to be taken literally or figuratively, the building of a road across the mountainous wilderness involves just such activities as are described: the leveling of hills and the filling in of valleys and depressions. While it may be anachronistic to think in terms of modern earth-moving and road-building equipment, nevertheless road-building in the ancient world was also a highly developed and technical undertaking. The peoples who could construct the pyramids and the great temples of the world also could and did build great roads. The opening words read as follows:

bammidbār pannû derek yhwh	In the wilderness prepare a road for Yahweh
yaššᵉrû bāʿᵃrābâ mᵉsillâ lēʾlōhênû	Make straight in the desert a highway for our God

We have a partial but impressive chiasm involving the first two words of each line: *bmdbr pnw // yšrw bʿrbh.* The last two words are strictly parallel. The words *drk* and *mslh* are roughly synonymous, although the second is more precise than the first, and the latter tells us more about the nature of the highway (i.e., built up). The other words, *yhwh* and *ʾlhynw,* reflect the breakup of a traditional expression, "Our God, Yahweh." The preposition before *ʾlhynw* serves double-duty and is retrospective (i.e., backward gapping). Thus we lose the rather difficult expression "the roadway of Yahweh," and gain instead a better parallel for "a highway for our God," namely, "a road for Yahweh." The purpose of the activity described here is to enable Yahweh to bring his exiled people back with him to their homeland. In this second Exodus, Yahweh will bring his people as a shepherd brings his flock, an image used often in connection with the first Exodus. That the return of the exiles to their homeland is a main theme of the poem, even though they are not mentioned as such, is confirmed in a number of other parallel and complementary passages in Exilic Isaiah: e.g., Isa. 35:8-10 and 51:11; 48:20-22, 52:1-12. Similar imagery is used in 49:8-26, although in that passage the exiles come from many different places.

Further responsibilities and activities of the road-builders are developed in related passages, such as Isa. 35:3-4 and 49:22-23. In this poem, however, they are given another and simultaneous assignment. As the roadway is being completed with its terminus in the holy land, and as Yahweh sets out with his ransomed people from the place of their exile, the same people who built the road, or a portion of them, are to bring word of the imminent arrival of Yahweh and his people in the land. For the next stage in the action, we must then return to Part I of the poem and the first two verses. The speaker in vv. 1-2 must be the same as in vv. 3-4, and it is the prophet concealed in the expression "Hark! One cries out" *(qwl qwrʾ).* So are those spoken to, who have a complementary assignment, to comfort Yahweh's people, those in the cities of Judah, and to speak directly to the capital city, Jerusalem. Just as they are to build a highway for Yahweh and the group he is bringing from exile, so they are to inform the people left behind in Jerusalem and Judah of their imminent arrival.

While we have tied all the elements in v. 1, including subjects, verbs, and object, to the actions in vv. 2 and 9, it may be that the force of the imperatives in v. 1 *(nḥmw nḥmw)* applies as well to the exiles, since they also are part of the people of Yahweh. Whereas in this poem the activity assigned to the comforters and strengtheners is limited to highway building in association with their return to their homeland, and their care and protection is undertaken by Yahweh himself as the Good Shepherd, in other passages these same people share in the latter tasks. Thus, in 35:3-4, they are told to "strengthen the weak hands, and make firm the stumbling knees; say to those whose hearts tremble, 'Be strong! Fear not! Behold your God!' " Actually, the language here is so close to that of Isa. 40:9 that the people of Jerusalem and Judah may be intended and not the exiles. The general content and context of Isa. 35 is the return of the exiles through the wilderness (cf. vv. 1 and 5-10), but the immediate context of the latter part of v. 2 and including vv. 3-4 may well be the cities of Judah. In Isa. 49:22-23, however, there is no doubt about the role of the nations in assisting and abetting the exiles as they return from the different parts of the world. The relevant portions read as follows: "Thus has said my Lord Yahweh: "Behold! I will raise my hand to the nations, and to the peoples I will lift up my banner. Then they will bring your sons in their bosom, and your daughters on their shoulders shall be carried. Their kinds shall be your foster-parents, and their princesses shall be your wet-nurses."

We may summarize the rest briefly. As the work on the highway progresses toward its culmination, the builders or their representatives have reached the border of Judah, and must carry out their other obligation, to announce to the people in Jerusalem, whose time of service has been fulfilled, and whose period of punishment is at an end, that Yahweh is coming with the people who were sent into exile. They, the people of Jerusalem, must spread the word of Yahweh's imminent arrival to the rest of the people in the cities of Judah. In the immediate future is the grand reunion of all the people of Yahweh and the glorious restoration of the holy land and holy city, with the permanent presence of Yahweh in the midst of his reunited people.

Then comes the end. The glory of Yahweh will be revealed and all flesh will see it together. "All flesh" includes the reunited people of Yahweh as well as the rest of humanity. It is these latter, the nations of the world, the other group making up the total of "all flesh," who are the unnamed subjects of the masculine plural imperative verbs of vv. 1-3. The chief clue in the poem is the occurrence of *kl-(h)bśr* (vv. 5-6, at the logical and chronological beginning and end of the sequence of events in the poem), showing that the whole of humanity is present throughout, including the people of Yahweh (*ʿmy* in v. 1 and *hʿm* in v. 7) and the rest of the nations. All of the participants are introduced in the opening section of the poem (considered chronologically). Thus in vv. 6-8, we have in order the first speaker (= the throne angel), the second speaker (= the prophet in all likelihood), all flesh (= the nations, to whom the prophet addresses the main message), the people (=

the people of Yahweh to whom the nations bring the message), and finally the word of Yahweh, which is the dominant factor and active force throughout, from beginning to end.

We propose, therefore, that the answer to the question posed at the beginning of this paper as to who the subjects of the plural imperative verbs in the first three verses were is the nations of the world. The principal data and arguments in support of the conclusion have been derived from the poem itself on the basis, essentially, of the juxtaposition of the terms *'am* and *kol-bāśār* and their respective roles in the verses under consideration. We now wish to call attention to data in the larger context of the book of Exilic Isaiah, and in particular the chapters in the immediate vicinity of ch. 40. There is a considerable number of second masculine plural imperative verbs in chs. 34, 35, 40, and 41. It is our claim that the subjects remain the same throughout. In some cases the subject is named, and it is always the same in the sense that a group of equivalent or complementary terms is used: *gôyīm, le'ummîm, 'iyyîm.* Where no subject is indicated, I believe it is the same as in the other passages, so that throughout all of these chapters the subject of the plural imperative verbs remains the same, unless specifically identified otherwise (e.g., Isa. 35:3-4, where two different groups are addressed by imperatives; only one of them can be the group we stipulate). To conclude the paper, we will sample the verses in which the imperative forms occur:

1. In Isa. 34:1 we read as follows:

qirbû gôyīm lišmōa'	Draw near, O nations, to listen
ûle'ummîm haqšîbû	and, O peoples, pay heed.

The remainder of the verse with its references to the earth and the world shows that all the nations (excluding his own people) are included.

2. In Isa. 34:16 there are two more plural imperatives, but the passage is obscure; it is not clear who is being addressed or what the connection with the surrounding verses is. The subject could well be the nations.
3. In Isa. 35:3-4, a passage already discussed, we find plural imperative verbs. The language here is very much like that of Isa. 40, especially vv. 1 and 9, and clearly they are related and have the same general scene in mind. The subjects of the verbs here are commanded to do for the people of Yahweh (whether those in exile or those in Judah) much the same as they are commanded in Isa. 40, in the context of the imminent return of the exiles and the revelation of the glory of Yahweh (Isa. 35:2, which corresponds to 40:5). The last bicolon of v. 2 immediately precedes the imperatives in vv. 3-4, and provides the context for them:

hēmmâ yir'û kebôḏ-yhwh	They will see the glory of Yahweh
hadar 'elōhênû	the splendor of our God.

The passage is a slightly different and perhaps more elegant version of Isa. 40:5. Several of the words are identical or almost so, while the passage in 35:2 makes use of the device of the breakup of a traditional formula in the same manner that we have seen several times in Isa. 40, namely the sequence *yhwh . . . 'lhynw,* which occurs in the same order, and also separated, in 40:3 and 40:7-8. Under the circumstances it is reasonable to suppose that the pronoun in 35:2 stands for the *kol-bāśār* of 40:5, or some equivalent expression, such as "the nations." The point is that all should be included, both Yahweh's people and the rest of the world, as in Isa. 40.

In 35:3-4 we read as follows:

ḥazz^{e}*qû yādayim rāpôt*	(3) Strengthen the limp hands
ûbirkayim kōš^{e}*lôt 'ammēṣû*	and the stumbling knees make firm.
'imrû l^{e}*nimh*^{a}*rê-lēb*	(4) Say to those whose hearts tremble,
ḥizqû 'al-tîrā'û	"Be strong! Do not be afraid!
hinnēh 'elōh^{e}*kem*	Behold your God!"

When compared with Isa. 40:1-2, 9-11, we find many structural similarities, although there are both resemblances and differences in vocabulary. We have the same quotation within a quotation structure, whereby the subjects of the first set of imperatives are commanded not only to do something (cf. 40:1, 3) but also to deliver a message (cf. 40:2 and 9). Thus, as also in Isa. 40, we have two sets of imperatives, one set addressed to the main subject, and the other addressed through them to another subject. In Isa. 40, the difference is marked because the second set is second feminine singular verbs, whereas the first set is second masculine plural verbs. Here all the verbs are second masculine plural, but the first group is clearly distinguished from the second, since the first group is supposed to strengthen and encourage the second, while the second is encouraged to be strong and not to be fearful (note the contrast between the piel *ḥazz*^{e}*qû* addressed to the first group in v. 3, and the qal *ḥizqû* addressed to the second group in v. 4 of ch. 35). Careful study shows that the first group in 35:3-4 is equivalent to the subjects of the imperative verbs in 40:1-3, whereas the second group in 35:3-4 corresponds to the last two groups in Isa. 40. The latter passage distinguishes between Jerusalem and the cities of Judah. Thus it is Zion/Jerusalem that is instructed not to be fearful in Isa. 40:9, whereas it is the cities of Judah to whom the announcement is made, "Behold your God!" In Isa. 35:3-4, there is just one group which is the recipient of both messages: "Do not be afraid" and "Behold your God!" They are the people of Yahweh, whereas in Isa. 40 there are subdivisions of this category. In conclusion we can say that the first group in Isa. 35 is the same as the first group, the subject of the plural imperative verbs in vv. 1-3 of Isa. 40. Whatever answer we give to the question in either place must be the same as in the other.

4. Passing by the imperative verbs in Isa. 40:1-3, we find the next pair in Isa. 40:26, which reads as follows:

śᵉʾû-mārôm ʿênêkem	Raise on high your eyes
ûrᵉʾû mî-bārāʾ ʾēlleh	and see who created these

This passage begins with v. 25, where we have another second masculine plural verb. The question is what is the subject, and to what noun or nouns do these verbs refer. The only viable possibilities are the following: *rôzᵉnîm,* "princes," and *šōpᵉṭê ʾereṣ,* "judges of the earth," in v. 23, or *gôyīm* and *ʾiyyîm* in v. 15 (cf. *kol-haggôyim* in v. 17). It is more likely to be the latter than the former given all the instances in which the nations // coastlands are addressed in the book. But in the end it does not matter very much, since the rulers of the nations are often surrogates or representatives of the nations.

5. In Isa. 41:1 we have another second masculine plural imperative verb, only this time the subjects are specified:

haḥᵃrîšû ʾēlay ʾiyyîm	Listen silently to me, O coastlands
ûlᵉʾummîm . . .	and peoples . . .

There is no equivalent verb in the imperative to balance *hḥryšw,* but clearly the words *ʾyym* and *lʾmym* form a complementary pair, presumably in a chiastic arrangement. These nouns may be compared with the subjects used in Isa. 34:1, already discussed. The arrangement there is also partially chiastic:

qirbû gôyīm lišmōaʿ	Draw near, O nations, to listen
ûlᵉʾummîm haqšîbû	and, O peoples, pay heed!

The pair *gwym* and *lʾmym* overlaps with *ʾyym* and *lʾmym* in 41:1; that they are intended to cover the same territorial and population groups is shown by the occurrence in the intervening material between 34:1 and 41:1 (we are speaking only of the four chapters: 34, 35, 40, and 41, which can and should be attributed to Exilic Isaiah) of the third possible combination of these terms. Note that in 40:15 we have the following:

hēn gôyīm kᵉmar middᵉlî . . .	Behold, the nations are like a drop from a bucket
hēn ʾiyyîm kaddaq yiṭṭôl	Behold, he lifts up the islands as though they were dust

On the basis of the evidence presented we would maintain that just as the subjects of the imperative verbs in 34:1 and 41:1 are the nations, peoples, and coastlands (or islands), so they are also the subjects of the unspecified plural imperative verbs in 35:3-4 and the second person plural verbs in 40:18-26 (including the imperatives in v. 26) following the specific reference to *kl-hgwym* in 40:17 (cf. *gwym // ʾyym* in v. 15). In particular they are the subject of the six masculine plural imperative verbs in 40:1-3. Collectively they make up the larger share of *kol-(h)bśr* mentioned twice in the poem (vv. 5, 6) and balance the other group, *ʿmy* and *hʿm* (vv. 1, 7), who make up the rest of "all flesh."

Table 7

Actual Arrangement	Sequential Arrangement
Part I: vv. 1-2	Part III: vv. 6-8
Part II: vv. 3-4	Part II: vv. 3-4
Part III: vv. 6-8	Part I: vv. 1-2
Part IV: vv. 9-11	Part IV: vv. 9-11

Table 8

Actual Arrangement	Sequential Arrangement
Part I: vv. 1-2	Part III: vv. 6-8
Part II: vv. 3-4	Part II: vv. 3-4
Center: v. 5	Part I: vv. 1-2
Part III: vv. 6-8	Part IV: vv. 9-11
Part IV: vv. 9-11	Finale: v. 5

According to our analysis, in contrast with the actual arrangement, the logical or sequential order of the main parts of the poem in Isa. 40:1-11 is as shown in Table 7. It will be seen that the poet has achieved his objectives of dramatic intensity and literary intricacy by a single switch: the interchange of Parts I and III. In addition, he has transferred the concluding line, a tricolon, to the center of the poem, where it serves as divider and focus of attention (v. 5). The full diagram is slightly more complex, but still essentially a matter of simple displacement (see Table 8). To show what the poem would look like and how it would read if we arranged the parts in which we believe to be their sequential order, we will present the text in translation only (see below). We add the cautionary note that the proposed arrangement is designed only to facilitate understanding and appreciation of the meaning and intent of the poem, and not to imply in any way that it is the arrangement the poet intended or produced, or that it is a superior way of organizing the material. On the contrary, the dramatic and literary qualities of the present arrangement are self-evident. Only they are so subtle and sophisticated that they have baffled and mystified readers and scholars for more than two millennia.

Isaiah 40:1-11 translated sequentially:

Part III

Hark! Someone says, "Cry out!" (6)
And another says, "What shall I cry out?"

All flesh is like grass
and all of their fidelity is like the flower of the field —
The grass has dried up the flower has faded (7)
because the breath of Yahweh blew on it;
surely the people were like grass.
The grass has dried up the flower has faded (8)
but the word of our God
will stand forever.

Part II

Hark! Someone cries out: (3)
In the wilderness prepare a road for Yahweh
make straight in the desert
a highway for our God.
Every valley shall be raised (4)
and every mountain and hill shall be lowered
and the bumpy ground shall become a plain
and the rough places a flatland.

Part I

Comfort, comfort my people (1)
says your God.
Speak to the heart of Jerusalem (2)
and cry out to her
because she has fulfilled her time of service
because her punishment is considered sufficient
because she has received from Yahweh's hand
double for all her sins.

Part IV

Upon a high mountain climb up for yourself (9)
O Zion, herald of good tidings!
Lift up with strength your voice
O Jerusalem, herald of good tidings!

Lift it up! Be not afraid!
Say to the cities of Judah:
"Behold your God!"
Behold, my Lord Yahweh! (10)
With power he comes
and his arm shall rule for him.
Behold, his payment is with him
and what he worked for is before him.
(He is) like a shepherd who feeds his flock (11)
who gathers the lambs with his arm
and in his bosom carries them
who guides the nursing ewes.

Finale

And the glory of Yahweh shall be revealed (5)
and all flesh shall see it together
for the mouth of Yahweh has spoken.

19

Patterns in Psalms 25 and 34

This paper will point out certain unusual features that Psalms 25 and 34 have in common and suggest that these coincidences can hardly be the result of chance. The commonalities should therefore be regarded as part of a planned, rather intricate, poetic structure. A brief rundown of these features follows.

1. As is generally known, Psalms 25 and 34 have the form of alphabetic acrostics in which each poetic unit begins with a different letter of the alphabet, beginning with the letter *aleph* and following the usual order, ending with *taw.* A minor variation which occurs in other alphabetic acrostic poems may be observed in Psalm 34. It has been suggested that the lines beginning with *ayin* and *pe* (vv. 16-17) should be reversed because of sense requirements; i.e., v. 16 (beginning with עיני יהוה) seems to fit better with v. 18 (beginning with צעקו) while v. 17 (beginning with פני יהוה) seems to go better with v. 15 (beginning with סור מרע). This alternate order of *ayin* and *pe* is attested elsewhere, particularly in the alphabetic acrostic poems of Lamentations (cf. Lam. 2:16-17 and 3:46-51; also 4:16-17). While the change may be justified, whichever sequence we adopt will be well within the range of actual usage in the biblical group of acrostic poems. Hence the possibility of a deliberate interlocking arrangement of these lines, departing from normal narrative prose style, should not be excluded. Other minor and presumably inadvertent deviations from the norm should also be noted. In Ps. 25:1-2 the official verse division violates the alphabetic order by placing the word אלהי at the beginning of v. 2 instead of at the end of v. 1. This error should be corrected by beginning the second line of the poem with the next word, בך, which conforms to the alphabetic pattern. In v. 18 of the same psalm we would expect, and the acrostic form would require, a word beginning with the letter *qoph* at the start of the line, whereas in fact the word ראה is in that position. Since the identical word occurs at the beginning of v. 19 which conforms to the

alphabetic expectation, it seems clear that an error has occurred at the beginning of v. 18, which we may describe as anticipatory vertical dittography — the scribe mistakenly copied the first word of the *resh*-line when he meant to copy the first word of the *qoph*-line. What the original initial word of the *qoph*-line may have been is not entirely clear, but the suggestion (BHS) that it was קְשֹׁב is as good as any. No similar minor lapses occur in Psalm 34.

2. Much more significantly, Psalm 25 entirely omits the *waw* line. While suggestions have been made to recover or restore such a line by detaching the third colon of the *he* line, emending the text slightly (by adding a *waw* at the beginning of the colon), and thereby supposedly restoring the original pattern of the poem, at best such a procedure is makeshift — no textual evidence supports such an emendation. Furthermore, the resulting hypothetical *waw* line is abnormally short (only one colon) and does not stand well by itself. It is much better to leave this colon where it is, a complement to the previous two cola of the *he*-verse as the MT has it. The clinching argument for leaving the text as it is and recognizing that the *waw* line has been omitted on purpose comes from Psalm 34, where the *waw* line is likewise absent. Psalm 34 not only omits one of the expected lines of the alphabetic acrostic poem, it omits the same line that is missing in Psalm 25. Any explanation of the phenomenon in either poem must take into account the same phenomenon in the other poem, so an ad hoc line of reasoning that might serve to explain the omission in one poem as inadvertent must also be applied to the other poem. It is going beyond the bounds of probability to suppose that the omission of a line, the same line, in both poems which have other features in common, resulted from coincidence or inadvertence. While we may not be able to give an adequate explanation of why this particular line was omitted, I think we must operate with the supposition that the omission was deliberate in both cases. The omission constitutes a deviation from the normal arrangement, but it also belongs to a larger consideration or configuration.
3. Yet another significant correspondence or correlation occurs between these two poems. As though to compensate for the omission of one of the internal lines of the acrostic poems (the *waw* line) at the end of each psalm, an additional line is appended after the *taw* line, normally itself the last line. While in principle such a line could begin with any letter, it is remarkable and impressive that in both cases the line begins with the same letter, constituting a second *pe*-line. The initial word in both cases derives from the same root פדה (the imperative verb in Ps. 25:22, פְּדֵה, and the masculine singular active participle in Ps. 34:23, פּוֹדֶה). If these phenomena had turned up in only one psalm, we might wonder about accidental omissions and possible inadvertencies, but when there are two psalms with so many identical points in common, it is clear that a deliberate program of alteration and adaptation has taken place in both cases. Whether or not we can explain the

underlying reasons or the overall objectives or purpose of such treatment, we must recognize that the procedures are deliberate and accept these altered psalms as belonging to a specific subcategory of the larger class of alphabetic acrostic poems in the Bible.

4. The simplest general solution to these curiosities is that the added line at the end of each poem serves as compensation for the omitted line in the body of each poem. It would appear that the added line was intended to make up for the omission of a line in the regular sequence, thereby retaining the normal and normative 22-line total for poems of this type: alphabetic acrostics. Alternatively and better, we could say that one of the internal lines of the poem has been omitted in order to allow for or to accommodate the addition of a final closing line. There is a very reasonable explanation for the supernumerary *pe*-line, the letter itself being part of and contributing to the interpretation. As expounded by Patrick Skehan, the initial *pe* of the last line of the poem was chosen deliberately in order to complete a combination with two other letters, namely, the *aleph* at the beginning of the first line, and the *lamedh* at the beginning of the twelfth or middle line of the poem.[1] These three letters in turn spell the word *aleph,* which stands for the whole alphabet (just as the combination of the first two letters stands for the whole sequence in Greek or English).[2] This little added twist serves to reinforce the special character of the poem in its alphabetic patterning. It also adjusts the structure of the poem to provide a 23-line arrangement, which thereby provides not only a first and last, but also a distinctive middle line, which the ordinary 22-line pattern would lack.

This last consideration raises a new question about these two psalms — asymmetry results from the loss of the *waw* line in each poem. This omission reduces the overall total to 22 lines, and therefore, strictly speaking, the *lamedh*-line is not in fact the twelfth line but the eleventh, and the mathematical precision of the superimposed pattern is somewhat marred. We may recognize, therefore, that the poet has created or allowed to persist a certain tension or inconsistency in trying to merge two patterns and to retain some features of the 22-line pattern while augmenting the poem to a 23-line pattern. In fact, the recognition of this apparent imbalance leads to further investigation of the phenomenon and to the acquisition of additional data bearing on a more comprehensive resolution to the remaining problems. In the end, however, why the *waw*-line was omitted in each instance may remain a mystery.

1. P. W. Skehan, "The Structure of the Song of Moses in Dt 32,1-43," *CBQ* 13 (1951): 153-163; repr. *Studies in Israelite Poetry and Wisdom.* CBQ Monograph 1 (Washington: Catholic Biblical Association, 1971), 74-75.

2. Cf. M. D. Coogan, "Alphabets and Elements," *BASOR* 216 (1974): 61-63; more recently, " '*'*LP*: "To Be an Abecedarian," *JAOS* 110 (1990): 322.

5. According to my analysis of the two psalms, the purpose of the poet regarding structure was twofold. On the surface, at least, he intended to maintain the appearance of a normal 22-line alphabetic acrostic poem, albeit with two obvious alterations in the regular sequence of the letters of the alphabet: the omission of one line (the *waw*-line in both poems) and the addition of a line at the end after the last line of the normal sequence (in both cases the added line begins with the same letter, *pe*). In both cases, therefore, the *waw* line has been dropped and a second *pe* line has been added at the end. On the one hand, the poet seems to have been at some pains to maintain the same profile for these poems as obtains for other poems with the normal sequence of the 22-letters of the Hebrew alphabet. On the other hand, these two poems share and exhibit other features that point to a 23-line structure, rendering these poems distinct from the other more normal set in various ways. In summary, while the poet(s) in both cases arranged their psalms to have 22 lines or alphabetic units, they also intended to project a larger or 23-line format. Surprisingly, both of these features appear in the poems as they have come down to us.

If we take a closer look at Psalm 25, we note that, while most of the lines are characteristically balanced with two half-lines or cola each (there are 20 of these), two lines uncharacteristically have an additional colon, making them tricola. Respectively vv. 5 and 7 (the *he*-line and the *het*-line) in effect bracket the missing *waw*-line (although not exactly, as the *zayin*-line [v. 6] intervenes). While scholars in the past, and some still in the present, regard such tricola lines as contrary to the requirements of Hebrew poetry and systematically eliminate one of the three cola in such lines in order to restore the original structure of the poem, that is an outmoded procedure. We now recognize that the occurrence and presence of tricola in biblical poetry is a frequent and, almost always, deliberate creation of the poet. The widespread occurrence of this phenomenon in Ugaritic poetry has especially persuaded most scholars that the phenomenon is deeply rooted in Northwest Semitic literary conventions. Therefore its widespread occurrence in biblical poetry is no accident and certainly not a persistent and repeated error to be corrected by excision or any other kind of manipulation. It thereby becomes apparent that the purpose of these two tricola in Psalm 25 is precisely to make up for the deficiency caused by the omission of the *waw* line. Immediately before the omission and almost immediately after it, and within the context of the first half of the poem, the addition of two cola, or the equivalent of one bicolon line, has made up for the deficiency created by the omission. The validity of this contention is borne out by the obvious way in which the number of cola for the poem as a whole, namely 46, equals 23 bicola or lines, while at the same time being restricted to 22 actual lines. A complete description of the poem would have to include both phenomena: the 22 actual lines and the 46 actual cola. The poet has combined these somewhat dissonant elements in the manner indicated: the poem consists of 20 lines of bicola and 2 lines of tricola, making a total of 22 lines and 46 cola. Furthermore, both of the additional cola occur in the first half of the poem, thereby balancing the different major segments of the poem:

Part I: vv. 1-10	10 lines	22 cola
Middle line: v. 11	1 line	2 cola
Part II: vv. 12-22	11 lines	22 cola
Total	22 lines	46 cola

To bring out the augmented alphabetic indicator, the first and last lines or verses could be isolated, and the following table produced:

First line: v. 1	1 line	2 cola
Part I: vv. 2-10	9 lines	20 cola
Middle line: v. 11	1 line	2 cola
Part II: vv. 12-21	10 lines	20 cola
Last line: v. 22	1 line	2 cola
Total	22 lines	46 cola

At the same time, the poem conforms to the standard pattern of 22 lines but equally gives the impression of an augmented alphabetic acrostic with an additional line appended at the end of the poem. Now we turn to a more precise count of words and syllables to show that the underlying pattern of this poem is the larger or augmented, rather than the normal one.

As I have shown elsewhere, the standard alphabetic acrostic poem has 22 lines or bicola, with an average or normative line length of 16 syllables, making a total for the poem of 352 syllables.[3] These numbers hold up well for the alphabetic acrostic psalms and poems in the Bible, along with a number of other poems of identical or similar structure which do not preserve or contain the alphabetic sequence (for example, Lam. 5 and Ps. 33).[4] In the case of Psalm 25, however, although the line total is the same (22), there are 46 cola (instead of the expected 44) and the syllable count is substantially higher than the normal and expected 352. In fact, while we must allow for some uncertainty in reproducing the actual pronunciation at the time of composition and also for some freedom on the part of the poet in matching words with metrical requirements, the total number of syllables for Psalm 25 could range from 363 to 382. The reason for the relatively wide range

3. D. N. Freedman, "Acrostic Poems in the Hebrew Bible: Alphabetic and Otherwise," *CBQ* 48 (1986): 408-431, especially the tables, 417-18; 424-28 [see above, Chapter 14]. An earlier, more provisional study appeared in my "Acrostics and Metrics in Hebrew Poetry," *HTR* 65 (1972): 367-392, esp. 392.

4. See Freedman, *CBQ* 48 (1986): 408-431. [See above, Chapter 14]

is the frequent and repeated occurrence of the 2nd masc. sg. pronominal suffix, which is almost always written as ךְ-, but in the MT, at least, is often vocalized as ךָ- rather than the shorter form ךְ-. While the spelling and the vocalization diverge throughout the MT, the existence of the two forms side by side can be demonstrated. While it may be possible to trace some evolution in the history of this form, originally ךָ-, it may well have lost the final vowel in certain situations and under certain circumstances. The survival of the longer form, especially in poetry, however, can be assumed. At the same time, the shorter form must have permeated the language so that in any given case it would be difficult to decide which form the author intended. The spelling in the manuscripts of the Massoretic tradition favors the short form, while the vocalization favors the longer. Many of the Dead Sea Scrolls confirm that the longer form was widespread — the so-called Qumran spelling, כה-, confirms the presence and pronunciation of the final vowel. Just what the poet intended in each case would be very difficult to determine, so we may leave the matter at this point and approach the question from the point of view of symmetry and structure. In Psalm 25 the suffixed forms occur as follows: vv. 1, 2, 3, 4 (twice), 5 (twice), 6 (twice), 7 (twice), 11 (twice: שִׁמְךָ and סלחת, where we have the comparable 2nd masc. sg. perfect form of the verb, mostly written ת- but occasionally תה- in the MT), 20, 21, for a total of 15 of these variable forms. The remaining instances of variable pronunciation and syllable-count occur where the MT elides a syllable in its vocalization and produces a lower count than would have obtained in classical pronunciation. The chances are that the older, longer pronunciation prevailed when the poem was written, but we must also allow for the poet to contract or condense words according to need or desire, and the MT offers a clue here as to how that might have been done. In my count, I do not include the numerous and uniform instances in which the MT expands the pronunciation of typical words, e.g., segolate formations, in conjunction with laryngeals, and so forth. There is no basis for these modifications in any ancient source, and they can be regarded as later and secondary additions to the text.

Given the numerous converging structural features of the two psalms, I conclude that the expected number of syllables for each poem as a whole would be 368 (e.g., 46 cola x 8 syllables = 368), which is clearly within the range noted above for Psalm 25 (363 to 382). If we suppose that the four Massoretic contractions (in vv. 7a, 9b, 14a, 18b) do not reflect the pronunciation at the time when the poem was composed and that we should therefore adopt the older and more original longer syllable count, the total would be 367. We could, then, suppose that none of the suffixed forms (2nd masc. sg. pronominal suffix) was given the long pronunciation, while the single case of the 2nd masc. sg. perfect verb would have had the longer count. This would add one more to the total, and it would come out exactly at 368. I make no claim that this is the technique the poet employed, or that the poem was actually counted out in this fashion. I simply suggest one plausible way in which the syllables could be counted to reflect the structure of the poem. As in the poetry of all languages and cultures, minor variations or deviations from the norm are only to be expected, but here we are very close to the mark. Regardless of the precise representation, I think it is clear that the text of Psalm 25, as it has come down to us, is an example of an augmented or enhanced alphabetic acrostic poem. The additional or second *pe* line was seen to be a plus, an extra line, with its own special significance for the enhanced structure, a signature or seal stamped on the original, as already discussed. The omission of the *waw* line in this poem is thus seen to be a separate matter, although part of the overall schema; but its loss is already compensated for by the addition of a third colon to the bicola in vv. 5 and 7, thus bringing the number of cola in the first half of the poem to 22 to match the 22 cola of the second half, and making a total of 44 before we reach the appended line at the end of the poem. The overall syllable count, which is a lot closer to 368 than to the expected 352 for the normal 22-line acrostic poem, supports this interpretation of these curious phenomena, and, as I have shown, the number 368 fits the poem quite reasonably.

Turning now to Psalm 34, we find a different arrangement and strategy for conforming to the metrical or quantitative norms or requirements of this type of poem. The basic features are the same as in the case of Psalm 25. Therefore I am predisposed to consider the second *pe*-line as an addendum or augmentation to the poem, while the loss of the *waw*-line will be compensated internally, i.e., within the alphabetic structure of the poem as a whole. Furthermore, we would expect the deficiency to be made up within the same half of the poem, as in the case of Psalm 25. In other words, while a line has been left out, nothing in fact is missing. In the case of Psalm 25, the missing bicolon was replaced by a third colon in each of two nearby lines; the poet of Psalm 34 does not employ that strategy, perhaps because it may have seemed a little too obvious and simple. Perhaps the same poet wished to employ a more subtle or intricate technique and not leave easy traces to follow. In any case, no cola have been added in this poem, and we have only 44 cola for the 22 lines extant. At the same time, the poem belongs to the augmentation group, as can be shown by matching the two poems and counting both words and syllables. The two poems are almost identical in length by whichever counting system used, and that can hardly be accidental either:

	Words	Syllables	
Psalm 25	158	363-382	(368)
Psalm 34	157	369-373	(371)

Given all the matching points between the two psalms, it seems clear that they were also designed to be of equal length, something that does not just happen accidentally. Furthermore, the length, as we have seen in the case of Psalm 25, corresponds to the pattern for an augmented or enhanced alphabetic acrostic poem, namely the 23-line or 46-cola type. In the case of Psalm 25, the 22-line, 44-cola, standard type has been expanded through the addition of two cola to existing lines, whereas in Psalm 34 the enhancement is spread over the whole poem by the addition of words and syllables here and there to achieve the desired totals of words and syllables. Thus Psalm 34 has a range from a minimum of 369 syllables to a maximum of 373, according to my count, which fits well within the range for Psalm 25 (363 to 382). If the count in Psalm 34 is adjusted along the same lines as for Psalm 25, we would come out with 371 (restoring the syllables elided by the Massoretes in vv. 8, 10, while opting for the short form of the 2nd masc. sg. pronominal suffix in v. 14 [twice]). This total is slightly higher than that for Psalm 25, and the latter total may be too low. If we averaged the minima and maxima for both psalms we would have slightly different numbers: 372.5 for Psalm 25 and 371 for Psalm 34. I think the numbers are close enough, however they are calculated, to show that the poems share the same pattern and structure. In the case of Psalm 34 the poet had a choice between the numbers 368, which was the norm for the 23-line, 46-cola, augmented acrostic poem, and 374, which would have been the norm for a 22-line, 44-cola acrostic poem augmented by adding a single syllable to each line, for a total of 17 syllables per line instead of 16 (which is essentially what this poet did). The resultant number, 371, is a compromise between the two norms (the average of 368 and 374). When we add in the special features of these alphabetic acrostic psalms, including the omission of the *waw* line, and the addition of the second *pe* line, it is clear that the poems have been created out of the same basic mold. But in reaching a common goal, the poet or poets proceeded along somewhat different paths and pursued different tactics. In the one case (Ps. 25), the poet simply added two cola to other lines of the poem to make up the desired total of 46 cola and 368 syllables, while in the other case (Ps. 34), the poet judiciously added enough syllables to the 22-line, 44-cola poem to reach the same goal.

Postscript

In the accompanying charts, I have given syllable and accent counts for both poems. Regarding the number and distribution of the accents, I have followed the MT almost slavishly, but here and there indicated alternate possibilities based on Massoretic usage in similar situations. As is generally known, there is considerable flexibility and leeway in the Massoretic accentual system, with the same or similar words receiving or not receiving accents (depending in part on whether they are connected through *maqqeph,* in which case the first word of the pair often loses an expected accent). Then there is the somewhat arbitrary use of the *metheg,* which may be regarded as a secondary accent. The same particles, such as כִּי, לְ, and so on, may stand alone and have an accent or be tied to the following word and each lose its accent; or in such cases the *metheg* may be used. So precision in the matter of recovering the plan of the original poet can hardly be expected or attained. Nevertheless, and especially because the accentual approach remains dominant in this field, it is worthwhile to record the results, which agree overall and quite emphatically with the basic argument presented here. If I am right in supposing that the basic pattern is a 23-line, 46-colon poem in both cases, then we would expect a total of 138 accents, corresponding to the 23 lines at 6 accents per line, or 46 cola at 3 accents per colon (these being balanced lines of 3 + 3 = 6 accents each). In the case of Psalm 25 there are 46 cola and a total of 138 accents, precisely as expected, although not distributed exactly evenly among the lines and cola (the principle of compensation seems to be at work here; i.e., if one line or colon has more than the expected number of accents, another line or colon will have fewer, and vice versa). In Psalm 34, with only 44 cola, the total number of accents nevertheless ranges between 133 and 139, so the results are not much different. It would not be difficult to reach a total of 138, which in any case seems to be the target number.[5]

5. One remaining alphabetic acrostic psalm has some common and different features when compared with the two psalms under consideration in this paper. One of the internal lines has been omitted from Ps. 145, although it is not the *waw*-line, as in the case of Pss. 25 and 34, but the *nun*-line, for which there is no other precedent. Other manuscripts (from Cave XI of Qumran) and versions supply a *nun*-line to make up for the apparent loss. In the light of our findings about the two psalms discussed in this paper, however, it is possible that the omission was deliberate. Furthermore, while Ps. 145 has only 21 lines, there is considerable evidence of augmentation, although there is no second *pe*-line at the end of the psalm. The number of words is less than the total for Pss. 25 and 34, 150 against 158 and 157, but the number of syllables is very close to the totals for the two earlier psalms: a range from 371 to 395 compared with 363 to 382 for Ps. 25 and 369 to 373 for Ps. 34. Applying the same general rules to Ps. 145 that we applied to the other psalms, we arrive at a total of 374 syllables for Ps. 145 (counting certain syllables that are elided in the MT, but also selecting the short form of the 2nd masc. sg. pronominal suffix against the MT vocalization), compared with totals of 368 for Ps. 25 and 371 for Ps. 34. A preliminary judgment would be that in Ps. 145 the poet uses the same basic mold of the augmented alphabetic acrostic poem, but has departed even more radically from the pattern observed in the two other psalms. Thus the poet has dispensed not only with one of the internal lines of the poem (though a different line from the one omitted in the other poems), but also with the added external *pe*-line observed in the other two poems. At the same time, syllables were added throughout. The author especially made up for the deficiency in the half of the poem in which one line was omitted, so that the 10 lines of the second half more than match the 11 lines of the first half, a circumstance already observed in both of the other poems. There is a family connection, although the resemblance between the third psalm and the other two has been attenuated. It is more like a second cousin, whereas the other two are more like siblings, but hardly twins.

Psalm 25

	Syllables					Accents			
	A	*B*	*C*	*Total*	***Verse***	*A*	*B*	*C*	*Total*
	4	7		11	**1**	2	3		5
	8	8		16	**2**	3	3		6
	8	9		17	**3**	4	3		7
	9	8		17	**4**	3	2		5
	13	8	8	29	**5**	3	4	3	10
	11	6		17	**6**	3	3		6
	13	8	6	27	**7**	4	2	3	9
	6	9		15	**8**	2	4		6
	8	9		17	**9**	3	3		6
	9	11		20	**10**	4	3		7
Sub-total	89	83	14	186	**1-10**	31	30	6	67
	6	11		17	**11**	3	4		7
	8	7		15	**12**	4	3		7
	6	6		12	**13**	3	3		6
	7	8		15	**14**	3	2		5
	7	8		15	**15**	3	5		8
	8	8		16	**16**	2	4		6
	8	9		17	**17**	3	2		5
	8	8		16	**18**	3	2		5
	8	9		17	**19**	3	3		6
	9	8		17	**20**	3	4		7
	7	4		11	**21**	2	2		4
Sub-total	82	86		168	**11-21**	32	34		66
	9	5		14	**22**	3	2		5
Sub-total	89	83	14	186	**1-10**	31	30	6	67
Sub-total	82	86	14	182	**11-22**	32	34	5	71
Totals	171	169	28	368		63	64	11	138

Psalm 34

	Syllables				Accents		
	A	*B*	*Total*	*Verse*	*A*	*B*	*Total*
	10	8	18	**2**	3	3	6
	8	10	18	**3**	3	3	6
	8	9	17	**4**	3	3	6
	10	11	21	**5**	3	3	6
	9	8	17	**6**	3	2	5
	10	9	19	**7**	4	3	7
	6	11	17	**8**	3	3	6
	9	7	16	**9**	4	3	7
	9	8	17	**10**	3	3	6
	9	12	21	**11**	3	4	7
Sub-total	88	93	181	**2-11**	32	30	62
	7	8	15	**12**	3	3	6
	8	7	15	**13**	3	4	7
	7	9	16	**14**	3	3	6
	7	8	15	**15**	3	3	6
	8	7	15	**16**	3	2	5
	8	7	15	**17**	4	3	7
	8	9	17	**18**	3	3	6
	9	8	17	**19**	4	3	7
	6	10	16	**20**	3	3	6
	6	9	15	**21**	2	4	6
	7	9	16	**22**	3	3	6
Sub-total	81	91	172	**12-22**	34	34	68
	8	10	18	**23**	4	4	8
Totals	177	194	371		70	68	138

Psalm 145

	Syllables				Accents		
	A	*B*	*Total*	*Verse*	*A*	*B*	*Total*
	9	12	21	**1**	3	4	7
	7	12	19	**2**	2	4	6
	10	7	17	**3**	4	3	7
	8	8	16	**4**	4	2	6
	6	10	16	**5**	3	3	6
	10	10	20	**6**	3	2	5
	7	8	15	**7**	3	2	5
	7	7	14	**8**	3	4	7
	5	8	13	**9**	3	3	6
	7	9	16	**10**	3	2	5
	8	9	17	**11**	3	2	5
Sub-total	84	100	184	**1-11**	34	31	65
	13	8	21	**12**	4	3	7
	9	9	18	**13**	3	3	6
	10	9	19	**14**	4	3	7
	9	13	22	**15**	3	5	8
	6	8	14	**16**	3	3	6
	9	7	16	**17**	4	3	7
	9	11	20	**18**	4	4	8
	7	11	18	**19**	3	4	7
	9	9	18	**20**	4	3	7
	9	15	24	**21**	4	6	10
Sub-total	90	100	190	**12-21**	36	37	73
Totals	174	200	374		70	68	138